Yale Law Library Series in Legal History and Reference

Lawtalk

*The Unknown Stories
Behind Familiar
Legal Expressions*

James E. Clapp

Elizabeth G. Thornburg

Marc Galanter

Fred R. Shapiro

Yale UNIVERSITY PRESS

New Haven and London

Published with assistance from the foundation established in
memory of Philip Hamilton McMillan of the Class of 1894,
Yale College.

Yale University Press books may be purchased in quantity for
educational, business, or promotional use. For information, please
e-mail sales.press@yale.edu (U.S. office) or sales@yaleup.co.uk
(U.K. office).

Set in Monotype Bulmer with Bauer Bodoni types by
Westchester Book Group.
Printed in the United States of America.

Library of Congress Cataloging-in-Publication Data

Lawtalk : the unknown stories behind familiar legal expressions /
James E. Clapp . . . [et al.].
    p. cm. — (Yale law library series in legal history and reference)
    Includes bibliographical references and index.
    ISBN 978-0-300-17246-1 (hardback)
    1. Law—United States—Dictionaries.   I. Clapp, James E.
(James Edward), 1943–.
    KF156.L39 2011
    340'.14—dc23

                                                        2011032372

A catalogue record for this book is available from the British
Library.

This paper meets the requirements of ANSI/NISO Z39.48–1992
(Permanence of Paper).

10   9   8   7   6   5   4   3   2   1

Contents

Preface ix

Note on Quotations and Sources xiii

Acknowledgments xv

Lawtalk

abuse excuse 1

affirmative action 5

age of consent 8

   Sidebar: Just Knitting 9

aid and abet (and the like) 12

   Sidebar: I Give You That Orange 14

attorney general 18

attorney vs. lawyer 21

badge of slavery 23

billable hour 27

   Sidebar: No Rest for the Weary 30

black letter law 31

   Sidebar: Blowing the Dust off the
   Black Letter Books 35

blackmail 36

blood money 39

blue laws 43

blue wall of silence 48

boilerplate 52

Chancellor's foot 54

charter party 58

Chinese Wall 59

color-blind 62

Comstockery 64

   Sidebar: Shaw and Comstock 66

corpus delicti 71

   Sidebar: Expecting the Unexpected 73

CSI effect 74

cut the baby in half 76

day in court 80

death and taxes 83

death tax 85

deep pocket 89

deliberate speed 93

electoral college 98

eye for an eye 103

fishing expedition 106

grand jury 109

green card 112

hanged for a sheep 117

   Sidebar: Baron Alderson's Remark 120

hearsay 121

hornbook law 125

hue and cry 129

indenture 132

indict a ham sandwich 136

jailbait 140

Jim Crow 141

kangaroo court 143

kill all the lawyers 148

   Sidebar: Dying Wish 149

the law is a ass 153

lawyers, guns, and money 157

make a federal case out of it 160

   Sidebar: Salt Seller 163

one-bite rule 165

one person, one vote 168

oyez 175

paper chase 178

penumbra 180

Philadelphia lawyer 182

   Sidebar: When You Really Need a Good Lawyer . . . 183

pierce the corporate veil 185

   Sidebar: Corporate Entity 188

play the race card 190

politically correct 193

posse 197

pound of flesh 202

rainmaker 205

rap 208

rap sheet 211

read the riot act 214

   Sidebar: Reading the Riot Act to a Rainmaker 216

RICO 216

rule of thumb 219

   Sidebar: Too Serious for God 223

scofflaw 225

separate but equal 230

shadow of the law 234

shyster 236

   Sidebar: Standard Operating Procedure 241

Star Chamber 242

testify 250

thin blue line 253

thinking like a lawyer 258

   Sidebar: The Legal Mind 261

third degree 262

three-fifths rule 268

versus 272

wall of separation 276

wet foot, dry foot 281

white shoe 285

the whole truth 288

   Sidebar: Not a Scholar 292

Notes 295

Index 339

Preface

Law is so much a part of everyday life that we scarcely notice it; it is a presence in everything from the simplest purchase at the corner store to the quality of the very air we breathe. Likewise, law-related language pervades our everyday speech; we use it all the time, often with little awareness of its origins or its actual legal significance. Even lawyers can be oblivious to the linguistic and cultural history embodied in the terms they use.

In this book we tell the stories behind the words. We delve into a wide range of what we call *lawtalk:* words and phrases—most of them familiar to nearly everyone—that have a particular connection with law or are used in talking about law. This is quite a different thing from mere legal terminology. This is *not* a book about insider jargon of the sort featured in a story purportedly told of a pompous judge and a wry local barrister in a nineteenth-century case in western Ireland:

JUDGE: Mr. Houlihan, is your client aware of the maxim *in pari delicto potior est conditio defendentis?*
COUNSEL: My Lord, in the bogs of Connemara they speak of little else.

Unlike that Latin maxim (which states that when the parties are "in equal fault, the position of the defendant is stronger," which is to say that the court will not come to the assistance of a plaintiff who is as much to blame as the defendant), the terms chosen for this book are generally well known—not in the nineteenth-century bogs of Connemara, perhaps, but in the twenty-first-century streets of America. Some are words that originated in law and expanded into nonlegal use; some are words from outside law that acquired special meaning in legal contexts. Some phrases are of ancient origin, some come from recent popular culture. Some terms had a life cycle that has run its course; some are still evolving. The one thing that they all have in common is that they have a story to be told—

though the stories themselves range from tragic to hopeful to comic, and often have elements of all three.

In each case, the information we present goes well beyond anything amassed before. For example, in tracing the origins of the terms, by using modern electronic databases available to universities we have been able to track many expressions back to dates considerably earlier than had previously been known—findings that will be of particular interest to linguists and lexicographers. In addition, we use original sources—both legal writings and nonlegal materials ranging from newspapers to literary works— to trace the evolution of terms under discussion and to highlight the differences between popular and legal understandings of these terms. (Of course, this isn't legal advice. General statements of legal principles are always subject to qualification in specific circumstances.) And we have drawn extensively upon contemporary scholarly writing in law and history to put these developments into context and flesh out the human events and concerns that underlie legal affairs. Our focus is on American law and language, but for history and comparison we often deal with England and occasionally discuss Europe or other English-speaking countries.

A great deal of popular discourse about law and lawyers is in the form of jokes and humor—and that, too, is lawtalk. Many of the entries, therefore, are augmented by sidebars containing jokes or historical material, usually lighthearted, related to the subject of the entry. And because urban legends and false etymologies about legal terms are also a kind of lawtalk (and a kind that is spread with particular ease in the Internet age), we have called attention to such myths and misconceptions and taken pains to separate fact from fiction.

Our object throughout has been to convey to general and specialized readers alike the history, the drama, and the humor behind these terms in an entertaining and readable form while providing new and reliable information that will be of interest to linguists, legal scholars, and others in the scholarly community. For the benefit of that community, we include appropriate documentation; for the benefit of readers who do not need such details, we consign the documentation to the back of the book.

The cumulative lesson from this venture is that legal history and linguistic history are, in the last analysis, cultural history. Language and law develop to meet the needs, accommodate the customs, and embody the morals of an evolving society. The accounts in this book, ranging as they do over a broad array of topics united only by the fact that there is something interesting to learn about them, collectively constitute a picture window on American cultural history.

JAMES E. CLAPP
ELIZABETH G. THORNBURG
MARC GALANTER
FRED R. SHAPIRO

Note on Quotations and Sources

Many historical quotations in this book are from times before spelling and punctuation became standardized. To capture the full flavor of the quoted passages, unless otherwise stated in the notes the spelling, punctuation, and capitalization of quotations are as in the original, except that the modern alphabet has been used (so that, when appropriate, *i* is rendered as *j*, and *u* as *v*, and *uu* or *vv* as *w*), and a truncated sentence at the beginning of a quotation may begin with a capital letter or, at the end of a quotation, may end with a period. Unless otherwise indicated, however, ellipses and bracketed material in quotations are our own.

Similarly, some older texts were very liberal and, to a modern eye, quirky in their use of italics. Any emphasis shown in a quotation is in the original unless otherwise stated in the notes. However, some quotations from court cases and from newspapers and magazines have been obtained from databases that provide only plain-text copies. In such cases our quotation might not include italics that appeared in the original printed text.

Conventional legal citation form is substantially followed for citations to statutes, court cases, and academic journals (mostly law reviews), though names of journals are spelled out for the benefit of those not accustomed to legal abbreviations. (In this style, the volume number precedes the name of the publication and the page number follows it, and reports of opinions of a state's highest court are usually indicated simply by an abbreviation of the name of the state.) For other sources a conventional humanities style is followed.

Except as otherwise noted, all quotations from Shakespeare are from *The Arden Shakespeare Complete Works,* edited by Richard Proudfoot, Ann Thompson, and David Scott Kastan (Walton-on-Thames: Thomas Nelson, 1998). And except as otherwise noted, quotations from the Bible are from the Authorized King James Version, edited by Robert Carroll and Stephen Prickett (Oxford: Oxford University Press, 1997), but with words in italics or small capitals rendered here in ordinary roman type. When a translation of the Bible into modern English is needed for clarity—particularly in quoting biblical law—we use the New Revised Standard Version.

Acknowledgments

This book was conceived of by Marc Galanter, who also was primarily responsible for the jokes and other sidebars. For history, context, and analysis of most of these jokes and many others, see Marc Galanter, *Lowering the Bar: Lawyer Jokes and Legal Culture* (Madison: University of Wisconsin Press, 2005). The illustrations and permissions were collected primarily by Fred Shapiro, who also provided research and coordination for the entire project. All the authors contributed to all the entries; however, primary and ultimate responsibility for each individual entry rests with the author who wrote it, whose initials appear at the end of the entry.

The authors wish to thank the many members of the Yale University Press staff who have helped to bring this book to fruition, particularly Mary Jane Peluso, Editorial Consultant, whose enthusiasm for the book induced the Press to take it on; Susan Laity, Senior Manuscript Editor, for many clarifications in the text; and Vadim Staklo, Reference Editor, who saw the project through.

We want particularly to thank the outside professionals who skillfully performed essential tasks that too often go unacknowledged, and did so under time pressure: our proofreader, Judy Kaplan, and our jacket designer, David Kopulos.

James E. Clapp acknowledgments

Throughout the years spanned by this project I benefited from the consultation and assistance of my friends Sue Spencer, William H. Roth, Esq., Nancy S. Erickson, Esq., and Lyle Pearsons. Their contributions were generous and invaluable, and instrumental in the creation of a book of this scope. My thanks, though inadequate, are profound.

I am very grateful to the following people who gave generously of their time to assist me with specific entries and issues: Professor John W. Cairns of the University of Edinburgh School of Law, for consultation on "corpus delicti"; Professor Bernard E. Harcourt of the University of Chicago, for making his work available for use in "indict a ham sandwich"; Symmes Gardner, Executive Director of the Center for Art, Design and Visual Culture at the University of Maryland, Baltimore County, for locating the image that appears in "one person, one vote"; Allen Barra, author of *Inventing Wyatt Earp,* for consultation on "posse"; genealogist Barbara Francis Terhune, for research leading to the correct identity of a leading character in "shyster"; Baila H. Celedonia, Esq., and Wendalyn Nichols, for consultation on several topics; Tracy L. Lowe, for meticulously cite-checking several entries; and photographer Dwight Primiano, for custom photography and consultation on image issues.

A research project of this scope requires great libraries, and I was privileged to have at my disposal the collections and knowledgeable staffs of some of the greatest: the New York Public Library, the library of the New York City Bar Association, and the Columbia University Libraries, including the Arthur W. Diamond Law Library at my alma mater, the Columbia Law School. My thanks go to the helpful reference and circulation librarians and other staff at all of these libraries, and in particular to the following individuals at Columbia University for their skillful and accommodating help with particularly difficult requests: Jane Rodgers Siegel, Rare Book Librarian, and Tara C. Craig, Reference Services Supervisor, at the Rare Book and Manuscript Library; Sabrina Sondhi, Special Collections Librarian, at the Arthur W. Diamond Law Library; and Erin Schreiner, Rare Books Assistant, at the Avery Architectural and Fine Arts Library. I also thank Justin Clegg, Curator in the British Library's Department of Manuscripts, for consultation regarding the manuscript shown in "Star Chamber," and Sue Walker and Caroline Fitzgerald of the British Library for helping us to obtain the image of that manuscript, presented here for the first time in such detail.

Above all, I thank my friend and colleague Enid Pearsons, who read every word I wrote with her keen critical eye and in ways large and small improved every entry for which I am responsible.

Elizabeth G. Thornburg acknowledgments

I am grateful to the SMU Dedman School of Law, which has provided a wide array of support, including a summer research grant, student research assistance, and the enormous resources of the Underwood Law Library. Huge thanks must also go to Greg Ivy, Laura Justiss, and Donna Bowman, the patient and resourceful reference librarians who supported my work in every way possible. All of them have tracked down countless obscure publications for me, always with a kind word and a sense of humor. My faculty colleagues at SMU generously suggested sources and ideas, as did participants in faculty workshops at Cornell and Northeastern law schools. In addition, I am grateful to a series of student research assistants who plunged into the wilds of historical research: Chris Smith, Stacie Cargill, Romit Cheema, Anthony Vecchione, Rachel Hass, Hamad Hamad, Sushovan Karki, Amy Moore, Christina Alvarado, and Tracy Lowe.

Thanks also to individuals who provided helpful information, especially Zachary Mann (then spokesperson for the Miami office of U.S. Customs and Border Protection), for helping me find Daniel Geoghegan; Daniel Geoghegan and Yves Colon for talking to me about the "wet foot, dry foot" story; and Jorge Chávez of Al Día for reflecting on current uses of *green card*.

Finally, and most especially, I thank my husband, John Thornburg, and daughter, Kate Betz, who cheerfully provided comments on drafts and loving encouragement along the long road to publication.

Lawtalk

abuse excuse

In eighteenth-century English law a woman who killed her husband was not just a murderer, but a traitor. Just as every British subject was deemed to owe unqualified allegiance to the crown, so a wife or servant owed complete loyalty to the husband or master. Therefore, just as it was treason to attack the king or the government, it was treason of a sort for a wife to kill her husband or for a servant to kill his master. As William Blackstone, the great expositor of English law in that era, explained, in all of these offenses the criminal is an "inferior [who] so forgets the obligations of duty, subjection, and allegiance, as to destroy the life of . . . his superior or lord."[1] Treason against the king—denominated *high treason*—was regarded as the worst possible crime, and the prescribed punishment was correspondingly grisly. (The sentences in particular cases varied, but typically included being hanged, cut down while still alive, and disemboweled—though the king could and often did reduce the penalty to mere beheading.) But the murder of a husband or master was not far behind. This was called *petit treason* (from the French *petit*, "small"—now often written *petty* in English). Whereas the penalty for mere murder was hanging, petit treason was punishable by burning at the stake.

Women have come a long way since then. The surge in awareness of the problem of wife beating in the 1970s (see RULE OF THUMB) led to the realization that there are times when killing one's husband is, if not exactly admirable, at least understandable. Lawyers for women charged with murdering their husbands began to raise as a defense what was referred to at first as the battered wife syndrome, later generalized to battered woman syndrome. The essence of the defense is that relentless physical, mental, or sexual abuse by a husband or lover was responsible for the conduct leading to his death. Depending upon the facts of the case and the state of the law in a particular jurisdiction, a defense of this type might be used to argue that the woman was driven to act irrationally (a temporary-insanity defense), that her judgment was impaired by extreme emotional disturbance (a diminished-capacity defense that would reduce the level of the crime), or that she reasonably concluded that the only way to save her own life was to kill the abuser (essentially a claim of self-defense). The frequency of news stories about women who were murdered by a former partner against whom they had obtained a legal order of protection shows that such fears can be well founded.

In the 1980s the battered woman syndrome defense increasingly found favor with courts, juries, and eventually governors. Within the space of two months in 1990 and 1991, the governors of Ohio and Maryland commuted the sentences of thirty-three women convicted of killing or assaulting abusive partners. Although the defense was controversial and by no means always successful, it inspired lawyers for defendants in other kinds of cases to mount similar kinds of defenses. But since defense lawyers must do the best they can with the facts they are given, a defense of this nature was sometimes raised in a case where, in the eyes of many observers, the facts were less than compelling or the defendant less than sympathetic.

One of the most famous of these cases went to trial in 1993: it was the case of Erik and Lyle Menendez, brothers who, at eighteen and twenty-one, had gruesomely slaughtered their multimillionaire parents at their home in Beverly Hills, and then managed to squander about a million dollars in the six months before their arrest. Their defense was that their father and mother, in various ways at various times, had abused them sexually and psychologically. At the trial the brothers testified that when they acted they believed that their parents were about to kill them to prevent them from disclosing this history of incest. The matter was tried in a joint trial before two juries—one for each brother. It was widely viewed as an open-and-shut case. But when the trial finally concluded the following year, the brothers' claims of parental abuse had sown enough doubt so that both juries deadlocked between convicting them of murder and convicting on a lesser charge of manslaughter. Not until 1996, after a retrial, were the brothers convicted of murder and sentenced to life in prison.

An equally celebrated case that arose in 1993 was that of Lorena Bobbitt, who became a folk hero in some circles when she reacted to what she described as a rape by her husband, John Wayne Bobbitt, by cutting off his penis while he slept, fleeing with it, and throwing it out her car window. (Amazingly, police found the penis in the general area where Lorena Bobbitt said she had thrown it, and surgeons reattached it in a nine and a half–hour operation.) Under the circumstances, both Bobbitts found it necessary to hire not only lawyers to defend themselves but also agents to manage interview requests and hoped-for book and movie offers. John Wayne Bobbitt's agency ultimately landed him a role in a pornographic movie in which he demonstrated what can be accomplished through microsurgery. Lorena Bobbitt's agency, Paradise Entertainment Corporation, for its part, released a statement—clearly guided by her lawyer—in which Lorena laid the groundwork for her temporary-insanity defense: "I was the victim of repeated emotional, physical and sexual abuse," she said. "Everyone has a limit, and this was beyond mine." In time, each of the spouses was tried for assaulting the other, and both were acquitted. In the first trial, against the husband, the jury was not convinced beyond a reasonable doubt that the sex on the fateful night was nonconsensual. But the jury in the second trial, against the wife, evidently was persuaded by her lawyer's argument that, as an abused woman, "Lorena Bobbitt believed she had no real means of escape. . . . In her mind, it was his penis from which she could not escape."[2]

The Menendez and Bobbitt cases were the subject of obsessive media attention and vigorous public debate throughout the second half of 1993. In this atmosphere, *abuse excuse* was a catch phrase waiting to happen. The phrase was probably coined independently by numerous people. It appeared, for example, in a letter to the editor of the *Dayton Daily News* in December 1993. And the previous month, in a somewhat different context, an editor at the *Chicago Tribune* had captioned a letter to syndicated advice columnist Ann Landers, "Sex-abuse excuse too often a copout."[3]

But it was Harvard law professor and media personality Alan Dershowitz who put this phrase on the linguistic map. In a hint of what was to come, Dershowitz dropped the phrase into a CBS network television interview on January 14, 1994, about the inability of the first Menendez jury to reach a verdict. Two days later, he released a syndicated column titled "The Abuse Excuse," discussing the "current rage among defense lawyers" for claiming a history of abuse as an excuse for violence, and concluding, "The popularity of the 'abuse excuse' poses real dangers to our safety and to the integrity of our legal system. . . . The time has come to place limits on testimony about excuses that are so subject to abuses."[4]

The phrase caught on immediately. Within a fortnight, legal commentator Fred Graham could be heard on a syndicated television talk show speaking as if it were an established legal term: "Well, of course, it's a very trendy defense these days, Geraldo. It's called the abuse excuse."[5] (Host Geraldo Rivera's lineup of guests for that episode illustrates the media frenzy at the time: it included a woman who had thrown acid over 69 percent of her husband's body, a man who had killed his wife with a punch to the head when she lunged at his genitals with a cavalry saber, a woman acquitted of murder after fatally shooting her abusive husband, and a female author who had become friends with John Wayne Bobbitt when he bought a copy of her book *How to Satisfy a Woman Every Time and Have Her Beg for More*.) Barely a week later, the phrase got a major boost when the ABC television network news show *Nightline* presented a "Nightline Town Meeting"—with Dershowitz as one of its guests—called "Is Abuse an Excuse?"

And the phrase was not limited to the popular media. Within four days after that *Nightline* special "abuse excuse" made its way into a legal newspaper, and within four months it appeared in the journal of the American Bar Association itself.[6] Although the public obsession with the issue has abated, the question of the extent to which past or ongoing trauma—whether in a war or in a family—should be considered as reducing or negating criminal culpability is an important topic in law, and the phrase *abuse excuse* has become a staple in law review articles on the subject. It remains a casual, slangy expression, however; it is never used as a legal term. Because the phrase has no specific legal meaning, it is almost never seen in judicial opinions, especially not in cases involving allegations of actual abuse, which are too serious for such dismissive language.

One appellate court in a different kind of case, however, was unable to resist a waggish reference to the phrase. In a sexual harassment case brought by a woman who had worked briefly as an assistant to the writing team for the popular TV sitcom *Friends,* the plaintiff asserted that the creative meetings she was required to attend were characterized by a pattern of stunningly crude and juvenile sexual talk and behavior. The defendants, including three of the writers, argued that this sort of locker-room banter and adolescent tomfoolery was an essential part of their job because it gave rise to many of their ideas for the often sexually oriented show. For example, one of the writers "admitted to pantomiming masturbation in the writers' room . . . but asserted '[i]t's part of the creative process' "—prompting the obviously skeptical court to observe in a footnote, "Reich's statement gives new meaning to the term 'abuse excuse.' "[7]

JEC

affirmative action

Affirmative action means doing something rather than doing nothing. It means taking steps to accomplish an objective instead of sitting on your haunches and hoping it will happen. If the goal is good and the means are not evil, affirmative action is a virtue. Yet in the context of efforts to end racial inequality, the concept has met with suspicion and resistance—not least in the Supreme Court.

Although at least one isolated occurrence of the phrase can be found as early as 1683 (in a rather convoluted theological discussion), the term *affirmative action* came into general use in the mid-nineteenth century; prior to that time the usual phrase was *positive action*. The phrase *affirmative action* proved particularly popular in legal discourse, and its use in the nineteenth century and beyond may even have originated there; it can be found in court cases as early as 1835.[1] But it was not until the 1960s that the idea of taking positive steps to overcome the nation's centuries of discrimination against minorities and women became thinkable; before then, simply ending legal *support* for such discrimination was a distant dream.

The first step occurred in 1961, when President John F. Kennedy issued Executive Order 10925 relating to government contracts. The order required government contractors to "take affirmative action to ensure that applicants are employed, and that employees are treated during employment, without regard to their race, creed, color, or national origin."[2] The individual responsible for the key phrase was Hobart Taylor Jr., the lawyer son of a wealthy black Houston businessman and political activist, who had become involved in the drafting at the behest of Vice President Lyndon

Johnson. Taylor later explained, "I was torn between the words 'positive action' and the words 'affirmative action.' . . . And I took 'affirmative action' because it was alliterative."[3] It says much about the status of African Americans in those days that three years later, when Johnson (who had become president upon Kennedy's assassination a few months earlier) named Taylor to his White House staff, it was such a stunning advance that the city's major newspaper printed the story under the five-column headline "Negro Named Associate Counsel to Johnson." It is similarly emblematic of the place of women in America in those days that a story about Taylor's wife in the same newspaper the following month consisted of a large photograph with the headline "Cited for Chic" and a caption identifying her as "Mrs. Hobart Taylor Jr., wife of the executive vice chairman of the President's Committee on Equal Opportunity, . . . wearing an at-home culotte of flowered French silk."[4]

By the time the Civil Rights Act of 1964 was passed, broadly outlawing many forms of discrimination on the basis of race and sex, it was clear that the unfair advantages that had accrued to the white citizenry as a whole over the centuries could never be overcome without affirmative action aimed at lowering obstacles to advancement for blacks. As President Johnson stated in a commencement address at Howard University in 1965, "You do not take a person who, for years, has been hobbled by chains and liberate him, bring him up to the starting line of a race and then say, 'you are free to compete with all the others,' and still justly believe that you have been completely fair."[5] Johnson therefore issued a new and stronger executive order (no. 11246) in 1965—expanded by a further order in 1967 to cover sex discrimination—not only calling for affirmative action in employment but also setting up an enforcement mechanism. Meanwhile, institutions of higher learning began to increase their black enrollment, and efforts to integrate public schools proceeded. At no time was it ever suggested that unqualified applicants should be chosen over qualified applicants; affirmative action was solely a device for enhancing representation of blacks in academia and in the workforce by increasing the number of blacks chosen from pools of qualified individuals.

Nevertheless, it took almost no time for whites to complain that they were being treated unfairly, and to mount court cases claiming that they were victims of "reverse discrimination." They averred that since they had not personally discriminated against blacks, they should not be made to yield any advantage to blacks, notwithstanding that their economic and educational advantages were the product of 350 years of violently enforced affirmative action in *their* favor. In his final sermon, delivered four days before his assassination, Martin Luther King Jr. described one aspect of that historical affirmative action:

> In 1863 the Negro was told that he was free . . . . But he was not given any land to make that freedom meaningful. . . . And the irony of it all is that at the same time the nation failed to do anything for the black man—through an act of Congress it was giving away millions of acres of land [to whites] in the West and the Midwest . . . . But not only did it give the land, it built land-grant colleges to teach them how to farm. Not only that, it provided county agents to further their expertise in farming: not only that, as the years unfolded it provided low interest rates so that they could mechanize their farms. And to this day thousands of these very persons are receiving millions of dollars in federal subsidies every year not to farm. And these are so often the very people who tell Negroes that they must lift themselves by their own bootstraps.[6]

Nevertheless, the Supreme Court has found the issue of affirmative action extremely difficult (one researcher found that in eleven affirmative action cases from 1978 to 1995 the Court generated fifty-five different opinions, among which there were only three that actually received the five votes necessary to represent a majority of the Court),[7] and has turned increasingly against it. This trend is supported by some intellectuals, who argue paternalistically that affirmative action undermines the self-esteem of those who benefit from it. Supporters of affirmative action are still waiting for those intellectuals to produce a single white male doctor or lawyer or business executive or construction worker racked by doubt about his self-worth because he got his start at a time when the system affirmatively favored white males over everyone else.

JEC

age of consent

The *age of consent* is the age at which a young man or woman can give legally effective consent to be married or to engage in sexual intercourse. Although the term had been around in legal writing at least since the early seventeenth century,[1] it exploded into general usage late in the nineteenth.

Generally speaking, a marriage entered into by a person who has not reached the age of consent for marriage can be annulled, and sex with a person who has not reached the age of consent for sexual intercourse is a crime (usually referred to as statutory rape). The legal details, however, can be very convoluted, as a Georgia high school student named Genarlow Wilson learned in 2004 when, at age seventeen, he was charged with "aggravated child molestation" for having received fellatio from an accommodating schoolmate two years his junior. Under Georgia law at the time, the minimum sentence for this act was ten years' imprisonment without the possibility of parole, followed by lifetime registration as a sex offender and lifetime restrictions on where he could live. Under the same law, if the pair had engaged in sexual intercourse instead of oral sex he would have been guilty only of a misdemeanor; and if in addition the boy had been the same age as the girl (fifteen) they both would have been guilty of misdemeanors—each one for having "raped" the other. As it was, Wilson served almost three years in prison before the Georgia Supreme Court narrowly decided that his sentence was so disproportionate to the crime as to constitute cruel and unusual punishment, and ordered him released.[2]

The separation of sexual maturity from legal capacity to consent to sex is the result of a cultural revolution that occurred not so very long ago. In earlier times, puberty signified marriageability. In England, a valid marriage could be contracted if the boy and girl had reached *anni nubiles* (Latin, "marriageable years": twelve for a girl, fourteen for a boy). Any girl who had reached this age was capable of legally consenting to sexual intercourse, a basic component of marriage. (Canon law, which governed marriage, allowed parents to marry off their children beginning at age seven, but then the children had the option of disaffirming the marriage

Just Knitting

This joke—found on the Internet as early as 1999 and widely circulated there since about 2003—captures the core idea of age-of-consent laws, though it fails to convey the variation and complexity of the statutory schemes of the different states:

A policeman was patrolling near midnight at a local parking spot overlooking a golf course. He drove by a car and saw a couple inside with the dome light on. Inside there was a young man in the driver's seat reading a computer magazine and a young lady in the back seat calmly knitting.

He stopped to investigate. He walked up to the driver's window and knocked. The young man looked up, obligingly cranked the window down, and said, "Yes, Officer?"

"What are you doing?" the policeman asked.

"What does it look like?" answered the young man. "I'm reading this magazine."

Pointing toward the young lady in the back seat, the officer then asked, "And what is she doing?"

The young man looked over his shoulder and replied, "I think she's knitting a sweater."

Confused, the officer asked, "How old are you, young man?" "I'm nineteen," he replied.

"And how old is she?" asked the officer.

The young man looked at his watch and said, "Well, in about twelve minutes she'll be sixteen."

upon reaching the age of twelve or fourteen. In practice, marriages at even younger ages were not unknown.)[3]

This principle was reflected in one of England's earliest statutes, the wide-ranging First Statute of Westminster (1275). Among other things, this promulgation by Edward I codified the law on "ravishment of women" by proscribing forcible rape or abduction of females of any age, and intercourse with any maiden under the age of twelve. In the words of an official nineteenth-century translation from the Anglo-French original, "The King prohibiteth that none do ravish, nor take away by force, any Maiden within Age, neither by her own consent, nor without; nor any Wife or Maiden of full Age, nor any other Woman, against her Will."[4]

In the sixteenth century, Parliament increased the penalty in rape cases to death (the penalty for felonies); and "for playne declaracion of Lawe" added, "That yf any person shall unlawfully and carnally knowe and abuse any Woman Childe under the Age of Tenne yeeres, everie suche unlawfull and carnall knowledge shalbe Fellonye." But while that made it plain that sex with a girl under the age of ten would be treated as a rape, the statute left it unclear whether previous lesser punishments were still available for cases where a child had reached the age of ten but not the age of twelve. The law was in this confused state when it was brought to America by the colonists; as a result, after independence some states pegged the age at which a girl could consent to intercourse at ten, others at twelve. In England the matter was clarified in 1828 by a statute continuing the death penalty for forcible rape and for carnal knowledge of a child under the age of ten and explicitly designating carnal knowledge of a child of age ten or eleven as a lesser crime punishable by imprisonment "for such Term as the Court shall award."[5]

In a general revision of England's criminal laws in 1861 the death penalty was abolished for such crimes, reducing the maximum sentence to penal servitude for life, or in the case of carnal knowledge of a girl aged ten or eleven, to penal servitude for three years—though in all cases the court had discretion to order a much lighter sentence.[6] As with all previous statutes on the subject, this involved no fundamental change in thinking about the crime: for at least six centuries, nothing had seemed more natural to lawmakers than that a child upon reaching sexual maturity thereby acquired the status of an adult so far as sexual matters were concerned.

But within the next half century a host of social, economic, philosophical, and political forces would combine to revolutionize the law. Industrialization and urbanization increasingly removed young women from the watchful eyes of their parents, at once freeing them to mingle unchaperoned with young men and subjecting them to unwelcome sexual pressures in the workplace. The romantic concept of children as the embodiment of innocence and purity mingled with Victorian notions of sexuality as a dangerous impulse in need of suppression (see COMSTOCKERY). The feminist movement and the woman suffrage movement, begun at the Seneca Falls Convention of 1848, called attention to the legal victimization of women. The temperance movement, and particularly the founding of the Women's Christian Temperance Union (WCTU) in 1874, called attention to the brutalization of women by men.

Many of these threads came together in what came to be called the "social purity movement," which was concerned, among other things, with what was perceived as an epidemic of prostitution and "white slavery." This concern represented a mixture of compassion for poor girls and women forced into prostitution by economic necessity, fear that "pure" women were being abducted or inveigled into lives of debauchery, and concern that "bad" women were luring virtuous young men into sexual vice. In England in 1885, the influential journalist and social purity advocate William Thomas Stead, with the support of Salvation Army Chief of Staff Bramwell Booth (who had helped his father found the Army a decade earlier) and the redoubtable social activist Mrs. Josephine Butler (wife of the canon of Winchester), investigated the London sex trade. Among other things, Stead contrived with several confederates to "purchase" a thirteen-year-old virgin and at least contract for the purchase of several more teenage virgins, all ostensibly for sexual purposes.

The resulting exposé, published as a week-long series in Stead's *Pall Mall Gazette*—and brilliantly promoted the preceding Saturday by means of a printed advisory that prudish readers should avoid reading the *Gazette* for the next few days—caused a sensation. An introductory essay argued for "raising the age of consent"—a theme to which the series repeatedly returned—and at once the topic was on everyone's lips.[7] The government was forced to respond, and within three months an act for "Protection of Women and Girls" had been whisked through Parliament. Among other measures, the act raised the age of consent from thirteen (to which it had been grudgingly increased from twelve a decade earlier) to sixteen. As his reward for exposing the complicity and involvement of powerful people and the legal system itself in the sex trade, Stead was convicted at the Old Bailey of child abduction and indecent assault and served three months in jail.

Stead's series was reprinted in the United States, where it proved as effective in selling newspapers, and almost as effective in arousing public sentiment, as it had in England. Suddenly people began to notice—and to be concerned—that the age of consent for girls in most American states was ten; in a few, twelve; and in Delaware, presumably because of confusion over the old canon law, seven. (In Arkansas the relevant criminal statute explicitly referred to the transition point as "the age of puberty"; but the state's supreme court held that an indictment for carnal knowledge of a twelve-year-old girl who allegedly had not yet reached puberty could not stand, for the common law had set twelve as the age of "legal puberty" so as to avoid the "indecently inquisitive" process of requiring a girl's underage status to be "proved by actual inspection.") In 1885 the WCTU established an official Social Purity Department to campaign for, among other things, a higher age of consent. Within five years, legislators in twenty-four states had responded to pressure from a wide range of sources by raising the age of consent for girls—most to fourteen, but a few to thirteen, fifteen, sixteen, and in one case eighteen. Opponents railed that such laws would put innocent boys at the mercy of conniving girls, and efforts were made to repeal the laws. But the activists pressed on, gaining higher and higher ages. By 1920 the lowest age of consent in the land was fourteen in a single state; in no fewer than twenty-one states it had reached the age of eighteen.[8]

By that time, World War I had rung down the final curtain on the Victorian era. The 1920s brought unprecedented freedom for young people, especially in the cities. It was the flapper era, the Jazz Age, the decade of speakeasies and bathtub gin and the Charleston. It was only in this post-Victorian atmosphere that a blunt expression acknowledging the sexuality of teenage girls—and wryly commenting on the legal dangers they now posed—could have taken root. The stage was set for the invention of a new word: JAILBAIT.

JEC

aid and abet (and the like)

One of the oldest complaints about lawyers is that they are, in a word, wordy. This trait has been the subject of ridicule and pleas for reform for centuries—and not just from outside the profession. Thomas Jefferson, who had used deliberately simplified language in his draft of new laws for the state of Virginia following the Declaration of Independence in 1776, alluded to that effort four decades later when he submitted a draft bill, in similarly straightforward language, to establish free public elementary schools throughout the state: "I suppose the reformation has not been acceptable, as it has been little followed. You, however, can easily correct this bill to the taste of my brother lawyers, by making every other word a 'said' or 'aforesaid,' and saying everything over two or three times, so that nobody but we of the craft can untwist the diction, and find out what it means."[1]

The most direct way in which lawyers say things two or three times over is by peppering formal documents with stock phrases that are—as such a document might put it—redundant and repetitive: "Aid and abet." "By and with." "Cease and desist." "Due and payable." You can go from A to Z and back again and find a different such expression for almost every letter. Here is a modern example, from a case against directors of a corporation named Midcom Communications who had signed a certain consent form, obviously drafted by the company's lawyer. As extracted by the court, this instrument

> "*authorized, empowered and directed*" the officers to "*do and perform* . . . all such *acts, deeds and things*, and to *make, execute and deliver* . . . all such other *agreements* . . . , *undertakings, documents, instruments or certificates* as any such *officer or officers* may deem *necessary or appropriate* to *effectuate and carry out* fully the *purposes and intent* of the foregoing resolutions and that any action [already] taken by any of the officers of MIDCOM . . . is hereby *ratified, confirmed and approved*."[2]

Meaning: the officers of Midcom are authorized to implement the board's resolutions.

It is often suggested that redundant legal expressions of this sort were created by pairing a native English word with a French-derived synonym in order to avoid any possible misunderstanding at a time when both languages were in common use in England. So in the Midcom consent form we have "do and perform" (from Old English and Old French, respectively), and likewise—though not always in the same etymological order—"act and deed," "make and execute," "agreement and undertaking."

I Give You That Orange

The classic send-up of legal verbosity is this, penned in the first half of the nineteenth century by an English campaigner for reform in the drafting of statutes by Parliament:

If a man would, according to law, give to another an orange, instead of saying:—"I give you that orange," which one should think would be what is called in legal phraseology, "an absolute conveyance of all right and title therein," the phrase would run thus:—"I give you all and singular, my estate and interest, right, title, claim and advantage of and in that orange, with all its rind, skin, juice, pulp and pips, and all right and advantage therein, with full power to bite, cut, suck, and otherwise eat the same, or give the same away as fully and effectually as I the said A. B. am now entitled to bite, cut, suck, or otherwise eat the same orange, or give the same away, with or without its rind, skin, juice, pulp, and pips, anything hereinbefore, or hereinafter, or in any other deed, or deeds, instrument or instruments of what nature or kind soever, to the contrary in any wise, notwithstanding," with much more to the same effect. Such is the language of lawyers; and it is very gravely held by the most learned men among them, that by the omission of any of these words the right to the said orange would not pass to the person for whose use the same was intended.

Arthur Symonds, *The Mechanics of Law-Making* (London, 1835), 75 (with a missing period supplied).

And there are many more French/English pairs that Midcom's counsel somehow failed to work in. Examples familiar to any lawyer include:

acknowledge and confess
annul and set aside
devise and bequeath
due and owing
fit and proper
free and clear

goods and chattels
[in one's] place and stead
maintenance and upkeep
ways and means

But any catalogue of French/English legal word pairs is far outweighed by the number of equally redundant phrases containing only words from dialects of French, only native English words, or other mixtures, including words (like *testament*) that bypassed French and came into English directly from Latin. For example, in the Midcom consent form, all six of the words in "documents, instruments or certificates" and "ratified, confirmed and approved" are from Old French. Other combinations entirely of French origin include:

aid and abet
cease and desist
custom and usage
due and payable
fraud and deceit
HUE AND CRY
necessary and proper
null and void
ordered, adjudged, and decreed
rest, residue, and remainder

and many more. Redundant legal phrases consisting entirely of words of Old English origin are somewhat unusual, but include *to have and to hold, [without] let or hindrance* (meaning without impediment), and innumerable combinations of prepositions (*by and between, through and under, from and after, over and above,* and so on).

Clearly this profusion of redundancies cannot be explained simply by an ancient desire to make writing clear to speakers of two different languages. Many other factors have played a role. Rigid adherence to unnecessarily complex and specialized verbal formulas helped the legal profession by making it necessary for people to hire lawyers to draft and interpret instruments. In addition, for some centuries court clerks, and sometimes even lawyers, were paid by the page for the papers they handled.[3] As late as 1818, John Adams, who apparently shared the views of his long-time political adversary Thomas Jefferson on the subject of legal language, wrote, "I hope . . . that common sense in common language will, in time, become fashionable. But the hope must be faint as long as clerks are paid by the line and the number of syllables in a line."[4]

The fundamental legal rationale for redundancy, though, is simply this: it is better to be safe than sorry. Lawyers are paid to make documents airtight, and they work with the knowledge that other lawyers down the line may be paid to try to poke holes in them. Including two or three words that mean essentially the same thing protects against a specious argument that some shade of meaning was not covered. And once a phrase has become common, omitting one of the usual words is even more dangerous. No lawyer relishes the prospect of explaining to a client that a deed proved ineffective, or a promissory note unenforceable, simply because the lawyer didn't think it would matter if some of the usual words were left out in the interest of brevity.

Most of these customary phrases in law are of very ancient vintage. In documents and ceremonies of great importance—wills, weddings, deeds, decrees, and so on—ritualistic and repetitive phrases, especially if they had a poetic quality in rhythm, rhyme, or alliteration, provided emphasis and underscored the significance and solemnity of the occasion. When a judicial pronouncement begins (as many still do), "It is hereby *ordered, adjudged, and decreed*," there is no doubt that it means business. The phrase *to have and to hold*—which resonates in any of the languages historically used in English law (Law French *aver et tener;* Latin *habendum et tenendum*)—was so well suited to this purpose that it was not just used in deeds of land: in 1549 it was incorporated into "The Forme of Solemnizacion of Matrimonie" in the Church of England's first Book of Common Prayer. And the human love of ritual is such that almost half a millennium later a great many couples still would not regard their marriage as suitably solemnized without these words. Similarly, most people would probably still find it unsatisfying to see the bare word *Will* at the top of their will. A document of such gravity cries out for a grander title: *Last Will and Testament.*

Even the Declaration of Independence, drafted by that resolute opponent of unnecessary repetition Thomas Jefferson, resorted to redundancy in the crucial concluding paragraph—the paragraph that actually declared independence and sealed the signers' fate as traitors to the king. As drafted by Jefferson, it would have stated that the people of the colonies "*reject and renounce* all *allegiance & subjection* to the kings of Great Britain, and all others who may hereafter claim *by, through, or under* them." The Continental Congress took out that language, but retained Jefferson's declaration that the colonies were "*free & independant* states," with "full power to levy war, conclude peace, contract alliances, establish commerce, & to do all other *acts and things* which independant states may of right do."[5] And in the most famously concise speech ever given by a politician, the Gettysburg Address, Abraham Lincoln knew that it would not do simply to say that it was "fitting" to dedicate a portion of the battlefield as a cemetery for those who died there; he said that it was "fitting and proper"—and not just that, but "altogether fitting and proper."

And here we come to the most basic fact of all about redundant phrases. Lincoln was not speaking in legalese; he was speaking in plain English. English, with its history of influences from multiple languages, is uniquely rich in vocabulary, and the stringing together of synonyms from this great store of words, especially when they rhyme or alliterate or match in meter, is a characteristic—and delightful—feature of the language.

The pattern is so pervasive that we are generally unaware of it. It certainly is not as fashionable as in centuries gone by; yet it still provides the language with much of its music: *First and foremost. One and only. Each and every. Any and all. All and sundry. Jot and tittle. Nooks and crannies. Whys and wherefores. Hem and haw. Moan and groan. Weep and wail. Hot and bothered. Cool, calm, and collected. High and mighty. Meek and mild. Fine and dandy. Hale and hearty. Safe and sound. Rest and relaxation. Part and parcel. Peace and quiet. Trouble and strife. Wrack and ruin. Blood and gore. Over and done with. Dead and gone.*

Even in this *day and age,* the list of everyday redundancies can go on almost *forever and ever.* At its heart, this pattern isn't lawtalk. It's just talk.

JEC

attorney general

For a considerable time now there has been a common practice, especially inside the Washington Beltway, of addressing attorneys general as "General." Some people may even think that the position of attorney general of the United States is a military position—a profound misunderstanding in a governmental system based upon civilian control of legal institutions and even of the military itself. Actually, the *attorney general* of a state or of the United States is the same thing as the *general counsel* of a corporation: it's the lawyer responsible for providing general legal advice and representation for the entity, as distinguished from attorneys retained for particular matters, who, depending on the circumstances, might have such titles as *special prosecutor, special counsel, independent counsel,* or, in the corporate context, *outside counsel.*

The potential for confusion lies in the reversal of usual English word order: an attorney general is a kind of attorney, not a kind of general. Not that this word order, with a postpositive adjective (an adjective coming after what it modifies), is by any means rare in English; we usually use it without giving it a thought. Some words are almost always modified postpositively (nothing *important,* anybody *suitable*); some adjectives can occur only after the word they modify (opportunities *galore,* a house *afire*); sometimes the position determines the meaning (the *present* members vs. the members *present*); sometimes the effect is arch or poetic (matters *mathematical,* love *undying,* creatures *great and small*).

Many such phrases, though, are simply fixed expressions that became established long ago under the influence of Latin and French syntax: *battle royal; time immemorial; body politic.* One area in which this pattern particularly tends to persist is in titles: *mother superior; poet laureate; heir apparent; princess royal; notary public; president-elect; sergeant major* (a sergeant, not a major). The single greatest repository of such formulas, however, is law—a field with deep linguistic roots in Latin and French and a particular propensity for hanging onto ancient technical expressions: *decree absolute* (a permanent decree); *chattel real* (a kind of property interest in real estate); *condition precedent* (a condition that must occur before a right can arise); *court martial* (a military court); *date certain* (a fixed date); *law merchant* (mercantile law); *letters testamentary* (a document authorizing an individual to act as executor under a will); *fee simple absolute*—an inheritable interest in land (a fee) that is unrestricted (simple) and cannot be divested (absolute).

In *attorney general* we have a twofer: both a long-established title and a legal term. The phrase, in its original French form, was already in use in England by the end of the thirteenth century as a term for a person with broad power to act on behalf of another, like the holder of a general power of attorney today. (It is found in the plural *attournez generals*—and distinguished from *attournez especials,* whose capacity was more limited—in a treatise on English law written, in French, in about 1292.)[1] By the end of the fifteenth century it had become customary for the king to designate a particular attorney as having the authority to represent him in all courts, and this position became formalized under the title *attorney general.* The title was carried over into the colonies and adopted by Congress when it established a similar position for the United States in 1789. The position at that time was viewed as a part-time job; no staff or office was provided. But the job grew as the government grew, and when Congress established a sort of vice–attorney general position in 1870, it again used the title of the corresponding position already established in England: *solicitor general.* Today the attorney general heads the entire Department of Justice, which includes United States Attorneys' offices throughout the country; the solicitor general is responsible for general supervision of appellate litigation and the handling of all Supreme Court cases on behalf of the United States.

In Washington legal and political circles—obsessed as they are with status and rank, and given as they are to extravagant (if not always sincere) expressions of respect—it has become usual to address those individuals as "General." For example, in the official transcript of a Supreme Court argument in 2007 between the attorney general of the state of Washington, Robert McKenna, and U.S. Solicitor General Paul Clement, one finds Chief Justice John Roberts thanking the first and calling upon the second by saying, "Thank you, General. General Clement." (The court reporter, even more finely attuned to status, identified the arguers as "General Clement" and "Mr. McKenna.") Most state attorneys general appear to have resisted the trend thus far, but some have embraced it, and at least one has gone so far as to allow himself to be referred to on his department's Web site simply as "the General."[2]

There is no way to determine how this all started. As the law professor who has dug most deeply into the phenomenon put it, "We will never know when the first sycophant tried it out on the first delighted megalomaniac." The inappropriately militaristic tone of the title is illustrated by a lighthearted but slightly ominous throwaway line early in the presidency of George W. Bush. After his election in 2000, President Bush proceeded (as all presidents do) to fill the ninety-three offices of U.S. Attorney with his own nominees. At the end of November 2001, when most of his nominees had been confirmed by the Senate, a conference of U.S. Attorneys was held in Washington and the president addressed them. In response to his introduction by Attorney General John Ashcroft he said, "Well, John, thank you . . . . I guess we call you General. [*Laughter*] That means you all are in the Army. [*Laughter*] And I am glad you are."[3]

Some of that laughter may have been nervous laughter. Even as a joke, the image of the U. S. Attorneys marching in lockstep at the command of the attorney general is somewhat disturbing; and for six of the new U.S. Attorneys who were confirmed in time to attend that meeting, the implication that they had better toe the line—whether intended or not—proved all too real when they found themselves among nine U.S. Attorneys sacked in 2006 by Ashcroft's successor, Attorney General Alberto Gonzales, for reasons that the Department of Justice itself later concluded were, at least in several cases, based upon "political partisan considerations."[4] The military analogy does not befit a department of justice in a democratic society. Although U. S. Attorneys are presumed to share the general priorities of the current administration, they must never be seen as soldiers in a partisan political campaign. They have a higher calling: to exercise independent judgment and seek justice in a scrupulously nonpartisan manner.

Likewise, the attorney general, as the chief lawyer for the nation and not just for the president, is much more than a general carrying out the political strategies of the commander in chief. In fact, in matters of diplomatic protocol, the attorney general of the United States, like the rest of the Cabinet and for that matter even the solicitor general, ranks above all military personnel of every stripe—which is exactly as it should be in a country ruled by democratically established laws rather than military might.[5] Perhaps one day we will see an attorney general, when addressed as "General Smith" or the like, reply, "I am not a mere general. You may address me as (Ms./Mr.) Smith if you like, but if you wish to identify me by my office, then please use the title to which I am entitled: Attorney General."

JEC

attorney vs. lawyer

A prominent characteristic of the English language is the frequent occurrence of two words with substantially the same meaning, one of Old English origin and one of French or Latin origin: *child* and *infant; buy* and *purchase; home* and *domicile; whole* and *entire.* So it is with *lawyer* and *attorney.*

Much of the credit or blame for this virtual doubling of the size of our lexicon goes to William the Conqueror. When he invaded England from Normandy in 1066, he launched two centuries of rule by French-speaking kings. Contrary to common belief, William and his successors did not impose the French language on English legal institutions. But the currency of French in royal circles gave the language importance in England, and this was enhanced by the growth of French as an international language and its consequent adoption, beginning in the thirteenth century, by the English legal profession. This foreign influence on English was compounded by the use of Latin as the international language of religion and scholarship in Europe in the Middle Ages. Together these influences resulted in the incorporation into English of a vast array of terms derived from Latin (either directly or by way of French) on top of the original English vocabulary—mostly Germanic in origin—handed down from before the Norman Conquest.

Law is part of that pre-Conquest vocabulary. It is derived from the Old Norse language that was carried to Britain by Viking invaders in the ninth century. As is common in early English, the word is short and simple. The *-yer* of *lawyer* is a variant of the *-er* of *miller* or *potter* or *hatter;* it signifies a person who practices a particular occupation. The *y* comes into play in -*er* words for professions whose names end with *w*—a phenomenon that seems to have affected only three professions: making bows, sawing wood, and practicing law. Thus we have (or at least used to have) bowyers, sawyers, and lawyers.

But even before there were lawyers, there were attorneys. This is a rare English-French pair of synonyms in which the imported French form appears to have entered the language before the home-grown English form. That is because, although there were certainly *laws* before the Norman Conquest, there was no such thing as a *profession* of law until the thirteenth century, and it was these new legal professionals—originally "a small band of pleaders practising in a corner of the king's palace"[1]—who made French the language of English law. It was therefore natural that the original word for such a professional would itself be taken from French. But whereas the meaning of *lawyer* is pretty obvious from the way the word is put together, the meaning of *attorney* is anything but.

The strange pronunciation of the word—as if it were spelled *atturney*—is a tipoff to its origins. The *torn* at the heart of the word goes all the way back to the Latin verb *tornāre*, "to turn on a lathe, round off," which in fact is indirectly related to the English word *turn*. Over the centuries the meaning of the Latin word expanded. Adding *ad* (to) as a prefix in medieval Latin produced *attornare* (by assimilation of the *d* and *t* in *ad-tornare*), which in Old French became *atorner*, meaning "turn to, turn over to, appoint." The participial form *atorné* (the person appointed) added a suffix that usually is rendered in English as -*ee*; for example, the French *employé* (the person employed) became the English *employee*. That -*ee* suffix is often seen in legal terminology (*assignee, donee, grantee*); but in *attorney* it is disguised. The word came into English before the -*ee* spelling became the norm—in fact, before there was any standardization of spelling at all—and of the various spellings that were used (citations in the *Oxford English Dictionary* include *atturney, attourneis, attorny, atorne, attornay, attourney, atturneye, attourneie, attornies*), somehow *attorney* is the one that stuck.

Putting it all together, we see that an attorney is a "turn-to-ee"—a person to whom you turn over your court case or legal matter. (More specifically, this is what we call an *attorney at law*. Another kind of attorney is an individual designated to act on another's behalf in matters not requiring legal training, referred to as an *attorney in fact*.) It is a convoluted etymology. In the past, even many lexicographers, though aware that *attorney* had some connection to the word *turn,* were unable to sort out the twists and turns that actually gave rise to the word, prompting this dry comment in the staid *Oxford English Dictionary:* "The statement found in the law dictionaries for the last 200 years, that the word means one 'who acts *in the turn* of another,' is a bad guess."

For centuries after the Norman Conquest, while English remained the mother tongue of nearly everyone in England, French—and in certain fields written Latin—was heavily used by the intellectual and social elite: scholars, clerics, lawyers, royalty. So it is not surprising that even today words of French and Latin origin are often regarded as somehow more elegant and sophisticated than short, plain Anglo-Saxon words with the same meaning. (In the most extreme cases, simple four-letter words for body parts and bodily functions, which have been part of the language for centuries, are actually taboo—or as close to taboo as anything is in this freewheeling age—and polite usage requires that multisyllabic Latin-derived words be substituted for them.) This phenomenon can be seen in the case of *attorney* and *lawyer.* Although both terms are perfectly acceptable in American English (in other English-speaking countries the terms tend to have developed distinct or specialized meanings and connotations), the French-derived term still has a little more cachet. Comedians never tell an "attorney joke"; it's always a "lawyer joke." But lawyers never put "lawyer" on a business card; they invariably style themselves "Attorney at Law."

JEC

badge of slavery

The word *badge* originally referred to an emblem or object identifying a knight or his followers. But the term was readily extended to anything that symbolizes or evidences an individual's status or personal qualities. For example, Shakespeare's character Falstaff, in a soliloquy in praise of alcoholic drink, lists among its benefits "the warming of the blood": cold blood, he says, leaves "the liver white and pale, which is the badge of pusillanimity and cowardice." At the other end of the bravery spectrum, in a novel about the American Civil War written three centuries after Shakespeare's play, the wounds of soldiers returning from battle are seen as "a red badge of courage."[1]

In the eighteenth century, a frequent rhetorical device for describing any practice regarded as oppressive to a class of people was to characterize it as a *badge of slavery* or *badge of servitude*. For example, the anonymous critic who called himself "Junius," whose brazen letters railing against the political establishment were published in a London newspaper from 1769 to 1772, had this to say about the tea tax that was so despised in the American colonies: "What is it then but an odious, unprofitable exertion of a speculative right, and fixing a badge of slavery upon the Americans?"[2]

In the nineteenth century, especially in the wake of the Civil War, the phrase took on a more literal meaning—and a specifically legal significance—in reference to the American institution of slavery and the caste system that perpetuated slavery's subjugation of blacks after the war. Although the Thirteenth Amendment, ratified in December 1865, abolished slavery and involuntary servitude except as punishment for a crime, every manner of law and practice was employed in the former slave states to keep the former slaves "in their place." In 1866, therefore, Congress adopted a civil rights bill granting blacks equal legal rights with whites in a wide range of areas and opening the federal courts to cases affecting individuals denied those rights. Senator Lyman Trumbull of Illinois, the bill's prime mover, explained it on the floor of the Senate as an implementation of the newly adopted antislavery amendment, saying that "any statute which is not equal to all, and which deprives any citizen of civil rights which are secured to other citizens, . . . is, in fact, a badge of servitude which, by the Constitution, is prohibited." Such laws, he said, "never would have been thought of or enacted anywhere but for slavery, and when slavery falls they fall also."[3]

But when a case based upon the Civil Rights Act of 1866 reached the Supreme Court a few years later, the Court began what was to become an eighty-year stretch of hostility and obstructionism regarding black civil rights by throwing out a murder case against two whites who had massa-

cred an extended black family—including a blind ninety-year-old grandmother—"as with a broad-axe." The case had been brought in federal
court under the Civil Rights Act because the witnesses, who were black,
were barred by a pre–Civil War Kentucky statute from testifying against
whites in state court. The Supreme Court held that the Civil Rights Act
did not apply to the situation because the case was not one "affecting" the
black witnesses or the black victims: only the parties to the case would be
legally affected by it, and they were all white. The two dissenters were
aghast. They said:

> To deprive a whole class of the community of this right [to testify], to
> refuse their evidence and their sworn complaints, is to brand them
> with a badge of slavery; is to expose them to wanton insults and fiend-
> ish assaults; is to leave their lives, their families, and their property
> unprotected by law. It gives unrestricted license and impunity to
> vindictive outlaws and felons to rush upon these helpless people and
> kill and slay them at will, as was done in this case.[4]

The majority of the Court was unmoved. Congress continued for a
while to try to extend basic civil rights to former slaves, but the Supreme
Court resolutely thwarted any progress. In 1875, Congress enacted another civil rights bill, this one outlawing racial discrimination in places of
public accommodation such as inns, public conveyances, and theaters. In
a group of cases ironically known as the *Civil Rights Cases,* the Supreme
Court struck down the Civil Rights Act of 1875. The Court conceded that
the Thirteenth Amendment gave Congress "a right to enact all necessary
and proper laws for the obliteration and prevention of slavery with all its
badges and incidents," but the majority could not perceive any connection between the country's history of slavery and the exclusion of blacks
from facilities open to all whites. To hold that "mere discrimination" was
a badge of slavery, it said, would be "running the slavery argument into
the ground." Justice John Marshall Harlan, a former Kentucky slave
owner who had come to despise the institution of slavery, was the lone
dissenter. Harlan's wife of fifty-seven years, in a memoir written after his
death, touchingly described how, to inspire him and help focus his mind

for the task of writing that dissent, she had secured and placed on his desk the very inkstand used by Chief Justice Roger Taney a quarter century earlier in writing the most infamous proslavery decision in the Court's history, the *Dred Scott* decision.[5]

Justice Harlan was to remain a voice in the wilderness on this issue throughout his thirty-four years on the Court. In 1896 he was again a lone voice in *Plessy v. Ferguson,* the case in which the Court endorsed the doctrine of SEPARATE BUT EQUAL. In his now-celebrated dissent, he wrote, "The arbitrary separation of citizens, on the basis of race, while they are on a public highway, is a badge of servitude wholly inconsistent with the civil freedom and the equality before the law established by the Constitution." Ten years later, when the Court held that Congress had no power to outlaw conspiracies to deprive blacks of employment through violence and intimidation, even Oliver Wendell Holmes Jr., recently elevated to the Supreme Court from his position as chief justice of the highest court of Massachusetts and destined to become known as "the Great Dissenter," went along with the majority. Justice Harlan was joined only by the Court's newest member, William Rufus Day, in arguing, in dissent, that the statute in question was constitutional under the Thirteenth Amendment because "the disability to make or enforce contracts for one's personal services was a badge of slavery"—the very essence of slavery, one might well say![6]

It was not until the height of the civil rights movement in 1968 that the Supreme Court changed its mind. In that year, the Court resurrected the Civil Rights Act of 1866, holding that it could properly be invoked to bar a real estate developer from refusing to sell a home to a person of color. "Congress," the Court decided, "has the power under the Thirteenth Amendment rationally to determine what are the badges and the incidents of slavery, and the authority to translate that determination into effective legislation."[7] In a bitter irony, the second Justice John Marshall Harlan— grandson and namesake of the great Justice whose passionate dissents all those years before were at long last being vindicated—dissented.

JEC

billable hour

Few terms hold more importance for a law firm's clients or its employees than *billable hour*—not a real hour, but sixty minutes of work that the lawyer can bill a client for. It is no accident that a popular lawyer joke on this subject made its first written appearance in a major federal case on attorneys' fees. As recounted by a dissenting judge,

> An immediately deceased lawyer arrived at the Pearly Gates to seek admittance from St. Peter. The Keeper of the Keys was surprisingly warm in his welcome: "We are so glad to see you, Mr. Smith. We are particularly happy to have you here, not only because we get so few lawyers up here, but because you lived to the wonderful age of 165." Mr. Smith was a bit doubtful and hesitant. "Now, St. Peter, if there's one place I don't want to get into under false pretenses, it's Heaven. I really died at age 78." St. Peter looked perplexed, frowned, and consulted the scroll in his hand. "Ah, I see where we made our mistake as to your age. We just added up your time sheets!"[1]

There it is in a nutshell—the public image of the lawyer as economic predator, billing more hours than there are in the day.

Lawyers didn't always bill by the hour (and some still do not). Early-twentieth-century lawyers used various methods for billing clients. Some matters were billed at a flat rate, some on a percentage basis, and many used a method called value billing. Bills were sent only sporadically and were not itemized, being only "for services rendered." Many lawyers were effectively bound by the "suggested" minimum fee schedules published by local bar associations until the U.S. Supreme Court rejected these as antitrust violations.

Lawyers initially kept track of time casually at best, not in order to bill by the hour but just to help determine a reasonable fee. Tracking time spent on a case also helped the firm analyze the productivity of individual lawyers, the profitability of various practice areas, and the appropriate work expectations for partners and associates—the salaried junior lawyers in a law firm. In 1940, Reginald Heber Smith wrote four articles for the *American Bar Association Journal* advocating a more organized approach to law-firm management. Among other things, he recommended a sort of billable-hour budget for each lawyer, with productivity documented through "Daily Time Sheet" forms.

The American Bar Association went on a crusade to promote hourly billing in 1958 with its pamphlet *The 1958 Lawyer and His 1938 Dollar,* pointing out that lawyers who kept track of their time and billed clients accordingly made more money than those who did not. The problem, said the ABA, was that by concentrating on "devotion to public interest," lawyers were failing as businessmen, and they needed to start recording and charging for their time, their "sole expendable asset." Billing by the hour gradually caught on, spreading from large firms to small ones. By the late 1970s, billable hours became the primary measure of client billing for most purposes.

The term *billable hour* seems to have crept into legal vocabulary as its adoption as a billing method became established. A 1968 case was the first to use *billable hour* with respect to lawyers, and it set the term in quotation marks and defined it. It seems likely, though, that bar association meetings and publications were the earliest adopters of this lingo, and those sources (even a law student's letter to the editor) routinely used *billable hour* without explanation by the early 1970s.[2]

The billable hour has some advantages as a management tool. Hourly bills are easy to prepare and easy for clients to understand and review. Time-based billing also provides a method to measure the unmeasurable: the value of the service rendered by the lawyer. This is particularly helpful in contemporary legal matters that are extremely complex or unpredictable, and that involve multiple lawyers from different sections of large firms. Billing by the hour can also be very profitable for the law firm: some matters can easily generate hundreds of thousands of hours in attorney work. As ethics expert Deborah Rhode noted sardonically, "Why not leave no stone unturned if you are charging by the stone?"[3]

Unfortunately, hourly billing also has significant disadvantages, some of which go to the heart of the profession. Legal ethicist Geoffrey Hazard has observed that with hourly billing a "subtle transformation occurred: The time sheet—created as a control on 'inventory'—now became the 'inventory' itself." In Hazard's view, the concept of the billable hour contributed to law firms' thinking of themselves primarily as businesses turning out commodities—measured in units of time.[4]

From the perspective of both law firm and client, the billable hour has some perverse consequences. First, hourly billing discourages efficiency. The lawyer who takes two hours rather than one to complete a task gets paid more; the partner who assigns three rather than two associates to a project creates a bigger pool of billable hours; costly improvements in technology that increase productivity (like computerized legal research and legal forms) increase overhead and decrease revenues. Hourly billing also discourages communication between lawyer and client (who may be billed at a minimum of .2 hour per phone call), shifts the cost of associate training and turnover to the client, and creates a potential conflict of interest between lawyer and client. The ABA now understands that it helped to create a monster, and in 2002 it tepidly recommended reform, defending hourly billing but identifying alternatives.

A 2007 survey showed a slight increase in alternative billing methods, and the protracted economic recession that began in December of that year encouraged further rethinking of billing practices, with the result that some large law firms reported using flat-rate billing more often by 2009. But the billable hour remained firmly entrenched. As one industry observer commented, "Alternative fees are like teenage sex. There are more people talking about it than doing it, and those that are doing it don't know what they're doing."[5]

A business model based on hourly billing leads to budgets based on expected billable hours, and those budgets include requirements that law-firm employees produce a certain number of billable hours every year. As salaries and other costs increased in the 1980s, law firms needed to increase either the billing rates or the number of hours worked (or both) in order to meet their budgets. As the years passed, billable-hour expectations skyrocketed. In its 1958 study, the ABA concluded that unless a lawyer worked overtime there were "only approximately 1,300 fee-earning hours per year." Today's large-firm associates would consider that part-time work, as official billable-hour expectations range from 1,800 to 2,300 billable hours per year, and billing 3,000 hours is not unheard of. Small wonder that a

No Rest for the Weary

Even time spent on a matter by paralegals is often billed by the hour. This joke, which entered circulation about 1997, must have been dreamt up by someone with firsthand experience of the pressure on law-firm employees to build up partner profits by piling up billable hours:

A paralegal, an associate, and a partner of a prestigious New York law firm are walking through Central Park on their way to lunch when they come upon a curious old oil lamp. They rub it and a genie comes out in a puff of smoke.

The genie says, "I usually only grant three wishes, so I'll give each of you just one."

"Me first! Me first!" says the paralegal. "I want to be in the Bahamas, driving a speedboat, without a care in the world."

Poof. He's gone.

In astonishment, "Me next! Me next!" says the associate. "I want to be in Hawaii, relaxing on the beach with my personal masseuse, an endless supply of piña coladas, and the love of my life.

Poof. She's gone.

"You're next," the genie says to the partner.

The partner says, "I want those two back in the office after lunch."

persistent legend in law-firm circles tells of an unknown associate who actually managed to bill more than twenty-four hours in one day by including work on a coast-to-coast flight across time zones.

While it may be hard to sympathize with associates at major law firms whose 2009 salaries started at $145,000, their compensation comes with significant tradeoffs. According to the Yale Law School Career Development Office, an associate could meet a target of 2,200 billable hours only by working twelve-hour days Monday through Friday (not counting commuting time), and seven-hour days most Saturdays, and spending none of that time on personal matters, nonbillable conversations with colleagues, community service, or business development. As to the quality of the work done: "No one working these kinds of sweatshop hours can give good legal service," says Rhode.[6]

In addition to maximizing legitimate billable hours, the pressure to meet quotas causes a few lawyers to blur ethical lines. Some "round up" their time to the next quarter hour, a practice approved by the ABA. Others "double bill"—charging multiple clients for the same time period, as when doing work for one client on an airplane while flying on a trip for another and billing both (the ABA declared this practice unethical, but it still occurs with some frequency). Some lawyers actually fabricate hours, charging for time they never worked. Which brings us back to Lawyer Smith chatting with St. Peter: his birth certificate makes him 78 years old, his time sheets make him 165—and after spending a career billing more than 2,000 hours annually he may feel as though his time sheets are right.

EGT

black letter law

Lawyers routinely use the phrase *black letter law* to refer to basic legal principles, principles that are too well settled—or so they are trying to claim—to be subject to reasonable dispute. (See also HORNBOOK LAW.) But few lawyers know why such principles are called "black letter," and fewer still know that the phrase used to have quite the opposite connotation.

Black letter is the English name for the style of type in which books were first printed. Also referred to as *Gothic* or *Old English* type (though Old English was never written in this style), it is now limited to ornamental use in newspaper logos, diplomas, and other specialized contexts. The style arose in the Middle Ages, when books were produced one letter at a time with a quill pen. Because it consisted mostly of thick vertical strokes very close together, it was economical and visually striking, though in extreme forms it could be fiendishly difficult to read. When Johannes Gutenberg invented printing with movable type in the mid-fifteenth century, he naturally adopted that familiar style, and when printing came to England in 1476, fonts using this typestyle came with it. This was therefore the style of all of England's earliest printed books, including the first printed reports and treatises on English law.

By the time printing reached Italy, however—well before it reached England—early Renaissance thinkers, who were rediscovering and celebrating their classical roots, had turned away from the "modern" style of writing used in the Middle Ages in favor of an earlier style that they believed (incorrectly, as it happens) authentically represented the writing style of early Rome. They gave the medieval script the deliberately unflattering designation "Gothic"—associating it with the Goths, the northern barbarians (as they saw it) who in 410 had sacked their beloved Rome. With the advent of Gutenberg's printing press the lettering style that they preferred, which they called *antica* or *antiqua* but which we call *roman,* spread throughout Europe: it was novel, it was philosophically fashionable, and above all it was legible. Within a century and a half the roman style predominated everywhere except Germany, which clung loyally to Gutenberg's style (in many variants generally lumped together under the name *Fraktur*) for three more centuries. Although to most Americans Fraktur is as emblematic of Nazism as the swastika, Hitler himself actually ordered it to be phased out during World War II because it was a hindrance to administration in occupied countries whose people could not read it. The death knell for this honorable old writing style as a general-purpose script was sounded on January 3, 1941, when party official Martin Bormann implemented Hitler's order in a memo, ironically typed on letterhead still written in Fraktur, denouncing the style as "*Judenlettern*" ("Jewish letters")—a description that would have come as a great surprise to the legions of medieval monks who spent their lives writing out Christian liturgical works in the script, and to Gutenberg himself, whose great printed work was the Christian Bible.[1]

The name *black letter* emerged in the first half of the seventeenth century, no doubt because the face's heavy strokes made the letters, and the

(opposite) The first page of *The Fift Part of the Reports of Sr. Edward Coke Knight, the Kings Attorney Generall* (London, 1612). Sir Edward Coke published an extremely influential eleven-volume set of case reports between 1600 and 1615. In this fifth volume, first published about 1606, he included a lengthy essay on the king's role as head of the church, printed in Latin and English side by side. The printer used fonts regarded at the time as appropriate for each language: roman for the Latin and black letter for the English. (Courtesy of Yale Law Library)

De Iure Regis Ecclesiastico.

Casus Caudrey.

Ermino Hillarij, Anno 33. Regni Elizabethæ Rotulo 340. *Robertus Caudrey* Clericus in ius vocauit *Georgium Atton* de actione transgressionis, quòd Clausum suum ad Northluffenham in Comit Rutlandię perfregisset die Septimo Augusti, anno regni prædictæ Reginæ tricesimo primo: Defendens respondit se minimè esse reum; Iuratores euocati & iurati, veredictum dederunt speciale, videlicet rem esse veram compererunt, de iure autem ad iudicium curiæ referentes in hanc sententiam, Compererunt Querentem ante transgressionem fuisse Rectorem Rectoriæ de Southluffenham in Comitatu prædicto, & locum in quo damnum fuit illatum, esse partem eiusdem Rectoriæ, compererunt item statutum factum anno eiusdem Reginæ primo, quo sancitum in hanc sententiam fuit. Quòd ea Ecclesiastica iurisdictio, quæ aliqua potestate spirituali, vel

Of the Kings Ecclesiasticall Law.

Caudreys case.

IN the Terme of S. Hillarie, in the 33. yere of the reigne of Q. Elizabeth, Rotulo 340. Robert Caudrey Clark brought an action of Trespasse against George Atton, for breaking of his close at Northluffenham in the Countie of Rutland, the 7. day of August, in the 31. yeere of the reigne of the saide late queene: The defendant pleaded not guiltie, and the Iurie returned and sworne for triall of this issue, gaue a speciall Verdict, that is, they founde the truth of the case at large, referring the same for the law to the iudgment of the Court, to this effect: They found that the Plaintife before the Trespasse supposed to be done, was Parson of the Rectorie of Southluffenhā, in the countie aforesaide, whereof the place wherein the Trespas is alleaged was parcell, & found the Statute made in the first yeare of the said late Queenes raigne, by which in effect it is enacted, That such Iurisdiction ecclesiasticall, as by any Spirituall or Ecclesia-

A   sticall

text as a whole, look very black in comparison with the roman type—which was sometimes referred to by way of contrast as *white letter*. By the eighteenth century the old black letter books were symbols of a bygone age. In 1768, the legal commentator William Blackstone observed that the earliest English law reports consisted of notes written in Law French—a species of French quite unlike the modern French of Blackstone's day—and ultimately "printed in that barbarous dialect; which, joined to the additional terrors of a Gothic black letter, has occasioned many a student to throw away his Plowden and Littleton [early legal writers], without venturing to attack a page of them."[2]

No one doubted the historical importance of the old books; but it is the nature of the common law to evolve continuously, and with every passing year the excruciatingly technical rules spelled out in those books became less relevant. Advocates who pinned their hopes on "black letter law" were apt to be met in equal measure with admiration for their scholarship and ridicule for bothering. The first biographer of Lord Mansfield, England's most eminent eighteenth-century judge, recounted an anecdote circulated in the press in 1760 regarding a "diligent book-read advocate" in Lord Mansfield's court who expounded upon

> several black-letter cases, to prove the genuine construction of an old woman's will:
>
> His lordship heard him with great patience for some time; at last he interrupted and quite broke the string of his learning, by asking him, 'whether he thought the old woman had ever heard of these cases? and, if not, what common sense and justice must say to that matter?' He therefore immediately gave judgement in favor of common sense against the black-letter-law, to the full satisfaction of the whole court.[3]

Nineteenth-century American cases were generally of the same tenor. A federal judge in Pennsylvania in 1812, when urged to apply ancient law that would have prevented a widowed mother from vetoing her minor child's enlistment in the military, refused to engage in such a "cold and cheerless submission to . . . the rude and rigorous principles of black letter jurisprudence." In 1848, the Supreme Court of Georgia said in the case of a family dispute over property, "Upon the proper construction of the conveyance . . . our opinion will be very brief, notwithstanding it has elicited such an admirable exhibition of 'complex and multifarious learning,' by the erudite and ingenious counsel . . . . We lack the necessary time, had we the inclination and the ability, to be 'raking in the ashes of antiquated cases,' . . . on this abstruse point of *Black-letter* lore." It was an admirable and forward-looking opinion, but for the fact that the property in question consisted of "a negro man slave named Jim, between forty-five and fifty years of age; also a negro girl slave called Eliza, about four years of age, with her future issue and increase."[4]

The twentieth century, however, spawned new generations of lawyers and judges who were vaguely aware of the phrase *black letter law* but entirely ignorant of its origins. Some assumed that it referred to the bold print with which some legal treatises highlighted their statements of fundamental principles, and wrote things like, "In the American Law Institute's

---

Blowing the Dust off the Black Letter Books

This legendary tale of shocking behavior by an English barrister has been told in various forms—and about various lawyers and judges—over the centuries. It evidently originated as a story about the celebrated barrister John Dunning (1731– 83), though this telling of it—the earliest we have found—appeared as an aside about Dunning in a book whose principal subject was the radical Irish lawyer John Philpot Curran, which led to the substitution of Curran's name for Dunning's in many of the subsequent retellings. Whether the incident actually happened cannot be known. What is certain is that the books referred to would have to have been the venerable old black letter law books:

There is a celebrated reply in circulation of Mr. Dunning to a remark of Lord Mansfield, who curtly exclaimed at one of his legal positions, "O! if that be the law, Mr. Dunning, I may *burn* my law books!"—"Better *read* them, my Lord," was the sarcastic and appropriate rejoinder.

Charles Phillips, *Recollections of Curran and Some of His Contemporaries* (Dublin, 1818), 41.

Restatement on the Conflict of Laws, the black letter of § 507 reads . . ."
(1940). The connotation thus shifted from ancient law of doubtful validity
to established principles of modern law, as in this from an appellate court
in 1971: "That a stockholder in a company which is a party to a lawsuit is
incompetent to sit as juror is so well settled as to be black letter law." The
final step was the dropping of any connection with either typestyles or
long-established law. In 2000, Chief Justice William Rehnquist carried
this to an extreme that would have left Lord Mansfield scratching his be-
wigged head. He invoked a rule regarding motor-vehicle checkpoints that
the Supreme Court had adopted as recently as 1976: "I begin," he wrote,
"with blackletter roadblock seizure law . . ."[5]

JEC

blackmail

Popular legend has it that the term *blackmail* originally referred to chain
mail, worn as armor by medieval knights, that had turned black or been
blackened. Various imaginative tales about the deeds and misdeeds of free-
lancing knights in not-so-shining armor are offered to explain how their
"black mail" turned into a term for the act of extorting money from a person by threatening to reveal some damaging secret.

Legal scholars writing in academic journals offer less entertaining explanations for the term. They link it to *mail* in the sense of written communications. Their theory is that criminals in early times took to transmitting
extortion threats by mail in order to circumvent the law against robbery,
which applied only to the taking of money or property through direct physical confrontation.

Both theories, though stated with great certainty, are wrong. *Mail* in
the sense of iron mesh comes from Latin *macula,* "spot" or "mesh" (of a
net). *Mail* in the sense of written communications is of Germanic origin
but comes to us by way of Old French *male,* a bag or pouch. The carrying
of letters in such a bag gave rise to the use of *mail* as a term for the letters
themselves—but not until well after *blackmail* had entered the language.
The *mail* in *blackmail* comes from a third source, Old Norse *māl,* "agree-

ment." In Old and Middle English the meaning expanded to include payments pursuant to an agreement and payments generally. When the Scots language and the English language (both of which grew out of Old English) diverged, this word largely died out on the English side. It survived in Scots, however, and also in dialects of English spoken near the Scottish border, as a term for any required payment of money or property, such as a rent or tax.

Sixteenth-century Scotland was a rugged place, and not just in the terrain. Farmers and small landowners were terrorized by brigands who hid out in the highlands and demanded, in the guise of rent, what we would today call protection money. Those who did not pay this "mail" (in money or goods) risked loss of their cattle, destruction of their property, and even harm to their persons. By mid-century these extorted payments had come to be called *black mail*—presumably because of the general association of the color black with matters of a dark and underhanded nature, as in the modern phrase *black market*. In 1567 and again in 1587 the Scottish Parliament enacted laws specifically aimed at controlling and punishing what the statutes referred to variously as "blak maill" and "blak meill." But at best this succeeded only in driving some of the practice over the border into England. In 1601, therefore, the English Parliament found it necessary to enact its own statute, applicable to the four northern counties of England, attempting to stamp out those practices by which "the Inhabitants . . . have bene inforced to pay a certaine rate of Money Corne Cattell or other Consideracion, commonlie there called by the name of Blacke maile." The statute made not only the receipt but also the payment of any such tribute punishable by death.[1]

But the most notorious era of blackmail in Scottish history was yet to come. In the Scottish highlands in 1671, an infant named Robert MacGregor was born to a younger brother of the chief of Clan MacGregor. Going by the name Rob Roy (Red Robert), he would rise to be chief of the clan and Scotland's most famous outlaw.

Rob Roy—who later had to change his last name to Campbell because the name MacGregor had been outlawed—became a legendary figure for his cattle-rustling, blackmailing, freebooting ways and his amazing ability to evade the law year after year. Despite his criminality, he had a deft public-relations sense, and with little if any justification eventually came to be regarded as something of a Robin Hood. Long after his death in 1734 he was celebrated by William Wordsworth, who had visited his burial site during a tour of Scotland in 1803, in a poem called "Rob Roy's Grave."

Wordsworth's poem was published in 1807. Ten years later, when the Scottish writer Walter Scott needed a title for a novel in which Rob Roy figured as a character—though by no means the main character—he chose one that he knew would attract the public: *Rob Roy*. The huge success of that novel, published on the last day of 1817, contributed to the author's being knighted less than three years later, becoming Sir Walter Scott. Like his father before him, Scott was a lawyer; he wrote the novel in his free time while holding the positions of sheriff-depute of Selkirkshire (essentially a county judge) and clerk of the Court of Session in Edinburgh. Fortunately for the literary world, in those days the courts were only in session for part of the year, leaving Scott plenty of time to write. In his book he included a long and amusing account of the practice—one might well say the custom—of "black-mail," as described by a Scotsman who conceded, "It's clean again our statute law, that must be owned, . . . clean again law; the levying and the paying black-mail are baith punishable: but if the law canna protect my barn and byre, whatfor suld I no engage wi' a Hieland gentleman that can?—answer me that."[2]

With the colorful Scottish term *black-mail* so prominently featured in so popular a book, its incorporation into English and its extension to other forms of extortion were inevitable. A recent example is the phrase that one author used as the title for a book—and then conveniently defined in the subtitle: *Emotional Blackmail: When the People in Your Life Use Fear, Obligation, and Guilt to Manipulate You.*[3]

The predominant meaning today—what has been pithily described as "the attempt to trade silence for money"—crept in gradually, as did the law's attention to it. It has long been illegal to demand money in exchange for silence about someone's criminal conduct (which one has at least a moral and often a legal duty to disclose) or to extort money by threatening to falsely accuse someone of a crime (which would be slander); but it took a while for the law to come around to the idea that it should be a crime to demand payment for keeping silent about a truth that one is perfectly free either to reveal or to keep to oneself. As Massachusetts Justice (later Supreme Court Justice) Oliver Wendell Holmes Jr. said in another context in 1896, "As a general rule . . . what you may do in a certain event you may threaten to do, that is, give warning of your intention to do in that event, and thus allow the other person the chance of avoiding the consequences." For example, as a general rule you have a right to add another story to your house even if it blocks your neighbor's view and an equal right to refrain from doing so if the neighbor is willing to pay you to preserve the view.[4]

Legal theorists have devoted vast amounts of paper to analyzing—and sometimes questioning—why it should be against the law to ask your neighbor for money (which you have a right to do) in exchange for keeping mum about his extramarital dalliance (which you also have a right to do). In one article a law professor painstakingly dissected no less than eight previous theories as to why, as it is often put, when it comes to blackmail "two rights make a wrong." He found them all wanting, and proceeded to enunciate a new theory of his own.[5]

The *practical* reason for the law against blackmail is much easier to divine. Everybody has secrets they would not like to see disclosed, and legislatures are made up of politicians whose status especially depends upon their public image. They can easily identify with the plight of anyone who is subjected to blackmail and can heartily agree that such exploitation should not be tolerated.

JEC

blood money

At least a dozen movies have been made with the title *Blood Money*. It's a good title because it evokes violence and avarice—the stuff of drama—and yet is vague enough so that you have to see the movie if you want to find out what it is actually about. This centuries-old phrase lends itself to so many meanings that one has to know the context to be sure what it represents.

Most commonly, *blood money* refers to a payment made to compensate and appease the family of an individual who has been killed, either intentionally or by accident. This has been a characteristic feature of countless cultures through the ages—especially clan- or tribe-based cultures, in which payment of blood money (or its equivalent in cattle, shells, or other things of value) can prevent retaliation and stave off a blood feud.

Among the legal traditions that embody this institution is Islamic law, whose concept of *diya* (spelled various ways but always translated as "blood money") permits the relatives of a slain person to accept payment instead of insisting upon the death of the slayer. This principle is seen as mitigating the harshness of the Old Testament law of EYE FOR AN EYE. Under Islamic law, killing or injury, whether intentional or accidental, is treated as primarily an offense against the individual victim and the victim's family rather than against the government, so it is primarily up to the family to insist upon retribution or compensation. It is therefore natural that a local leader in Iraq, when given an opportunity to meet with the American official in charge of reconstruction projects there in the wake of the invasion of 2003, would ask for payments of "blood money" directly to the families of seventy-five members of his tribe said to have been mistakenly killed in a U.S. air raid.[1] The United States, though rejecting most such requests, has nevertheless paid out tens of millions of dollars in "compensation" and "condolence payments" for deaths, injuries, and property damage suffered by Iraqi civilians as a result of American military actions.[2]

Substantially the same legal principle prevailed in Britain in Anglo-Saxon times under the name *wergild* (also written *wergeld* or *weregild*)—literally, "man payment"—with the amount to be paid depending upon the rank of the person slain. Over time, English law came to the view that murder was not just a personal offense but a "breach of the king's peace," and therefore a crime punishable by the government. Even so, it remains true today that the family of a person who is killed through the negligence or intentional misconduct of another can sue the person responsible and demand compensation. A notable instance of this occurred in the celebrated case of O. J. Simpson, who was accused of slashing his ex-wife, Nicole Brown Simpson, and her friend Ronald Goldman to death in 1994. Even though Simpson was acquitted of the crime, in a subsequent civil case he was held responsible for the killings and ordered to pay Goldman's parents $8.5 million as "compensation for the loss of love, companionship, comfort, affection, society, solace, [and] moral support," and an additional $12.5 million to each family as punitive damages.[3] The American legal system has its own version of the Islamic diya; we just don't call it blood money.

In fact, the original meaning of *blood money* in English was completely different. The first recorded instance of the term occurred in connection with an even more celebrated case, but the money in question was paid to bring about the death rather than to compensate for it. The victim in that case was Jesus Christ. As told in the biblical book of Matthew, the priests who wanted to do away with Jesus paid Judas Iscariot thirty pieces of silver to lead them to him. After the deed was done, Judas had an attack of conscience, threw the money at the priests in the temple, and hanged himself. The priests took the silver pieces back, but were in a quandary about what to do with them because—in the words of the King James translation (Matt. 27:6)—"it is not lawful for to put them into the [Temple's] treasury, because it is the price of blood." (This was a rather surprising scrupulousness about the law, considering that receiving money that had been paid to bring about a death could scarcely be worse than paying out the money for that purpose in the first place.) This phrase—"the price of blood"—is a literal translation from the Greek and has been used in most English-language versions of the Bible, beginning with the earliest manuscript versions. But when Miles Coverdale published the first printed translation of the entire Bible into English in 1535, he chose a more pungent expression: "it is bloudmoney."

Either Coverdale was using an existing colloquial expression or he was being creative. In any case, it was in this sense of "money paid to help condemn a person (especially an innocent person) to death" that *blood money* was to become a familiar phrase in Anglo-American law. In England it became common to offer a reward for evidence leading to conviction in a capital crime. This made it financially advantageous to witness such a crime. A dictionary of slang and underworld jargon published in London in 1785 indicates that some people made something of a profession of being in the right place at the right time. That dictionary, written at a time when any substantial theft was punishable by death (see HANGED FOR A SHEEP), included an entry for *thief takers,* who it explained were "fellows who associate with all kinds of villains, in order to betray them, when they have committed any of those crimes, which entitles the persons taking them to a handsome reward, called blood money. It is the business of these thief takers, to furnish subjects for a handsome execution."[4]

But not everyone who took such money went to the trouble of actually witnessing the crime; after all, the money was just as good if the person hanged was entirely innocent. Charles Dickens, always ready to skewer the injustices of nineteenth-century English justice, referred to this in his 1865 novel *Our Mutual Friend,* in which one character threatens to expose another for having "conspired against an innocent man for blood-money." The threat evokes this self-justification: "I may have been a little over-eager for the cause of justice, or (to put it another way) a little over-stimulated by them feelings which rouses a man up, when a pot of money is going about, to get his hand into that pot of money for his family's sake."[5]

In America as in England it was usual in those days for prosecutions to be conducted by private attorneys hired by the victim or the victim's family. As with paid witnesses, the lawyers were paid to gain a conviction, creating an incentive to accomplish that result by almost any means. In the eyes of some nineteenth-century legal commentators, taking money to help put a person to death was no more appropriate for a private attorney than for a paid witness; they felt that prosecution of such cases should be left to the state. An esteemed Philadelphia lawyer put it bluntly to his brethren at the bar: "Private counsel should never prosecute a capital charge—NEVER TAKE BLOOD MONEY."[6]

Although the use of privately retained attorneys to assist in prosecution of criminal cases has diminished (but not disappeared),[7] the rewarding of witnesses in order to obtain convictions—even in capital cases—remains a prominent feature of American law. In the modern context, the witness is often a "jailhouse snitch"—a character of dubious credibility who claims to have heard the defendant admit to committing the crime. And the witness is compensated not in money but in something more valuable: favorable treatment in the witness's own criminal case. A study of 130 cases of individuals exonerated by DNA evidence as of July 2003 found that in 16 percent of the cases the wrongful conviction was obtained with testimony from a jailhouse snitch or similar informant.[8] The federal criminal code, sentencing guidelines, and rules of criminal procedure specifically provide for imposition of shorter sentences, or reduction of sentences already being served, in exchange for "substantial assistance" in the prosecution of another person,[9] thus institutionalizing the practice of rewarding criminals who can lie convincingly. Dickens would recognize this at once as just another form of blood money.

In addition to the two main meanings of *blood money*—compensation for the loss of a life and reward for helping to condemn a person to death—the phrase lends itself to myriad other uses. At least two of these are particularly related to law. One is the repeated use of the term by John Ashcroft, the first attorney general in the administration of President George W. Bush, in reference to money collected by Muslim charities accused of supporting terrorism. Another is the informal use of the term by some personal injury lawyers to refer to money collected in lawsuits from individual defendants as opposed to DEEP-POCKET insurance companies.[10]

But the phrase need not always be so metaphorical. It is also employed sardonically by some writers discussing paid blood donors or the cost of blood for people who need it.[11] When all is said and done, sometimes blood money is like lunch money or taxi money—it's just money paid for blood.

JEC

blue laws

Blue laws—government regulation of behavior intended to enforce moral values—are both ancient and relevant to contemporary debates. The term is most often used to refer to laws governing behavior on Sundays, but it also includes laws enforcing other religion-based prohibitions. While some of the issues seem trivial (why can you buy beer on Sundays at noon but not at 11:50?), in a larger sense the debate about blue laws is part of the debate about the proper role of religion in American law.

Although restrictions on Sunday activities date back to a decree of the Roman emperor Constantine in 321 C.E., the term *blue laws* probably originated in the American colonies. The two earliest-known written instances of the phrase—both indicating that the term was already familiar—occurred there in unrelated but uncannily complementary contexts in the mid-eighteenth century. The centuries-old religious debates between adherents of the Church of England (Anglicans) and dissenters, which had led many Puritans to leave England and settle in what became New England, were still going strong in America. Among the many issues that divided Anglicans and Puritans (mainly Congregationalists) in the northeastern colonies was that the latter believed much more strongly in regulating people's private conduct—especially on Sundays and religious holidays. In 1755 a writer in New York, where Anglicanism was the established religion, published a bitterly satirical attack on Congregationalism, the established religion of neighboring Connecticut, in which he recounted an imagined dream of life twenty years in the future. In this dream, Congregationalists had come to power in England, the colonies of New York and Connecticut had been merged under their rule, and life had become a nightmare of Congregationalism run rampant and ancient Puritanical laws restored. As a newspaper report in the dream put it, "Since . . . the Revival of our old Blue Laws, we have the Pleasure to see the Lord's Work go on with Success"—a success evidenced by accounts of an endless string of outrages against Anglicanism, from the selling off of church lands to the severe whipping of one "John Faithful, an old Man of the Church of England, aged 85" for refusing to attend Congregationalist services.[1]

The Congregationalists gave as good as they got. In 1762, the minister of the First Congregational Church of Stamford, Connecticut, anonymously published a wickedly wry and witty pamphlet purporting to be a "letter to a young gentleman" explaining why the gentleman should abandon the dissenting religions and join the Church of England. The moral strictures of the dissenters, he wrote, are so extreme that "I have heard that some of them begin to be ashamed of their blue laws at *New-Haven*." Nevertheless, "If a gentleman drinks a little freely, or happens to love a pretty girl somewhat *too warmly*, nothing will content these *rigid bigots*, but they must stand on the *stool of repentance*, or in the *broad-alley*, and make a *long whining confession*." This discipline, he said, "is chiefly levelled and contrived to *pester* and afflict polite gentlemen, to whom *women* and *wine* are far from being disagreeable." In such ways the writer slyly criticized Anglicanism as the religion of "gentlemen" (read: the idle rich), who viewed moral rules as a pesky nuisance contrived to interfere with their pleasure, and who therefore chose a church that tolerated their licentiousness.[2]

It was the Reverend Samuel Peters, an Anglican with an ax to grind, who popularized the term *blue laws*. Peters, an ultraconservative, high-church Anglican priest in colonial Connecticut, consistently and publicly supported British rule, opposed independence, and criticized the Congregationalists who ruled the colony. He fueled the wrath of his opponents through the scathing tone of his many editorials. He further irritated them by dressing "ceremoniously and expensively" like a British squire. Repeatedly attacked by mobs, threatened with hanging, and with a price on his head, Peters abandoned his property (including his slaves) and fled to London at the end of 1774.[3]

Angry and short of money, Peters published *The General History of Connecticut* in England while the Revolutionary War still raged back home. The book continued his attack on the Puritans and his defense of Anglican loyalists, and Peters hoped it would also attract the favorable attention of potential benefactors. The *General History* recited titillating tall tales, such as a story of bullfrog armies invading a Connecticut town so that "old and young, male and female, fled naked from their beds," and described the colonial practice of bundling, by which courting couples shared a bed while remaining clothed. Similarly, Peters breathlessly revealed the "truth" about the "Connecticutensians" and their "wanton and barbarous persecutions, illegal practices, [and] daring usurpations." His book claimed that the Colony of New Haven, before its merger with Connecticut Colony in 1662, had adopted a set of laws so harsh that "even the rigid fanatics of Boston, and the mad zealots of Hertford, put to the blush, christened them the *Blue Laws*." Some of Peters's provisions paralleled actual laws in Britain and the colonies. Some, however, were largely fanciful:

No one shall run on the Sabbath-day, or walk in his garden or elsewhere, except reverently to and from meeting.

No one shall travel, cook victuals, make beds, sweep house, cut hair, or shave, on the Sabbath-day.

No woman shall kiss her child on the Sabbath or fasting-day.

No one shall read Common-Prayer, keep Christmas or Saints-

Days, make minced pies, dance, play cards, or play on any instrument of music, except the drum, trumpet, and jews-harp.

Every male shall have his hair cut round according to a cap.

Peters was eager to make life in the colonies look as rigid and silly as possible, and many English readers were happy to believe the worst of the rebellious colonists. Later confusion led some to apply the title "Blue Laws of Connecticut" to the genuine Connecticut code of 1650, but neither that code nor the original New Haven code contains the forty-five "laws" reported by Peters.[4]

Of all the possible epithets for rigid religious laws, why *blue?* The most popular explanation—that they were printed on blue paper—is certainly incorrect, although that story appears as early as 1788 in the debates over Virginia's adoption of the Constitution. Historians point out the lack of printing presses in Connecticut at the time, the expense of blue paper, and the fact that no one has ever produced a printed copy of the alleged laws, blue or otherwise. Peters himself admitted that his purported laws "were never suffered to be printed" but invented a colorful etymology of his own. Apparently on the theory that his British audience would readily accept the idea that *blue* could be a euphemistic shortening of the offensive word *bloody*—and would enjoy a bit of sensationalism as well—Peters declared that these "were very properly termed *Blue Laws; i.e. bloody Laws;* for they were all sanctified with excommunication, confiscation, fines, banishment, whippings, cutting off the ears, burning the tongue, and death." Other theories associate the color blue with religion, specifically with non-Anglican faiths, but there appears to be no support for a link between the use of blue as a symbol of Protestant dissenters and the term *blue laws.*[5]

Although Peters's account was a sham (either his own invention or repetition of existing scuttlebutt), there were indeed laws in the American colonies prohibiting various Sunday activities. Many combined Sunday closing provisions with laws aimed at other perceived vices. Pennsylvania's laws, for example, targeted public profanity, gambling, intoxication, dueling, and billiards. While the blue laws were often ignored, nineteenth-century religious movements repeatedly called for the expansion and enforcement of Sunday closing laws, as well as for bans on the sale of alcohol and tobacco, and for censorship of books, plays, and films. During the heyday of the blue laws, forty-six states had some kind of Sunday closing statute.

Most people associate blue laws with enforcement through government penalties. Sunday closing laws, however, affected disputes between individuals as well. For example, defendants in contract cases could try to get out of their deals by arguing that contracts made on Sunday were illegal and therefore unenforceable. Initially, state courts agreed and refused to enforce Sunday contracts as both immoral and illegal. As the nineteenth century progressed courts began to look for exceptions, and by the end of the century, Sunday contracts were usually enforced.

As time went by, courts became less comfortable with upholding blue laws on explicitly religious bases and instead began to ground them in secular arguments. Sunday closings were justified as a decision to create a common day of rest and recreation. (Why Sunday? because that was the day the majority of Americans rested.) The shift in the stated purpose of the blue laws allowed them to survive objections based on the religion clauses of the First Amendment. In 1961 the U.S. Supreme Court decisively upheld the statutes, even while conceding that the origin of the blue laws was religious.[6]

Despite surviving religion-based challenges, Sunday restrictions became increasingly unpopular as the twentieth century progressed, and legislatures carved out more and more exceptions at the request of businesses wanting to operate on Sundays and citizens wanting more "recreation" than "rest." By the middle of the twentieth century, the remaining patchwork became impossible to explain as promoting either rest or religion. A good example is Connecticut, the focus of Peters's hoax. By the 1950s, its general prohibition on secular activities contained exceptions for the sale of milk, bakery products, fruit, ice, ice cream, confectionery, nonalcoholic beverages, tobacco in any form, smokers' supplies, newspapers and other periodicals, drugs or supplies, and car parts. The 1978 version created even more exemptions, including twenty-four types of exempted businesses and all manufacturing. One study of the law found that it allowed two-thirds of the labor force of Connecticut to work on Sundays.

Today only a few areas in the United States maintain and enforce broad-based blue laws. In addition, a few states cling to blue-law remnants such as prohibitions on the sale of liquor or automobiles on Sundays. There are still groups who advocate a return to the days of Sunday closings, and who do so on explicitly religious grounds, but the American passions for shopping and professional football are probably insurmountable. Other religious groups have turned their efforts to incorporating other faith-based prohibitions into the law in other ways, such as forbidding embryonic stem-cell research and restricting the right to divorce. While most of us can now spend Sundays at the mall, debates about the extent to which the law should prohibit religiously disapproved behavior are as current today as they were in the 1600s.

EGT

blue wall of silence

Most city police in America are outfitted in blue uniforms—a custom so widely followed that for more than a century the word *blue* has evoked images of the police in contexts ranging from references to the THIN BLUE LINE to the names of the television cop shows *Hill Street Blues* and *NYPD Blue*.

Before the nineteenth century, peacekeeping and crime control in England and America depended heavily upon private and volunteer activity—and in England, for major disturbances, the military. London's Metropolitan Police Force, established by Parliament in 1829, led the way to a new model of policing—professional, publicly funded, and serving the citizenry at large. London's "new police" wore top hats and blue tailcoats—a style similar to that of English gentlemen of the day, and a color that stood out while clearly distinguishing the police from soldiers, who wore red. Starting in 1839, the new policing concept was expanded to other parts of England, despite resistance from some townsfolk who resented supporting—and being monitored by—what they called "Blue Devils," "blue plagues," and "Blue Locusts."[1]

New York City's police department, formally organized in 1845, was one of the first such departments in the United States. For a considerable time the members were identified only by a copper star. As a member of the force in the 1850s later explained, his compatriots refused to wear uniforms "because, they said, it would give them the appearance of footmen. . . . We all unanimously declared [uniforms] to be a badge of servitude." This resistance was finally overcome, and 1857 saw the introduction of a winter uniform of blue with a white stripe on the pants and a dapper summer outfit featuring white pants, white vest, and a Panama hat.[2]

For well over a century the color's association with the police appears to have had only favorable connotations in America, although the police themselves were not always paragons of virtue. Stories of significant police corruption or other wrongdoing can be found by the 1870s. Along with them came stories of collusion: police refusing to expose the wrongdoing of fellow officers.

In the 1960s this aspect of police solidarity began to attract widespread attention, and when it did, there was no lack of vivid imagery to characterize it. At first, the preferred image was of a curtain shielding police misconduct from scrutiny, as in 1965 when Congressman Robert N. C. Nix, at the time the only black ever elected to Congress from the state of Pennsylvania, urged white Alabamans to "lift the curtain of silence behind which their brutal police hide." Describing metaphorical curtains erected by the police as blue was irresistible; for example, a sociological study published in 1967 referred to "the 'blue curtain' of secrecy" inhibiting studies of police culture, and in 1968 city officials in Detroit complained that "a 'blue curtain' of silence" was hampering investigation of alleged attacks on black youths by off-duty policemen in the city.[3]

But the curtain metaphor was too flimsy to convey the power of the culture of silence when a massive police-corruption scandal erupted in New York City in 1970. Police officers David Durk and Frank Serpico took their story of institutionalized graft and extortion in the police department to the *New York Times* after years of fruitless efforts to get action from police authorities—one of whom helpfully advised Serpico to drop the matter or "be found floating in the East River, face down." In the investigation that followed, the phrase most often used was one that had long been associated with the Mafia: the "code of silence." As one officer was later reported to have testified in 1971, "It is said that there is a code of silence among police that is greater than the *omerta* of the underworld." This phrase—sometimes in the form "blue code of silence"—is still common in discussions of police coverups.[4]

The most common metaphor for police secrecy today, however, is more concrete than a code and more solid than a curtain: it is the *blue wall of silence*. Possibly the first occurrence of the phrase was in 1975. In that year, police officers in the Bronx savagely beat two men in their custody, leaving one with a shattered jawbone protruding through his cheek and the other—a twenty-five-year-old with a four-year-old daughter and a pregnant wife—dead. Several policemen in the precinct, despite their feelings of loyalty toward their fellow officers, decided to answer investigators' questions—an act characterized by one reporter as a "breach in the blue 'wall of silence' at the 44th Precinct."[5]

Neither the phrase nor the spirit of cooperation caught on. Ten years later, when three police officers in a patrol car slammed into two elderly pedestrians—critically injuring one and killing the other—and then fled the scene, later falsifying reports to conceal their involvement, the Manhattan District Attorney complained of a lack of cooperation not only by the officers directly involved but also by three of their superior officers. The chief of the police department's internal anticorruption efforts explained, "They call it the 'code of silence' or 'the blue wall of conspiracy.' There's a natural affinity of cops to stick with one another. But I don't see that as different from any other profession. Hey, it's not the American way to be a rat." This comment overlooked two crucial distinctions between policing and other professions: first, that the purpose for which police exist—their raison d'être—is to prevent crime and bring wrongdoers to justice; and second, that sociological studies had shown that the police "ethic of secrecy" was not just ordinary solidarity among co-workers, but a core value of police culture.[6]

Less than a month later, in yet another borough of New York City, the phrase *blue wall of silence* reemerged to stay. This time several officers of a precinct in Queens were accused of using stun guns to torture confessions out of prisoners. Queens district attorney John Santucci, discussing efforts to investigate the charges, stated that "there is some degree of a blue wall of silence, the so-called code of silence," but added hopefully: "there are cracks in the wall, some penetration, and some officers have come forward to tell us things." Any hope for a significant breakthrough was soon dashed, however. When grand jury indictments against five officers were handed down eight days later, Santucci admitted (as paraphrased by the *Times*) that "the inquiry had been hampered by a lack of cooperation from other officers" and in particular that "about 40 other officers who were on duty in the precinct at the times of the purported assaults declined to be questioned." But if the case accomplished nothing else, it fixed the phrase *blue wall of silence* in the language—so much so that a couple of weeks later even the president of the Patrolmen's Benevolent Association (the police union) used it in a statement on the case: "There is no 'blue wall of silence,'" he declared—ironically demonstrating the very behavior he was denying.[7]

Both the metaphor and the phenomenon of the blue wall—so familiar now that the phrase is sometimes used without "of silence"—have survived every effort to stamp out the practice. This was vividly demonstrated in the case of Abner Louima, who had the misfortune to be mistaken by New York City police officer Justin Volpe for someone who had landed a punch on Volpe in a melee outside a Brooklyn nightclub on a summer night in 1997. Back in the station house, Volpe broke a broomstick over his knee, took Louima into the bathroom in a station full of police officers, and with the help of a fellow officer beat and kicked Louima and then shoved the broomstick into his rectum with such ferocity that it perforated both his colon and his bladder, requiring an initial hospital stay of two months and multiple surgeries. Yet when other officers accompanied Louima to the hospital they attributed Louima's injuries to "abnormal homosexual activity" before his arrest. Ultimately four officers cooperated with the investigation, but investigators reported that they had "learned virtually nothing from scores of other officers who have been granted limited immunity from prosecution." Prosecutions of the two officers regarded as most responsible for obstructing the investigation collapsed in part because the wall of silence held; and although Volpe himself ultimately pleaded guilty, he clung to the code of silence by refusing to testify against his apparent accomplice. In the end prosecutors had to settle their case against the likely accomplice by accepting a guilty plea to a charge of perjury.

This brought the case to a close after more than five years of investigation and litigation, as noted in the *New York Times*, "without resolving one of the biggest questions of the five-year legal ordeal: the identity of the second officer in the Brooklyn police station bathroom"—all because of "the longstanding tradition that police not testify against one another. Without that tradition, the police who were on duty on the night of the attack could have eliminated all the questions about who was involved. The 'blue wall of silence' did not serve either the department or the public in this case."[8] But then, it never does.

EGT

boilerplate

In the beginning, *boilerplate* was just about boilers. Steam engines required boilers made of iron or steel, and by the early nineteenth century iron foundries were making standard-sized plates of rolled metal that were then made into steam boilers. These sheets were (and often still are) called boiler plates—or collectively, boiler plate. As industrialization progressed, boiler plate was used in the construction of everything from boilers to bridges to battleships. Given the pervasiveness of the product, it is not surprising that beginning in the second half of the nineteenth century, the term cropped up in all sorts of court opinions, especially in patent claims, contract cases, and insurance disputes. This was an age in which industrial development outpaced industrial safety, and well into the twentieth century "boiler plate" featured prominently in personal-injury cases arising from boiler explosions and industrial accidents.[1]

News syndicates also developed in the late nineteenth century. These and other companies supplied local newspapers with prewritten items— news, press releases, puff pieces, and other tidbits—to be inserted as desired. The stories were supplied in the form of metal plates. Because these printing plates reminded people of the sheets for making boilers, they too were called boiler plates, and it was natural to begin referring to the stories themselves—and by extension any preset, unvarying text, like the masthead—as *boiler plate*.[2]

Decades later, boiler plate became a legal metaphor. In legal usage, the term—now usually written as the single word *boilerplate*—refers to the formulaic language found in contracts, wills, insurance policies, and other legal documents. Like its newspaper analogue, boilerplate can be slotted into documents as needed. Thus the term entered law by analogy to the standardized newspaper components. A popular explanation, however, holds that this legal usage is related to the personal-injury claims that used to arise so regularly from boiler accidents. Because steam boilers could be very dangerous to people working around them, the story goes, the boiler manufacturers' lawyers put warnings in small print on a metal plate attached to the boilers themselves in an effort to avoid liability for the injuries caused. Hence *boilerplate.* It's a creative idea, but it's not true.

The newspaper term popped up as a legal metaphor in an isolated 1923 case when a lawyer—presumably of some eminence, because he was also a former U.S. senator—attempted to explain the absence of crucial language from a contract by saying that he had "dictated certain special clauses to his stenographer and then left to her the incorporation of what he termed 'boiler-plate' provisions." But this sense of the term did not appear in legal writing with any frequency until the 1960s; it then entered popular culture as well, as in Ed McBain's 1965 police procedural, *Doll:* "The rest of the will was boilerplate. Meyer scanned it quickly."[3]

The term did not appear in a U.S. Supreme Court opinion until 1964, in a dissent by Justice Hugo Black in a landmark case read by many first-year law students, *National Equipment Rental, Ltd. v. Szukhent.* The case involved an obliquely worded clause slipped into the fine print of an equipment lease by the leasing company's lawyers—and approved by the 5–4 majority of the Court—enabling the company to sue a father and son in New York over their lease of farm equipment in Michigan. Noting that small-time customers have little bargaining power in dealing with a large corporation, Black decried "a system of law that would compel a man or woman from Hawaii, Alaska, or even Michigan to travel to New York to defend against civil lawsuits claiming a few hundred or thousand dollars growing out of an ordinary commercial contract," and warned that similar clauses would "soon find their way into the 'boilerplate' of everything from an equipment lease to a conditional sales contract."[4] Not only was Justice Black right about the future of contracts, he also was prescient in his use of the word *boilerplate,* which in the years since has become a fixture of legal terminology, appearing not only in hundreds of judicial opinions each year but even in formal contexts such as statutes, administrative regulations, and court rules.

Legal boilerplate suffers from the same flaws as its newspaper cousin: it is standardized, used over and over, and often inserted in larger documents without careful review. Further, boilerplate contract language is often written in fine print, and invariably is drafted in an effort to favor the powerful entity imposing the terms of the contract. Even in negotiated contracts, lawyers may use the *boilerplate* label as a strategic ploy to signal that the terms are not negotiable or are so standard that only a fool would question them. The wise lawyer, though, will rise above the metaphor and never approve a contract without checking the boilerplate.

EGT

Chancellor's foot

We all know what a foot is, but fewer modern Americans know about a judicial officer called a "Chancellor," and even fewer care to imagine what might be wrong with the *Chancellor's foot.* Ingrown toenails? Foot-and-mouth disease? No. But to understand why twenty-first-century lawtalk might refer to a judge's appendage requires a brief tiptoe through English legal and political history. The office of the chancellor (*cancellarius* in Latin) goes back to the courts of the Roman emperors and the Roman church, and it also existed in Britain at the time of the Saxon kings; but our story begins in the 1300s.

Court systems do not spring into being fully formed and ready to try cases, applying preexisting laws and using fixed rules of procedure. Instead, like other branches of government, they develop over time as the power of the state adapts to changing social and economic conditions. So it was with the courts in England. Centralized power resided with the king and his council, but over time bits of decision-making authority were spun off to bodies that became courts and which began to develop what we now think of as rules of law. Some of the courts that administered these rules became known as the *law courts,* and both the rules themselves and the procedure for enforcing them became quite rigid over time.

Sometimes the law courts were not up to the task of providing justice in particular cases because a powerful person chose to ignore the rules. The king, in whom justice was thought to reside, reserved the power to intervene and provide just decisions. He often delegated this power to the chancellor, one of the most powerful of the king's advisors. By the 1300s, petitions to the chancellor and his office (called Chancery or, later, the Court of Chancery) complained of various "outrages" committed by people whose power put them above the law, and the chancellor responded by dealing with these discrete cases on an ad hoc basis rather than by making "law."

By the sixteenth century this Chancery function had expanded beyond correcting individual abuses of power to addressing situations in which limitations in the law as enforced in the law courts prevented a fair or sensible solution. For example, it was Chancery that came up with a way to enforce an unwritten contract and created the legal concept of a trust. The Court of Chancery accordingly expanded its jurisdiction and grew increasingly important, although unlike similar courts in Europe, England had only one chancellor and the chancellor's staff was too small to deal with the onslaught of litigation.

The Chancery court eventually became known as an *equity court,* and the flexible principles the court administered came to be called the *rules of equity* (in this context a term of art and not a general reference to fairness). Thus England developed two sets of competing, and somewhat overlapping, types of court: "law" and "equity."

Under the Stuart kings in the early seventeenth century, Chancery became one of the flashpoints in the power struggles between the kings and Parliament. Each chancellor was still closely allied with the king who appointed him, and each depended on the king to remain in power. Critics of James I and Charles I (the first two Stuart kings) believed that the chancellor's power was abused for political ends, as was the power of the STAR CHAMBER. Chancellors were up to their necks in the political intrigue that led to the English Civil War, the execution of Charles I, the rule of Oliver Cromwell and, eventually, the restoration of the monarchy.

Power struggles between the law courts and equity court went public at this time, particularly because the equity court granted relief from the law courts' judgments, and because the law courts released people who were being held for refusing to obey the decrees of the equity court. While this was going on John Selden, a prominent lawyer and opponent of the Stuart kings, pronounced a devastating critique of equity as administered by the chancellor, and he did it with a catchy image—the *Chancellor's foot:*

> Equity is a Roguish thing. For Law we have a measure, know what to trust to; Equity is according to the Conscience of him that is Chancellor, and as that is larger or narrower, so is Equity. 'Tis all one as if they should make the Standard for the measure we call [a Foot], a Chancellors Foot. What an uncertain measure would this be! One Chancellor has a long Foot, another a short Foot, a Third an indifferent Foot: 'Tis the same thing in the Chancellors Conscience.[1]

Nor was Selden alone in his criticism. Throughout this period, equity's critics depicted Chancery as inconsistent, while its supporters emphasized the universality of equitable principles and the need to tailor rules to the different situations of different cases.

The equity court regularized its procedures and became less unpredictable during the seventeenth century. These reforms had already begun by the time Selden spoke, and were largely in place before his remarks were published. Early in the 1600s, for example, chancellors had begun using reporters to record equity decisions, and equity judges came to treat earlier cases as precedent that would guide the outcome of later decisions. By the end of the seventeenth century, Chancery had become a conventional court with its own system of rules and procedures.

In the early 1800s equity had become so standardized that its Chancellor, Lord Eldon, felt comfortable replying to Selden's critique: "I cannot agree that the doctrines of this Court are to be changed with every succeeding judge. Nothing would inflict on me greater pain, in quitting this place, than the recollection that I had done any thing to justify the reproach that the equity of this Court varies like the Chancellor's foot."[2] While Lord Eldon had the issue of unbridled discretion more or less under control, the equity court under his guidance had other problems. Formalization may have decreased discretion, but it also created a maze of rules that could make equity as inflexible as the law courts.

It was the equity court under Lord Eldon, after all, that Charles Dickens satirized in *Bleak House* (1853), in which protracted litigation caused all the disputed money in an inheritance to go to the lawyers. Dickens warned: "This is the Court of Chancery . . . which gives to monied might, the means abundantly of wearing out the right; which so exhausts finances, patience, courage, hope; so overthrows the brain and breaks the heart; that there is not an honourable man among its practitioners, who would not give—who does not often give—the warning, 'Suffer any wrong that can be done you, rather than come here!'"[3] Dickens's criticism, like Selden's, came after Chancery reform had already begun, and by the 1870s many of the problems had been fixed. England, and later the United States, merged "law" and "equity" into a single court system, having the powers of both the old law courts and the old equity system.

Nevertheless, modern equity power is still limited in ways that reflect its historical roots. Selden's admonition survives to curb equity's ability to evolve, and *Chancellor's foot* acts as shorthand for the argument that equity is an unfortunate interference in the regular course of the law. As recently as 1999, U.S. Supreme Court Justice Antonin Scalia wrote an opinion that quoted Selden. Federal trial courts, he wrote, may not issue pretrial orders designed to preserve the defendant's assets so that funds will be available to pay a judgment if the plaintiff wins. In his view, to allow such an order merely because it is necessary to ensure that justice can be done would "deserve the spirited rebuke of Seldon" for giving individual judges too much discretion. Unlike in England, U.S. equity courts may not use their flexibility to expand their procedural options; the preservation order was "unavailable from a court of equity" in 1789, and so it is unavailable today.[4]

Yet the case was a close one, with four Justices dissenting. Noting that the defendant in the case was clearly liable and was busily disposing of its only assets, Justices Ginsburg, Stevens, Souter, and Breyer preferred the chancellor's flexibility. Quoting the judge whose order the Supreme Court majority was voting to overturn, Justice Ginsburg asked why the defendant should be allowed "'to use the process of the court to delay entry of a judgment as to which there is no defense? Why is that equitable?' . . . The Court gives no satisfactory answer."[5] Four centuries after Selden, echoes of the ancient tension between the certainty of "law" and the flexibility of "equity" still reverberate in the halls of justice.

EGT

charter party

To a lawyer, a *charter party* is no party. It is the term used in maritime law for a contract to hire a vessel. "Although *charter party* sounds like an afternoon of fun in a rented boat, it is actually a very dry document filled with an ocean of fine print."[1]

The *charter* part of this phrase is familiar enough. A charter is a kind of legal document, especially one granting a privilege. In a ship charter the owner of the ship gives someone the right, upon specified terms, to use the ship for a span of time or for a particular voyage. The word comes from Old French *chartre*, which came from Latin *chartula* (a little piece of paper)—a diminutive form of *charta* (paper, papyrus leaf), from which we also get the English *chart* and *card*.

It's the *party* that comes as a surprise. To understand where that comes from, consider the plight of a shipowner and a ship charterer some centuries ago: having reached agreement on the terms of the charter, each of them wanted to make sure that the other would not alter the contract or substitute a forged copy during the time—possibly years—that they were separated. The solution was to write out the charter in duplicate on a single piece of parchment and then cut it in two, often through the title. That way each individual could keep a copy and any forged substitute would be detectable because the two pieces would no longer fit neatly together. (For a similar antifraud strategy, see INDENTURE.) The result was, in French, a *chartre partie,* or "divided charter." *Partie* (from Latin *partīta*) means "parted, divided into parts." The phrase was absorbed into English with only a slight respelling (and with no change in the French noun-adjective word order), and in the tradition-minded field of law it has survived over the centuries even as word processors, copy machines, and contracts running to scores of pages have replaced the parchments it referred to.

JEC

Chinese Wall

For millennia the Great Wall of China has stood as a symbol of strength, permanence, and impenetrability. In the 1970s lawyers seized upon the familiar image of the Chinese Wall to give concreteness to an important new concept in legal ethics—and opened the door to a linguistic controversy.

Lawyers have an extremely high duty of loyalty to their clients. Among other things, except in very extraordinary circumstances (such as to prevent a serious crime), they must never allow confidential information acquired from a client to be used against that client. To prevent this from happening—even accidentally—when a lawyer moves from one law firm to another, the courts traditionally had a simple rule: if a law firm on one side of a case hires away a lawyer from an opposing firm, the hiring firm has to get off the case. As one court explained in 1976, even if the lawyer will not be working on the case and fully intends to preserve the former client's secrets, disqualifying the entire firm "frees lawyers from the difficult task of erecting Chinese walls in their own minds between what is confidential and what is not."[1]

By 1976, however, changes in the profession were bringing the old rule into question. As law firms grew larger and the legal workforce more mobile, it was becoming increasingly common for litigants to bring disqualification motions as a tactical maneuver, and increasingly impractical and unfair to disqualify an entire firm solely because one of its hundreds of lawyers was tainted by a prior relationship with an opposing party. In 1977 a court held for the first time that if the individual lawyer in question could be effectively screened from any involvement or influence in the case then the entire firm need not be disqualified.[2] Over time, more and more courts— though by no means all—came to accept this general principle.

Even in courts that accept the concept of screening, though, in order to defeat a motion for disqualification in this situation a law firm must convince the court that it has established a truly effective set of internal rules and procedures to ensure that the tainted lawyer can neither contribute to nor profit from any work by the firm that is contrary to the interests of the lawyer's former client. Not surprisingly, right from the start firms fighting to stay on a case (and keep the fees rolling in) chose the strongest metaphor they could think of to characterize their screening procedures. As was said in a case where a large firm found itself with two groups of attorneys with potentially conflicting loyalties, "Morgan Lewis takes the position that such adverse representation within a firm of their size does not require disqualification because a 'Chinese Wall' was built in the firm between those attorneys representing Fund of Funds and those representing Andersen."[3] The term was already in use in other industries, such as securities and banking, where entire departments having different functions were forbidden to share certain kinds of information with each other,[4] and it quickly became the standard metaphor for similar procedures in law firms.

The appropriateness and effectiveness of such a screening arrangement is subject to debate and litigation in case after case. What has occasionally been debated with even greater passion, however, is the appropriateness of the name itself. The debate was launched by a single state court judge, a Californian of Chinese ancestry named Harry Low, who learned of the metaphor in 1988 and wrote an entire separate opinion in a case for the sole purpose of expressing his "profound objection" to it. "Chinese Wall," said Justice Low, is a "piece of legal flotsam which should be emphatically abandoned. The term has an ethnic focus which many would consider a subtle form of linguistic discrimination. Certainly, the continued use of the term would be insensitive to the ethnic identity of the many persons of Chinese descent."[5]

Now, no lawyer or judge wants to offend another judge in the same state, especially in the delicate area of ethnic sensitivities. Within a few years after Justice Low declared it anathema, the term *Chinese Wall* had virtually disappeared from California state cases, largely replaced by *ethical wall* or *ethical screen*. Outside of California, however, *Chinese Wall* (with or without the capital *W*) remains the prevailing term. A court in neighboring Oregon explained: "We agree with [plaintiff] that 'Chinese wall' is an appropriate term and that it does not have the pejorative connotations that made some expert witnesses uncomfortable in using it. As one of humanity's greatest engineering achievements, the Great Wall of China suggests the kind of solidity and impermeability that a potential conflict of interest situation requires." One law student, writing a law review note on the subject of ethical screening in law firms, neatly hedged his bets: he announced at the outset that "due to the potentially offensive and linguistically discriminatory potential of this term" he would not use it in his article, but he nevertheless worked it into his title ("The Art Formerly Known as the Chinese Wall . . .") so that researchers looking for articles on the subject would be sure to find his.[6]

It is understandable that any phrase beginning with a national or ethnic identifier should be viewed with suspicion: this pattern often represents a deliberate slur—or, perhaps worse, a casual and unthinking one—as in the phrase "Chinese fire drill" formerly regarded as an amusing way to describe a chaotic situation. But like *French wine* and *Egyptian pyramids*, the phrase *Chinese Wall* evokes a specific item generally regarded as the most impressive of its type.

It is true that this is a somewhat informal appellation, and in some sense not the "real" name for the wall. In China it is called *chángchéng*, "the long wall," or more formally *wànlǐ chángchéng*, "the 10,000-li-long wall." (One li now equals half a kilometer, or about a third of a mile.) In English the wall itself is often referred to rather formally as the Great Wall of China or Great Wall; but when invoked as a metaphor, the more colloquial *Chinese Wall* has always been the phrase of choice.

In 1851, for example, a Massachusetts minister invoked the metaphor in his response to the publication of a proslavery sermon by another northern clergyman. He argued that the use of religion to justify slavery was even more dangerous than the conduct of those who actually take others into bondage, for "such kidnappers can never corrupt public sentiment, nor sanctify the sin of slavery, nor build around it a Chinese wall for its defence." And when slavery was finally ended, the former slave Frederick Douglass wrote of the need to reunite the republic: "No Chinese wall can now be tolerated. The South must be opened to the light of law and liberty."[7]

Occasionally the metaphor has been more literal. In the wilderness along the Continental Divide in Montana lies a thousand-foot-high, twelve-mile-long escarpment known as the Chinese Wall. But in all of its uses over the

years, however literal or fanciful, the phrase *Chinese Wall* has always signified awe for this wonder of the world.

In fact, the qualities attributed to the Great Wall by those who use this
term in some ways exceed those it actually possessed. In its twenty-plus
centuries of existence, the Great Wall has had a mixed record. Wall-like
defenses from Troy to the Maginot Line have seldom proved invincible, and
there are those who argue that ethical quarantines in law firms are equally
vulnerable. But everyone agrees that the original Chinese Wall is a glorious
structure. Those who have used its name as a symbol over the centuries, far
from demeaning anyone, pay the wall and its makers homage.

JEC

color-blind

A popular metaphor for the dream of a culture and legal system in which
race does not matter is that they should be *color-blind.* Of course, race
does matter in our culture, and the legal system cannot blind itself to that
reality. In 1900, W. E. B. Du Bois presciently observed that "the problem
of the Twentieth Century is the problem of the color-line";[1] and with that
century of struggling with the problem behind us it appears that another
century of effort may be needed to mitigate the effects of the country's
long history of legally enforced racism. Early in the twenty-first century,
however, the Supreme Court threatened to undermine those efforts by
converting a catchy slogan into a rule of law.

This image of racial equality is identified with the abolitionist Wendell
Phillips, who as the Civil War neared its end argued that the vote must be
extended to blacks in the former slave states: "reconstruction . . . must be
color-blind; unable to tell a white man from a black; able only to distinguish between loyalty and disl[o]yalty." Two decades later the orator
Robert Ingersoll, protesting the Supreme Court ruling striking down the
Civil Rights Act of 1875 (see BADGE OF SLAVERY), invoked the same ideal,
declaring that by the constitutional amendment abolishing slavery "the
Supreme court became color blind, and now justice had no right to tear the
bandage from her eyes to see whether a person was white or black."[2]

The first Justice John Marshall Harlan, the lone dissenter from the decision that Ingersoll was attacking, employed the metaphor himself thirteen years later when, again alone among the Justices, he dissented from the even more infamous decision in *Plessy v. Ferguson,* which enshrined the SEPARATE BUT EQUAL doctrine: "In view of the Constitution," he wrote, "in the eye of the law, there is in this country no superior, dominant, ruling class of citizens. There is no caste here. Our Constitution is color-blind, and neither knows nor tolerates classes among citizens." Of course Harlan was not so blind as to think that he was describing social reality; quite the opposite: he was deliberately voicing an ideal. In no small part because of the *Plessy* decision, that ideal was scarcely any closer to reality sixty-seven years later when Martin Luther King Jr. voiced the same aspiration in his most famous speech: "I have a dream that my four little children will one day live in a nation where they will not be judged by the color of their skin but by the content of their character."[3]

As soon as the law actually began to change, however, the rhetorical use of this metaphor changed dramatically. As legal historian Paul Finkelman put it, "the dancers pirouetted, and suddenly the advocates of civil rights wanted a racially conscious Constitution that would support AFFIRMATIVE ACTION. Meanwhile, the traditional opponents of civil rights—people who had openly opposed integration just a few years earlier—unexpectedly praised the notion of color blindness in constitutional adjudication."[4] There is nothing surprising in this: those who longed for a society characterized by racial equality realized that the social, economic, and legal structures put in place by centuries of slavery and segregation—ranging from specific practices such as preferential university admissions policies for children of alumni to broad and crushing economic and educational disparities—would perpetuate inequality indefinitely in the absence of positive measures to overcome them; and those who wanted to preserve the privileged status of whites realized exactly the same thing.

In reality the Constitution was never color-blind, even in theory. Even in the Fourteenth Amendment, Congress rejected calls for language declaring that "no State shall make any distinction among its citizens on account of race or color," and opted instead for deliberately flexible language about "equal protection of the laws."[5] In 2007, however, the Supreme Court barred two school districts from taking race into account so as to preserve a degree of racial balance and diversity in schools throughout the district. In a concurring opinion, Justice Clarence Thomas—ironically himself the beneficiary of a race-conscious selection process, having succeeded to the "black seat" on the Court upon the retirement of Justice Thurgood Marshall—argued at length for the theory of a strict "color-blind Constitution," and three of the four Justices who joined him in voting against the school district apparently concurred. In the view of those who take this position, after 350 years of legal subjugation of one race to another, a mere 50 years of affirmative legal measures to remedy the resulting damage is plenty.

Only one of the five Justices in the majority felt that disregarding America's racial history would be too simplistic and inflexible an approach to Constitutional interpretation. Referring to the statement that "our Constitution is color-blind" in Justice Harlan's ringing dissent in *Plessy* more than a century earlier, Justice Anthony Kennedy wrote: "Fifty years of experience since *Brown* v. *Board of Education* . . . should teach us that the problem before us defies so easy a solution. . . . [A]s an aspiration, Justice Harlan's axiom must command our assent. In the real world, it is regrettable to say, it cannot be a universal constitutional principle."[6]

JEC

Comstockery

In September 1905, George Bernard Shaw wrote to a *New York Times* correspondent about the removal of his works, including his play *Man and Superman,* from the open shelves of the public library. "Nobody outside of America is likely to be in the least surprised. Comstockery is the world's standing joke at the expense of the United States. Europe likes to hear of such things. It confirms the deep-seated conviction of the Old World that America is a provincial place, a second-rate country-town civilization after all." Shaw, knowing the commercial value of being thought lewd, went on to comment, "I can promise the Comstockers that, startling as *Man and Superman* may appear to them, it is the merest Sunday school tract compared with my later play . . . with which they will presently be confronted." And although the *Times* had actually used the word *Comstockery* ten years earlier, this letter rightfully gets the credit for popularizing the term.[1]

Anthony Comstock, the source of the label, was quick to reply to Shaw's letter when questioned by a reporter: "Shaw?" said Mr. Comstock reflectively, "I never heard of him in my life. He can't be much." After the reporter showed Comstock a copy of Shaw's letter, Comstock rose to the bait: "I had nothing to do with removing this Irish smut dealer's books from the public library shelves, but I will take a hand in the matter now. . . . You say he has plays also and some of them have been presented and liked in New York City? Well, they will be investigated, and the plays and the playing people will be dealt with according to the law."[2] Comstock was as good as his word, and arranged to have Shaw's play, *Mrs. Warren's Profession,* closed by New York police on opening night. When courts declined to ban the play as obscene (it dealt with the social and economic issues surrounding prostitution), it became the hottest ticket in town.

Comstockery signifies a prudish, self-righteous censorship based on a desire for sexual purity. Legally, it is inextricably intertwined with the law of obscenity and its First Amendment limits. But who was Comstock, and how did his name come to be associated with priggish overreaction?

Anthony Comstock was born in 1844 in the farming community of New Canaan, Connecticut, and reared in the Congregational church, at that time strongly influenced by the evangelical fervor of the Second Great Awakening. He did not go to college and did not read widely. His idealism led him to join the Union Army and fight in the Civil War to help free the slaves. Comstock was shocked by the rough behavior of his fellow soldiers, and tried to get them to pledge to abstain from rum, tobacco, and profanity. His diaries reflect a man haunted by constant temptation. At age twenty, he wrote: "Sin, sin. Oh how much peace and happiness is sacrificed on thy altar. Seemed as though Devil had full sway over me today, went right into temptation, and then, Oh such love, Jesus snatched it away out of my reach. How good is he, how sinful am I . . . . O I deplore my sinful weak nature so much."[3]

After the war, Comstock found work in a dry goods store in New York. His passion, though, was to protect the young from temptation. He got a job

Shaw and Comstock

On the day after the New York Times *reported Comstock's threat to take action against George Bernard Shaw's plays, the paper published an editorial that included the following words to the wise for "our esteemed fellow-citizen, Mr. Anthony Comstock, the guardian and arbiter of the public morals in these parts." (The "late fifties" and "early sixties" refer, of course, to the 1850s and 1860s, but it is easy to imagine virtually the same scenario having taken place in the late 1950s or early 1960s.)*

Let us tell Mr. Comstock an authentic anecdote of the late fifties or the early sixties in New York. A foreign firm of art dealers had consigned to this country a painting which they expected to make a sensation in this new and unsophisticated world. The agent to whom it was consigned hired a room in which to exhibit it, and modestly advertised it as a work of art. But nobody came to see it. Discouraged, the agent repaired to the office of a newspaper in which he happened to be persona grata, and requested permission to write a notice of his exhibit. This being granted, he recited that a picture was now openly insulting the public moral decency at the apartment in question, and loudly demanded to know where were the police. In consequence the next morning there was a queue of ticket buyers to the exhibition extending half way around the block. Does Mr. Comstock see the point? We can assure him that Mr. Shaw beholds it vividly.

Editorial, "Shaw and Comstock," *New York Times,* Sept. 29, 1905, 8.

with the Young Men's Christian Association (YMCA) and became its agent in fighting vice in New York City—a task consistent with the organization's campaign to outlaw alcohol and to enforce the BLUE LAWS. In 1872, the YMCA created the Committee for the Suppression of Vice (soon replaced by the Society for the Suppression of Vice) and put Comstock in charge.

A provision of the Post Office Act of 1865—included in response to concerns that the mails were increasingly being used to convey sexually oriented materials, often to soldiers—already made it a crime to send any "obscene book, pamphlet, picture, print, or other publication of a vulgar and indecent character" through the U.S. mail. Comstock, though, wanted a more powerful tool to clean up America, so he went to Washington (toting a bag full of examples of lewd books, items that claimed to increase sexual potency, and materials on contraception and abortion) and lobbied for changes in the law.

Congress gave Comstock what he wanted, in 1873 passing "An Act for the Suppression of Trade in, and Circulation of, obscene Literature and Articles of immoral Use," which became popularly known as the Comstock Act. The act prohibited the sale or distribution of obscene or indecent material as well as any information about birth control or abortion. The penalty for mailing any of these items was increased, and offending material could be seized and burned.

Two days after the Comstock Act was passed, the postmaster general appointed Comstock himself as an unpaid special agent with a free-wheeling mandate to enforce the act, and he dove in with zeal. Comstock's early attacks were aimed at lowbrow books for the working class but stayed clear of serious literature and art. In addition to racy books about Wild West exploits or big-city crime ("devil-traps for the young"), Comstock seized and suppressed novels such as *The Lustful Turk, The Curtain Drawn Up; or, The Education of Laura,* and *The Confessions of a Voluptuous Young Lady of High Rank.* He also declared war on visual erotica, particularly postcard reproductions of paintings and photos. By January 1874, he had seized 194,000 pictures and photographs; 14,200 stereopticon plates; 134,000 pounds of books; 60,300 "rubber articles" (condoms); and 5,500 sets of playing cards.[4]

Comstock later began to attack more literary and artistic works. He had no more respect for classics than for French postcards. "To set our youth wild with passion by the lascivious products of ancient writers, or to fasten the picture of lust painted by some 'old master' upon their imagination to defile it, is none the less a crime because these records of crime have outlived their day," Comstock said. He campaigned against Walt Whitman's *Leaves of Grass* and did his best to suppress *Tom Jones, The Canterbury Tales, The Arabian Nights,* and works of Balzac, Rabelais, and Zola. He even prohibited certain anatomy textbooks from being mailed to medical students. Comstock also censored public discussion of contraception or abortion, including Margaret Sanger's attempts to educate immigrant and working women. And he enthusiastically engaged in his spat with Shaw.

Two years before his death in 1915, Comstock boasted that he had convicted thousands of people and driven fifteen people to suicide. Even Comstock's own statistics understate his impact: the threat of prosecution caused many publishing houses to self-censor to avoid actual prosecution. By the end of his career, however, Comstock had extended his purity campaign so far that he had lost the support of the mainstream. (He did attract the attention of a young law student named J. Edgar Hoover, who was interested in Comstock's causes and enforcement methods.) Even supporters of censorship no longer supported Comstock: "The trouble with Anthony Comstock," noted one newspaper editorial, "in spite of the good work he has done, is that he has sought so long for impurity that he finds it in everything he looks into. For this reason he is no longer able to judge things impartially."[5]

As public opinion evolved, so did the definition of obscenity. Comstock was able to censor broadly because the definition of *obscene* under which he operated, taken from the 1868 English case of *Regina v. Hicklin,* was so wide. Under *Hicklin,* material was judged obscene on the basis of its presumed effect on "those whose minds are open to . . . immoral influences," including "the young of either sex." The work's intended audience was irrelevant, as was the work's overall artistic merit. Exactly one hundred years after the passage of the Comstock Act, the Supreme Court recast the legal test and limited obscenity to "works which, taken as a whole, appeal to the prurient interest in sex, which portray sexual conduct in a patently offensive way, and which . . . do not have serious literary, artistic, political, or scientific value."[6] Nevertheless, much of the Comstock Act remains on the books today.

After his death, Comstock's successors continued his work. As each new medium made the dissemination of erotic or obscene material easier, groups that disapproved of the content lobbied the government to censor it. As the twentieth century progressed, officials undertook to regulate comics, television, recorded popular music, video games, and the Internet.

The perennial push and pull between popular culture and censorship not only persists in the twenty-first century; in some ways it has intensi-

Drawn by Robert Minor.

"Your Honor, this woman gave birth to a naked child!"

Satirical cartoon by Robert Minor, from the September 1915 issue of the socialist magazine *The Masses*. The corpulent and extravagantly mustachioed Comstock, who died unexpectedly later that very month, would have been immediately recognizable to readers. (Courtesy of Beinecke Rare Book and Manuscript Library, Yale University)

fied. In response to complaints about occasional obscenities uttered on television during hours when children might be watching—most notoriously by the celebrities Bono, Cher, and Nicole Richie during live broadcasts of award shows in 2002 and 2003—the Federal Communications Commission, which is authorized by Congress to penalize "indecency" in radio and television broadcasting over the air (but not via cable), changed its decades-old policy of disregarding "fleeting expletives" and began to hold broadcasters accountable for such isolated occurrences.

On February 1, 2004, modest public consternation over such incidents erupted into widespread furor when, at the climax of the Super Bowl half-time show before some 90 million TV viewers, a carefully choreographed "wardrobe malfunction" caused singer Janet Jackson's breast to be exposed for nine-sixteenths of a second. This triggered an organized campaign of viewer complaints, to which the FCC responded by launching what a writer in *Broadcasting & Cable* magazine, in an article headlined "Federal 'Comstockery' Commission," characterized as "an enforcement program that has all the earmarks of a Victorian crusade." The commission imposed $8 million in fines for "indecency" violations in 2004 (versus $440,000 in 2003) and in 2006 fined CBS television stations a total of $550,000 for the Janet Jackson episode alone. Shortly thereafter, Congress got into the act by increasing the maximum fine tenfold and making it possible, with multiple fines, for a single such incident to cost a network millions of dollars. Television networks, in turn, challenged the FCC's new policies and actions in court, causing a cascade of judicial rulings, appeals, remands, and further rulings that at this writing are still far from reaching a final resolution. It is perhaps not an encouraging sign for the TV networks, however, that in one of those opinions Supreme Court Justice Antonin Scalia, demonstrating his well-known love of Latin, added a Latin feminine ending to an English word and used it to deride pop culture icons such as Cher and Nicole Richie as "foul-mouthed glitteratae from Hollywood."[7]

Anthony Comstock has been dead for almost a hundred years, but the issues he raised remain with us. Society is still debating what role the government should play in limiting communications about sexuality—when (if ever) ignorance is better than information, when regulation is necessary to protect the vulnerable, and when sexual material is so inherently harmful that it should be prohibited even to adults.

EGT

corpus delicti

Corpus delicti wins the prize for the legal term that is at once most misunderstood by nonlawyers and most misspelled by lawyers.

The misunderstanding is understandable. The Latin translates literally as "the body of the crime," a meaningless phrase in English. In law the phrase *corpus delicti* refers to the essential elements of a crime—the facts showing that a certain kind of crime, such as murder or larceny, has occurred, without regard to who might have committed it. The term appeared in Scots law at least as early as 1705,[1] and remained almost exclusively a Scottish term for at least a century. Under Scottish law, as explained in an 1811 treatise, circumstantial evidence linking the accused to a supposed crime could not be considered "unless there be proof of the *corpus delicti*," that is, proof "that a *crime has been committed.*"[2]

In England the importance of establishing that the crime in question actually occurred was stressed (though without the Latin terminology) by the seventeenth-century jurist Sir Matthew Hale. In an influential treatise that he was still working on at his death in 1676 (finally published sixty years later), Hale cited as object lessons such cases as that of a man who was put to death for the murder of a niece he had been bringing up (on land that belonged to her but that he would inherit if she died), who had disappeared after being heard to cry, "Good uncle do not kill me," during a beating. It turned out that she had run away to escape his beatings; after his execution, she waited until she came of age and then coolly returned and claimed her land.[3]

In the nineteenth century the Scottish term caught on in England and America. And because of experience with wrongful convictions based on a false confession, the courts and legislatures in America uniformly adopted the "corpus delicti rule," under which, at least in murder cases, no one can be found guilty solely on the basis of a confession; there has to be independent evidence that the crime really happened. In recent decades, the crucial importance of such a rule has become ever clearer as understanding has grown of the many ways in which false confessions can be produced—through false memory, depression, delusion, a desire for celebrity, and the plain old THIRD DEGREE. Beginning in the 1950s, however, this rule has been steadily weakened as Americans have become more concerned with making sure that every guilty person is convicted and less concerned with making sure that every innocent person goes free.[4]

In a murder case, whether in Scotland, England, or America, the best possible evidence that the crime really happened is a dead body with a knife in its back. The fact that the corpus delicti in a murder case is most often established by the corpse itself gave rise to the belief among many nonlawyers that *corpus delicti* is just a fancy name for the corpse. This process was aided by the fact that "corpus" *sounds* like "corpse"; in fact, the two words are related, although *corpse* came from *corpus* by a round-about route in which, among other things, the *p* dropped out in Old French and then got reinserted in English. A final factor in the growth of *corpus delicti* as the conventional term for the corpse in murder mysteries and the like is that even for those who know perfectly well what the term means in law, it has a catchy, jocular quality that makes it irresistible to authors. As a result, when a mystery writer takes pains to use the term in the technical legal sense—as when Agatha Christie wrote that "Inspector Maine . . . had painstakingly and accurately compiled the corpus delicti"[5]—it has a strikingly unconventional tone.

This common misunderstanding had uncommon consequences for one John George Haigh and the nine people he ultimately claimed to have murdered in England in the 1940s. Haigh started his criminal career as a dapper, engaging con man, and ended it swinging from the gallows as the "Acid Bath Murderer." During an early stint in prison his fellow inmates had dubbed him "Old Corpus Delicti" for his fascination with the notion that all one needs to get away with murder is a foolproof way to make the body disappear, because (he explained) "there would then be no *corpus delicti*." Experiments on mice convinced Haigh that he had found the solution he was looking for. He thereupon took to supporting himself by murdering people for their valuables, stuffing the victims into an oil drum, steeping them for several days in sulfuric acid, and pouring out the resulting sludge. When evidence linked him to the disappearance of a certain wealthy matron, he told the police, "Mrs. Durand-Deacon no longer exists. . . . I have destroyed her with acid. You will find the sludge which remains at Leopold Road. . . . How can you prove murder if there is no body?" He went on to describe several other such murders and added, for good measure, that he had drunk a glass of the blood of each victim before dissolving them—apparently in the hope of adding an insanity defense to the defense of "no corpus delicti."[6] Neither defense worked. The lesson for would-be murderers is: learn your legal vocabulary before you embark upon the perfect crime.

Expecting the Unexpected

The Haigh case shows that the corpus delicti in a murder case—that is, the fact that a person has died—can sometimes be established without a body. But doing so can be a challenge for the prosecutor, as this joke, first attested in 1992, suggests:

A noted criminal defense lawyer was making the closing argument for his client accused of murder, although the body of the victim had never been found. The lawyer dramatically turned to the courtroom's clock and, pointing to it, announced, "Ladies and gentlemen of the jury, I have some astounding news. I have found the supposed victim of this murder to be alive! Within the next thirty seconds, she will walk through the door of this courtroom."

A heavy quiet suddenly fell over the courtroom as all waited with bated breath for the dramatic entry.

But nothing happened.

The lawyer continued, "The mere fact that you were watching the door, expecting the victim to walk into this courtroom, is clear proof that you have far more than even a reasonable doubt as to whether a murder was actually committed."

The jury was instructed, filed out, and filed back in just ten minutes with a guilty verdict.

When the judge brought the proceedings to an end, the dismayed lawyer chased after the jury foreman: "Guilty? How could you convict? You were all watching the door!"

"Well," the foreman explained, "most of us were watching the door. But one of us was watching the defendant, and he wasn't watching the door."

But just as the similarity of *corpus* to *corpse* confuses nonlawyers, another pronunciation issue has led many lawyers into confusion. The word *delicti,* the possessive of the Latin *dēlictum* (crime, fault), at a casual glance is reminiscent of the much more common but completely unrelated English word *delectable* (from Latin *dēlectābilis,* "delightful"). It is therefore common for people to read the word with a short *e* sound in the middle instead of the short *i* sound; and having got that stuck in their minds, they write it the same way: "delecti." This linguistic crime is compounded when others see or hear the word in that form and faithfully reproduce the error in their own writing. Of course this seldom happened back in the days when lawyers knew Latin, but those days are long gone. A look at the relative incidence of "corpus delicti" and "corpus delecti" in American judicial opinions since the first occurrence of "corpus delicti" in 1809 shows that the incidence of "corpus delecti" hovered around 2 percent up through the 1930s, averaged 4 percent to 5 percent for the 1940s through the 1960s, rose to 7 percent in the 1970s, then leapt to an average of about 12 percent for the 1980s, 1990s, and first decade of the 2000s. The legal profession is known for clinging to its ancient Latin locutions, but this one may prove to be an exception: a Latin expression whose form changes through use.

JEC

CSI effect

The television show *CSI: Crime Scene Investigation* debuted in the fall of 2000. Its heroes are scientists—called forensic scientists because they use scientific techniques to provide information for the legal system—who analyze the trace evidence found at crime scenes to help the police identify and apprehend criminals. The show is enormously popular and has spawned so many similar shows that television viewers can see hours of forensic science–based fiction every day. That much is clear. What is debated, however, is whether these shows have an impact—the *CSI effect*—on real juries in real criminal cases.

Television does influence the way viewers see the world around them, including their perception of the legal system. *Perry Mason,* for example, often showed Mason approaching a witness and leaning against the rail during the examination, not because that's what lawyers did but because it allowed the television camera to capture both lawyer and witness in a single frame. Lawyers, believing that juries expected this kind of confrontation, began doing likewise. *Dragnet* showed TV viewers the way *Miranda* warnings ("You have the right to remain silent . . .") interact with police interrogation. And even before *CSI* came along, a show called *Quincy*, about a medical examiner, raised concerns that jurors would expect forensic evidence in every case.

CSI and similar shows depict trace evidence being analyzed by earnest, attractive, well-dressed technicians. The results are portrayed as fast, cheap, objective, and completely reliable. This incomplete fictional portrait worries both prosecution and defense lawyers, though for different reasons. Prosecutors believe that the *CSI* effect has led to an increase in acquittals, as jurors demand more than the prosecution can realistically provide. Juries, they fear, are conditioned by television to expect helpful trace evidence at all crime scenes, and so they perceive a lack of scientific evidence as a failure of proof. *CSI* gives them no appreciation of the dearth of testable evidence, the multi-thousand-dollar price tag of full DNA testing, or the months-long backlog at the lab. Prosecutors worry that disappointed juries will acquit because they expect evidence of complete scientific testing in every case, no matter how routine.

Defense lawyers, in contrast, argue that the *CSI* effect helps the prosecution. Television science gives the illusion of objectivity, rarely making clear that the analysis of most forensic evidence involves subjective judgment calls. "The evidence never lies," repeatedly proclaims the show's charismatic lab director, Gil Grissom. The characters are experts in their fields and work in spotless labs stocked with cutting-edge technology. The *CSI* plots do not involve degraded samples, faulty lab work, undertrained technicians, or overstated certainty. Nor do they disclose that real scientists have serious doubts about the reliability of techniques claiming to match hair, fibers, and bite marks—all staples of the fictional criminologist. On television the person identified as the criminal at the end of the episode indisputably *is* the bad guy. In real life, statistics from the Innocence Project show that fully half of the wrongful convictions later overturned by DNA evidence were based at least partly on "unvalidated or improper forensic science." So while prosecutors fear that the *CSI* effect causes jurors to ask too much of scientific testimony, defense lawyers fear that it encourages jurors to give it too much deference.[1]

Whether the *CSI* effect is a fact or a media creation, lawyers and judges have begun to act as though it were real. For example, one Delaware judge allowed the prosecution to introduce evidence of the extent of its investigation, including tests that produced no relevant results, in order to counteract potential defense arguments that additional testing might have exonerated the defendant. Said the judge, "For sure, juries are instructed to decide the case on the evidence presented, but perforce, in this atmosphere, juries sometimes decide cases on 'evidence' not introduced, such as, scientific analysis not sought or done. To believe otherwise is folly. Juries are also told not to speculate, and to reduce the risk of that happening, potential areas of speculation should be minimized."[2] Judges have also begun to allow lawyers to question potential jurors about their television-viewing habits, and lawyers for both sides refer to *CSI* in opening and closing statements to the jury. Some judges have even ordered jurors not to watch *CSI*.

Perhaps most ironically, there may be a *CSI* effect that kicks in even before the police arrive. One accused multiple murderer allegedly used bleach to wash blood off his hands, spread blankets in his car to avoid contaminating it with the victims' blood, and burned the bodies and his own clothing to try to eliminate all trace evidence. Where did he get these ideas? From *CSI*.[3]

EGT

cut the baby in half

This phrase, or words to the same effect, is used in reference to a compromise of any kind; it means to "split the difference." In a business story about a ruling of the Federal Communications Commission, for example, we read: "From Northpoint's perspective, the F.C.C. took a 'split the baby in two' approach. 'They feel good when everyone is equally unhappy,' Ms. Collier said." And turning from business to recreation we find: "In *State v. Fly* the North Carolina Supreme Court crafted an intricate opinion that in essence split the baby or at least the two groups of buttocks exposers. In a unanimous opinion, the Court held that the mooner was guilty of indecent exposure, but stated that the thong and g-string bikini wearer would not be."[1] The allusion in each case is to the compromise that King Solomon threatened to impose on the parties in what is sometimes referred to as the world's first recorded child-custody case.

Solomon, the third and last king of the twelve tribes of Israel, reigned in the mid-tenth century B.C.E. He is legendary as a man of wisdom, as exemplified by his handling of this dispute. As the story is told in the Bible, two prostitutes appeared before the king in his capacity as a judge. The women shared a house, became pregnant at about the same time, and gave birth within three days of each other. But then, according to the petitioner, "this woman's child died in the night; because she overlaid it. And she arose at midnight, and took my son from beside me . . . and laid her dead child in my bosom. And when I rose in the morning to give my child suck, behold, it was dead: but when I had considered it in the morning, behold, it was not my son, which I did bear." The respondent denied the allegations, saying, "Nay; but the living is my son, and the dead is thy son." After considerable argument, none of which added any new evidence, Solomon made his ruling. He summarized the inconclusive state of the evidence, called for a sword, and ordered: "Divide the living child in two, and give half to the one, and half to the other." At that point one of the women relented, "for her bowels yearned upon her son, and she said, O my lord, give her the living child, and in no wise slay it. But the other said, Let it be neither mine nor thine, but divide it." This was all Solomon needed to hear; we can imagine the king pointing dramatically to the first woman as he issued his final judgment: "Give her the living child, and in no wise slay it: she is the mother thereof."[2]

It may seem overblown, even callous, to invoke this emotional human drama as a metaphor to describe everything from the most prosaic business decisions to the most amusing legal hairsplitting, but the vividness and familiarity of the story make it a natural subject to draw upon. As long ago as 1880 we see a court resolving competing claims to a certain fund of money by saying, "We think that the shortest, wisest, best way to get rid of it, is to divide the child between them . . . . The decree of the court, therefore, is that this fund be equally divided."[3]

Occasionally a pedant objects to such language—as when one federal appeals court criticized another for describing an equal division as "Solomon-like" on the ground that, in the end, Solomon did not actually divide the baby in half.[4] This objection overlooks the fact that idiomatic expressions are typically used more for color than for logic. It is bootless to criticize someone for saying "That book knocked my socks off!" on the ground that, as a matter of historical fact, the socks did not actually leave the feet.

More fundamentally, this objection overlooks the fact that, according to the story, Solomon did indeed order the baby to be cut in half. As a man who had consolidated power by ruthlessly and systematically liquidating his competitors—even to the point of spilling blood at the very altar of the tabernacle[5]—Solomon was not given to squeamishness or idle threats. The women in the story were right to take him at his word. A judicial order to divide something in half *is* Solomonic, for the simple reason that this is exactly the order that Solomon issued. Some references to the story are almost uncomfortably close to the original, as in a dispute between a decedent's family and his gay partner over how his remains should be disposed of. The court wrote: "Before a decision could be rendered on this issue, the parties reached a resolution which this court applauds. Displaying the wisdom of King Solomon . . . , the parties agreed . . . to cremate Stanton's body and split the ashes."[6]

But the Solomon story is too profound and too deeply rooted to serve merely as an occasional rhetorical flourish. It is, in the words of constitutional scholar Paul Gewirtz, "perhaps our culture's central myth about judicial wisdom," and as such it has been the subject of no end of legal and academic analysis—and no small amount of criticism. The story has been interpreted variously as a "biblical blood test" to determine the biological mother, as a "best interests of the child" test to determine which woman would make the best parent, as a symbol of the helplessness of children at the mercy of adult whims, and as an example of the helplessness of women at the mercy of an arbitrary and violent male legal system.[7]

On a procedural level, Solomon's apparent impatience with the matter and ultimate resolution on the basis of simplistic psychological assumptions have been criticized repeatedly—though nowhere more vividly than in Mark Twain's 1884 novel *Huckleberry Finn*. Huck's traveling companion, the escaped slave Jim—the seemingly naive character through whom Twain often speaks—insists that Solomon "*warn't* no wise man, nuther. He had some er de dad-fetchedes' ways I ever see." Jim dramatizes the point for Huck by playing the role of Solomon with a dollar bill in the role of the child:

> What does I do? Does I shin aroun' mongs' de neighbors en fine out which un you de bill *do* b'long to, en han' it over to de right one, all safe en soun', de way dat anybody dat had any gumption would? No—I take en whack de bill in *two,* en give half un it to you, en de yuther half to de yuther woman. Dat's de way Sollermun was gwyne to do wid de chile. Now I want to ast you: what's de use er dat half a bill?[8]

From a modern perspective, one of the most interesting yet least discussed aspects of the Solomon story is that the litigants were prostitutes. Of course, the parties had to be unattached women for the story to work; otherwise the litigation would have been between their husbands. The notion that a married woman herself might have some claim to custody of her child would not come along for at least another twenty-eight centuries. Nevertheless, the story is strikingly advanced in its recognition that a prostitute is no different from any other woman in her capacity to be beside herself with grief at the loss of a child or to be struck with gut-wrenching horror when faced with the prospect of such a loss.

Admittedly, it would have ill-befitted Solomon to be scornful of such women. According to the Bible, he himself was descended from a former prostitute—the harlot Rahab of Jericho, who had helped the Israelites by sheltering two of Joshua's spies and so was spared when Joshua destroyed the city. Moreover, Solomon was reputed to have, in addition to his seven hundred wives (many of them given to him to seal diplomatic alliances), some three hundred concubines. But even so, the story's underlying respect for the maternal rights of a prostitute stands in marked contrast to U.S. law, in which any involvement with the world's oldest profession could subject a woman to being "declared an unfit mother and deprived of the custody and visitation of her children."[9]

Almost three thousand years after the event, it appears that we still could learn a thing or two about justice from King Solomon.

JEC

day in court

The idea that a person accused of a crime or involved in a legal dispute is "entitled to his *day in court*" is at the same time fundamental to the Anglo-American concept of justice and constantly evolving. The principle—though not in those words—was born at Runnymede, a meadow on the river Thames, on June 15, 1215. King John's barons, fed up with oppressive taxes, harsh enforcement, capricious justice, and official corruption, had revolted against the king and captured London. After several days of negotiation at Runnymede, John ended the revolt by affixing his seal to a long list of concessions demanded by the barons. Within days, the king's scribes put these "Articles of the Barons" into the form of the formal royal grant that came to be known as the Magna Carta (Great Charter). Notable among its provisions were promises that henceforth no one would be put to trial except upon evidence from credible witnesses, and no free man would be imprisoned or deprived of property or rights "except by the lawful judgment of his peers or by the law of the land."[1]

This was the cornerstone of the edifice known as due process of law. William Blackstone, writing 550 years later, explained its fundamental position in English law: "for if once it were left in the power of any, the highest, magistrate to imprison arbitrarily whomever he or his officers thought proper, . . . there would soon be an end of all other rights and immunities. . . . To bereave a man of life, or by violence to confiscate his estate, without accusation or trial, would be so gross and notorious an act of despotism, as must at once convey the alarm of tyranny throughout the whole kingdom." The principle of due process was subsequently carried over into the United States Constitution (particularly the Fifth, Sixth, and Fourteenth Amendments). In the words of the Supreme Court, "A person's right to reasonable notice of a charge against him, and an opportunity to be heard in his defense—a right to his day in court—are basic in our system of jurisprudence; and these rights include, as a minimum, a right to examine the witnesses against him, to offer testimony, and to be represented by counsel."[2]

The origin of that phrase *day in court* is lost in the mists of time, but it was certainly well established by the beginning of the eighteenth century, when legal treatises routinely remarked that a person cannot be deprived of property rights if "he hath no day in Court" to defend his interest.[3] Centuries ago the expression could have been taken quite literally: one of the king's judges would visit a town a few times each year and hear any cases that had accumulated since the last visit; a trial, even several trials, could easily be completed in a day. Even in twenty-first-century America, more than 40 percent of civil trials and more than 50 percent of criminal trials in the federal courts are completed within a day, and the percentages in state courts, which handle many small cases, are probably higher.[4] But the use of *day* to refer to an indefinite period of time—not just a calendar day—extends back at least to the fourteenth century; the saying that a "dog will have his day" was a well-worn proverb long before Shakespeare used it.[5] So there is nothing inappropriate about referring to a trial spanning weeks or even months as the plaintiff's or the defendant's "day in court."

In 1900 the Supreme Court described the principle that a person with a legal claim or defense is entitled to a day in court as a "truism"[6]—and then proceeded to hold that the party before it was not entitled to any such thing. There are in fact many legal doctrines that can bar a person from maintaining an action or a defense in court, including jurisdictional rules, requirements of standing, statutes of limitations, and a host of others. And on a practical level, the economics of the legal system ensure that well-heeled litigants have far greater access to the courts than the poor. Moreover, although the number of cases filed has grown year by year, the number of trials has dramatically declined. In the state courts for which statistics are available, fewer than 16 percent of the civil cases disposed of in 2002 were tried, and only 3.3 percent of the criminal cases. In the federal courts, by 2004 barely 4 percent of criminal dispositions, and a mere 1.7 percent of dispositions on the civil side, were the result of trials.[7] Whatever they may believe about being entitled to their day in court, civil litigants are heavily pressured to settle their cases. And for criminal defendants it's worse: they are threatened with more severe charges and more severe punishment—even death—if they insist upon their right to a trial. This practice was specifically approved by the Supreme Court in a 1978 ruling upholding a life sentence (under a "habitual offender" statute) for a defendant charged with forging a check for $88.30, as a penalty for his refusal to plead guilty to forgery and accept a five-year sentence.[8]

In the twenty-first century a new front opened in the battle begun by King John's barons. In the invasion of Afghanistan in 2001, the United States captured, or had handed over to it, some 650 individuals suspected of having some involvement with or information about terrorists. In early 2002 the captives were transported to the American naval base at Guantánamo Bay, Cuba, where they were later joined by other detainees. The administration of President George W. Bush took the position that it had the right to hold these prisoners indefinitely, without charge, without the protections accorded to prisoners of war by the Geneva Conventions, and without any other rights. In June 2008, the Supreme Court held that the prisoners were entitled to challenge their detention in federal court. But the court expressly left open the core issue in any such challenge—the "extent of the showing required of the Government" to justify their continued imprisonment.[9]

Less than a year later, the new president, Barack Obama, announced that, like his predecessor, he intended to continue to hold at least some of the prisoners indefinitely without trial. These would be individuals who, though believed to be dangerously anti-American, would probably be released if given a trial, "in some cases because evidence may be tainted"— a veiled reference to accusations and admissions procured by torture or other coercion. And a year after that, in May 2010, the administration released a report concluding that forty-eight of the Guantánamo detainees should be held indefinitely without trial "because either there is presently insufficient admissible evidence to establish the detainee's guilt beyond a reasonable doubt . . . or the detainee's conduct does not constitute a chargeable offense." In a reversal that would have stunned King John's barons, the absence of reliable evidence of criminality, rather than being a reason *not* to hold prisoners, has become a reason to keep them locked up.[10] As we approach the eight hundredth anniversary of the Great Charter, we can predict that the Supreme Court will be called upon yet again to clarify the scope and meaning of the ancient right to one's day in court.

JEC

death and taxes

The Constitution of the United States was ratified in 1788, and the new government went into operation the following year. Benjamin Franklin, whose final act of public service had been to participate in the framing of the Constitution, wrote of the achievement to his longtime friend and fellow scientist Jean-Baptiste Le Roy, with whom he had presented a report to the French Academy of Sciences on the subject of lightning rods for a cathedral. "Our new Constitution is now established," Franklin wrote, "and has an appearance that promises permanency; but in this world nothing can be said to be certain, except death and taxes." In regard to the first of these certainties, he added, "My health continues much as it has been for some time, except that I grow thinner and weaker, so that I cannot expect to hold out much longer."[1]

Franklin was correct; he died less than six months later. But his popularity in America and abroad was unabated. So there was a ready market in 1817 when Franklin's grandson published *The Private Correspondence of Benjamin Franklin,* a collection that included this letter. Inevitably, people picked up on Franklin's remark, as in a famous speech in England in 1831 on the occasion of the defeat of a parliamentary reform bill, which the speaker correctly predicted would ultimately succeed: "I have no more doubt . . . that this bill will pass, than I have that the annual tax bills will pass, and greater certainty than this no man can have, for Franklin tells us, there are but two things certain in this world—death and taxes."[2] More than two centuries after Franklin penned his letter, it is still cited with great regularity—especially by legal writers. Any number of scholarly articles on tax law have led off with the Franklin quotation, and the Supreme Court itself has cited what it calls "Franklin's aphorism" or "Franklin's adage" in three different cases.

Franklin would be astonished. When he wrote those words, he could not have imagined that he would come to be viewed as the originator of that old saw about death and taxes. In a book of proverbs published thirty-three years earlier it had been coupled with another familiar proverb and explained:

Many Things happen between the Cup and the Lip; *or,* Nothing is certain but Death and Taxes.

This is a prudent Precaution, and applicable to all such as are too warm and sanguine, too unmindful of future Contingencies; and build their Hopes of Success too frequently on a sandy Foundation.

And the proverb was old even then. We find it, for example, in a popular farce staged forty years before, in which a wife starts to tell her husband that she is sure about something and is cut off with, "You lye, you are not sure, for I say, Woman, 'tis impossible to be sure of any thing but Death and Taxes,—therefore hold your Tongue."[3]

But the irony of Franklin's truism is not so much that it is not Franklin's as that it is less and less true. Legions of lawyers and accountants work to help corporations and wealthy individuals avoid taxes, while many politicians work to reduce and even eliminate the very taxes that principally affect the wealthiest classes. The late twentieth and early twenty-first centuries have seen significant reductions in marginal income tax rates (whose greatest effect is on the highest incomes), capital gains taxes (on profits from buying and selling stocks and bonds), taxation of dividends (on income received from holding stock), and estate taxes (on transfers of very large estates—see DEATH TAX). Serious proposals have even been made to eliminate the capital gains, dividends, and estate taxes entirely. In 2004, *Newsweek*'s Wall Street editor, Allan Sloan, pulled no punches in laying out what this would mean for the magazine's readers: "The income tax will become a misnomer—it will really be a salary tax." People with sufficient assets to make their money through investments rather than by working for a paycheck, instead of merely paying reduced taxes on their income, would pay none at all, creating "a new class of landed aristocrats who could inherit billions tax-free, invest the money, watch it compound tax-free and hand it down tax-free to their heirs."[4]

The ancient adage may have to be revised. For the very wealthy, it seems, nothing is certain but death.

JEC

death tax

In the U.S. presidential elections of 2000, 2004, and 2008, the official platform of the Republican Party called for a permanent end to the "death tax." In fact, the "death tax" was cited as a particular evil, on average, four times in each platform, despite the fact that there has never been a federal tax by that name. How this name came to be used, and used so insistently and repeatedly, tells us a lot about the role of language in modern campaigns for legal change. Rhetoric has been the subject of formal study since at least the fourth century B.C.E., but it was not until the latter part of the twentieth century that political rhetoric was changed from a high art into a low science. Both major parties in the United States now use market research to shape their messages.

The tax in question is the federal estate tax (Chapter 11 of the Internal Revenue Code), which is a tax on transfers of large accumulations of wealth at death. As of 2009, this tax applied only to the richest one-fourth of one percent of Americans, was assessed only on a portion of the wealth left over after they had consumed all they wanted for themselves and given away as much as they wished to charity, was not collected until nine months after their death, and left a large enough portion of their estates untaxed to enable even the poorest of them to leave millions of dollars to their heirs— and the richest to leave billions. Unlike sales and payroll taxes, which fall disproportionately on people of modest means, and income tax, which taxes wage earners at higher rates than people who are rich enough to make their money simply by investing what they already have, the estate tax has always been the one significant tax targeted specifically at those best able to afford it. Since 2002, it has been literally a tax that applies only to millionaires—or in the case of married couples with a little basic estate planning, multimillionaires. For the few affected individuals whose wealth might be tied up in a family farm or other family-operated business, the family could choose to pay the tax a little at a time over a period of fourteen years. In sum, as taxes go, this is as painless as it gets.

Small wonder that the estate tax, a fixture of the American tax system since 1916, was long viewed as unassailable. In the "Contract with America" signed by Republican candidates for the House of Representatives as an election-year campaign tool in 1994—when the minimum size of an estate subject to the tax was $600,000 (or $1.2 million for a married couple)—the farthest the party felt it could go was to tuck into one of its promised bills a provision "increasing the estate tax exemption from $600,000 to $750,000." And in the presidential campaign of 1996, the party's platform was even less assertive on the subject, promising only to take steps to "assure that no one who inherits a small business or farm has to sell it to pay inheritance taxes."[1]

Yet just three years later, in the summer of 1999, Congress passed a sweeping tax bill that, among many other things, would have phased out the estate tax completely. President Bill Clinton vetoed the bill, but the following summer the estate tax phaseout was passed again, only to be vetoed again. A few months and one presidential election later, in the spring of 2001, this provision was passed a third time, and the new president, George W. Bush, signed it.

This stunning turnabout was the product of a superlative campaign to change public opinion, financed by a group of extremely wealthy families. And the linchpin of the campaign was recharacterizing the estate tax as a "death tax" to make it sound as if it applied to ordinary people rather than just the very rich. As Grover Norquist, president of the antitax coalition Americans for Tax Reform, explained: "Estates are what British people hunt foxes on. Death is what everybody does."[2]

Several antitax activists have been credited with coining "death tax" in the mid- to late 1990s, but in fact the expression has been used for at least a century as a general term for taxes on the transfer or acquisition of property at or after the death of its former owner. Andrew Carnegie, one of the world's wealthiest men at the end of the nineteenth century and a strong believer in the principle that those who profit the most from the American system should contribute the most to it, wrote in 1900, "The writer believes in collecting the revenues, as far as possible, from the rich, and favors heavy death taxes upon estates in lieu of income tax. There is no reason why the necessary expenditures of the government should not come chiefly from this class through such taxes, and through the tariff. . . . To tax foreign luxuries heavily and to collect a high percentage of death duties upon estates should be the policy."[3]

But it was not until the 1990s that the power of this phrase to transform public perception of the estate tax was recognized. By most accounts, it was Jim Martin, founder of a conservative senior citizens' organization called the 60 Plus Association, who first seized upon the phrase for this purpose around 1993. But the person generally credited with making it the official language of the anti–estate tax movement is the pollster, market researcher, and language consultant Frank Luntz. Luntz uses focus groups to determine how conservative messages can be phrased to make them resonate with the largest possible segment of the electorate, and then works with his clients and contacts in Congress and industry to spread the language that works best. As Merrie Spaeth, formerly director of media relations in President Ronald Reagan's White House, explained in a different context, in public policy debates "words often determine the outcome. He who gets the good words first, wins." In the mid-1990s Luntz tested "death tax" and found that it evoked a much stronger negative reaction than "estate tax." He also found that once people have formulated a negative opinion on the basis of such language they rarely change their opinion on the basis of any facts learned subsequently.[4]

Luntz became an evangelist for the term "death tax," promoting it both to private antitax organizations and to leading Republican politicians. He found a receptive audience. Legend has it that linguistic discipline was enforced by "pizza funds," in which anyone in an office who slipped up and uttered the phrase "estate tax" had to contribute a dollar to a fund to buy pizza for the office. This regimen purportedly started in lobbyists' offices, was picked up in the office of House Speaker Newt Gingrich, and spread to other congressional offices.[5] The terminology was reinforced by repetition in interviews with news media and by death imagery. In 1999, Luntz issued a memo suggesting that Republican members of Congress hold anti– "death tax" press conferences at their local mortuaries;[6] a photograph in *USA Today* showed an antitax activist on Capitol Hill dressed as the Grim Reaper.[7]

The campaign was a smashing success. By 2001, nearly 20 percent of Americans believed that they would have to pay the tax, though at that time only 2 percent were affected by it; by 2003, a survey found that 49 percent of Americans believed that most families have to pay the tax.[8] Luntz, who deserves much of the credit for this mushrooming misunderstanding, is not a diffident man, and not above creating the impression that the phrase "death tax" was his idea right from the start. In a television documentary, he said,

> Look, for years, political people and lawyers—who, by the way, are the worst communicators—used the phrase "estate tax." And for years they couldn't eliminate it. The public wouldn't support it because the word "estate" sounds wealthy. Someone like me comes around and realizes that it's not an estate tax, it's a death tax, because you're taxed at death. And suddenly something that isn't viable achieves the support of 75 percent of the American people. It's the same tax, but nobody really knows what an estate is. But they certainly know what it means to be taxed when you die. I argue that is a clarification; that's not an obfuscation.[9]

Not surprisingly, pro–estate tax writers see it differently: "Presenting the tax as one on death—and not as one on wealth—obscures its true nature. Everyone dies; not everyone is wealthy."[10]

Be that as it may, under the law passed in 2001 the federal estate tax expired—at the age of ninety-three—at the end of 2009. But to spare the 2001 Congress from having to account for the resulting long-term revenue loss, that same law provided for the estate tax to spring back to life (for estates exceeding $1 million for individuals or $2 million for couples) exactly one year later. This left it to future Congresses to decide whether to allow the estate tax to be automatically resurrected or to kill it off for good. In the last month of 2010—just days before the old estate tax was to come back into effect—the pro- and anti–estate tax factions in Congress agreed to CUT THE BABY IN HALF: in a compromise designed to last two years, the tax was revived, but in a greatly—almost mortally—weakened state. The estate tax rate for 2011 is far lower than at any time during the "phaseout" period from 2001 to 2009, and it does not apply at all to estates worth $1 million or $2 million—or even $3 million or $4 million—but only to those that rise above $5 million for individuals or $10 million for couples. And for 2012 those exemptions will be further increased by a "cost-of-living adjustment" based upon the Consumer Price Index—probably the first case ever of a cost-of-living increase for dead people.

The contest between those who believe in the estate tax and those who resent it has thus been extended at least through 2012. At this writing the opponents of the tax have had the upper hand for more than a decade, in no small part because of their control of the language in which the battle has been waged. It will be interesting to watch as they undertake to drive the final nail into the coffin of the "death tax."

JEC

deep pocket

While the concept of a pocket is simple, the concept of a *deep pocket* is fraught with political overtones. The word *pocket*—a pouch sewn into clothing to keep things in—easily became a symbol of the money kept in the pocket—a person's financial resources. A *deep* pocket is capable of holding a lot. In 1888, for example, a certain gambling gentleman was said to be "in the habit of carrying a 'private bank,' i.e., a deep pocket in an under waist-coat, whence he drew any supplies that he was in need of."[1] When lawsuits are the topic of discussion, *deep pocket*, used figuratively, implies that a defendant is being sued because he is rich rather than because he is at fault. Claims that juries will be prejudiced against deep-pocket parties can be found in cases as long ago as the early 1800s and as recently as last week. Social scientists tend to doubt that there is, in fact, a deep-pocket effect, but the debate continues in the popular press.

The phrase *deep pocket* has often functioned as a symbol of wealth. As long ago as 1730, the saucy English playwright and novelist Henry Fielding, in a play called *Rape upon Rape; or, The Justice Caught in His Own Trap*, portrayed a corrupt judge—aptly named "Squeezum" for his practice of extorting money from defendants—sizing up a potential victim. Told that the man is very tight with his money, Squeezum concludes that he must be rich; contrasting the stinginess of the rich with the generosity of the poor, he remarks, "Deep Pockets are like deep Streams; and Money, like Water, never runs faster than in the Shallows." But it was in the latter half of the twentieth century that the expression became widespread. Residents of

Aspen, Colorado, for example, worried in 1965 that a new road might cause them to lose the "deep-pocket visitors" they coveted, leaving them stuck instead with "hot-dog tourists." In the world of politics, "deep-pocket donors" contributed to President George W. Bush's second inaugural celebration, while in the world of sports, fans hoped for deep-pocket team owners who could fund the high salaries demanded by star players.[2]

The earliest cases referring to the relevance of those metaphorical deep pockets dealt with the issue of damages: what evidence should a jury be allowed to consider in deciding how much money to award someone who has been harmed? The first historical judge known to have used the phrase was that colorful English jurist Baron Alderson (see HANGED FOR A SHEEP sidebar). Sitting on a malicious prosecution case in 1836, Alderson refused to allow evidence of the defendant's wealth, saying, "It is nothing to the purpose that damages are taken from a deep pocket." His catchy turn of phrase was perpetuated in later cases—though often misattributed to an even more prominent judge, Lord Mansfield. In most of those later cases husbands or fathers were seeking damages from seducers of their wives or daughters. The earliest such opinion referring to "deep-pocket" defendants was the English case of *Hodsoll v. Taylor* (1873), in which the court stated that "the true measure of damages is the amount of compensation to be paid to the plaintiff for the injury he has sustained by the seduction of his daughter," and therefore "it should be immaterial, as Lord Mansfield said, whether the damages came out of a deep pocket or not."[3]

Lord Mansfield, in a 1770 case in which a husband demanded compensation from another man for "criminal conversation" (that is, sexual intercourse) with the plaintiff's wife, had instructed the jury that "the rank of the plaintiff in this cause makes no manner of difference, as to the injury or satisfaction he is entitled to; for an injury done to the bed of any commoner of England, is as much an injury to him, and to his domestic peace, as to a peer of the realm." Likewise, "whether the defendant is rich or poor, that is not to measure the damages." Mansfield did not, however, use the term *deep pocket*. It's not surprising that Mansfield's association with this issue stuck in people's minds, though. The plaintiff in that adultery case was a prominent peer, his younger wife (Lady Grosvenor) a famous beauty, and the defendant—with extraordinarily deep pockets—the younger brother of King George III. The salacious details of the case (complete with incriminating letters, the testimony of innkeepers and servants, and tales of catching the couple in flagrante delicto) were the talk of London.[4]

Unlike in England, American cases allowed evidence of wealth because the damages for seduction included exemplary damages—damages designed to punish the wrongdoer. In 1880 the Virginia Supreme Court respectfully quoted the recent British decision in *Hodsoll* and then proceeded to disagree with every word of it: "The jury in fixing the amount of the recovery, may and ought to have reference to the pecuniary circumstances of the defendant. In all such cases the wrong is aggravated in proportion to the wealth and position and rank of the guilty party. All of which may be the instruments by which he more readily accomplishes his purposes. . . . At all events it is better to place the jury in full possession of all the facts as to the condition and circumstances of the parties, than to leave them to grope their way in the dark, and to base their verdict upon fanciful conjectures and rumors."[5]

The U.S. and English cases differ both in their assessment of relevance and in their trust in the jury. Whereas the English judges feared that jurors would improperly give higher damages against a rich man, the Virginia court argued that a fully informed jury would use its discretion to fix damages in a way that would best accomplish the law's goals.

In the modern age the use of the phrase morphed a bit, as deep-pocket defendants claimed the label as a rhetorical tool of the "tort reform" movement. Picking up on the complaints of defendants and their insurers, media stories alleged that plaintiffs' lawyers were purposely choosing defendants based on their assets. At times this was portrayed as a pragmatic issue: there was no point in suing a defendant who could not pay a judgment. "Indeed, the strongest case will not get [the lawyer's] attention unless there is a deep pocket . . . from which the defendant's damages can be paid," commented one newspaper writer.[6]

By the mid-1980s, defendants were claiming that the only reason they were sued was those deep pockets. "Manufacturers and insurance companies are mounting a major drive to halt or at least reduce huge awards won by people who are injured by defective products. They say the current system has led to excessive jury awards to litigants, not so much because the maker of the product was at fault but rather because he had 'deep pockets' and could afford to pay."[7] Just as the nineteenth-century English judges distrusted juries' reactions to seduction claims, twentieth-century defendants argued that juries' treatment of deep-pocket defendants reflected their willingness to disregard legal rules in order to help sympathetic plaintiffs at the expense of wealthy litigants.

Does such a bias exist? Probably not, at least not in the simplistic way the media describe. Social scientists have researched the impact on juries of a defendant's resources. Although studies occasionally show higher awards against corporations than against individual defendants, there is no evidence that this is based on prejudice against those with deep pockets. Rather the studies tend to show that a jury's knowledge or belief that the defendant is a large institution has a more complex, less predictable impact. If anything, a higher award is the result not of bias but of jurors' findings that large institutions have a greater capacity to foresee and prevent harm, as well as a greater capacity to cause harm when their behavior fails to live up to reasonable standards.[8]

Potential defendants also argue that a component of tort law is unfair to wealthy parties who were only part of the cause of the plaintiff's injuries. Under a traditional doctrine called *joint and several liability,* successful plaintiffs may collect the full amount of their judgments from any of the defendants the jury finds to have negligently caused (at least in part) the damages. The paying defendant(s) may then seek reimbursement from all defendants until each defendant has paid only for the percentage of damages it caused. The plaintiff is thereby fully compensated for his or her injuries so long as at least one defendant is able to pay the amount of damages specified in the judgment. The alleged unfairness arises when one of the defendants can't pay its share, leaving the wealthier defendant to foot the bill. Defendants dislike this result, preferring in such cases that the victim go unpaid.

Joint and several liability thus became another target of tort reformers, but it was hard to rally public opinion when talking about a doctrine no one understood. Corporate public relations campaigns therefore gave the old common-law doctrine a new title, the *deep-pocket rule.* The supporters of a 1986 California referendum limiting joint and several liability, for example, used this illustration in the state's official voter brochure: "A drunk driver speeds through a red light, hits another car, injures a passenger. The drunk driver has no assets or insurance. The injured passenger's trial lawyer sues the driver AND THE CITY because the city has a very 'deep pocket'—the city treasury or insurance. He claims the stop light was faulty. The jury finds the drunk driver 95% at fault, the city only 5%. It awards the injured passenger [full damages]. Because the driver can't pay anything, THE CITY PAYS IT ALL . . . . THAT'S THE 'DEEP POCKET' LAW AND IT'S UNFAIR!" Not only did the illustration use the inflammatory example of the drunk driver and the 95/5 split, it also failed to explain one important meaning of the jury's finding of joint liability: that the city's faulty stoplight was a cause of the innocent plaintiff's serious injuries. Similar language choices entered academia when tort-reform advocate Victor Schwartz became the senior author of a torts casebook. One reviewer noted that Schwartz's version of the book adopts "the pejorative use of code words like 'deep pocket.' In asking whether joint and several liability should be abrogated, the reference is even to Mr. Deep Pocket."[9]

Based on arguments like the one in California and those by Schwartz's American Tort Reform Association, the common-law doctrine of joint and several liability has frequently been modified. As of 2011, forty-five states had enacted some type of legislation limiting defendants' liability to their own percentage of fault, thus leaving the injured party to bear the cost of damages caused by a defendant who did a lot of harm but has no money. Corporate defendants and their insurers saw the value of metaphor and changed the lawtalk: the "deep-pocket" label played a large role in this campaign to change the law.

EGT

deliberate speed

In perhaps the most celebrated decision in Supreme Court history, the May 17, 1954, ruling in *Brown v. Board of Education,* the Court confidently and forcefully declared racial segregation in public schools unconstitutional—and then, in its final paragraph, suddenly wavered. Instead of directing the states to end school segregation, it directed the parties to come back in a few months with suggestions as to what should be done about the problem. In response, the National Association for the Advancement of

Colored People, representing the black children who were the plaintiffs—who had already waited years for a decision—argued that schools should be desegregated forthwith. The school districts, states, and federal government (which maintained segregated schools in the District of Columbia) argued for a gradual approach. The Court, fearing a backlash if southern states were ordered to integrate precipitously, attempted to fashion an order that would require steady progress toward desegregation while allowing a degree of flexibility. Its follow-up opinion (referred to as *Brown II*), issued on May 31, 1955—already more than a year after the original decision—acknowledged the plaintiffs' interest in admission to the schools from which they had been excluded "as soon as practicable" and required defendant school districts to make "a prompt and reasonable start toward full compliance" with the 1954 ruling. The decision allowed lower courts to permit delays in individual situations but only to the extent "consistent with good faith compliance at the earliest practicable date." As to the specific children who were the plaintiffs in the case, the Court ordered that they be admitted to public schools on a nondiscriminatory basis "with all deliberate speed."[1]

It was this last phrase that caught everyone's attention. Never mind that it was limited to a small aspect of the case and clearly intended as just another way of saying "as soon as practicable"; its poetic sound and elusive meaning immediately made it a catchphrase forevermore associated with the *Brown* case.

Lawyers promptly set to work trying to pin down the origin and significance of *with all deliberate speed*. And as Supreme Court materials from the *Brown* years have gradually become available, scholars have made a cottage industry of working out how and why the phrase made it into the *Brown* order. Although the Court in *Brown* spoke only through its Chief Justice, Earl Warren, this was actually a pet phrase of Associate Justice Felix Frankfurter, who had used the expression *deliberate speed* in five different opinions since joining the Court in 1939. The only other Supreme Court Justice to have used the phrase—and the source from whom Frankfurter got it—was Oliver Wendell Holmes Jr., who in 1911 had written, "A State cannot be expected to move with the celerity of a private business man; it is enough if it proceeds, in the language of the English Chancery, with all deliberate speed." (The English Chancery court had a tradition of flexibility in fashioning remedies. See CHANCELLOR'S FOOT.) Holmes too was smitten with the expression; in a 1909 letter to the English legal historian Sir Frederick Pollock, he had referred to "your chancery's delightful phrase, with all deliberate speed."[2] Pollock must have been mystified, because the phrase had in fact never been used in England's courts.

The conventional wisdom now is that Holmes, the son and namesake of an eminent poet, must have gotten the phrase from "The Hound of Heaven," published in 1893 by the English poet Francis Thompson, which described God as pursuing the human soul relentlessly, "with unhurrying chase, / And unperturbèd pace, / Deliberate speed, majestic instancy." But that alone could not account for the phrase *with all deliberate speed* and its association in Holmes's mind with English Chancery practice. If the reference to "deliberate speed" in that poem influenced Holmes at all, he must have conflated it with a longer phrase that had long been in use in English law, and for that matter in American law as well: "with all convenient speed." Indeed, the British and the Americans joined in using that expression in the 1783 peace treaty ending the American Revolution, which provided that "his Brittanic Majesty shall with all convenient speed, and without causing any destruction, or carrying away any Negroes or other property of the American inhabitants, withdraw all his armies, garrisons, and fleets from the said United States."[3]

But there is no reason to assume that Thompson's poem was the source for the word *deliberate* in this phrase. The well-read Justice Holmes might have encountered it in the writing of Sir Walter Scott, whose 1817 novel *Rob Roy* referred to a lawsuit that "proceeded, as our law-agents assured us, with all deliberate speed."[4] Or if Holmes was indeed interested in poetry, he might have read the published diaries and letters of the poet Lord Byron, a fan of *Rob Roy,* who latched onto Scott's phrase and used it repeatedly.[5] Or the phrase might have sprung into Holmes's mind spontaneously. There is nothing surprising or novel about the concept of deliberate speed. The phrase can be found throughout the nineteenth century in such contexts as newspaper stories about advancing trains, hurricanes, and cold fronts; an 1802 essay on the importance of disease prevention (a principle to which the writer predicted "converts will . . . come over with deliberate speed"); and an 1844 Mississippi Supreme Court case referring to the desirability of settling decedents' estates "with all deliberate speed."[6]

Whatever factors combined to plant the phrase in Holmes's mind, it was Justice Frankfurter's relentless devotion to it that landed it in the *Brown* decree. In April 1955, Frankfurter revised a draft decree by striking out "forthwith" and inserting "with all deliberate speed" and sent the reworded draft to Chief Justice Warren for consideration. The next month, when Warren circulated his own draft calling for compliance "at the earliest practicable date," Frankfurter sent the chief a memo proposing that his pet phrase be used instead and that the Court cite the 1911 Holmes decision from which it came. If the result "may suggest that it takes time to get enforcement," wrote Frankfurter, "that is a good intimation." Three days later Frankfurter spoke to Warren in person about the phrase, then followed up with yet another memo.[7] Warren never completely capitulated; he kept his own strong language, but he did insert Frankfurter's phrase as well.

The rest is history—and a sorry history it is. Despite its spirit of "reasonableness" and flexibility, the *Brown* decree met with implacable resistance in the South; the "deliberate speed" language, intended to signify steady progress, simply provided additional arguments for delay. Thurgood Marshall, lead attorney for the NAACP in *Brown* and later the first African American to sit on the Supreme Court, would come to say, "I've finally figured out what 'all deliberate speed' means. It means '*slow*.'" In 1960, six years after the original decision in *Brown*, not a single one of the 1.4 million African American children in six Deep South states was attending an integrated school. In 1963, nine years after the fact, Prince Edward County, Virginia, one of the defendants in the *Brown* cases, had no students of any color; the county had closed its schools rather than integrate them. In 1964, after a full decade of southern stonewalling, the Supreme Court abandoned Frankfurter's beloved but disastrous formulation: "The time for mere 'deliberate speed,'" it said, "has run out." Chief Justice Warren himself is reported to have "concluded that he had been sold a bill of goods when Justice Frankfurter induced him to use the phrase. It would have been better, he later said, to have ordered desegregation forthwith."[8]

But the phrase has an undeniable appeal. It can now be found even in Chancery decisions in England, where Holmes and Frankfurter thought it

not refused admission to any school where they are situated

similarly to white students in respect to (1) distance from school,

(2) natural or manmade barriers or hazards, and (3) other relevant

educational criteria.

5. On remand, the defendant school districts shall be required

to submit with all appropriate speed proposals for compliance to

the respective lower courts.

6. Decrees in conformity with this decree shall be prepared

and issued forthwith by the lower courts. They may, when deemed by

them desirable for the more effective enforcement of this decree,

appoint masters to assist them.

7. Periodic compliance reports shall be presented by the

defendant school districts to the lower courts and, in due course,

transmitted by them to this Court, but the primary duty to insure

good faith compliance rests with the lower courts.

[handwritten marginal and interlinear edits throughout, including:] with all deliberate speed, after ... due hearing ... on the relevant issues ... detailed findings

Justice Felix Frankfurter's markup of the final page of a draft order dated April 8, 1955, regarding implementation of the public school desegregation decision in *Brown v. Board of Education.* Frankfurter changed "Decrees in conformity with this decree shall be prepared and issued *forthwith* by the lower courts" to "Decrees in conformity with this decree on the basis of detailed findings shall be prepared and issued by the appropriate lower courts *with all deliberate speed,* after due hearing is had on the relevant issue." Frankfurter sent a polished version of this revised draft to the Chief Justice on April 14, 1955. (Courtesy of Library of Congress) had come from in the first place. And where do *they* say the phrase comes from? *Brown v. Board of Education.*[9]

JEC

electoral college

Strangely for a country that holds itself out to the world as a model of democracy, the United States does not provide for direct, or even proportional, election of its presidents by the people. Instead, it uses the convoluted mechanism known as the *electoral college.*

When delegates from most of the thirteen confederated states set out in the summer of 1787 to "form a more perfect Union,"[1] one of the thorniest issues they grappled with was how to choose the "national executive" or "chief magistrate" or "executive magistrate" or—as they finally called the office—"president." Should it be one individual or a triumvirate? A member of Congress or a separate branch of government? A lifetime office or a limited term? A renewable term or nonrenewable? Selected by the Congress, by the states, or by the people? Small states favored election by a count of the states; large states favored a process based on population. The most democratically inclined delegates favored direct election by the people (meaning white male landowners); others favored intercession by the state legislatures or Congress.

And as with almost every issue the convention dealt with, there was the complicating factor of slavery. James Madison, a slave owner from Virginia—far and away the most populous state, if you counted the nearly 40 percent of its people who were slaves—believed that "the people at large was . . . the fittest" body to choose "an Executive Magistrate of distinguished Character." But as he saw it, there was "one difficulty . . . of a serious nature attending an immediate choice by the people," and that was that the southern states "could have no influence in the election on the score of the Negroes." Hugh Williamson, a delegate from North Carolina, put the Virginian's concern more bluntly: "The people will be sure to vote for some man in their own State, and the largest State will be sure to succede. This will not be Virginia however. Her slaves will have no suffrage."[2]

The compromise finally agreed to—more out of exhaustion than any conviction that it was a good plan—remains to this day the most round-about method for choosing a chief executive in the world. Each state legislature appoints a set of *electors* to vote for president. The number of electors is equal to the combined number of senators and representatives allocated to that state in Congress. Each state's electors then convene in their respective states and cast their ballots. Congress collects the ballots from all the states (and, pursuant to an amendment ratified in 1961, also from the District of Columbia) and counts the votes. If no candidate gets a majority—which some delegates assumed would normally be the case—Congress chooses one of the top few vote getters as president, with each state having a single vote regardless of population.

This cobbled-together scheme gained sufficient support among the delegates to make its way into the Constitution (Art. 2, § 1) for three principal reasons: it allowed the small states a disproportionate share of electoral votes by including a fixed number of two electors per state corresponding to their representation in the Senate; it allowed the slave states a bonus by incorporating the THREE-FIFTHS RULE for apportionment of seats in the House of Representatives; and it allowed everyone to avoid the issue of how electors should be chosen, by leaving it to the state legislatures to choose them any way they please. (As recently as 2000, in the case of *Bush v. Gore*, the Supreme Court reaffirmed that "the individual citizen has no federal constitutional right to vote for electors for the President.")[3]

The framers did not, however, provide a name for this method of election. They would certainly not have used the term *electoral college*, for in those days (and for more than a century before that), that phrase referred primarily to the handful of German princes empowered to elect the emperor of the Holy Roman Empire—one of whom was Georg Wilhelm Friedrich, the elector of Hanover, who happened also to be known as George III of England, the very king against whom the American colonies had so recently rebelled. But the concept of electors gathering to vote for a leader was similar, so at least as early as 1800 we find a senator speaking of the "different Electoral colleges" of the various states. The *college* terminology made its way into the U.S. statutes in 1845, where it remains today in a law providing that each state may fill any vacancies "in its college of electors when such college meets." (Another section of the same law, in what must be a great help to alphabetically challenged legislators, provides that Congress is to count the electoral votes "in the alphabetical order of the States, beginning with the letter A.")[4]

The framers of the Constitution feared conspiracies and cabals among electors, and so intentionally designed this mechanism in such a way that the electors from the different states would never meet. The concept of a college—a united body—therefore does not apply so well to the entire collection of electors from all the states. But that needed a name too. At least one writer in 1800 distinguished that body from the state electoral colleges by calling it "the grand electoral college"; but it probably took little time for the phrase *electoral college* by itself to be extended to the entire body, and even Congress used it that way in an 1865 resolution declaring that the eleven states that were in rebellion on election day in 1864 were "not entitled to representation in the electoral college" for that election.[5] Today the term is used—often confusingly—both for the separate state electoral colleges and for the whole body of electors.

Some of the framers might have expected that when the state electors met they would engage in a collegial discussion of the merits of possible presidential candidates. Within fifteen years after the convention it was clear that any such thought, though charmingly idealistic, was hopelessly naive. Electors were not chosen for their wisdom; they were chosen for their loyalty to a particular candidate. And it took almost no time for the dominant party in each state to realize that it could appear to allow the voters a democratic choice and yet ensure that every single electoral vote in the state would go to the party's favored candidate. All the party leaders had to do was have the legislature organize the voting not district by district, which would have resulted in minority party electors being chosen in some districts, but on a statewide basis. This so-called general-ticket or unit-voting or winner-take-all plan ensured that the minority voters would be outnumbered.

In 1800, the Virginian Thomas Jefferson realized that if he wanted to win the presidency his state would have to play the same game. If the northern states were going to prevent him from getting even a single electoral vote in their region, then he had to deprive his northern adversary, John Adams, of electoral votes in Jefferson's own state. "All agree," he wrote, "that an election by districts would be best if it could be general but while ten states choose either by their legislatures or by a general ticket, it is folly and worse than folly for the other states not to do it."[6] That change in the Virginia system for choosing electors, together with the bonus electors provided by the state's enormous slave population under the three-fifths rule, enabled Jefferson to squeak into the presidency.

When Virginia abandoned its proportional system for choosing electors in 1800, the legislature described the move as a temporary expedient "until some uniform mode of choosing a President and Vice-President of the United States shall be prescribed by an amendment to the Constitution."[7] Virginia and the nation are still waiting. In the meantime, the electoral college and the winner-take-all system combine to distort the electoral process and even, in several elections (most recently the election of 2000), install as president a candidate who lost the popular vote by a wide margin.

The system hangs on because small states believe that their citizens benefit from the extra voting power provided by the fixed two-seat-per-state bonus in the electoral college and large states believe that their citizens benefit from the huge voting block that the winner-take-all system gives them. They are both wrong. Consider the two states at the ends of the population spectrum, which should, if these presumed advantages hold water, receive the greatest attention in an election. In 2004 and 2008, using apportionment population figures from the 2000 census, Wyoming's citizens individually had 3.74 times the voting power of California's citizens in the electoral college, while California's electoral college delegation collectively had 18.3 times the voting power of Wyoming's.[8] Yet neither state received anything beyond token attention from the candidates because the outcome in both was a foregone conclusion: California would vote Democratic and Wyoming Republican. In modern presidential elections, the only states whose voters matter to the candidates are the handful of so-called swing or battleground or undecided states where the contest is close enough so that people's votes can actually make a difference. The rest—the overwhelming majority—are mere "spectator states."

The framers of the Constitution were struggling to forge a nation out of

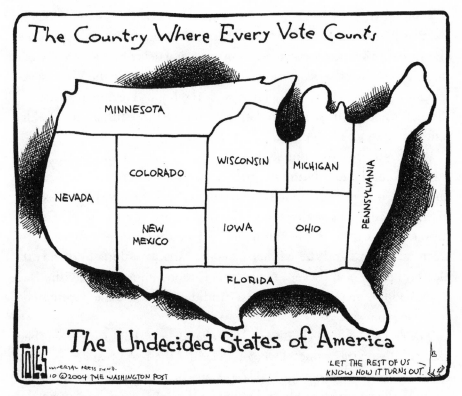

The Country Where Every Vote Counts

MINNESOTA

WISCONSIN   MICHIGAN

COLORADO

NEVADA

NEW
MEXICO   IOWA   OHIO

PENNSYLVANIA

FLORIDA

The Undecided States of America

LET THE REST OF US
KNOW HOW IT TURNS OUT.

Cartoon by *Washington Post* political cartoonist Tom Toles, published on October 18, 2004, fifteen days before Election Day in the presidential race between George W. Bush (seeking his second term as president) and Senator John Kerry. Bush took six of these ten states, and with them the election. (Courtesy of *The Washington Post*)

a confederation of independent states at a time when state loyalties reigned supreme and distrust between regions—especially over the pervasive issue of slavery—overshadowed all. Most citizens now think of themselves as Americans and share a belief in the principle of ONE PERSON, ONE VOTE. No wonder surveys show that most now favor direct election of the president. That would make everyone's vote equal, and every vote matter. It would make every state and every region important in every election. It would make the president truly the president of all the people. It would form a more perfect Union.

JEC

eye for an eye

"An eye for an eye, and a tooth for a tooth" sounds like a grisly rule from some video game or the words of an action hero plotting revenge. The maxim's Latin name, *Lex Talionis,* could be a long-clawed character who is Superman's next nemesis. Instead, *lex talionis* (the law of retaliation in kind) is a theory of retributive justice—punishment that focuses on retaliation against the wrongdoer rather than on compensation for the victim. Yet this principle of measured retaliation acts not as a license to maim but as a limit on punishment. Its earliest uses came in elaborate systems prescribing privately administered penalties for various offenses. This served the social purpose of discouraging escalation of conflicts into violent feuds.

Although it is widely assumed that the phrase originated in the Bible, the law of *eye for an eye* is much older. Its earliest known appearance is in the Code of Hammurabi. Hammurabi, the sixth king of Babylon, reigned in the eighteenth century B.C.E. His code is one of the first known written laws. It consists of 282 numbered laws carved in 49 columns on a basalt stone slab. Laws 196, 197, and 200 are the sources for *eye for an eye.* They read, "If a man has destroyed the eye of a free man, his own eye shall be destroyed. If he has broken the bone of a free man, his bone shall be broken. . . . If a man has knocked out the teeth of a man of the same rank, his own teeth shall be knocked out." Other rules provide for similar parallel punishments:

> If a man accuses another man of a capital offense, but cannot prove his charges, the accuser will be killed.
>
> If a man cannot pay his debt, he can sell himself, his wife, his son and his daughter to work for three years.
>
> If a builder builds a house, and the house falls in, killing the owner, the builder will be killed. If the son of the owner dies, the son of the builder shall be killed.[1]

Punishments varied depending on the social status of the offender and the victim. So, for example, "if a man strike the body of a man who is great above him, he shall publicly receive sixty lashes with a cowhide whip," whereas striking someone of the same rank resulted only in a payment of money. In fact, money payments were often substituted for the literal physical violence of the law. (See BLOOD MONEY.)

The principle of an eye for an eye does figure prominently in biblical lists of laws, however. One instance is in the book of Leviticus: "Anyone who maims another shall suffer the same injury in return: just as he has done, so it shall be done to him: fracture for fracture, eye for eye, tooth for tooth; the injury inflicted is the injury to be suffered."[2] Although the rules sound harsh to modern ears, they were at the time a way of imposing proportional rather than excessive punishment. This in turn could help prevent escalating cycles of revenge and protracted violence.

These Old Testament rules of controlled retribution are rejected by Jesus in biblical accounts of the Sermon on the Mount, especially the version found in the book of Matthew: "You have heard that it was said, 'An eye for an eye, and a tooth for a tooth.' But I say to you, Do not resist an evildoer. But if anyone strikes you on the right cheek, turn the other also."[3] Christ is thus reported to have urged his followers not merely to limit retaliation but to reject the principle of retaliation altogether.

Occasionally Jesus's view of the matter finds some favor in the courts. The first U.S. Supreme Court opinion quoting "eye for an eye" came in 1945. The Illinois State Bar had refused to license Clyde Wilson Summers because of his faith-based antiwar beliefs, and Summers appealed to the Supreme Court. The Court upheld Summers's exclusion from practicing law, but four Justices dissented. Justice Hugo Black, speaking for the four dissenters, noted that Summers's opposition to the military draft relied on Christ's teaching against "an eye for an eye" and commented sardonically, "It may be, as many people think, that Christ's Gospel of love and submission is not suited to a world in which men still fight and kill one another. But I am not ready to say that a mere profession of belief in that Gospel is a sufficient reason to keep otherwise well qualified men out of the legal profession."[4]

Much more commonly, *eye for an eye* is invoked to justify punishment in the legal system. Indeed, U.S. Supreme Court Justice Thurgood Marshall (no fan of capital punishment) pointed to the Code of Hammurabi as the original justification for capital punishment in homicide cases. The principle continues to be influential, and the phrase *eye for an eye* is often recited by death penalty proponents. Cultural understandings of the maxim influence jurors as well.

The facts underlying three recent appellate cases on behalf of prisoners on death row show how powerful this influence can be. In Colorado, when a sequestered jury returned to its hotel after deliberating late into the evening without reaching agreement on a penalty, several jurors looked up passages advocating an eye for an eye in their hotel Bibles; the next morning some brought the Bibles to the jury room (in violation of the judge's order not to consult extraneous materials) and discussed the passages, and "by noon that day, the jury returned a unanimous verdict imposing the death penalty." In North Carolina the extraneous material was actually supplied by a court official: a bailiff provided a Bible to a juror, who then read aloud a passage about "eye for an eye" to "convince other jurors . . . that they should change their position from one favoring a life sentence to one favoring a death sentence." And in the most extreme case, in Oklahoma an entire trial was held in a courtroom featuring, on the wall over the judge's bench, a wooden carving of a sword emblazoned with the legend "An Eye for an Eye & A Tooth for A Tooth." The prosecutor specifically directed the jury's attention to the carving in his closing argument, saying, "It's above Judge Winchester. The sword there. You live by the sword, you die by the sword, folks." In the first case, the Colorado Supreme Court set aside the death sentence; but in the other two cases, federal courts left the death sentences intact. None of the three courts remarked upon the irony that in the overwhelmingly Christian culture in which these cases were tried, no one involved referred to Christ's views on the subject.[5]

Calls for vengeance in global affairs also rely on the concept of an eye for an eye. A man whose father died in the September 11, 2001, attack on the World Trade Center bemoaned the failure of the jury in the case of Zacarias Moussaoui, an alleged co-conspirator in the plot, to sentence Moussaoui to death: "I know why the jury made the decision that they did, but I believe in an eye for an eye. Heck with lethal injection. Here's to hoping someone in jail gets to him." Often the phrase is invoked as purported justification for particularly bloodthirsty vengeance, as when one American expressed disappointment that the leader of Al-Qaeda in Iraq had merely been killed in a bombing raid: "My only regret is that he didn't live long enough for some real 'eye for an eye' treatment. . . . We should have given the Iraqis a rusty, dull knife and assembly instructions in five languages."[6]

But revenge tends to beget revenge. In 2009 a Muslim man charged with fatally shooting a military recruit in Arkansas said, "U.S. soldiers are killing innocent Muslim men and women. We believe that we have to strike back. We believe in eye for an eye. We don't believe in turning the other cheek." The last word on retaliation as a theory of justice—personal or international—is the one often attributed to Gandhi: "An eye for an eye makes the whole world blind."[7]

EGT

fishing expedition

When controversial radio host Rush Limbaugh was arrested for abuse of prescription pain killers, he decried the state attorney's investigation as a "fishing expedition." When the Securities and Exchange Commission tried to investigate allegations of fraud involving financier Bernard Madoff, he headed them off by complaining that they were "fishing." Clearly the authorities were not approaching Limbaugh or Madoff with rod and reel, so what were they complaining about? In criminal cases, a *fishing expedition* is an investigation not justified by adequate suspicion and thus an abuse of government power. In civil cases, the fishing metaphor refers to a wide-ranging request for discovery of documents and information from an opposing party, or to a lawsuit filed before the claim can be proved, but commenced in the hope of uncovering the necessary evidence.

Ever since its first recorded use in law, the fishing metaphor has served as a way to limit unpopular kinds of cases. In eighteenth-century England, accusations of "fishing" turned up in cases challenging people's title to their land, including cases in which title turned on claims about illegitimate children and ugly disputes among family members. These cases were filed in the equity courts (see CHANCELLOR'S FOOT for the distinction between courts of equity and courts of law), and the written requests for information in the cases were called bills of discovery. In the first case to employ the "fishing" epithet, in 1752, the judge flatly rejected a request for discovery of deeds and other records pertaining to the defendant's purported title, telling the plaintiff, "You cannot come by a fishing bill in this court." In this and other property cases, courts feared that the threatened fishing would reveal private information and upset the stability of land ownership. As another judge put it decades later: "This is another of the fishing bills, that I do not like to see in this Court. A spirit of prying into titles has got into the Court, that is highly dangerous to the title of every man in *England*."[1]

In the United States, accusations of "fishing" arose particularly in debtor-creditor disputes. The first American case to characterize a request for information in this way came in New York in 1801. In that case, a widow filed a bill of discovery in equity against a creditor who had sued her in a law court for money allegedly owed by her late husband. The widow claimed that she had no personal knowledge of the debt, and she believed it to be spurious. The creditor, she argued, had never tried to collect his claim during her husband's lifetime and there was no written proof of the debt. The widow wanted the court to force the creditor to give her all of the facts regarding the origin of the alleged debt so that she could "safely proceed to a trial" of the action at law. The court held that she was not entitled to the information and called her request a "mere fishing bill."[2]

It wasn't necessary for a request to be burdensome, or to invade anyone's privacy, for it to be condemned as fishing. In Mississippi in 1893, a certain Mr. Solomon sued because he had paid his rent twice, once to Mr. Ragsdale and then to Mrs. Ragsdale, owing to a dispute as to whether Mr. Ragsdale had been acting as his wife's agent when collecting the $1,000 rent. Solomon knew that either Mr. or Mrs. Ragsdale owed him a refund, but he needed more information to determine who should repay him. The court refused to help and called his case "a pure and simple fishing bill, [where Solomon] angles in the broadest water." Since the unhappy Solomon could not say which defendant owed him the money, he was entitled to no help from the court.[3]

As U.S. state courts after the Civil War began to adopt new mechanisms by which litigants could obtain relevant information from their adversaries before a trial—going beyond what had been permitted through the old bill of discovery—the epithet began to change from "fishing bill" to "fishing expedition." The Supreme Court of Kansas was the first to use the term in a reported opinion. A bank was trying to use a newly available deposition procedure to question a debtor before trial, and the court rejected an attempt to prevent the deposition from taking place: "It is . . . said that this permits one to go on a 'fishing expedition' to ascertain his adversary's testimony. This is an equal right of both parties, and justice will not be apt to suffer if each party knows fully beforehand his adversary's testimony."[4]

In the 1930s, a procedural reform movement in the United States resulted in congressional authorization of the Federal Rules of Civil Procedure. The rules established a system that reduced the formal barriers to suing and allowed much wider discovery of information in the hands of opponents. The purpose of these changes was to increase access to justice by providing more evenhanded sharing of relevant information. The U.S. Supreme Court enforced the new policy by rejecting the old lawtalk, declaring: "No longer can the time-honored cry of 'fishing expedition' serve to preclude a party from inquiring into the facts underlying his opponent's case." For a while, it seemed that the fishing metaphor was finally going away. One prominent treatise writer emphasized: "That the proceeding may constitute a 'fishing expedition' is not a valid objection. . . . As a matter of fairness, if there appears to be a reasonable probability or even possibility that there may be fish in the pond, there is no reason why the litigant should not be permitted to endeavor to catch them."[5]

In the 1970s, however, the tide shifted, as powerful forces expressed their concern about the costs involved in defending lawsuits. Chief Justice Warren Burger of the U.S. Supreme Court appointed a commission to consider problems in the justice system, and its report claimed that "wild fishing expeditions . . . seem to be the norm." Today the metaphor is back with a vengeance and is more than capable of preventing discovery and heading off lawsuits altogether. Courts and defendants frequently accuse plaintiffs of trying to fish, particularly in antitrust, securities fraud, civil rights, intellectual property, and product liability cases.[6]

Fishing expedition is code language used to condemn. It conjures images not of artful fly fishing but of outsized nets that catch dolphins instead of tuna. The metaphor is often embroidered with further adjectives: *vexatious, mas-*

sive, burdensome, expensive, invasive, spurious, wide-ranging, transparent, blind, old-fashioned, unbridled, experimental. Courts sometimes do an entire riff on the fishing theme: one court, in refusing to enforce a litigant's sweeping demand for production of documents from the opposing party, stated: "Instead of using rod and reel, or even a reasonably sized net, IBM would drain the pond and collect the fish from the bottom."[7]

As a useful metaphor, fishing has far outlived its usefulness. It has been trite for more than two hundred years. A number of recent writers even fail to see that they are using a (mixed) metaphor: "The trial court [should not] allow plaintiffs to embark on a wide-ranging fishing expedition in hopes that there may be gold out there somewhere"; "The trial court cannot be faulted for slamming the door on this transparent fishing expedition"; "This allows a product liability plaintiff to go on a 'fishing-expedition' in the defendant's records in the mere hope of finding a 'smoking gun.' " While those who accuse others of "fishing" act as though the word has some kind of concrete historic meaning, in fact it is little more than name-calling and more likely to distract the court than to be helpful. As Lord Mansfield, the great eighteenth-century British judge, is often said to have warned: "Nothing in law is so apt to mislead as a metaphor."[8]

EGT

grand jury

What is so grand about a grand jury? Answer: its size. The *grand jury* (from Old French *grand,* "great," "large") typically consists of sixteen to twenty-three citizens convened to investigate criminal activity or to bring charges against those believed by the prosecutor to be responsible. The jury of twelve that actually determines guilt or innocence at trial is a *petty jury* or *petit jury* (both from Old French *petit,* "small"). It just sounds better to use the Old French names than to call them "the big jury" and "the little jury."

The American tradition of using grand juries to charge people with crimes was started in England by King Henry II in 1166, in a statute called the Assize of Clarendon. Sixteen men in each locality were to be put under oath (making them a *jury,* from Old French *juree,* "sworn") and then called upon to identify anyone in their region believed to be a murderer, robber, or thief, or to have harbored such a criminal. The king's judges would then give the accused a fair trial by the time-honored method of tying him up and throwing him into the nearest pond. If the water "received" him—that is, he sank—he was innocent. If he was not only innocent but lucky, he would still be alive when they fished him out. The surviving copies of the Assize of Clarendon do not say what happened to the guilty—those unlucky enough to float—but it becomes clear in a follow-up statute promulgated ten years later, the Assize of Northampton. That statute increased the range of crimes to be ferreted out by the jury and also increased the penalty: in addition to losing a foot, as before, the guilty would lose their right hand. And be banished. And since the personal property of the condemned fell to the king, it is safe to say that no jury was ever criticized by his majesty for overzealousness in making accusations.

Long after trial by ordeal fell out of general use (though it continued in cases of alleged witchcraft up to 1712), the grand jury remained a feared institution. But by the end of the seventeenth century the grand jury had begun to show some independence from the crown. In a celebrated case in 1681, grand juries resisted pressure from Charles II to indict the earl of Shaftesbury and one of his followers, Stephen Colledge, for treason. The king simply convened a more malleable grand jury, got his indictment against Colledge, and executed him. Shaftesbury avoided the same fate only by fleeing the country.[1]

In the United States to this day, if a federal prosecutor does not get a desired indictment from one grand jury he or she can just try again with a new grand jury. Nevertheless, during the colonial period in America the grand jury earned a reputation as a shield against the crown. Most famously, in 1734, when the widely despised royal governor of New York, William Cosby, sought to have a printer named John Peter Zenger prosecuted for "seditious libel"—the publication of material tending to bring the government (namely, Cosby) into disrepute—two successive grand juries refused to indict him. (The governor had Zenger arrested and charged anyway, but when he was finally brought to trial after more than eight months of confinement, the trial jury defied both the evidence and the law and declared him not guilty. For more on the case, see PHILADELPHIA LAWYER.) Grand juries in Massachusetts were especially stubborn; thus in 1773 the governor of Massachusetts, Thomas Hutchinson, was thwarted in his hope of identifying and prosecuting the instigators of the Boston Tea Party when the Colony Council directed that any evidence be submitted for action to the grand jury for the county in which Boston is situated—which the Council well knew was filled with supporters of that rebellious action.[2]

So it was that by 1789, when the Constitution was adopted, the grand jury as an institution was riding high in public esteem, viewed as—in the Supreme Court's words—"a protective bulwark standing solidly between the ordinary citizen and an overzealous prosecutor."[3] Understandably, then, the institution was enshrined in the Bill of Rights: the opening words of the Fifth Amendment are "No person shall be held to answer for a capital, or otherwise infamous crime, unless on a presentment or indictment of a Grand Jury" (save in certain military cases). This clause applies only to federal criminal cases, but all states have had their own grand juries for state cases. "Infamous crime" has been held to mean a felony, that is, any crime that might result in a prison sentence. The power to make presentments— reports or criminal charges issued on the jury's own initiative rather than at the behest of the prosecutor—was removed from federal grand juries by rules that took effect in 1946. This leaves federal grand juries with the right only to say yes or no to the prosecutor's request for an indictment—a charge initiated and drawn up by the prosecutor.

Unfortunately, as a human rights institution, the grand jury peaked in 1789. Since then, the federal grand jury has regressed. The rules under which it operates, which allow the prosecutor to present evidence selectively and without regard to standard rules of reliability or fairness, ensure that the jury will almost always see things the prosecutor's way, either indicting or failing to indict as the prosecutor wishes. (Sometimes a prosecutor finds it politically expedient to be able to say that a failure to bring charges, or to bring more serious charges, against a certain individual was the "grand jury's decision.")

Even critics of the institution acknowledge that the federal grand jury is a powerful instrument—too powerful, some say—through which to conduct criminal investigations. But as a shield against unfair accusations, the

role envisioned by the Fifth Amendment, it is widely seen as virtually pow-
erless. Students of the institution fall over each other reaching for suitably
evocative phrases to describe it: "rubber stamp," "fifth wheel," "tool of the
executive," "total captive of the prosecutor," "indictment mill," "prosecution lapdog," "ignominious prosecutorial puppet," "playtoy," "little more
than an elaborate ritual used only to justify by ceremony the decisions of the
government."[4] (See also INDICT A HAM SANDWICH.) England itself substantially abolished the grand jury in 1933, finding a brief open hearing before a
magistrate to be a more efficient and more reliable method for determining
whether there is sufficient evidence to justify a serious criminal charge.
Even in the United States—much more wedded to English legal tradition
than England is—slightly over half the states have followed suit by abolishing the indicting grand jury or significantly limiting its use. But the grand
jury remains a time-honored tradition in America, just as ordeal by water
was in England in 1166. Most scholars believe that it equally deserves to be
consigned to history.

JEC

green card

It hasn't been green since 1964, but the name has stuck. A *green card* is a
document that attests to a noncitizen's right to live and work in the United
States indefinitely. The nickname refers both to the physical card (now
Form I-551 and called a Permanent Resident Card) and to the holder's
status as a legal permanent resident. In addition to granting permission to
live and work in the United States, the card entitles its holder to apply for
citizenship after a period of legal residency.

The United States has always been a nation of immigrants (even Native
Americans may have come by crossing the land bridge from Asia), and its
more established citizens have always been ambivalent about the presence
of the most recent arrivals. The country's first law providing for something
like an alien registration card was enacted less than a decade after the
adoption of the Constitution. A wave of anti-French panic, triggered by a
diplomatic crisis and the prospect of war with France, led Congress to

enact the infamous Alien and Sedition Acts of 1798. Among other things, those acts authorized the president to deport any foreigner he viewed as dangerous, or to issue a "license" permitting the alien to remain in the country only "for such time . . . and at such place as [the president] may designate."[1]

The first across-the-board alien registration requirement was much more recent, and it came in response to a fear of foreign Communist and anarchist influences in the United States. The Alien Registration Act of 1940 required that all aliens over the age of thirteen report to a post office to be fingerprinted and registered, and that parents and legal guardians register alien children thirteen years of age and younger. Registrants received a numbered Alien Registration Receipt Card proving registry and were required to carry this card with them at all times. This registration did not distinguish between "legal" and "illegal" aliens; everyone registered, and each received the same type of receipt, which was printed on white paper.

Beginning in 1946, registration became part of regular immigration procedure and occurred at the port of entry. Those admitted for permanent residency received the I-151 form, which was printed on green paper. This was the original green card, and it remained some shade of green until 1964, when the color was changed to light blue.

In retrospect it might seem inevitable that once this registration card became green it would acquire the nickname "green card." But that is not what happened. This name did not enter the English language until just before the card stopped being green, and when it did enter the language, it did so from an unexpected source and entirely by chance.

We all carry all sorts of cards in all sorts of colors, yet we seldom refer to them by their color; instead we identify them by their function: social security card, library card, driver's license, and so on. And so it was with this green-colored card for the first sixteen years of its eighteen-year life. When it came up in judicial opinions or newspaper articles it was referred to as an "I-151 card" or "immigration card" or "alien card" or "alien permit" or the like, and occasionally even by its formal name at the time: an "alien registration receipt card." Occasionally the color was mentioned in the course of describing the card (as, for example, "a small green card sandwiched between two pieces of transparent plastic").[2] But in those cases "green card" was merely an incidental description; the phrase was not used as a name for the card.

For Mexican nationals working in the United States or wishing to do so, however, the color was crucial. In early 1953, for example, Spanish-language newspapers in Texas carried an article discussing the Immigration and Nationality Act of 1952 and advising readers who still held the old white card ("la antigua tarjeta blanca") to exchange it for the new green-colored card ("la nueva tarjeta verde").[3] And among themselves, the phrase *tarjeta verde* became a convenient shorthand name for this important document.

But it required another decade for the name to cross over into English. Near the end of 1962, the *Los Angeles Times* published a groundbreaking four-part series by reporter Ruben Salazar on the political, economic, and humanitarian issues raised by migrant and seasonal farm labor in California. In the first installment, Salazar wrote of " 'green-card' carrying legal residents of the United States" who continued to live in Mexico, where housing was affordable, and crossed the border every day to work in the fields. Salazar's quotation marks around "green-card" have a dual significance: they indicate both that he knew the term was new to his Anglo readers and that he was quoting—actually, translating—from his Mexican interviewees. Accordingly, as the article went on Salazar elaborated for his readers on the significance of this card ("the 'green-card' of an immigrant—with most privileges of an American citizen except voting") and quoted at length from a Spanish-language interview with a green-card holder, highlighting and translating key terms as he went: "The moridas (literally 'bites,' that is, bribes) I had to pay Mexican bureaucrats came to 600 pesos, but luckily I was able to borrow it from my brother who had just returned home from Texas as a mojado (wetback) . . . . I finally got a tarjeta verde (green card) and was made an emigrado (immigrant)."[4]

Salazar used the term *green card* throughout that series and in many subsequent articles, and gradually it began to spread (though for a considerable time only in articles about immigrants in southern California)—undoubtedly abetted by others' contacts with the same Spanish-speaking population. Two years later the green immigration card was history, but the term *green card* had taken root in English.

In sum, though nothing sounds more English than "green card," it is clear that the term is actually of Spanish origin. It is what linguists clas-

sify as a "loan translation": a phrase or compound created by literal translation of each element of an expression in another language—like the
English phrase *moment of truth,* from Spanish *momento de la verdad* (the
moment before the final, fatal plunge of the sword in a bullfight). Loan
translations are relatively rare in English because the language so readily
absorbs foreign words and phrases in their original form, as with the
French *carte blanche*—literally, "white card." (This absorption is referred
to as "borrowing" a foreign word, and the resulting English expression is
classified as a "loanword.") But *green card* stands out even among other
loan translations, in that a non-English expression is the source for the
popular name of a quintessentially American object—a government-
issued card permitting the holder to live in the United States.

Ironically, today Spanish speakers in the United States are likely to refer to the card not as a "tarjeta verde" but as a "tarjeta de residencia" (its
more technical name) or by using the English label: "green card." This
undoubtedly is a result of the linguistic phenomenon called code switching: the alternate use of multiple languages in the same discourse—in this
context better known as Spanglish. Two 2009 stories in the Dallas-based
Spanish-language newspaper *Al Día* are good examples. Even in a relatively technical context, a column giving immigration advice notes that
"Con un poco de ayuda legal, usted debería conservar su residencia y
obtener una green card 'permanente'." (With a little legal help, you should
be able to keep your legal residency and obtain a permanent green card.)
And in an article about a church helping visitors regardless of immigration
status, the pastor uses "green card" in English but "red card" in Spanish:
"No me importa si en su cartera traen una *green card* o una tarjeta roja o
no tiene tarjeta." (It doesn't matter to me whether in their wallet they carry
a green card or a red card or don't have a card.) The newspaper's copy
chief, Jorge Chávez, reports, "We believe that at this point 'green card' is
a term understood by all our readers. . . . Most Spanish speakers use 'green
card' in their everyday lingo, and not 'tarjeta verde.' That's why we try to
stay away from using 'tarjeta verde,' although it sometimes gets published."
Chávez also explains that "tarjeta verde" is used only to refer to the physical
card and not to immigration status.[5]

In a final evolutionary step for the phrase, the English form acquired
by Spanish speakers in America has traveled with them back to Mexico

and other Latin American countries, where it all started. While "tarjeta verde" can still be found in Mexican newspapers, "green card" is now more common. Often it appears in quotation marks, signifying that the term in this form is still relatively new or exotic; but often it is treated as an ordinary Spanish term, as in this newspaper story: "En la legislación estadounidense, quien obtiene una green card tiene derecho a vivir y trabajar de manera permanente en cualquier lugar de EU." (Under American law, anyone who obtains a green card has the right to live and work permanently anywhere in the U.S.)[6] Thus *green card* has become a Spanish term (and in Mexico, at least, the prevailing Spanish term) for *tarjeta verde* in the sense of a U.S. Permanent Resident Card—having made a complete circuit from Spanish to English (by way of loan translation), to Spanglish (through code switching), and then in its English form back into Spanish (as a loanword from English).

Although a green card is the next best thing to citizenship for people who wish to reside in the United States, green-card holders, unlike citizens, can still be deported if they commit a serious crime. As an agent of the Department of Homeland Security explained with apparently unconscious wit, some immigrants erroneously "think that when they get a green card they have carte blanche."[7] Historically, many have found that the next best thing to a green card is a counterfeit green card. For decades, the format and color of the green card have been altered repeatedly to combat counterfeiting; as a result, the "green card" has at different times been light blue, dark blue, and pink. The current off-white plastic card contains myriad security measures such as digital images, holograms, microprinting, and optical memory strips with embedded laser-etched data that can be read only by government machines. But in a whimsical tip of the hat to the familiar name, the designers have repeated the formal name "Permanent Resident Card" on the back—on a token strip of green.

The expression *green card* has a prominent place in modern global culture. It has gone from a literal reference to a green piece of paper, to a figurative reference to the permanent resident alien status the piece of paper represents, to a broader invocation of the dreams and identity of immigrants. Caught in Americans' ambivalence about newcomers, immigrants are poised somewhere between the Statue of Liberty's "Give me your tired, your poor, your huddled masses yearning to breathe free" and television ads that depict a group of American citizens looking at a desolate region of the Mexican border and asking, "Where's the fence?"

EGT

hanged for a sheep

"As good be hang'd for an old sheep as a young lamb." This saying—meaning that once you have decided to do something risky or improper you might as well get as much out of it as you can—was already old and familiar enough to be included in a book of English proverbs in 1678,[1] and neither the form nor the meaning has changed much in the centuries since. To a modern gourmet the saying might seem backward: surely anyone with taste would prefer succulent young lamb to tough old mutton. But to a medieval peasant with a starving family, the best catch from the lord's pasture was the biggest sheep he could make off with.

The most common form of the saying today is, "Might as well be hanged [less often, hung] for a sheep as a lamb." The choice between *hanged* and *hung* is a matter of tradition and personal preference. The modern English word *hang* represents a fusion of three different etymological threads—two from Old English and one from Old Norse—complicated by dialectal differences among different regions of England in centuries past. One form of the word added -*ed* to form the past tense and past participle (*hang, hanged, hanged*); another took the form *hing, hang, hung*. During roughly the sixteenth century, the blended form *hang, hung, hung* became predominant—except in reference to executions.

The law is always linguistically conservative, and never more so than in such somber ceremonies as the pronouncing of a death sentence. Therefore, for centuries after the past participle *hung* had become generally accepted in other contexts, the age-old courtroom ritual remained unchanged: the judge donned the fateful "black cap" (a square of black silk laid on top of his white wig), addressed the prisoner by his full name, and intoned: "You are sentenced to be taken to a place of execution and hanged by the neck until you are dead. May the Lord have mercy on your soul." The language in America was essentially the same, though the proceeding was sometimes a good deal less formal. One of the many tales told of the legendary West Texas judge Roy Bean, who operated a combined court and saloon in the 1880s and 1890s, concerns his sentencing of a Mexican man—who might well have been guilty of little more than being Mexican—in the following terms: "Carlos Morales . . . it is the order of this court that you be taken to the nearest tree and hanged by the neck until you are dead, dead, dead, you saddle-colored son-of-a-gun."[2] To this day, although *hung* continues to gain ground, *hanged* remains the conventional form when referring to hanging as a form of execution.

Today the proverb about being hanged for a sheep is often used light-heartedly; in centuries past, it had a grimmer sound. For England did indeed execute people for crimes as small and desperate as stealing a single sheep. The British legal system's historical obsession with the death penalty—particularly as a means of protecting property interests—is legendary. Recorded cases of individuals being hanged for sheep stealing go back at least to the year 1276. During the eighteenth century, more and more crimes against property were designated as capital offenses; by the early nineteenth century, over two hundred capital crimes had been defined, including "uprooting a shrub in a public park; being in the company of gypsies; damaging a rabbit warren; forgery; highway robbery; theft from a dwelling if the value of the item exceeded one shilling; shoplifting . . ."[3] More often than not, ways were found to avoid carrying out the penalty; but even so, more than enough people were hanged—often in groups as a public spectacle—to earn that period in English law its nickname as the era of the "Bloody Code."

The American colonies (and later states), while accepting most of the common law of England as their own, uniformly rejected the Bloody Code and generally restricted the death penalty to crimes against the person. In England, campaigns to reform the Bloody Code began to gather steam in the early 1800s, and in 1832 the death penalty for sheep stealing was repealed and replaced with transportation to Australia for life. In 1845 a defendant charged with stealing a "sheep" attempted to avoid the penalty on the ground that the animal was less than a year old and therefore was only a lamb. The jury agreed that "in common parlance, according to the usual mode of describing such animals in the country, it would be called a lamb." The judges of the court conferred on the matter and ruled, by a vote of six to five, that this made no difference; in essence, they held that the defendant could as well be banished for a lamb as a sheep.[4]

In early-nineteenth-century England there were even efforts to abolish the death penalty entirely, but the country was scarcely ready for such an about-face. It is emblematic of old-guard resistance to radical reform that in 1840 the great Romantic poet William Wordsworth, seventy years old and soon to become the country's poet laureate, published "Sonnets upon the Punishment of Death," a series of poems arguing in favor of the death penalty for murder and treason. Over the next century and a half, however, the death penalty was gradually whittled away in Britain. The last two executions there—still by the traditional method of hanging—took place simultaneously in two different prisons at 8:00 A.M. on August 13, 1963. In 1999, the United Kingdom took the final step by acceding to Protocol 6 of the European Convention on Human Rights, which abolishes the death penalty except for acts committed in time of war or imminent threat of war.

The United States, where technology is king, took a different path to the end of hangings—replacing hanging in almost every state by electrocution, and that in turn by lethal injection. But while hanging is no more, the proverb "hanged for a sheep" remains popular in legal discourse. It is invoked by judges, legislators, scholars, and legal observers because it so vividly highlights fundamental issues of proportionality, grading, and deterrent effect in the drafting and interpretation of criminal laws and penalties.

For example, when the federal appeals court for the District of Columbia held, by a vote of six to five, that a defendant could be convicted only for a single violation of a federal statute that makes it a special crime to use a gun in connection with a drug conspiracy even though he had used the gun four times, the dissenters wrote: "Under the Court's interpretation . . . every use after the first use is a free use. That is, once a drug conspirator has used his gun once in furtherance of the conspiracy, he may as well use, carry, display, brandish, and fire his weapon throughout the conspiracy, for no matter what he does with his firearm, he can be punished

---

Baron Alderson's Remark

The insouciance with which English judges condemned people to death or transportation for life simply for stealing a sheep is demonstrated by an anecdote about Sir Edward Alderson, a judge in England from 1830 to 1856. As recalled with amusement by Sir Henry Hawkins, a barrister when Alderson was on the bench and subsequently a judge himself, Baron Alderson (as certain judges were titled) was sitting on the case of an accused sheep stealer against whom the crown's evidence was very weak. The prisoner's counsel made the mistake of admitting that certain bones found buried in the defendant's garden were those of a recently deceased sheep but argued that the sheep could have become entangled in a fence and, in its struggle, cut its own throat. According to Sir Henry, Baron Alderson—said by others to have been known for his irrepressible (if sometimes inappropriate) jocularity—seized upon the argument:

"Yes," said Baron Alderson, "that is a very plausible suggestion to start with, but having commenced your line of defence on that ground, you must continue it, and carry it to the finish; and to do this you must show that not only did this sheep in a moment of temporary insanity—as I suppose you would allege in order to screen it [that is, shield it from blame]—commit suicide, but that it skinned itself and then buried its body, or what was left of it after giving a portion to the prisoner to eat, in the prisoner's garden, and covered itself up in its own grave. You must go as far as that to make a complete defence of it. I don't say the jury may not believe you; we shall see. Gentlemen, what do you say—is the sheep or the prisoner guilty?" The sheep was instantly acquitted.

Richard Harris, ed., *The Reminiscences of Sir Henry Hawkins, Baron Brampton* (London: Edward Arnold, 1904), 1:246.

---

under § 924(c)(1) for only one use. He has the same perverse incentive that a thief faced when at common law . . . virtually all felonies were punishable by death: 'As well be hanged for a sheep as a lamb.' "[5]

JEC

hearsay

Broadly speaking, *hearsay* is just secondhand information. But the term has special meaning in law, where its role is complex, controversial, and commonly misunderstood.

The word itself is of mixed origin: though the verbs *hear* and *say* are English, their use together as a noun is a French grammatical construction. We owe the combination to Giles Du Wes, a French tutor in the court of Henry VIII. In about 1533, Du Wes published *An Introductorie for to Lerne to Rede to Pronounce and to Speke Frenche Trewly*. This textbook on the French language includes a set of practice readings with word-for-word translations into English in small print between the lines. One reading is styled as a dialogue between the king's seventeen-year-old daughter Mary and her almoner (a cleric in the royal household). The almoner undertakes to introduce Mary to science by explaining the properties associated with the four elements—earth, water, air, and fire—though he admits that this is not his field. He says,

je nen scay rien que par ouir dire,

meaning "I know nothing about it except by hearing it said," but for Du Wes's educational purposes rendered word for word as:

I knowe nothyng of it but by here say.[1]

The book was a hit, and before long the phrase "by hear say"—in various spellings—started appearing in English writings. By the end of the century, *hearsay* (or *heresay*) was a single word and was being used in other constructions as well, without the *by;* it had become an established English loan translation from French. (See GREEN CARD on loan translations.) In French, likewise, the words merged over time: although *ouïr* (related to *oïr;* see OYEZ) is no longer the usual word for "to hear," the modern French word for "hearsay" is *ouï-dire*.

In ordinary English, *hearsay* connotes "gossip," " 'rumor," " scuttlebutt"—information of uncertain or unreliable origin, as likely to be wrong as right.

But in a U.S. court even the most authoritative treatise on a subject would be classified as hearsay. This is because, for purposes of the legal "rule against hearsay" (or "hearsay rule"), the term has a specialized and far from intuitive meaning. In a nutshell, *hearsay* in the legal sense encompasses any out-of-court assertion—oral, written, or nonverbal—offered as evidence of the fact asserted. This includes many things that were never overheard: a statement in a book or police report, a nod of the head, the pointing of a finger. At the same time, it *excludes* much that *was* overheard. A witness can testify that he heard somebody yell, "Don't shoot," because "Don't shoot" is not an assertion but rather a command or plea. Even an overheard rumor—classic hearsay in the normal sense—might not be hearsay in the legal sense: if a witness testifies that she heard John say "The boss is having an affair"—not as evidence that the boss was having an affair but as evidence that John is a gossip—then that overheard assertion is not offered as evidence of the fact asserted, and so does not count as hearsay.

The rationale for excluding hearsay evidence is to shield juries from statements that were not made under oath, subject to cross-examination, and under the jurors' scrutiny. But there have always been exceptions to the rule. For example, it is impossible to testify from firsthand knowledge about the identity of one's ancestors, or even the date of one's own birth; so an early exception allowed the use of written records of births and marriages to prove family relationships in cases about inheritance. As the hearsay rule developed in the courts of England and the United States, more and more special exceptions were carved out. By the first half of the twentieth century the law relating to hearsay could aptly be characterized as "an old-fashioned crazy quilt made of patches cut from a group of paintings by cubists, futurists, and surrealists."[2]

For decades, scholars called for reform of the patchwork of often ill-thought-out rules and exceptions. The perfect opportunity arose in the early 1970s, when Congress was considering what was to become the Federal Rules of Evidence—a comprehensive set of rules for the federal courts, adopted in 1975. This enactment reduced the complex hearsay rule to a single simple sentence: "Hearsay is not admissible except as provided in these rules or by other rules." The statute then proceeded to itemize twenty-seven specific and two general exceptions to the rule, declare eight kinds of statements covered by the definition of hearsay to be "not hearsay," and, in notes by the drafting committee, list ten other rules and statutes under which hearsay could be used as evidence. Small wonder that in a survey of prosecuting attorneys, 68 percent stated that judges did not understand the hearsay rule and frequently misapplied it. (The researcher spared the prosecutors embarrassment by not surveying judges on how well they thought *attorneys* understood the rule.)[3]

Even when properly applied, the hearsay rule often defeats its own purpose of helping the jury reach a just verdict based upon the most reliable evidence. It sometimes permits evidence of very doubtful reliability, as in the "excited utterance" exception, which allows into evidence statements made under the stress of a startling event. The theory is that a person under such stress would not have the presence of mind to lie about it; but the fact is that stress and shock distort perception and preclude the calm reflection required for accurate understanding of a startling event.

More often the rule excludes useful evidence. Notably absent from the statute is any broad exception for previous statements by people with first-hand knowledge of a matter who are unavailable at the trial—because they are sick or missing or dead, for example. A striking illustration of the problem was provided in the O. J. Simpson murder trial of 1995. Simpson was accused of murdering his former wife, Nicole Brown Simpson, and her friend Ron Goldman. The prosecution wanted to introduce evidence of a pattern of stalking and violence directed at Nicole that had caused her to fear for her life. Nicole had written in her diary of an incident in which Simpson "beat me up so bad that he tore my blue sweater and blue slacks completely off me"; she had told at least five different people of incidents of stalking and her fear of Simpson; and five days before her murder a woman calling herself "Nicole" from West Los Angeles (where the Simpsons lived) had called a battered women's hotline expressing fear of her ex-husband, who was stalking her.[4] Any one of these statements by itself might have been of little weight and questionable reliability, but cumulatively they were substantial and—unless Nicole was planning to be stabbed to death and wanted to frame Simpson in advance—credible. In a decision uniformly regarded by commentators as legally correct, the trial judge, Lance Ito, held this entire body of evidence to be inadmissible hearsay. He explained: "To the man or woman on the street, the relevance and probative value of such evidence is both obvious and compelling, especially those statements made just days before the homicide. It seems only just and right that a crime victim's own words be heard, especially in the court where the facts and circumstances of her demise are to be presented. However, the laws and appellate court decisions that must be applied by the trial court hold otherwise."[5]

In most countries, a flat rule barring large categories of relevant evidence would be unthinkable. In contrast to the Anglo-American tradition, in which only those facts the lawyers choose to bring out may be considered in a trial (see WHOLE TRUTH), the legal system that prevails in continental Europe and many other countries places paramount value on "identifying what actually happened—indeed, the investigating judge is duty bound to seek the actual truth."[6] To this end, although there are protections for criminal defendants, as a general rule all relevant evidence is considered. At the same time, the system provides safeguards against overvaluing hearsay: when juries are used they sit as a panel with the judge or judges, who can help make sure that evidence of doubtful reliability is not given undue weight. Moreover, "in Continental legal systems it is regarded as a fundamental requirement of due process that the court disclose the grounds of its decision . . . both to deter abuse and to facilitate review for error."[7] In this way, contrary to the Anglo-American tradition, verdicts based upon weak evidence, or a misunderstanding of the evidence or the law, or emotion rather than reason, can be corrected.[8]

But even among the countries that share America's legal tradition, the hearsay rule has fallen on hard times. In Canada the rule was substantially liberalized in the early 1990s by a series of Supreme Court decisions, including one case specifically concerned with statements made by a homicide victim shortly before her murder. Scotland abolished the hearsay rule for civil cases in 1988. Even England, where it all began, finally made hearsay fully admissible in civil cases (with certain safeguards to give opposing parties an adequate opportunity to meet it) in 1995. Discussing the change, a British writer summed up: "It may be felt that any rule which prevents a witness being able to give evidence of his own age is ripe for reform, and there will be few . . . who will mourn the passing of this least understood and most unloved of rules."[9]

JEC

hornbook law

In the common-law tradition that America inherited from Britain, "the law" on most subjects is not a statute or code; it is the consensus of a body of judicial opinion, sometimes stretching back for centuries. What gives this system continuity and coherence is a reverence for precedent. Even in modern times—when nearly every area of the law is governed by statutes— lawyers and judges are expected to justify their legal arguments and decisions by reference to past court decisions involving similar issues. Yet some legal principles are claimed to be so basic, so well established, so far beyond dispute, that even the most diligent practitioner or jurist would not think it necessary to cite cases for them. Lawyers refer to these as BLACK LETTER LAW or *hornbook law.*

A hornbook, in its original sense, was a type of primer used in England and America from the sixteenth through the eighteenth centuries for teaching young children the rudiments of reading and writing. It consisted of a wooden tablet with a handle—rather like a small ping-pong paddle—on which was pasted a single sheet of parchment or paper inscribed with the alphabet and whatever extras would fit, such as a separate list identifying the vowels, perhaps some simple words or syllables, and often a Bible verse or the Lord's Prayer. This was not what we would recognize as a book; it was a "book" only in the obsolete sense of "document, writing." Nor would most of us recognize the "horn" part: through a laborious process of soaking, boiling, peeling, and flattening, an animal horn was transformed into a hard protective transparent laminate, which was put over the writing so that the primer would hold up under use by child after child.

Only Shakespeare could have teased any literary value out of a hornbook. In *Love's Labour's Lost,* he put it into the hands of a mere page, named Moth, as a tool to cut a pompous teacher, named Holofernes, down to size. Noting that Holofernes "teaches boys the horn-book," Moth challenges him: "What is a, b, spelt backward, with the horn on his head?" and then answers his own question: "Ba! most silly sheep with a horn." Holofernes, correctly suspecting that he has just been insulted, indignantly demands to know whom Moth is calling a silly sheep, and Moth's

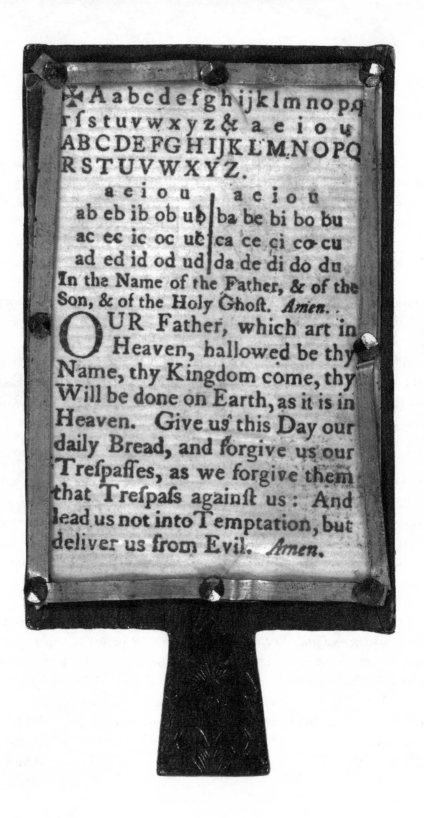

✠ A a b c d e f g h i j k l m n o p q
r ſ s t u v w x y z & a e i o u
A B C D E F G H I J K L M N O P Q
R S T U V W X Y Z.

a e i o u a e i o u
ab eb ib ob ub | ba be bi bo bu
ac ec ic oc uc | ca ce ci co cu
ad ed id od ud | da de di do du

In the Name of the Father, & of the
Son, & of the Holy Ghoſt. *Amen.*

OUR Father, which art in
Heaven, hallowed be thy
Name, thy Kingdom come, thy
Will be done on Earth, as it is in
Heaven. Give us this Day our
daily Bread, and forgive us our
Treſpaſſes, as we forgive them
that Treſpaſs againſt us : And
lead us not into Temptation, but
deliver us from Evil. *Amen.*

sassy reply again uses the hornbook: "The third of the five vowels, if you repeat them; or the fifth, if I"—in other words, the silly sheep is *I* if Holofernes reads the vowels from the hornbook (*a, e, i, o, u*), or *U* (*you*) if Moth reads them.[1]

Like the idea of the primer—which has given us books described as "primers" on everything from astrophysics to zoning—the hornbook concept naturally lent itself to an expanded or metaphorical sense referring to any book of rudiments or set of basic principles for a subject. And the term was used that way from time to time, as in *The Gull's Horn-Book,* an irreverent guide to contemporary social behavior for innocents ("gulls" in the language of the day) published in Shakespeare's own lifetime.[2] But the concept never really caught on the way *primer* did—except in law.

The first recorded use of the term in a legal context in America was by the attorney general of Missouri in 1832. He was arguing to the state's supreme court that a slave accused of murder was not entitled to have his trial moved to another county merely because the judge in the county where he was charged happened to be his own master. The attorney general argued that a change of venue could occur only if the judge might have some bias against the defendant; surely the slave's master would have nothing but the kindliest of feelings toward him. It was all so obvious, he said, "it is like attempting to prove that two and two make four. [The defendant's argument] would be going back to the horn book of the law"—that is, it would rewrite the most basic principles of the law.[3] The court, to its credit, disagreed, and ordered the slave, who as it happened had already been tried and sentenced to death by his kindly master, retried in another county.

This was an early demonstration of two principles that remain true today: (1) sometimes an appeal to "hornbook law" is just an admission that you can't find any specific authority supporting your position, and (2) courts are not much impressed with "hornbook law"—unless of course they themselves are citing it. When a lawyer argued to the Illinois Supreme Court in 1844 that it would be "a most solemn farce" to allow a technical

(opposite) Replica of a typical hornbook, one of which was included in a pocket in the first volume of each copy of *History of the Horn-Book* (London, 1896) by the English printer and antiquarian Andrew W. Tuer. (Courtesy of Rare Book and Manuscript Library, Columbia University. Photograph by Chris Antkowiak.)

detail about the form of the action to determine the outcome, the court was not amused: "As 'solemn a farce' as it may seem to counsel, . . . yet it is a distinction upon principles laid down in the very horn books of the law. And there would be more wisdom in addressing the sarcasm to the law-making, than to the law administering department of the government."[4]

The particular technical distinction involved in that case—between "law" and "equity" (see CHANCELLOR'S FOOT)—has long since been abolished, illustrating another enduring fact about hornbook law: today's fundamental principles can be tomorrow's obsolete ideas. The Pennsylvania Supreme Court demonstrated this particularly well—albeit inadvertently—in an 1871 case about a horse:

> The case falls clearly within the common law . . . and must be determined by its well-established rules; and it is horn-book law that by marriage the husband becomes the immediate and absolute owner of the personal property of the wife, which she has in possession at the time of the marriage in her own right, and it never can again revest in the wife or her representatives. She can acquire no personal property during coverture [that is, while married], and if she obtains any by gift or otherwise, it becomes immediately, by operation of law, without any act on his part, the property of the husband. Her acts of ownership are his acts of ownership, and her possession is his possession, and so is the property. It follows that upon the delivery of the horse in question to the husband for his wife, it became immediately the property of the husband.[5]

But even the judges themselves can disagree about what is a "hornbook principle." In an 1880 opinion in the United States Supreme Court, Justice Stephen Field wrote that the indictment of a Virginia judge for violating the Civil Rights Act of 1875 by refusing to seat blacks on juries should be thrown out because it did not specify any qualified blacks who were excluded. The doctrine that indictments must be drawn with specificity, Field said, "is only common learning; it is found in the hornbooks of the law; it is on the pages thumbed by the student in his first lessons in criminal procedure." What is noteworthy about this is that it was a dissent.[6] The majority of the Court obviously read the metaphorical "hornbooks of the law" differently, because it found no problem with the indictment.

As these examples illustrate, references to "hornbook law" seldom referred to an actual book. In the 1890s, however, a legal publishing company realized that with the growth of the legal profession, the rise of law schools, and the increasing complexity of the law, there was bound to be a market for a series of one-volume summaries of different areas of the law, such as contracts or criminal law. And some marketing genius, seizing upon all the connotations of *hornbook law*—basic, appropriate for the student, indisputable—named it the "Hornbook Series," a series that is still going strong today.

The success of this series ensured the permanence of the terms *hornbook* (for any one-volume summary of an area of the law) and *hornbook law* (for basic, purportedly indisputable principles) in American legal language. The terms appear with great frequency in law reports, and now references to "hornbook law" are often backed up by citations to actual books, as when the clerks for U.S. Supreme Court Justice Antonin Scalia went to the trouble of looking up a certain principle in not one but two different works in the Hornbook Series so that he could write, "This time-of-filing rule is hornbook law (quite literally) taught to first-year law students in any basic course on federal civil procedure."[7] Even so, four of the nine Justices on the Court and two of the three judges in the court below disagreed with Justice Scalia's understanding of the rule. In a legal argument, calling the rule one favors "hornbook law" never persuades the other side.

JEC

hue and cry

We all know what a cry is; but what's a hue? The answer is: it's a cry. *Hue and cry*—now a general expression for any public clamor, uproar, or outcry—started out as a legal term and is one of the law's many redundant expressions (see AID AND ABET). It goes back to the time when the language of English law was a form of French. The Old French verbs *huer* and *crier* both meant "to hoot, shout, cry out": the first—like the English *hoot*—is presumed to be imitative of the sound it represents and it still exists in modern French with the meaning "to boo"; the second is from a Latin word meaning "to scream, wail, cry out" and still exists with that meaning in modern French and in the English word *cry*. The corresponding noun phrase *hu e cri* (with variable spelling) —which evolved into the English *hue and cry*— therefore is just another way to say "hooting and hollering."

In the late Middle Ages this phrase had great legal importance for every one of the king's subjects, and especially for able-bodied males. From time immemorial it had been the natural inclination of communities to join in chasing down and meting out justice to anyone seen to be stealing or committing some other serious offense. In time this became a formal requirement. The concept of a police force would not be developed for centuries; therefore if criminals were to be brought to justice, it was essential that anyone seeing a crime raise a "hue and cry" to alert the neighbors, who then had an obligation to join in the chase.

But as medieval society grew more complex, the system seemed to be breaking down. In 1285, in response to a perceived increase in crime and decrease in the citizenry's enthusiasm for dropping everything to chase after criminals, Parliament enacted a statute making the people of each local administrative region collectively responsible for compensating the victim of a robbery in their midst if they failed to turn the thief over to the king's representatives within forty days. The larger towns were required to appoint watchmen to monitor the activities of passing strangers; and in the event that one was believed to have committed a crime and attempted to flee, the watchman was to "levy Hue and Cry [*heu e cri* in the original language of the statute] upon them" and follow them "with all the Town, . . . and so Hue and Cry shall be made from Town to Town" until the suspect "be taken and delivered to the Sheriff." Every man between the ages of fifteen and sixty was required to keep weapons for use in the chase.[1]

The requirement of a hue and cry was not entirely repealed until 1827. But well before that—and despite its name—it had evolved in at least some circumstances into a formal *written* process. A statement of English law in effect in the colony of Virginia in 1704 illustrates how this worked:

If any Negro, Mulatto, Indian Slave or Servant for life, run away, and shall be pursued by hue and cry, it shall be lawful for any Person endeavouring to take them, to kill or wound them, if they resist; provided such Negro, &c. be named and described in the hue and cry, and that the same be signed by the Master or Owner of the Run-away. And if it happen that such Negro, &c, die of such Wound received, the Master or Owner shall receive satisfaction from the Publick for his Negro, &c. so dying . . . . And all such Negroes shall be valued at 4500 *l.* [pounds] of Tobacco and Cask a piece, *Indians* at 3000 *l.* of Tobacco and Cask.[2]

Later in that century the eminent legal commentator William Blackstone inadvertently spawned a recurring legal and linguistic misconception about the phrase. Blackstone wrote, "An hue (from *huer,* to shout) and cry, *hutesium et clamor,* is the old common law process of pursuing, with horn and with voice, all felons."[3] Some writers have taken this to mean that the blowing of a horn was an integral part of the process, or at least that the word *hue*—and especially its Latinized equivalent *hutesium*—could mean "horn" or "the sound of a horn." But Blackstone was just being vivid in his depiction of the chase; while a hunting horn (or more likely a banging pot) might come into play if someone happened to have one at hand, this was scarcely an essential element of the process. And the Latin-educated readers of Blackstone's day would not have confused *hutesium* with *horn* (Latin *tuba* and other words); the word is simply a Late Latin term for *hue.*

The original meaning of "hue and cry" is now barely remembered except by legal historians; but occasionally, especially in England, it resurfaces. In a Scotland Yard detective's 1938 memoir of solving the sensational case of the "North London Cellar Murder"—in which a certain Dr. Crippen had carved up his wife with surgical precision, buried parts of her in the coal cellar of their home at 39 Hilldrop Crescent, and then vanished with his young mistress Ethel Le Neve—the author wrote: "There has never been a hue and cry like that which went up throughout the country for Crippen and Miss Le Neve." Even in the twenty-first century an English political columnist can be found commenting wryly about the British home secretary, "Mr Reid is nothing if not attuned to public concerns. If there is a hue and cry, he can be found leading the chase."[4] But the most entertaining context for the phrase in modern times was a 1947 film produced by Britain's Ealing Studios, in which a group of street children figure out that a comic strip is being used by a criminal to convey instructions to his gang. The police do not take the children seriously, but after many plot twists the children themselves—with the help of a great mob of other children notified by word of mouth—succeed in capturing the gang. The name of the movie: *Hue and Cry.*

JEC

indenture

An *indenture* is a type of written contract. The word, like *contract* itself, came to us from Latin by way of Old French in the fourteenth century, and the similarity to the word *denture* is no coincidence. It's all about teeth.

The indenture was invented to deal with a perceived risk in agreements that were of sufficient importance or complexity to be put into writing: if you write out the contract in duplicate so that each party can keep a copy, how can you be sure that neither party will substitute a different writing and then make a claim based upon that? The solution was to write out two copies of the agreement side by side on the same piece of parchment, and then cut them apart with a zigzag cut so that each would fit only with the other. For extra security, the cut could be made through a vertically written alphabet or line of text. The resulting copies had jagged edges like the teeth of a saw, which could be matched up for authentication. (Similarly, see CHARTER PARTY.) If the document was long, or there were several parties so that more than two copies were needed, multiple copies of the agreement could be piled up and the cut made across the top; the copies would then have matching serrated or scalloped top edges.

A document processed in this way was said to be *indented,* from the Latin root *dens, dentis* (tooth). To *indent* is to "entooth"—put teeth in, furnish with teeth, make jagged (like the left margin of a page of text when the first line of each paragraph is indented). The result of indenting is *indenture,* in the same way that the result of *sculpting* is *sculpture* and the result of *discomfiting* is *discomfiture.*

It seems likely that indenting was always more significant as a ceremonial act than as an anti-forgery device, but it provided a convenient way of distinguishing ordinary deeds from two-sided contracts. Since an ordinary deed was a one-way transfer of property, only the transferee needed to keep a copy, so as to be able to prove ownership. That kind of deed would be "polled," or cut off cleanly across the top (*poll* being an old word for "shear," "crop," "cut off"). But if a deed also embodied some mutual obligations, both parties would need authentic copies to establish their rights in the event of a dispute; those deeds would get the zigzag or scallop treatment. This distinction between a *deed poll* and a *deed indented,* though of little practical significance and never a legal requirement, was maintained by lawyers and conveyancers even into the nineteenth century.

Although the practice of indenting contracts died out long ago, the term *indenture* has hung on in a few specialized areas. For example, when a corporation or governmental entity borrows money from the public by issuing bonds, its agreement with the bondholders (represented collectively by a trustee) is called an indenture.

The indentures of greatest historical significance in America, however, were long-term personal service contracts. The English tradition of apprenticeship involved turning over a young man to a craftsman for a number of years, during which time the craftsman would house and feed the youngster and teach him a trade and the youngster would do whatever work the master required. The success of the arrangement depended upon the good will of the master; the indenture that sealed the bargain made the apprentice a virtual slave and provided no way out. This tradition was carried over into America—Benjamin Franklin was apprenticed to his brother to learn the printing trade—and to this day apprenticeship contracts, though much more fair, are still referred to as indentures.

The early growth of America depended upon a labor arrangement called indentured servitude. During colonial times, this made it possible for people—especially young men—who wanted to seek a better life in America to make the trip even if they could not afford passage. They paid for the trip by selling themselves as servants, typically for four to seven years, to someone already in America. The agreement was similar to an apprenticeship indenture except that the indentured servant would not be learning a trade. Sometimes the indenture was entered into in advance;

Portion of an indenture dated November 22, 1729, by which one party transferred to the other an interest in certain property in East Greenwich, Kent County, England. The parchment was preprinted with the words "This Inden-

the two & twentieth day of November in the third year of the Reign
efender of the faith &c. Anno q3 Dni 1729 Between ara
nd in the two severall Messuages or Tenements and Hereditaments
unty of Great Gardner of the other part Witnesseth that for o
Edwards to the said Nathaniel Northern in hand paid at or before
in possession of the undivided Moyety or half part and par
nds with the appurtenances the receipt and payment whereof
tt and discharge the said Thomas Edwards his heirs Extors C
and by these presents Doth grant bargain sell release and re
aniel Northern for one whole year for five shillings consideratio
hereof and by force of the Statute for transferring uses into possess
) of All those two Messuages or tenements and Gardens therem
ations of Edward Howard and Humphry Bredo their assigns or un
Hereditaments and appurtenances whatsoever to the said Moye
joyed as part parcell or member thereof or of any part thereof o
thull Street in East Greenwich aforesaid And the Reverton an
tle Interest use Trust property Claime and Demand whatsoever
erting or concerning the said Premises which are now in the possess
delivery of the said Nathaniel Northern or for his use and which
part and purparty of the said two Messuages or Tenements an
to the said Thomas Edwards his heirs and Assigns to the only

ture" and completed by hand. Note the "indenting" of the top margin. See also
the 1504 indenture at STAR CHAMBER. (Courtesy of Yale Law Library)

sometimes it was arranged after arrival. In either case, the proceeds went to the ship's captain. These immigrants were joined by convicts who were sold into indentured servitude and transported out of England as punishment for a crime.

All told, it is generally calculated that at least half of the white people who came to America before the Revolution came as indentured servants. Like apprentices, they were at the mercy of their masters; like slaves, they (or their indentures, which amounted to the same thing) could be bought and sold. But for many reasons, particularly the rise of slavery, the institution of indentured servitude waned after the Revolution. Today, a personal service contract from which one cannot escape if the situation turns out to be intolerable would be prohibited by the Thirteenth Amendment to the Constitution, which abolished slavery and involuntary servitude.

JEC

indict a ham sandwich

In an episode of the popular TV series *Law & Order: Criminal Intent,* a defense attorney reacted to the prosecutor's statement that his indictment of her client was warranted by the evidence: "Oh, right. Was my client indicted before or after the ham sandwich?"[1] Viewers unfamiliar with the phrase must have found it a bit mystifying. Even among those who are familiar with it, however, few know the real-life context in which it arose and the tragic irony that followed.

New York, where the drama was set, is one of the minority of states that still require all serious criminal cases to be initiated by indictment by a grand jury. The state has clung to this traditional but much-criticized system (see GRAND JURY) despite its substantial cost and the damning descriptions of the process by grand jurors themselves,[2] and despite a vigorous bipartisan campaign in the 1980s and 1990s to abolish the system, backed by the state's chief judge at the time, Sol Wachtler.

In the 1960s, Wachtler was an ambitious New York Republican in the mold of then-governor Nelson Rockefeller. He was elected to a seat on the state's highest court, the Court of Appeals, in the Nixon landslide of 1972 after an aggressive television campaign echoing the "law and order" theme of Nixon's campaign. His commercials showed him slamming a prison door on "thieves and muggers and murderers." Once on the bench, he proved to be a respected, temperate judge and the author of many forward-looking opinions, especially on civil rights and women's rights issues, including most notably a pathbreaking decision overturning the ancient law under which a man had a right to force sexual intercourse upon his wife. Wachtler was often mentioned as a serious contender for the office of governor; but in late 1984 New York's Democratic governor, Mario Cuomo, eliminated him as a potential opponent by elevating him to the position of chief judge.

Wachtler seized upon that position as an opportunity to effect, or at least to advocate, sweeping modernizations in the state's judicial system. Within days after his confirmation he gave an extensive interview to the New York *Daily News*. The topics ranged from case management to sentencing policy, but what made the headline was his proposal to replace grand jury indictments with preliminary hearings to determine whether a suspect should stand trial. Not that there was anything new to say on the subject; a dozen years before, a respected senior federal trial judge, William J. Campbell, had said of the indicting grand jury: "This great institution of the past has long ceased to be the guardian of the people . . . . Today it is but a convenient tool for the prosecutor—too often used solely for publicity. Any experienced prosecutor will admit that he can indict anybody at any time for almost anything before any grand jury." But Wachtler had a way with words that had eluded those who came before him. As the newspaper reported it, "Wachtler . . . said district attorneys now have so much influence on grand juries that 'by and large' they could get them to 'indict a ham sandwich.'"[3]

Apparently pleased with the effect, Wachtler repeated the statement at a press conference that coincidentally occurred on the same day that his remark was published in the *Daily News,* giving the *New York Times*—which would never have quoted the *Daily News*—a chance to pick it up.[4]

From then on there was no stopping it. The line became an almost mandatory element in scholarly articles on the grand jury system. Wachtler's friend and college classmate Tom Wolfe cited it as "the famous phrase of Sol Wachtler" in his best-selling novel *The Bonfire of the Vanities*.[5] Within a decade it was being referred to as an "old saw" and a "courthouse cliché." Recalling the story years later for language researcher Barry Popik, Wachtler, who is Jewish, said that his one regret was that he did not say "corned beef."[6]

Unlike Judge Campbell, a former prosecutor, Judge Wachtler had no personal experience with grand juries when he made his statement. But this was to change. At about the same time that he was made chief judge, Wachtler was designated in a will as trustee of a trust for the benefit of a step-cousin of his wife's, a woman seventeen years his junior named Joy Silverman. By all accounts it was Silverman—a thrice-married socialite already growing disenchanted with her third husband—who pressed to turn their quasi guardian-ward relationship into an affair. It was Wachtler who turned the affair into the subject of a federal grand jury proceeding.

The affair alone would likely have been enough to end Wachtler's career; but by 1991 it was mixed with increasingly bizarre behavior—noticed by his colleagues but, as so often happens, not recognized as a sign that he was becoming mentally unhinged until it was too late. When Silverman, impatient with Wachtler's vacillation over whether to leave his wife, took up with somebody new—a lawyer whom she described to Wachtler as both richer and handsomer than he was—Wachtler began to imagine that he could win Silverman back by discrediting the other man, or that he could frighten her into coming back to him for protection. What followed was a spiral of increasingly deranged acts, including letters and phone calls made in the role of characters—a crude Texas private investigator named "David Purdy" and a devout Roman Catholic woman named "Theresa O'Connor"—that Wachtler invented and then acted out.

Wachtler was so wildly out of touch with reality that at one point, as "Purdy," he sent Silverman a photocopy of a pornographic playing card and attempted to convince her that it was one of a series of photographs secretly taken of Silverman herself with her new friend. What finally brought the spiral to an end was his arrest for threatening—again in his

"David Purdy" persona (by this time he had taken to dressing up in a cowboy hat and string tie and going around Manhattan as "Purdy")—to kidnap Silverman's fourteen-year-old daughter unless he were paid twenty thousand dollars.[7]

Wachtler was, in a word, insane. But over the course of the last third of the twentieth century America largely abandoned the practice of sending mentally ill individuals to mental institutions, and took to imprisoning them instead. (This shift has been quantified and graphically illustrated by University of Chicago professor Bernard E. Harcourt, as shown in the accompanying figure.)[8] Accordingly, under the direction of United States Attorney Michael Chertoff (later to become the nation's second secretary

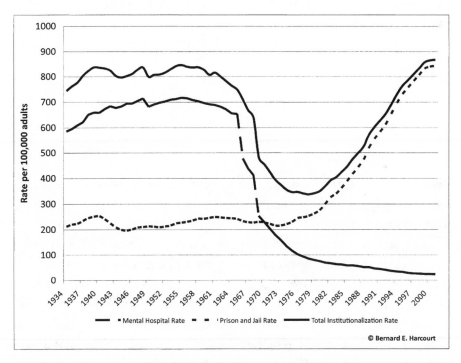

Graph showing rates of institutionalization in the United States per hundred thousand adults from 1934 to 2001. The rates are shown for mental institutions (falling line), penal institutions (state and federal prisons and county jails—rising line), and the two combined (solid line). (Courtesy of Bernard E. Harcourt)

of homeland security), a federal grand jury in New Jersey dutifully indicted Wachtler for extortion and other crimes—thereby demonstrating that a prosecutor can indeed get a grand jury to indict, if not a ham sandwich, at least an individual with no more power of rational thought than a ham sandwich.

In the end, Wachtler pleaded guilty to sending threats through the mail, served thirteen months in prison and two more in a halfway house, and finished up with five hundred hours of community service. Four months into his prison term, NBC broadcast an episode of *Law & Order* partially inspired by his case. Six and a half years after his release, the Court of Appeals announced that, by unanimous consent, it had commissioned a portrait of Wachtler to hang alongside those of Benjamin Cardozo and all the other chief judges of that court. Said Chief Judge Judith Kaye: "We felt it was time."[9]

JEC

jailbait

Jailbait (or *jail bait*) is a slang term for an adolescent girl who has not yet reached the legal age for sexual intercourse. It is a vivid warning that no matter how attractive or provocative the girl might seem to a man, if he attempts any sexual contact with her he could find himself behind bars.

The earliest appearances of the term found by lexicographers occur in the grittily naturalistic stories and novels of James T. Farrell published in the first half of the 1930s. Farrell's writing, which began in earnest around the time that he entered the University of Chicago in 1925, was based on his experience and observation of life in the city's Irish working-class neighborhoods and was noted for its documentary quality; it is therefore probable that the term existed as street slang, at least in Chicago, in the 1920s. Probably by confusion with the primary meaning of the term, *jailbait* also acquired a secondary meaning referring to a person, especially a young man, who seems destined to land himself in jail.[1] The original meaning, however, remains by far the most common today.

The unknown person who coined this expression had a keen instinct for language, creating a graphic and disturbing metaphor by a novel juxtaposition of the plainest of words. The expression quickly became a staple of hard-boiled American fiction, in lines like "Look, even if I wasn't on the level, yuh think I'd be stupid enough to mess with jail bait?" and "You're wasting your time, Gran'pa, I'm jailbait."[2]

In real life, however, the term is best used sparingly and with considerable caution: if intended or perceived as a slur upon the character of a girl or of girls in general it is offensive. For example, one of the allegations against a teacher accused of sexual molestation and harassment of a thirteen-year-old student was that he had "referred to Barbara as 'jail bait,' or 'San Quentin jail bait' in front of students, his friends, band parents and student teachers."[3]

The fundamental principle underlying this expression is the separation of sexual maturity in the biological sense from sexual maturity in the sociological sense. This concept is now so firmly established that it is somewhat surprising to realize that it is barely a century and a quarter old. For the story of how it came about, see AGE OF CONSENT.

JEC

Jim Crow

Jim Crow is the name now used to refer to the legal and social system of racial segregation and subjugation that prevailed throughout much of the United States during the century following the Civil War. Jim Crow is America's apartheid.

The name was popularized long before the Civil War, however, by an entertainer named Thomas Dartmouth Rice. "Daddy" Rice, as he came to be called, is often regarded as the father of the American minstrel show. He was not the first white performer to apply burnt cork to his face and cavort onstage to the amusement of other whites, but when he took to the stage in about 1828 with a song-and-dance routine called *Jump Jim Crow,* he set off a cultural chain reaction whose ripples still permeate American language and culture. With blackened face, ragged costume, a catchy tune,

a quirky dance step, and enough verses of "Negro dialect" for virtually un-
limited reprises and encores, Rice enchanted audiences in city after city—
Cincinnati, Pittsburgh, Philadelphia, New York, even London and Dublin.
By many accounts *Jim Crow* was America's first international hit song. The
refrain was soon known far and wide:

> Weel about and turn about and do jis so,
> Eb'ry time I weel about I jump Jim Crow.

Legend has it that Rice got his idea by watching the dancing of a stable-
hand owned by a gentleman named Mr. Crow. Legend also has it that
the original Jim Crow was a slave in Louisville. Or Charleston. That Rice
saw him performing on the street in Baltimore. Or New Orleans. That Jim
Crow was a crippled old man whose awkward movements Rice was imitating. Or a young boy. That the song was actually originally a slave song. In
the absence of real evidence for any of these stories, the most plausible theory is simply that Rice was inspired by the singing and dancing of slaves
generally, and that he concocted the name "Jim Crow" by combining a
common slave given name with a last name associated with blackness. (The
word *crow* as an epithet for a black person had already appeared, for example, in James Fenimore Cooper's *The Pioneers*.)[1]

The name was initially associated with Rice's caricature of a black
man—a contemporaneous illustration shows "Mr. T. Rice as Jim Crow"—
but it soon became a generic and derogatory term for black people generally.
Meanwhile, Rice's success spawned countless imitators, who performed
similar turns based upon similar characters, and this form of entertainment
evolved into the minstrel show, a staple of American theater throughout the
last half of the nineteenth century. The grotesquely demeaning portrayal of
blacks in the minstrel theater both reflected and shaped white attitudes for
generations.

At the same time that the caricature of blacks as "Jim Crow" was perpetuated through popular culture, barriers to legal and social advancement were maintained through rigid policies of segregation, enforced by
custom in the North and by law in the South. The Supreme Court gave its
blessing to all such laws and customs in 1896 when it formally approved a
state law restricting blacks to separate cars on trains, popularly referred to

as Jim Crow cars. (See SEPARATE BUT EQUAL.) From then on more and more laws were passed throughout the South consigning blacks to separate (and inevitably inferior) "Jim Crow" facilities; naturally these were referred to as Jim Crow laws. By the 1920s this systematic segregation of blacks was being referred to as Jim Crowism, and finally, in the 1940s, the term completed its evolution, with the entire system of subjection of blacks to white control being referred to simply as Jim Crow.

JEC

kangaroo court

A *kangaroo court* is a trial or tribunal that makes a mockery of justice. It can be a genuine judicial proceeding, an exercise in vigilante justice, or a mock trial conducted for fun. Whatever the context, the outcome is a foregone conclusion—the defendant will be found guilty.

The word *kangaroo* entered the English language on August 4, 1770. Captain James Cook and a small band of naturalists were two years into a three-year voyage of discovery sponsored by the Royal Society of London for the Promotion of Natural Knowledge and had put into shore in Australia for repairs following an unfortunate encounter with the Great Barrier Reef. This allowed them their first good look at a creature so strange that they were at a loss to classify it. As Captain Cook noted in his journal on August 4, the animal was "called by the Natives Kangooroo, or Kanguru."

Later visitors to Australia, however, found that the name drew a blank with the local people they encountered. In time the following explanation evolved: Captain Cook, not knowing the local language, had pointed to the strange animal and asked what it was called. A native, not knowing Captain Cook's language, replied in his own language, "I don't understand." Captain Cook transcribed what he heard as best he could into his journal, and the rest is history.

It is a great story—so good that it has endured for some 150 years and now permeates the Internet. It even appeared on the television quiz show

Hollywood Squares. (Question: "What does *kangaroo* mean?" Correct answer: "I don't know.")[1]

It is also complete hokum. Captain Cook was not an idiot. Linguists now know that there were some two hundred indigenous languages in Australia when Europeans settled there, and that the particular people with whom Cook and his shipmates interacted during their layover were speakers of Guugu Yimithirr, whose word for a species of large kangaroo was indeed *gangurru*.[2]

But if *kangaroo* has finally been established as authentically Australian, the same cannot be said of *kangaroo court*. That expression comes from, of all places, Texas. By 1849 the term was familiar as far away as Mississippi, where a letter to a newspaper referred to a proceeding motivated by "a love of sport" and "gotten up some what in imitation of a 'Kangaroo Court.'" The first explanations of the term came slightly later, in lengthy descriptions of "kangaroo court" proceedings (also referred to in early days as "mestang" or "mustang" courts, after a similarly uncontrollable animal) published for the entertainment of the reading public. One described a mock trial conducted as a jovial evening's entertainment in a "frontier county town" in the Southwest; another—a reminiscence of events in San Felipe, Texas, "some time in the year 1831, or '32"—recounted a more elaborate and meaner proceeding carried out to haze a newcomer to that town. Both ended, however, with camaraderie, conviviality, and drinks all around. In such early accounts—most notably in the one describing events as far back as 1830—the judge of the mock court was sometimes referred to as "the kangaroo."[3]

A wealth of information on the use of the phrase in Texas and cattle ranges to the north in the second half of the nineteenth century is preserved in oral histories of old-time Texas range hands collected in the 1930s by the Federal Writers' Project, one of the many government job programs for the unemployed during the Great Depression. These interviews show that the term was used for at least three types of ad hoc "court": courts run by the ranchmen to enforce rules of the cattle business, courts run by the cowboys to enforce their own protocols (one old-timer remarked, "It sure stopped this smutty yarn talk in camp"), and most of all, courts simply for hazing and entertainment. As one interviewee said:

They used to deal out misery to the green hands. Sometimes they'd hold Kangaroo Court, and of course find the accused one guilty of some made-up crime. Then he had to take his punishment. Often they'd whip him with leggins, or make him ride a buckin' horse.

Another elaborated:

There would be some of the dangest pleading of cases in those kangaroo courts you ever heard in your life. There would be a lawyer there and a fellow prosecuting the cases. Laugh! It would tickle a dog. The attorneys would do some of the darndest arguing you ever heard . . . . I bet I've helped whip a thousand old boys.

In the more civilized environments the punishment might be "to buy candy for the ladies or cigars for the men"; but cowboys were a rough lot, and whipping with leather chaps was the standard punishment. And a harsh punishment it was; as one interviewee cheerfully recounted, "They didn't tie me down, but they knew I wasn't goin' to stand after the first lick."[4]

By the end of the nineteenth century, however, a more sinister form of kangaroo court had become established. As reported in *Harper's* magazine in 1895, "The Kangaroo Court" was a common institution in county jails even as far away as New York. It was organized principally for the purpose of relieving each day's crop of new inmates of cash, which was then given to the jailer to buy tobacco to be shared by all the prisoners. The mechanism was a mock trial for a crime such as "havin' boodle in yer pockets." In the *Harper's* account it was a reasonably friendly affair conducted in a mock-serious manner; but the seeds of violence were there: "If a prisoner insults the court he is punished very severely."[5]

The institution of prisoner-run kangaroo courts expanded, and there arose a symbiotic relationship between the jail keepers and the thugs who naturally gravitated to positions of power in the kangaroo courts: the thugs, while satisfying their lust for power and violence, helped the jailers maintain order and discipline. Real courts were called upon repeatedly to deal with the consequences of this institutionalized mayhem, and for the most part they acquitted themselves well, awarding damages to individuals

THE KANGAROO COURT.

Illustration by A. B. Frost from *Harper's New Monthly Magazine,* April 1895 (p. 717), depicting a session of the kangaroo court in a county jail in the 1890s. Everyone has a role: the defendant—the newest inmate—is standing; the "judgeship" is seated; the "searchership" is performing his duties; and the "juryship"—everyone else—awaits the evidence. (Courtesy of Rare Book and Manuscript Library, Columbia University. Photograph by Enrique Ortiz.)

who were grievously, sometimes permanently, injured by beatings—or to the heirs of those who were killed.

Cases arising from jailhouse kangaroo courts continued at least into the 1950s—in one case despite the enactment of a state statute (still on the books) expressly defining the term "kangaroo court" as a mock court conducted by prisoners and making it unlawful for prison officials to permit such courts to exist.[6] By that time, however, the final phase of evolution of the phrase *kangaroo court* was under way: its use as an epithet to describe actual, legally constituted courts perceived to be proceeding in an outrageously unfair manner.

Even lawyers, who have a professional obligation to uphold the dignity of the courts, have been known to use the phrase this way. One lawyer single-handedly created a whole vocabulary list of variations on this phrase, first referring to the courts of Nebraska collectively as "Kangaroo Courts" and one of the judges as "the old Kangaroo himself," and then answering the resulting disciplinary charges with papers referring to a "Kangaroo judge" and a "Kangaroo action." He climaxed this linguistic exercise with a rare use of *kangaroo* as a verb, claiming that a certain judge had been imported "to Kangaroo this respondent, and prevent this respondent from having a fair trial." He was disbarred. (Note to lawyers: in the event that you do let the "kangaroo court" epithet slip out in a moment of frustration, it will not help your case to follow up, as one lawyer did, by addressing a judge of the court as a "horse's ass.")[7]

A glance at the Internet shows that there is no shortage of theories to explain how an irregular legal proceeding came to be identified with the kangaroo: The action jumps from accusation to sentencing. The defendant is bounced from the court to the gallows. The proceedings are as unorganized as a kangaroo hopping about. They are as vicious as a cornered kangaroo. They defy the law just as the kangaroo seemed to defy the laws of nature. And so on. Anyone can play this game; feel free to make up your own "etymology." There will be as much evidence for it as for any of the others.

The truth is, no one knows where this came from. In the realm of slang and idiom, however, it can be sheer quirkiness (often assisted by alliteration) that causes a phrase to catch on. This phrase came into being when the kangaroo was still a novelty everywhere on the planet outside of Australia, exotic in every sense of the word. To Texas pioneers in the 1830s, it had to be the silliest, most unlikely, most fall-down-funny critter imaginable—with a name to match. No one needed labored logic to associate the kangaroo with high jinks. All they needed was to visualize a sober judge as a silly kangaroo.

JEC

kill all the lawyers

One of Shakespeare's best-known lines comes from one of his least-known plays, *Henry VI, Part 2:* "The first thing we do, let's kill all the lawyers." The line is so popular that mugs inscribed with it are among the best-selling items in the museum shop of the Folger Shakespeare Library, on a par with "velvet hats of the sort Shakespearean jesters wear." Even New York mob boss John Gotti was apparently taken with the phrase; in one of the surreptitiously taped conversations with his confederates that finally got him put away for life, he summed up an expletive-laden exchange about the high cost of legal representation by saying, "I'd like to kill all the lawyers."[1]

The line is generally regarded as simply a Shakespearean witticism. One columnist, so tickled by it that he used it twice in the same column, added: "Notice to lawyers and their hypersensitive bar representatives: The Shakespeare line is a joke—A JOKE!"[2] But a bit of lawyerly sensitivity might be forgiven; after all, lawyers *are* sometimes killed just for being lawyers. To their credit, though, lawyers in America are assaulted about twice as often by opposing parties as by their own clients; they can take satisfaction in knowing that they are more often killed for doing their job too well than for not doing it well enough.[3]

Although the line is spoken by a character in a play, the anti-lawyer sentiment is often attributed to Shakespeare himself, as when the editor in chief of the *Washington Times,* commenting on certain judicial decisions with which he disagreed, thoughtfully observed, "Shakespeare got it only half right: 'First, we kill all the lawyers.' He might have started with judges." Not surprisingly, the lawyers and judges have a different take. Supreme Court Justice John Paul Stevens spoke for them when he wrote in a dissent, "Shakespeare insightfully realized that disposing of lawyers is a step in the direction of a totalitarian form of government."[4]

So how exactly *did* Shakespeare expect us to take the line: Was it an attack on lawyers, a backhanded compliment to the profession, or just a throwaway joke?

Dying Wish

Although humor aimed at lawyers is as old as the legal profession itself, jokes about killing lawyers off—now a fixture on the Internet—are for the most part a recent development, having blossomed quite suddenly during the 1980s. This relatively nonviolent one, dating from 1995, is actually an adaptation (with the addition of a gibe about lawyers collecting their fees) of a story that had been told in various forms—always with one or another religious or political group as the target—since the 1920s:

The old man was critically ill. Feeling that death was near, he called his lawyer.

"I want to become a lawyer. How much is it for that express degree you told me about?"

"It's $50,000," the lawyer said. "But why? You'll be dead soon; why do you want to become a lawyer?"

"That's my business! Get me the course!"

Four days later, the old man got his law degree. His lawyer was at his bedside making sure his bill would be paid.

Suddenly the old man was racked with fits of coughing, and it was clear that this would be the end. Still curious, the lawyer leaned over and said, "Please, before it's too late, tell me why you wanted to get a law degree so badly before you died?"

In a faint whisper, as he breathed his last, the old man said, "One less lawyer."

Even without reading the play we can be sure that Shakespeare did not personally favor extermination of lawyers. Lawyers were his friends and patrons; his plays were sometimes performed at the Inns of Court (those combinations of law school and bar association that were and still are the center of Britain's legal establishment); two of his earliest works were even dedicated to a lawyer, his patron Henry Wriothesley, the third earl of Southampton. Moreover, Shakespeare's plays taken as a whole give every indication that he shared the overwhelming attitude of his time—that nature and society are inherently hierarchical and that authority should be respected and order maintained. And then as now, law and order went hand in hand.

But in interpreting any specific line, the play's the thing. This play deals, in fictionalized form, with a decade in the middle of the tumultuous reign of England's pious but ineffectual king Henry VI—approximately the years 1445–55. The fourth act of the play is devoted to an uprising that occurred in 1450, about 140 years before Shakespeare was writing. That rebellion, led by one Jack Cade, sought political reforms on behalf of small landowners. In a proclamation of grievances the actual rebels of 1450 took pains to state, "We blame not . . . alle men of lawe," but only "such as maye be ffounde gilty by a just and a trew enquere by the lawe."[5] For purposes of his play, however, Shakespeare drew upon chronicles of an earlier rebellion, the Peasants' Revolt of 1381, led by Wat Tyler. That was an uprising *against* the landed classes and their support structure, including lawyers and written records obligating serfs to their lords. Thus in Shakespeare's fictional version of Jack Cade's rebellion the rebels are not landowners, but tradesmen and peasants who imagine a classless utopia in which all land is held in common and there is no educated class to lord it over the workers.

In Shakespeare's hands, the rebels simultaneously provide comic relief, exemplify the chaos that looms when established government is weak and divided, and air understandable grievances against the privileged classes. To mark their low-class status, Shakespeare renders their speech in prose rather than the blank verse used for more aristocratic characters. This down-to-earth, un-"Shakespearean" quality contributes to the current appeal of the line "First thing we do, let's kill all the lawyers": unlike "Wherefore art thou Romeo" or "To be or not to be," it sounds as right coming from the mouth of a modern mobster as from a member of Jack Cade's mob of rebels.

The scene in which this famous line occurs features an extended sequence of jokes and puns at Cade's expense—a virtual vaudeville routine of setups and one-liners—but then turns serious as Cade launches into a rabble-rousing speech to whip up support for his campaign to overthrow the king. His speech, like those of many a rising dictator right up to modern times, is filled with crowd-pleasing promises ranging from the plausible (lower prices: "There shall be in England seven halfpenny loaves sold for a penny") to the idealistic (no private ownership of land: "All the realm shall be in common") to the humorous ("I will make it felony to drink small [weak] beer"), to the ominous ("I will apparel them all in one livery [all will wear a standard uniform], that they may agree like brothers, and worship me their lord"). It is at this point that Dick—a butcher by trade who later proves himself an eager and able butcher in the rebellion as well—is overcome with fervor and leaps up with his call to begin the program of reform by killing all the lawyers.

Lest anybody in the crowd think this is just a joke, Cade responds, "Nay, that I mean to do." Straightaway the mob produces the first candidate: not a lawyer but a clerk, which is bad enough. He is accused of being able to "write and read and cast accompt [add up figures]," and even "make obligations, and write courthand [the shorthand used for recording judicial proceedings]." When with ill-considered pride the clerk acknowledges that he signs documents with his name rather than a mark such as ordinary people use (this in an age when most people could not read and write), Cade dispatches him with his first command as leader of the rebels: "Hang him with his pen and ink-horn about his neck." Cade's—which is to say Shakespeare's—mastery of mob psychology has enabled him to move the crowd from passive and lighthearted to frenzied and murderous in one scene.

As the rebellion proceeds Cade's utopian vision becomes more mad, the violence he inspires more horrific. Lawyers and clerks are just the beginning; as a messenger later reports to the king, "All scholars, lawyers, courtiers, gentlemen, They call false caterpillars [parasites] and intend their death" (act 4, scene 4). Shakespeare leaves no doubt that individuals like his character Cade—charismatic, megalomaniacal, anti-intellectual, and ruthless—threaten the very foundations of civilized life, a lesson that the world has learned again and again in such cataclysms as the Cultural Revolution in China under Chairman Mao and the killing fields of Cambodia under Pol Pot.

But Shakespeare is too sophisticated to present such events as unmotivated. He knows that rebellion is spawned by discontent with the existing order, and eloquently presents the rebels' point of view: they see the workers as the honest folk of the country; they criticize officials who send others to war but stay out of danger themselves; they are outraged at the sight of an aristocrat whose horse is dressed in a finer cloak than any working man could have.

Given the tapestry of humor, lawlessness, and legitimate grievance in which Dick the Butcher's line about killing all the lawyers is embedded, several interpretations are possible—and several are ruled out. Chief among the latter is the simplistic notion that this is just Shakespeare speaking his own mind. Although the line suggests starting with the lawyers, it is understood and acted upon as encompassing the death of all who can read and write. It is fair to assume that the playwright did not actually believe that slaughtering writers is a good plan for improving society. Likewise the idea that this line is just a joke is nonsense. This is the pivotal line marking the transition from mere speech to bloody action—converting political fantasy to actual carnage.

On the most straightforward level—the level upon which Cade and his followers understood it—the remark is an expression of outrage toward lawyers as tools of the rich and the powerful. Shakespeare may not have shared that outrage, but he clearly understood it. Conversely, from the viewpoint of those who favor the established order (or indeed any modicum of civil order at all), the line, coming as it does from a character bent on violent revolution, can be read as an unintentional compliment to lawyers as guardians of law, order, civility, and reason in human affairs.

There is no need to choose. Shakespeare's greatness lies in part in his genius for ambiguity and complexity. He would no doubt agree with both interpretations.

JEC

the law is a ass

This may be one of the few statements about law that nearly everyone can agree upon. For even though most people respect the law as a whole, there are few indeed who could not point to particular aspects of the law that strike them as asinine.

The sentiment is occasionally traced to an obscure seventeenth-century English play called *Revenge for Honour*. In this exotic tale of imagined political intrigue in far-off Arabia, the eldest son of the caliph, through the connivance of his half brother, is accused of ravishing another man's wife, for which he may have to be condemned by his own father to have his eyes put out. A supporter of the elder son, dismayed at the harshness of the penalty (and not much troubled by the charge of rape), says:

> . . . what, hoodwink [blindfold] men like sullen hawks
> for doing deeds of nature! I'me asham'd
> the law is such an Ass.[1]

But it was Charles Dickens, writing two hundred years later, who tagged our own legal tradition with this epithet—in an even blunter form that lawyers and nonlawyers alike have gleefully quoted ever since. Dickens was almost certainly unaware of that centuries-old play when, in 1839, he penned the words "the law is a ass" for the character of Mr. Bumble in the next-to-last installment of his second novel, *Oliver Twist*.

The law was a constant thread and sometimes the main subject of Dickens's writing. His keen eye and ear for pomposity and absurdity found ample raw material when, as a teenager in the 1820s and early 1830s, Dickens worked first as a clerk in a solicitor's office, then as a court stenographer in several courts, and ultimately as a reporter in Parliament. Later, as a young man in the mid-1830s, Dickens worked for a newspaper that actively promoted the reformist ideas of Jeremy Bentham. Consequently, although Dickens's actual understanding of the law was superficial and sometimes wrong, when he stumbled into a career as a novelist he came equipped with both a wealth of colorful material for humorous legal caricature and a genuine sense of outrage at injustice perpetrated in the name of the law.

This particular statement about the law, however, was certainly more an expression of humor than of outrage. Mr. Bumble is not a character whose words are to be taken seriously. He is a hypocritical and venal man, and a henpecked husband as well. He stands by while his wife, for a payment of twenty-five pounds, gives over to Oliver Twist's evil half brother, Monks, a stolen locket containing the only evidence of Oliver's true parentage—and then watches as Monks throws the locket into the river so as to secure for himself the inheritance that rightfully belongs to Oliver. When the truth comes out and first Monks and then Mrs. Bumble confess their part, Mr. Bumble characteristically continues to evade responsibility:

> "It was all Mrs. Bumble—she *would* do it—" urged Mr. Bumble; first looking round to ascertain that his partner had left the room.
>
> "That is no excuse," returned Mr. Brownlow. "You were present on the occasion of the destruction of these trinkets, and, indeed, are the more guilty of the two in the eye of the law, for the law supposes that your wife acts under your direction."
>
> "If the law supposes that," said Mr. Bumble, squeezing his hat emphatically in both hands, "the law is a ass—a idiot. If that is the eye of the law, the law's a bachelor, and the worst I wish the law is, that his eye may be opened by experience—by experience."[2]

The rule of law referred to was one aspect of the principle summarized by the great commentator William Blackstone almost seventy-five years earlier: "By marriage, the husband and wife are one person in law: that is, the very being or legal existence of the woman is suspended during the marriage, or at least is incorporated and consolidated into that of the husband." In a legal system capable of thinking this way, it seemed a logical corollary that the husband should take responsibility for his wife's actions. Thus, "if a woman commit theft, burglary, or other civil offences against the laws of society, by the coercion of her husband; or merely by his command, which the law construes a[s] coercion; or even in his company, his example being equivalent to a command; she is not guilty of any crime: being considered as acting by compulsion and not of her own

"The Evidence destroyed": one of the twenty-four illustrations made by George
Cruikshank to accompany the twenty-four installments in which *Oliver Twist*
was first published. This illustration, from the December 1838 issue of *Bentley's
Miscellany,* depicts the furtive nighttime meeting between Monks and Mr. and
Mrs. Bumble in a decaying old factory built out over the river, into which
Monks throws the telltale locket obtained from Mrs. Bumble. (Courtesy of Bei-
necke Rare Book and Manuscript Library, Yale University)

will."—though in fairness it should be noted that some exceptions were made. For example, "a wife may be indicted and set in the pillory *with* her husband, for keeping a brothel: for this is an offence touching the domestic oeconomy or government of the house, in which the wife has a principal share; and is also such an offence as the law presumes to be generally conducted by the intrigues of the female sex."[3]

Bentham had railed against legal fictions—knowingly false assumptions that permeated the common law—calling them "a syphilis, which runs in every vein and carries into every part of the system the principle of rottenness"; and in Mr. Bumble's speech Dickens ridiculed the fiction that a husband and wife are one person.[4] But few men in the 1830s—and certainly not Dickens—would have questioned the law's basic view of the roles and status of men and women in marriage; and in any event, even today Mr. Bumble would be regarded as at least equally guilty with his wife, as an accessory or co-conspirator. It is not the law but the aptly named Mr. Bumble that is the primary subject of ridicule here, because of his dialect, his foolishness in entering into a bad marriage, his inability to control his wife, and his eagerness to blame others for his shortcomings as a man.

There is another respect in which this scene can be read as a barb at the law, however—not at the substance of the law, but at the language of the law: in no other field is personification elevated to so high an art. In the brief quotes from Blackstone above, for example, we find "the law construes . . ." and "the law presumes . . ." When Dickens had Brownlow say "in the eye of the law" and "the law supposes," he was capturing perfectly the way lawyers really talk; and in having Bumble pick up on those expressions and elaborate upon them at such length—even to the point of using the masculine pronoun to refer to "his eye"—Dickens was having good fun at the expense of legal convention.

The most common use of Mr. Bumble's opinion of the law among lawyers today is in characterizing an adversary's legal argument or a judicial opinion with which one disagrees. Occasionally emotions run so high that the phrase comes perilously close to being a characterization not of the law but of the judges themselves, as in this terse statement by a dissenting judge when ten of his eleven colleagues on a federal appellate court voted not to reconsider a certain decision by a three-judge panel: "The panel's holding makes Mr. Bumble correct. Happily the panel's holding is not the law."[5]

Rare indeed is the judge who will admit that a decision the judge is voting to *uphold* is absurd. Justice Harry Blackmun of the United States Supreme Court did so in an opinion concurring in the court's refusal to review a case in which the Supreme Court of Pennsylvania had, because of an even split over the reasons why a certain award of damages was inappropriate, ended up affirming the award even though all six Pennsylvania justices agreed that it was unjust. Justice Blackmun went along with the decision not to take up the U.S. Supreme Court's time with the matter, but added somewhat plaintively, "I must confess, however, that when a State's highest court unanimously agrees that a judgment is wrong but nevertheless affirms that judgment by an equally divided vote, I am left with substantial discomfort. . . . There ought to be some way on the state side . . . for this obviously, and concededly, unjust result to be corrected. Otherwise, I fear that there will be new recruits to be added to those members of the public who already are inclined to agree with Mr. Bumble's well-known remark."[6]

JEC

lawyers, guns, and money

Singer-songwriter Warren Zevon (1947–2003) repeatedly wrote of unrepentant rogues and pampered young sociopaths who failed to learn from their mistakes or worry about consequences. His songs include "Roland the Headless Thompson Gunner" (narrating the exploits of a fictional Norwegian mercenary who fights in a guerrilla war in the Congo, then is betrayed and murdered by his comrade, whose ghost seeks revenge); "Werewolves of London" (portraying a dapper werewolf who preys on old ladies and likes Chinese food); and "Excitable Boy" (telling the story of a boy who rapes and murders his junior prom date). In "Lawyers, Guns and Money" (1978), Zevon voiced the woes of a man in trouble, including waitress-spies, gambling losses in Cuba, and Latin American hideaways, concluding:

Now I'm hiding in Honduras
I'm a desperate man
Send lawyers, guns and money
The shit has hit the fan.

While only a few people can still hum the tune, the triad of *lawyers, guns, and money* is so catchy and versatile that it has caught the imagination of many writers, and is particularly popular as a headline. Individuals, groups, and entire nations in desperate straits can almost always use money; depending on the nature of their plight they may also need either legal help or weapons. What makes Zevon's phrase so arresting is its linking of lawyers and guns. Despite the common metaphor of litigation as war (as in "battle of the experts" or "scorched-earth litigation"), providing advice and advocacy within the framework of a system of law is generally at odds with the idea of providing a gun so that people in trouble can try to shoot their way out.

Nevertheless, Zevon's phrase is sometimes just the thing for describing what is needed or involved in a situation. A 2004 law review article called "Lawyers, Guns, and Money: Warlords and Reconstruction after Iraq" proposed a three-pronged strategy to bring the warlords under control by using legal, military, and financial pressure. And the phrase is almost irresistible in books and articles discussing lobbying and litigation on gun issues, which are given to titles like "Lawyers, Guns, & Money: The Rise and Fall of Tort Litigation Against the Firearms Industry."

The step from literal to metaphorical uses is a small one. In early 2009, for example, the president of the Boston Bar Association seized upon Zevon's song to dramatize her appeal to the association's members to volunteer their services and contribute money to legal aid programs to help poor people hit by the ongoing national recession. She titled her appeal in the association's journal "Send Lawyers, Guns, and Money"—but with a line through the word "Guns" lest anyone interpret her plea a little too literally. In such nonliteral or only partially literal uses, the phrase becomes a metaphor for all-out effort or no-holds-barred conflict. Thus one scholar contrasts businesses that attempt to resolve cases quickly and minimize litigation costs with those in which "the incentive is to fight with all the tools available—'lawyers, guns and money.'" Another labels the situation in which disputing parties "call in the litigators and unleash their fury" as "going into Warren Zevon mode." These lawyers may be doing their jobs, but their behavior is portrayed as somewhat regrettable.[1]

For those who dislike lawyers in general, or plaintiffs' lawyers in particular, *lawyers, guns, and money* becomes a symbol of self-interested litigiousness. One editorial writer used Zevon's words in a somewhat nuanced context when criticizing out-of-town lawyers arriving in a small town after a disaster: " 'Send lawyers, guns and money' was the familiar refrain of a Warren Zevon song from the 1980s. There's a time and a place where lawyers are absolutely essential . . . . There is something repulsive, however, in the scenes of lawyers flocking to Bogalusa like buzzards zeroing in on road kill." More hostile was this 2009 blog comment: "Lawyers, guns and money. A bloodsucking lawyer will sue for anything over anything. You need the money to hire a man with a gun to kill all the lawyers. A life without lawyers, hard to imagine, but we can only hope!!"[2]

In a case of life imitating art, the combination of lawyers, money, and offspring in jeopardy led a judge in New York to invoke Zevon's lyric to express sympathy but deny relief. A woman named Cornelia Sage had died in 1972, and her will created a trust for her son Henry and his children. The will provided only a limited power to spend the principal of the trust. In 1976, Henry's son Ricky Sage and Ricky's wife, Karen, were jailed in Brazil and charged with illegal possession of drugs. They were held in prison conditions conceded by the judge to be "horrible . . . barbaric . . . primitive . . . brutal . . . [and] including murders, sexual assaults, torture and abuse." Henry paid $85,000 to lawyers in Brazil to secure special treatment for Ricky and Karen, for their release, and for dismissal of the charges. The New York judge, concluding that the payments were in fact used to pay bribes, refused to allow the trust funds to be used to repay Henry. The judge waxed eloquent about trusts as "a sacred legal creation which cannot be soiled." He did not question the "motives of a father's decision to employ this means to free his children from such intolerable and life-threatening prison conditions. No father could do less. The lyrics of contemporary rock music capture the ageless seeking of a child for a parent's help—'Send lawyers, guns and money / Dad, get me out of this.' And while Dad did answer and get his children out, this Court cannot indorse the methods employed."[3]

While the judge did not allow trust funds to pay for the release of Ricky and Karen, he did let the trustee use trust money to pay the attorneys' fees of the many lawyers involved in the dispute over the trust. Perhaps the judge thought the song just said, "Send lawyers money."

EGT

make a federal case out of it

In common parlance, to *make a federal case out of* something means to blow it out of proportion—to make a mountain out of a molehill. Anything requiring the attention of a federal court is a serious matter, the saying implies, and the problem at hand is not that serious. Although many of society's most serious legal matters—rape, robbery, extortion, and murder, to name a few—are dealt with almost exclusively in the state courts, those courts also must deal with small claims, petty crimes, and local disputes, whereas most cases in the federal courts are of greater gravity. It does seem odd, though, that an expression having to do with the jurisdiction of the federal courts made it into everyday slang. The groundwork for the phrase was laid by developments in the legal system; but for the phrase itself we can thank a group of vaudeville comedians.

Under the Constitution, not just any old case can be brought in federal court: criminal cases there concern only federal crimes (usually involving interstate activities); civil disputes must either arise under federal law or be between citizens of different states and involve a fairly large amount of money. From the country's earliest days, lawyers and prosecutors who had reason to believe that a state court would be unwilling or unable to provide real justice in a particular case would try to frame their allegations in such a way as to bring the suit within federal jurisdiction. But the legal community's sense of the importance and prestige of the federal courts increased dramatically in the first half of the twentieth century. Whereas in the nineteenth century the federal courts often had to meet in state courthouses or hotels, and federal judges were paid less than their state counterparts, the twentieth century brought better support and greater recognition. Arguments (by federal judges) that the federal courts were too important for ordinary matters blossomed in the 1920s and 1930s. During that time, the federal courts were confronted with an increasing volume of cases involving national law and took steps to professionalize their administration. The United States Supreme Court, which for seventy-five years had met in a room in the Capitol, acquired a monumental building of its own in 1935; and in 1938 it adopted distinctive rules of procedure to be used uniformly throughout the federal judicial system. All these events helped solidify a feeling that federal courts were different, better, and more important than other courts. The general public may have become more conscious of the distinction between federal and state authority during this period as well, particularly in light of the expansion of federal anticrime efforts in the 1930s, as when prosecutors brought down the notorious gangster Al Capone by making a federal case against him for income tax evasion, and Congress adopted a federal kidnapping statute—the "Lindbergh Law"—in response to the public furor over the abduction and murder of the aviation hero's twenty-month-old son.[1]

An early example of this expansion of federal power was the colorfully named White-Slave Traffic Act of 1910 (also known as the Mann Act), which prohibited taking a woman across state lines for immoral purposes. Thus a 1936 story in the *Chicago Daily Tribune* told the tale of a twenty-one-year-old Colorado cowboy named Buster Barton who ran off to Chicago with the sixteen-year-old daughter of a sheepherder. When the sheriff back home found out where the young lovers were staying, he notified Chicago police of the romance and the elopement and added: "Please arrest and hold these parties, as the girl's folks are about crazy. If there is no [state] law to hold Barton on we'll make a federal case of it."[2]

The jocular use of "making a federal case out of it" emerged in the 1940s, in the New York vaudeville-comedy-radio scene. Former vaudevillians became radio personalities, no doubt recycling jokes from popular vaudeville routines. Jimmy Durante was among the most successful, and he is the first person known to have uttered the phrase, in a comedy sketch broadcast in January 1944. On *The Camel Show* (named for his cigarette-company sponsor) Durante was making fun of grand opera:

Now take Romeo and Juliet, Romeo has to leave Juliet . . .
But does he say . . . Shoo-Shoo Baby? No . . . in opera he says . . .

(OPERATIC CHORD)
I have but a moment to spend with you.
A moment my dear to spend with you,
A moment to spend, a moment to spend,
A moment, a moment . . . a moment . . . a moment . . . a moment . . .
   a moment
A moment . . . a moment.

He's got one moment to spend and he's taking three hours to tell her
   about it.
Why the guy's making a federal case out of it.

Durante repeated essentially the same skit—with the same line—on his
show a few months later and again in 1949, and it was quoted in a book on
radio comics in 1945. Other comics and writers about comedy started using the line. A December 1945 magazine story had comedian Lou Holtz
using the phrase. In 1949, borscht-belt comic and writer Joey Adams used
the expression as dialogue in a novel—and coincidentally explained how
it was spreading: "Baby, you're making a federal case out of this thing.
You know as well as I do that every one of those comedians steal from
each other."[3]

In 1948 the phrase was picked up by the most widely read newspaper
writer of the day—the powerful New York gossip and show-business columnist Walter Winchell. A frequent target of gibes in *Time* magazine for
spreading stories that turned out not to be true, Winchell—portraying himself as a humble working man—groused in his syndicated column that *Time*
was holding him to the standard set by Winston Churchill, who had just
completed another volume of his monumental history of World War II:
"Time mag brags that Churchill had a squad of experts to detect errors in his
memoirs. . . . When a colyumist (with a daily grind) occasionally fluffs—this
same mag makes a Federal case of it."[4]

Despite the nationwide popularity of Durante's radio show and Winchell's
newspaper column, the expression did not catch on outside the New York
show-business community until a newer medium came along to popularize it.
In an early demonstration of the cultural power of television, yet another
former vaudevillian (who had worked with Durante) played the decisive

Salt Seller

In 1945, a New York–centered magazine called Stage Pictorial *interviewed comedian Lou Holtz to get humorous material for a column. Holtz, who had been a vaudeville, Broadway, and radio personality since the 1920s, told character-driven stories, often with at least one character speaking in Jewish dialect. This story grew out of the premise that Holtz believed that salt would cure colds. As recounted in the magazine, the story begins as Holtz walks into a grocery store to buy a bit of salt:*

"Have you any salt?" he asked the grocer.

The other looked up at him. "Have I got salt?" he challenged. "Will you please come with me in the back-room?"

Holtz was reluctant to go, but finally acceded to the grocer's invitation. Here, before his eyes, was 40,000 pounds of salt.

"That's a lot of salt," commented Holtz.

The other gave him a disdainful look. "Come with me in the cellar," he urged.

"Look," fired back the nettled Holtz, "I got a little cold and I want five cents worth of salt. Why are you making a Federal case out of this?"

But once again the persuasive grocer prevailed upon him to march down the cellar where the man showed the astonished Holtz 150,000 pounds of salt. Holtz was truly bewildered.

"Do you mean you can sell all this stuff?" he asked incredulously.

"No," said the grocer, "but the man who sold it to me, can he sell salt!"

"Broadway Raconteur: Lou Holtz Spins Some Jokes . . . ," *Stage Pictorial,* Dec. 1945, 8.

role. Fatso Marco—really Marco Marcello, a three-hundred-pound veteran vaudeville straight man—began appearing on Milton Berle's *Texaco Star Theater* in 1948 and became a featured performer in 1949. Within a couple of seasons, Marco gave Durante's old expression a negative spin, put it into a punchy, memorable form, and made it his catchphrase: "Don't make a federal case out of it!" Just as later shows would capture the public's fancy with "Sorry about that"(*Get Smart*), "Sock it to me" (*Laugh-In*), or "Is that your final answer?" (*Who Wants to Be a Millionaire*), "Don't make a federal case out of it" became enormously popular.[5]

In fact, *make a federal case out of it,* in various permutations, was omnipresent in the 1950s. The earliest appearance of the phrase outside showbusiness circles that we have found to date was in a horse-racing report published in the *Washington Post* on December 30, 1950; in wording clearly referring to Fatso Marco's admonition, the writer began, "I'm not trying to make a Federal case of it, but Mi Scandal and Petty Larceny won the two chief races on the Friday program." The phrase appeared in publications from *Life* magazine (a 1957 ad for Smirnoff vodka) to mainstream fiction such as Allen Drury's *Advise and Consent* (1959) and James Michener's *Hawaii* (1959). A popular "Personal Health" column in the *Hartford Courant* often suggested that readers not "make a federal case" out of their ills. There was even a successful race horse named Federal Case. And in yet another horse-racing story, the *Washington Post* reported in 1952 that the track announcer calling a race had accidentally identified the horse named Petty Larceny as "Grand Larceny," prompting a fan to ask him, "What were you trying to do, make a Federal case of it?"[6]

In the 1960s and 1970s, *federal case* came full circle as the courts themselves began to combine literal and figurative uses. A federal appellate court in 1976 refused to award attorneys' fees and costs to an antipoverty organization called the Vermont Low Income Advocacy Council in an action that the organization admittedly had a right to bring in federal court, because the facts showed that there was no need for the lawsuit. "As every lawyer should know," the court said, "the fact that a party is legally entitled to invoke the aid of the courts does not demonstrate that a rush to the courthouse door is always reasonable. . . . It was VLIAC that had decided to make a 'federal case' out of a matter that . . . had promise of amicable resolution."[7] The court's use of quotation marks signaled—just in case there was any doubt—that it meant the term *federal case* not only in its legal sense, but also in the colloquial sense made popular by Marco Marcello.

Although the phrase has become less ubiquitous in everyday conversation over the ensuing decades, in the courts it has only become more common. It is used by lawyers and judges alike to characterize legal claims and disputes as overblown. Nevertheless, the concept underlying *make a federal case out of it* implicitly recognizes that serious disputes have a place in federal court. Television catchphrases have moved on from "don't make a federal case out of it" to the less eloquent "D'oh!" but the federal courts remain an essential part of our country's government and vital guarantors of our rights as citizens. In 1945, just as *make a federal case out of it* was becoming comic hyperbole, federal judge Alfred P. Murrah wrote in a case concerning the rights of free speech and freedom of assembly for workers under a state labor law passed in the midst of a world war, "We yet like to believe that wherever the Federal courts sit, human rights under the Federal Constitution are always a proper subject for adjudication."[8]

EGT

one-bite rule

"You only get one bite at the apple" is a familiar expression warning that sometimes we only get one chance. The exact origin of the metaphor is unclear. Bryan Garner, in the *Dictionary of Modern Legal Usage,* observes that until the 1940s both British and American lawyers regularly said "one bite at the cherry." In the twentieth century, however, *cherry* had taken on an additional meaning in the United States as a slang term for the hymen or for a virgin. As Garner notes, "*one bite at the cherry* may well be the only legal idiom that has changed because its users felt embarrassment over a newfound double entendre."[1] Unfortunately, the substitution takes an image that made sense (a cherry is normally consumed in one bite, so you can't have another bite) and replaces it with one that does not. Usually you get lots of bites at an apple!

After the metaphor changed from cherry to apple, it led some judges to associate *one bite* with the Bible. The judge in a 1990 Illinois case noted that the defendant was "only entitled to a third bite on the apple of innocence, not the right to swallow it. If there were divine constitutional rights of due process, Adam and Eve, and maybe the rest of us, would still be in the Garden of Eden." Similarly the U.S. Tax Court once held that "we can only give petitioner one bite at the apple. After that, like Adam, petitioner knew what he was doing."[2]

The phrase *one bite* or *one-bite rule* has two primary uses in the legal context. One refers to the liability of the owner of an animal for the damage done when that animal attacks someone. Under the traditional rule, a dog owner is not liable to a person bitten by the dog unless the dog has previously demonstrated vicious tendencies—usually by biting someone else—so that the owner should have been aware of the need to take precautions to avoid further attacks. This leads judges to say that the dog is entitled to "one bite," or "one free bite." The rule both protects the owner the first time and imposes liability for repeat offenses. The first bite may be free, but after that the owner had better get out the checkbook. Although some states retain this rule, others have replaced it with statutes that take away the free bite, making owners strictly liable for all injuries caused by their pets.

The moral and legal principle embodied in this one-bite rule is ancient indeed. The traditional rule for dogs finds an exact parallel in the Old Testament in connection with another domestic animal—the ox. Exodus 21:28–29 laid down what might be called the "one-gore rule." That biblical law, in the modern English of the New Revised Standard Version, states: "When an ox gores a man or a woman to death, the ox shall be stoned . . . ; but the owner of the ox shall not be liable. If the ox has been accustomed to gore in the past, and its owner has been warned but has not restrained it, and it kills a man or a woman, the ox shall be stoned, and its owner also shall be put to death."

The second use of the phrase *one-bite rule* in law is more metaphorical (no actual biting here), but it too refers to a single chance. In this context *one bite* precludes repeated assertions of the same legal claim. In civil cases the limit is embodied in a doctrine called *res judicata* (Latin for "a thing adjudicated," and therefore not open to further litigation). In the words of one legal scholar: "A litigant is entitled to one, and only one, 'bite' of the litigation 'apple.' After the litigant has taken that bite, the [law] precludes the litigant from trying another apple to see if it tastes better."[3] Plaintiffs cannot sue for damages in a car wreck, lose, and then sue all over again in hopes of winning the second time. Nor can they sue, win modest damages, and then sue again to try for more money. In both cases the plaintiffs have had that one bite at the apple. This rule applies not only to claims that were actually litigated but also to related claims that could have been included. Car wreck plaintiffs cannot, therefore, sue once for claims for personal injuries and a second time for the damages to their cars. That would be two bites.

This second type of one bite/one chance rule applies in criminal cases as well, and it applies to both defendants and prosecutors. One court, for example, refused to allow a defendant to repeatedly raise the same challenge to his conviction, noting that he was only "guaranteed one bite at the apple, not a feast." Prosecutors are limited to one bite by the double-jeopardy clause of the Fifth Amendment to the Constitution: "nor shall any person be subject for the same offence to be twice put in jeopardy of life or limb." Therefore, when an appellate court reversed an aggravated rape conviction for insufficient evidence, the state was not allowed to re-prosecute the defendant for the (nonaggravated) rape of the same victim in the same incident. The court rejected the district attorney's argument that he was merely asking for "a new bite to replace the bite which [the defendant] took away through his successful appeal."[4]

Occasionally, the two uses of *one bite*—one chance to get away with something bad/one chance to obtain something good—can be confusing. In a particularly contentious case, a California judge was faced with multiple motions and numerous disputes about discovery. In response, the judge mixed his *one bite* metaphors, threatening: "I don't know how to say it in some legal sense, but I just don't want to be doing this any more unless I absolutely have to, so if I come to some conclusion that somebody is just wasting my time I'm not going to be so reasonable next time. So everybody is put on notice that they use their respective one bite of the apple or every dog gets to bite somebody or however that legal phrase is used."[5] When despite this warning one of the parties ignored several discovery orders, severe sanctions followed. Cherries, apples, or dogs, the lawyer had used up his free bite.

EGT

one person, one vote

To the modern ear, *one person, one vote* sounds like a self-evident expression of a fundamental principle of democracy. But in fact, the phrase has come into common use only within the past few decades, and the principle itself is still evolving.

The concept has two components: *universal suffrage* (virtually all adults may vote) and *equal suffrage* (everyone's vote has the same weight). Despite the rhetoric in the Declaration of Independence about all men being created equal, neither of these complementary concepts would have been regarded as self-evident by America's founders. The franchise in those days was an attribute of the landed class. Few of the revolutionaries—least of all the Virginia slaveholder who penned the Declaration—dreamt that nonwhites would ever be allowed to vote. And as to women, the famous exchange of letters between Abigail and John Adams in the spring of 1776 tells the tale. Abigail implored her husband and his fellow delegates to the Continental Congress to "Remember the Ladies" in establishing legal rights in the new nation. She slyly co-opted the revolutionaries' own slogans: "If perticuliar care & attention is not paid to the Laidies we are determined to foment a Rebelion, and will not hold ourselves bound by any Laws in which we have no voice, or Representation." John spoke for all the founding fathers when he replied to his wife's suggestion that women should have some voice in government: "I cannot but laugh."[1]

When the Constitution was adopted thirteen years later, it purported to guarantee every state "a Republican Form of Government" (Art. IV, § 4)—that is, a government elected directly or indirectly by the people—but left it to the states to decide who could vote and how their legislatures should be apportioned. At the national level, the Constitution embodied three major compromises of democratic principle whose effects are with us still. One was the United States Senate, in which each state would have exactly two votes regardless of population. Another was the ELECTORAL COLLEGE, which gave the people in the least populous states the greatest voting power in proportion to their numbers in presidential elections. Most infamously, the Constitution was built on the THREE-FIFTHS RULE, which greatly enhanced the political weight of white voters in the slave states as against voters in other states.

The Fourteenth Amendment, enacted to extend civil rights to former slaves in the South and ratified in 1868, abolished the three-fifths rule, but it did not extend to the former slaves a constitutional right to vote—for the simple reason that most northern states did not allow blacks to vote either. Instead, Congress passed Reconstruction acts requiring southern states to allow blacks to vote as a condition of the states' readmission to the Union. In the election of 1868, however, the Republicans—the party of Lincoln—realized how useful the black vote was to them; to protect the electoral advantage those votes gave them, they adopted the Fifteenth Amendment, giving blacks in all states the right to vote on an equal basis with whites.

For a while, there was a good deal of black voting in the South. But the white majority devised means to stamp out this vote, including poll taxes, literacy tests, and felon disenfranchisement laws (disqualifying anyone convicted of a felony from ever voting again). When combined with policies that kept blacks poor and uneducated, and a system of justice that contrived to convict them disproportionately of crimes, these laws disqualified the vast majority of blacks from voting. A Florida politician boasted in 1872, regarding his role in promulgating a new state constitution that included both felon disenfranchisement and strategic malapportionment of the legislature, that he had kept the state from becoming "niggerized."[2] And for blacks who were not barred by such legal measures, there was always physical violence to dissuade them from voting. It was not until the 1960s, a century after the Civil War, that the situation would improve.

Meanwhile, other groups were struggling for the vote as well, and likewise learning how strongly those who have the vote resist sharing it. A Rhode Island state legislator named Thomas Dorr found this out in the 1840s when he led a movement to replace the state constitution, which limited the franchise almost entirely to landowners, with one that enfranchised all adult white males. The complicated series of events that ensued—including a couple of armed scuffles known as Dorr's Rebellion—culminated in his being convicted of treason and sentenced to solitary confinement at hard labor for life. He was released after twenty months' imprisonment, his health irretrievably broken.

A few years later, in 1848, a women's rights convention at Seneca Falls, New York, adopted resolutions calling for a number of legal reforms, including woman suffrage. The call for suffrage was widely regarded as so preposterous as to discredit the entire work of the conference. Twenty-four years later, in 1872, Susan B. Anthony had the temerity to cast a vote in the presidential election—for which she was arrested, convicted, and fined. The territory of Wyoming had extended suffrage to women in 1869, but it stood alone for almost a quarter of a century; and it was a quarter century more before women nationwide would get the vote.

The march of democracy was equally halting in England. As early as 1780, the English parliamentary reform advocate John Cartwright listed 110 political principles he deemed fundamental, one of which was: "One man shall have one vote." But universal suffrage and substantial equality of voting power were achieved there only through a long series of incremental reform bills beginning in 1832 and extending to 1948. One of these was enacted in 1867, and in the agitation for that bill there arose, apparently for the first time, the pithy slogan "One man, one vote."[3] The phrase showed up occasionally in American publications in stories about England, but it did not catch on in the United States, where the focus for the next half century was on votes for women.

Ratification of the woman suffrage amendment in 1920 put to rest for a while the issue of universality of suffrage in the United States; it would take about forty more years before the plight of disenfranchised blacks would capture the attention of the nation as a whole. In the meantime, the issue of voter inequality came to the fore.

The United States was founded at the dawn of the Industrial Revolution. America was largely an agrarian society: cities were small, the population spread out. But virtually from the day of the nation's founding, the growth of industry and commerce created ever greater differences in population density between urban and rural areas. In most states, the drawing of congressional and legislative district lines did not keep up with population shifts. Moreover, many state legislatures were apportioned at least in part on the basis of geography rather than population—sometimes on the model of the U.S. Senate. As a result, voters in rural areas acquired ever increasing voting power relative to those in urban areas. And of course, the representatives they elected, whether at the state or national level, had every incentive to perpetuate the imbalance in electoral districting that had elevated them to their high office.

In 1946 the Supreme Court was faced with a challenge to congressional apportionment in Illinois, where the population disparity between districts had reached nine to one—and turned its back. Writing for the Court, Justice Felix Frankfurter dismissed legislative districting as a "political thicket" that the courts "ought not to enter," and directed victims of the system to seek their remedy from the legislative branch—that is, from the very politicians whose careers depended upon the unfair system.[4]

Over the next decade and a half, however, two important changes occurred. First, postwar social and economic trends dramatically accelerated the demographic shift toward urban and suburban concentration, and the consequent malapportionment of legislative districts. By the 1960s, a nine-to-one differential in voting power was nothing; virtually every state could point to much greater discrepancies. In Vermont, for example, the population ratios among state legislative districts exceeded *nine hundred* to one, with thirty-eight residents in one small town having the same representation as the entire city of Burlington.[5] Second, the nation finally began to awaken from nearly a century of slumber on the issue of racial equality and black civil rights. The problem of malapportionment had an obvious racial component that, while seldom discussed, could not escape notice in the civil rights–conscious atmosphere following the Supreme Court's 1954 school integration decision. African Americans in the North were heavily concentrated in the cities; underrepresentation of the urban population meant underrepresentation of the black population.

Faced with these changed circumstances, the Supreme Court changed its mind. In 1963 the Court held inequality of voting power to be a violation of equal protection of the laws. The Court's opinion, written by Justice William O. Douglas, concluded: "The conception of political equality from the Declaration of Independence, to Lincoln's Gettysburg Address, to the Fifteenth, Seventeenth, and Nineteenth Amendments can mean only one thing—one person, one vote."[6] In using *person* instead of *man,* Douglas may consciously have included women, but he was certainly not yielding to some concept of POLITICALLY CORRECT language. There was no sensitivity to sexist language in those pre–women's liberation days. Douglas was just being literal.

A series of follow-up cases made it clear that the principle of one person, one vote would apply to every kind of election at every level of government with the sole exception of elections for the U.S. Senate and the presidency. Among other things, the legislature of every state would have to be reapportioned on a strict population basis—a prospect greeted with relief by proponents of racial equality and fairness in government, and with howls of dismay by the political power structure. The next several years saw continuous efforts to nullify the one person, one vote rule, including a petition for the calling of a constitutional convention (adopted by thirty-two of the necessary thirty-four state legislatures) and a proposed constitutional amendment (twice falling only seven votes short of the necessary two-thirds vote in the Senate).[7] America's politicians heard the clarion call of *one person, one vote*—and they fought it tooth and nail.

This extreme resistance was obviously motivated in significant part by fear of the civil rights movement. In 1962, the Student Nonviolent Coordinating Committee (SNCC, pronounced "snick")—the most youthful, energetic, and confrontational civil rights organization of its day—had made voter registration its top priority. In those days the old English slogan "one man, one vote" was a rallying cry among political activists in the British colonies of Africa, and this inspired SNCC to take up the phrase. On September 24, 1963, SNCC's young chairman, John Lewis, and about fifteen other individuals picketed the Selma, Alabama, courthouse carrying signs emblazoned with those words—"the first appearance," Lewis later wrote, "of what was now SNCC's official slogan."[8]

In that time and place, these were viewed as fighting words. Literally. The marchers were arrested, herded into a school bus with electric cattle prods, and jailed for a week. The stated crime: engaging in actions that would "so outrage the sense of decency and morals or so violate or transgress the customs, patterns of life and habits of the people of Alabama as to be likely to cause a riot or breach of the peace." SNCC's position on voting rights was aggressive even by the standards of some civil rights supporters at the time. The civil rights bill then being promoted by the Kennedy administration would have extended voting rights only to individuals with at least a sixth-grade education. As recounted by Lewis, "We were outraged at that. Here were these Southern states that had for so long denied black children the right to a decent education, and now, beyond that denial, these children were to be *punished* for that neglect when they reached voting age. The only qualifications to vote, we believed, should be age and residence, period."[9]

For many reasons, "one man, one vote" made a better slogan than "one person, one vote." It fit better on a sign, it worked better as a chant, and it

SNCC poster (ca. 1963), with photograph by Danny Lyon. At the time, people of color throughout the South were prevented from voting by voter "qualification" procedures including poll taxes and discriminatorily administered literacy tests. This poster, featuring a man who was apparently a typical hardworking but poor and undereducated sharecropper, aggressively put forth SNCC's position that all adults, regardless of race, class, or educational opportunity, have an equal right to a say in who will govern them. (Courtesy of Danny Lyon and Magnum Photos. Photograph by Wisconsin Historical Society.)

reinforced one of the major themes of the civil rights movement, which was to restore dignity to black males who grew up—and even grew old—being treated as a hybrid of simpleton child and dangerous animal. "One man, one vote" became the usual expression—in newspapers, among politicians and the public, and even in much legal writing—for the rule that the Supreme Court had carefully called "one person, one vote." The resurgence of the women's rights movement beginning in the late 1960s engendered a new sensitivity to language, however, and over time the Supreme Court's more prosaic but more precise wording prevailed in legal writing. Amusingly, when some writers, habituated to the word *man* in the phrase, saw "one person, one vote" in post-1960s Supreme Court opinions, they assumed that the Court was *changing* the phrase as a "linguistic bow to women's liberation."[10] But of course the Court was simply adhering to its original language.

America has traveled far on the tortuous road toward voting fairness. Certainly when the young John Lewis was repeatedly arrested and beaten in the voter-registration drives of the 1960s he could not have imagined that he would go on to become one of the most senior members of the United States House of Representatives—representing the southern state of Georgia, no less. But no one would claim that the journey is complete. Among other things, the United States has no general system of runoff elections to prevent election by a minority of those voting. (The "instant runoff" system, in which voters are allowed to number the candidates in a multicandidate election in order of preference, would substantially solve that problem.) Felon disenfranchisement laws still disproportionately disqualify blacks from voting, and counting prisoners who cannot vote as part of the population of the district where the prison is located adds to the voting strength of the local population in the same way that counting slaves who could not vote added to white voting power before the Civil War. Needlessly burdensome voter-registration and identification laws disproportionately restrain voting by the young, the poor, and first-time voters. The census figures used for apportionment are still limited to the numbers of people that census takers are able to track down, and are not adjusted scientifically to come as close as possible to the "actual Enumeration" called for by Article I, section 2, of the Constitution. The U.S. Senate is vastly more disproportionate than at the nation's founding: as of the 2010 census, citizens of the least populous state, on a per person basis, have 65.7 times the voting power in the Senate of citizens in the most populous state. And the ELECTORAL COLLEGE is so flawed that in presidential elections the voters in most states, large and small, are little more than spectators.

Democracy in America will always be a work in progress.

JEC

oyez

The Honorable the Chief Justice and the Associate Justices of the Supreme Court of the United States!

Oyez! Oyez! Oyez! All persons having business before the Honorable the Supreme Court of the United States are admonished to draw near and give their attention, for the Court is now sitting. God save the United States and this Honorable Court!

So cries the Marshal of the Supreme Court to announce the entrance of the Justices and proclaim the commencement of each day's proceedings. Similar solemnities attend the openings of courts throughout the United States—though in at least one court this time-honored proclamation suffered the addition of a modern ending that gives new meaning to the word *anticlimax:*

Oyez! Oyez! Oyez! The Honorable the Seventeenth Judicial District Court of the State of Louisiana in and for the Parish of Lafourche is now open. Judge _____ presiding. God save the State and this Honorable Court. Please be seated. No smoking allowed.[1]

The cry of *oyez*—called out two or three times to command attention—comes to us from the Norman dialect of French that crossed the English Channel with William the Conqueror in 1066 and grew into a distinct dialect known as Anglo-Norman or Anglo-French. *Oyez* is a plural imperative form of the Anglo-Norman verb *oir* (Law French *oyer*), "to hear"; so its literal meaning is "Hear ye." Unlike most words, whose meanings evolve over the years, this one means today exactly what it meant a thousand years ago.

Many American courts—probably most of them—long ago substituted "Hear ye" for "Oyez" in their ceremonies. We can thank the more traditional courts, which have resisted the change, for some of the most imaginative legal defenses ever raised. In one, a defendant convicted of first-degree murder argued that he had never been properly indicted, on the ground that "the indictment was not here returned in open court because the sheriff failed to recite 'Oyez, Oyez, Oyez,' to announce that court was formally open." In another, a man accused of improperly trying to influence one of the jurors in a case against his brother-in-law testified that he had spoken to the juror only because he "wanted to find out what the words 'Oyez! Oyez!' meant." (Neither defense was successful.)[2]

The wording of the Supreme Court Marshal's proclamation has not changed (give or take a "the" or two) in at least a century, and probably much longer.[3] The *sound* of the proclamation, however, has changed. The most common pronunciation of *oyez* today, and that used in the Supreme Court, is "Oh yay! Oh yay!" When uttered with suitable solemnity, the effect is of a dirgelike football cheer. This twentieth-century development is a decided departure from previous centuries.

The Norman language that William the Conqueror brought to England in 1066 was, like all dialects of French, descended from the Latin language that Caesar brought north when he conquered Gaul in 58–50 B.C.E. The evolution of French spelling and pronunciation is in many respects a story of gradual but inexorable reduction and simplification of the original Latin words and sounds. The word at hand is a good example: *oyez* is descended from the Latin *audīre* (to hear) and the Latin second person plural ending *-tis*. In early Anglo-French the pronunciation of *oyez* was "oyets," the Latin *-tis* ending having been shortened over time to a *-ts* sound. This process of simplification continued, and in later Anglo-French the final *-ts* sound was reduced to an *-s* sound. Accordingly, the usual spelling of this word when it began to appear in English writing in the fifteenth and sixteenth centuries was *oyes*—and for a time the spelling and the pronunciation were in agreement.

Meanwhile, back in France, the Parisian dialect was evolving into modern French. The writing system became relatively stabilized in the fourteenth and fifteenth centuries, with *-ez* as the second-person plural ending (the one that started out in Latin as *-tis*). By the seventeenth century, *oyez* began to appear alongside *oyes* in English writing, undoubtedly as a result of the growing prestige of Parisian French. This Frenchified spelling of what was by then a perfectly good English word smacks of pretentiousness and over-correction, but it gradually caught on. In France, however, the changes in pronunciation went further than in England—to such an extent that the final consonant sound in this ending completely disappeared, so that *oyez* would be pronounced "oy-yay." With the English word *oyes* respelled as if it were Parisian French, it began to seem as if the longstanding English pronunciation was "incorrect." Even the historically knowledgeable legal commentator William Blackstone complained in 1769 of "abuse of . . . legal terms of antient French," as in the case of "the prologue to all proclamations, '*oyez*, or hear ye,' which is generally pronounced most unmeaningly 'O yes.'"[4]

But this standard English pronunciation had been passed down as a part of centuries-old oral tradition. The criers and bailies and tipstaffs who used it were not concerned with how the word was spelled, and were unlikely to be experts in modern French pronunciation in any event. Perhaps for this reason the venerable "O yes" pronunciation so puzzling to Blackstone remained dominant well into the twentieth century. In fact, if dictionaries showed a pronunciation other than "O yes," it was the logical "O yez."[5] It was not until 1961 that a dictionary—the new Merriam-Webster Third International—added "O yay" to the two more traditional pronunciations. Almost three centuries after it was first introduced, that Frenchified *-ez* ending had finally given rise to a correspondingly Frenchified pronunciation.

Language change tends to snowball: as more people adopt a new spelling or pronunciation or construction, the pressure increases on the rest to go along so as not to seem wrong. In this case, factors beyond the mistaken illusion of "correct" pronunciation of an old Anglo-French term may have helped tip the balance. Saying "Oh yay!" avoids the impression—which bothered even Blackstone—that one is saying "Oh yes! Oh yes!" Moreover, "Oh yay!" has an almost biblical gravity; it sounds like "O yea!" One almost expects the next word to be *verily*.

Ironically, *yea* means "yes," as in the parliamentary step of "calling for the yeas and nays"; so "O yea!" would actually mean the same thing as "Oh yes!"—a coincidence that, as one politician has shown, can be a source of humor. When the electronic tally board in the Connecticut State Senate failed just before the final vote on an important bill, the senators had to vote the old-fashioned way, by voice. According to a newspaper report, a long-time advocate of the bill "drew laughter from his colleagues as he cast his vote in the manner of a courtroom bailiff: 'O yea, O yea, O yea,' he said."[6]

Sometimes, however, the rendering of *oyez* as "O yea" or the like is done in complete seriousness, as in a newspaper description of the expected procedure in a crucial Florida Supreme Court argument over disputed balloting in the 2000 presidential election: "Inside the white-pillared Supreme Court building in Tallahassee, Fla., the justices will enter the courtroom in order of seniority, as the court marshal calls out 'Oh yea, oh yea' to bring the proceeding to order."[7]

The history of *oyez* is one of repeated change—either of spelling to conform to pronunciation or of pronunciation to conform to spelling. Does this erroneous use of *yea* signal the beginning of a new round, which will once again change the written form to correspond better to the sound of the cry? Check back in a hundred years.

JEC

paper chase

The phrase *paper chase* began popping up in American judicial opinions in 1975, and has appeared with regularity ever since. Judges came late to the phrase; it originated in the mid-nineteenth century as another name for the game or sport of "hare and hounds," in which one team (the "hares") was given a head start and led the other (the "hounds") on a chase by leaving a trail of torn-up pieces of paper. The game, which could be played on foot, on horseback, or later even on motorcycles with side cars, originated in England and had made its way to America by the 1870s. For decades, stretching well into the twentieth century, this was a popular pastime of the horsey set, frequently reported on in the society pages of the newspapers. "The New-York Hare and Hounds Club will celebrate Thanksgiving Day with its usual 'cross-country paper chase . . . over the picturesque hills and valleys of Westchester County," the *New-York Times* reported in 1883. "Mrs. Astor in Paper Chase," ran a breathless headline in 1916, "Finishes Among the First at Aiken—A Throng at Tea."[1]

The analogy between this game and the following of clues to track down a killer led the mystery writer Elizabeth Linington, writing under one of her pen names, Lesley Egan, to title a 1972 crime novel *Paper Chase*. It is less clear what prompted John Jay Osborn Jr. to name his novel about the life of a Harvard Law School student (published in 1971, the year after his graduation from the school) *The Paper Chase*. It is generally assumed that this was a reference to the quest for a law school diploma—quite a different thing from the original meaning of the term. When Hollywood began work on a film adaptation, the *New York Times* conflated the two books and reported that John Houseman, who would go on to win an Academy Award for his performance as a professor in the film, was "playing the dean of the Harvard Law School in a suspense film to be called 'Paper Chase.'"[2]

The film (actually called *The Paper Chase*, like Osborne's book) opened on October 16, 1973, to mediocre reviews—and promptly became a huge hit. It provoked interest and discussion in the legal world as in the moviegoing world at large. Suddenly the phrase *paper chase*—heard only sporadically since the heyday of hares and hounds—was on every lawyer's lips.

In early 1975, the phrase found its way for the first time into a reported American judicial opinion: a Georgia appellate court complained of having to wade through pages and pages of irrelevant documents merely because lawyers found it easier to photocopy them all than to determine which ones were relevant. "In calling this 'paper chase' to the attention of the bar we do not intend to be critical of the lawyers involved in the instant case," the court said. "They have done only what has become common usage in today's Xerox world." But the court asked the bar to be more selective in the future.[3]

Less than a month later, the Supreme Judicial Court of Massachusetts, discussing standards under new rules of pleading that were intended to avoid the technical requirements of the old rules, declared itself "loath to renew the futile paper chase for the supposedly exact pleading."[4] The phrase has appeared in court after court ever since. But as those first two judicial uses illustrate, the circumstances seldom bear any similarity either to the hares and hounds game or to the struggle to attain a diploma. In fact, as used in judicial opinions, *paper chase* has almost no identifiable meaning at all. It generally serves only to attach a vaguely negative connotation to some aspect of a case having to do with documents or court papers. Decisions were clearer before judges got this phrase into their heads and started throwing it into their opinions.

JEC

penumbra

Courts have sometimes used the word *shadow* as a metaphor for the scope or coverage of a law. (See SHADOW OF THE LAW.) But the precise boundaries of the law are not always clear. Law is not a mathematical science; it deals with human behavior, which is infinitely variable, and it must be expressed in words, which are always inexact. A statute or legal principle is like a shadow with fuzzy edges—there is a core area that it obviously covers, and then there are areas around the edges where the applicability of the law is debatable. It is the job of judges to decide, in cases at the margin, whether the law should be interpreted as covering the situation. From time to time legal writers have invoked a particular kind of shadow to express this concept—the *penumbra*. In a solar eclipse, the penumbra is the area of partial shadow surrounding the dark shadow where the eclipse is total. Thus in a 1957 case regarding the application of a certain statute, the Supreme Court held that federal courts must apply not only the specific words of the law but also "the penumbra of express statutory mandates."[1]

Constitutions, which lay out broad principles of governance in deliberately vague terms, are particularly in need of interpretation. As Supreme Court

Justice Oliver Wendell Holmes Jr. put it, "The great ordinances of the Constitution do not establish and divide fields of black and white. Even the more specific of them are found to terminate in a penumbra shading gradually from one extreme to the other."[2]

The penumbra analogy reached its peak in 1965, in the case of *Griswold v. Connecticut,* in which the Supreme Court struck down a Connecticut law banning the use of contraceptives by married couples. Although the Constitution does not mention contraception, Justice William O. Douglas, writing for the Court, noted that the Bill of Rights has been interpreted as creating many protections not expressly referred to in the Constitution. This, he said, shows that "specific guarantees in the Bill of Rights have penumbras, formed by emanations from those guarantees that help give them life and substance." The Court held that several different provisions in the Bill of Rights, taken together, create zones of privacy that the government simply may not intrude upon—and surely none more private than the marital bed. "Would we allow the police to search the sacred precincts of marital bedrooms for telltale signs of the use of contraceptives?" the Court asked. "The very idea is repulsive to the notions of privacy surrounding the marriage relationship."[3]

Justice Douglas's flowery language about penumbras and emanations turned out to be an easy target for ridicule by those opposed to expansive interpretation of constitutional rights, especially in the area of sex and reproduction; and the Supreme Court soon backed away from it. Within two years after Douglas retired because of poor health, a unanimous Supreme Court chastised litigants for basing their arguments upon "the shadows cast by a variety of provisions in the Bill of Rights."[4] The court still must interpret the general language of the Constitution and determine its scope, just as it always has; but it no longer uses the apt metaphor of the penumbra when it does so.

JEC

Philadelphia lawyer

For well over two centuries the phrase *Philadelphia lawyer* has signified masterful lawyering and a keen ability to analyze and understand complex legal or factual situations. "It's so complicated, you need to be a Philadelphia lawyer to even understand it," says a senior citizen about a newly enacted Medicare prescription-drug program. "We were bombarded by a flurry of information that only a Philadelphia lawyer could sort out," writes a reporter regarding procedures for homeowners seeking federal disaster relief. A local individual discussing the case of a man declared dead by paramedics and a county medical examiner, shipped to the morgue in a body bag, and placed in a refrigerated drawer, only to be found alive when the bag was opened an hour or so later, remarks to a reporter, "This case won't take a Philadelphia lawyer. A country lawyer could do it."[1]

Of course, being a shrewd lawyer is not always regarded as an admirable trait. Hence the phrase is sometimes used as an insult: "Those developers talk faster than Philadelphia lawyers on acid," says a county commissioner. A sports columnist critical of an American Bowling Congress official's interpretation of certain rules asks, "Is Mordini attempting to imitate a Philadelphia lawyer, or is he practicing to become a political speech writer?"[2] But lawyers—especially those in Philadelphia—will be happy to learn that, despite the modern popularity of jokes and barbs aimed at lawyers, our review of newspaper stories containing the phrase in recent years indicates that the image of a "Philadelphia lawyer" is still overwhelmingly invoked in a positive sense rather than a negative one.

The phrase is generally assumed to have been inspired by one particular Philadelphia lawyer, the justly celebrated Andrew Hamilton. Born in Scotland about 1676, Hamilton came to Virginia as an indentured servant around 1700, later established himself in Philadelphia, and ultimately rose to become the most eminent attorney of his day in the colonies. Hamilton's crowning achievement was his successful defense of New York publisher John Peter Zenger in 1735.

Zenger's paper, *The New-York Weekly Journal,* had assailed the governor of the province of New York, William Cosby, for his manipulation of

When You Really Need a Good Lawyer . . .

Sometimes only a Philadelphia lawyer will do, as in this joke that has been in circulation since the 1890s:

Defendant: "Before I plead guilty or not guilty I would like to ask the court to appoint a lawyer to defend me."

Judge: "You were caught in the actual commission of a crime, with the merchandise on you, a gun in your hand, and your victim on the floor. What could a lawyer possibly say in your defense?"

Defendant: "That's just it—I'm curious also to hear what he could possibly say."

the legal system—setting up juryless courts with sympathetic judges to do his bidding. Cosby responded to the attacks by having Zenger arrested, held in prison for ten months, and then put on trial for "seditious libel," that is, words tending to undermine the government. When Zenger's New York lawyers argued that Cosby's handpicked judges should disqualify themselves from sitting in the case, the judges responded by disbarring the lawyers. Hamilton, who haled from the safer and more enlightened province of Pennsylvania, then stepped in and assumed the defense for no fee. His principal argument, advanced with great eloquence, was that no one should be punished for publishing the truth about the government. The law at that time, and for a considerable time thereafter, was to the contrary. The crime was one of stirring up sentiment against the rulers; if the statements were true, that only increased the risk that publishing them would undermine the government. In the words of a common-law maxim, "the greater the truth, the greater the libel." To the consternation of the judges, however, the jury was won over by Hamilton's long and dramatic summation, and declared Zenger not guilty.

The Zenger case did not change the law—at least not in any direct or immediate way—but Hamilton's oration to the jury was widely reprinted and eagerly devoured, not only throughout the colonies but even in Mother England. The case led the way to an open and vigorous press in the colonies, which in turn led the way to revolution. In the end, the principle of free press advanced by Hamilton was embodied, long after his death in 1741, in the First Amendment to the Constitution—a charter drafted and signed, like the Declaration of Independence before it, in the Pennsylvania State House (later dubbed Independence Hall) on land formerly owned by Hamilton himself and sold to the province as a location for the building.

There are just two problems with the theory that Andrew Hamilton was the model for *Philadelphia lawyer* as a term meaning a really smart lawyer. First, there is no evidence for it. And second, on the evidence we have, it is not plausible.

The earliest known use of the term with this meaning occurred in 1788—almost half a century after Hamilton's death—in a letter reporting on the "Manners and Fashions of London" published in a Philadelphia magazine. Referring either to London generally or to its legal community in particular (the letter is unclear on the point), the writer noted, "They have a proverb here, which I do not know how to account for;—in speaking of a difficult point, they say, *it would puzzle a Philadelphia lawyer.*" (The same pattern is still in use; today we read, for example, "The form for collecting from the Microsoft settlement . . . would baffle a Philadelphia lawyer.")[3] That 1788 use was far too remote in time from the 1730s, when Hamilton was a celebrity, to suggest a connection. Moreover, the nature of the usage actually suggests a lack of connection: it refers to a generic Philadelphia lawyer rather than intimating that a particular Philadelphia lawyer was regarded as especially astute. (Compare the modern expression "It doesn't take a rocket scientist," referring to scientists in general, with "You'd have to be an Einstein to understand it," invoking the brilliance of a specific scientist.)

Most significant of all, however, is that Hamilton occupied an entirely different world from the Philadelphia of 1788, when this expression was first noticed. In 1788, Hamilton was a historical figure from a bygone colonial era; since his time the world had undergone a revolution unimaginable in Hamilton's day, with Philadelphia as its political heart. Beginning thirty-three years after Hamilton's death, Philadelphia had become, in turn, the seat of the First Continental Congress (which took the first united political action by the colonies against England), the first seat of the Second Continental Congress (which shepherded America through the Revolutionary War), and, upon independence, the first seat of Congress under the Articles of Confederation. And just the year before this phrase was reported from London, Philadelphia had been the site of the greatest conclave of legal minds the New World had yet seen: the Constitutional Convention of 1787, which produced the Constitution that was at that very moment going through the process of ratification by the states. Many in London would still have been resentful about the loss of the colonies and dismissive of the American political experiment; but if there were any Londoners inclined to think of American lawyers as particularly clever or wily, they would not have been harking back to the antediluvian days of Andrew Hamilton but referring to the bright lights of the day—the Philadelphia lawyers of their own time.

JEC

pierce the corporate veil

Law students get a verbal jolt when taking a class on business organizations. There, in the middle of officers, directors, and the Securities Exchange Act of 1934, is a sexy little metaphor: piercing the corporate veil. *Veil* conjures up images of chaste women or of courtesans who arouse their audiences by hiding behind a diaphanous veil (either way, piercing or lifting the veil has sexual overtones). Both *pierce* and *veil* have been used metaphorically for centuries—but how did they come to be associated with the mundane world of corporations?

A business corporation is a company formed for the purpose of making money for its owner or owners, whose proportional interest in the company and its profits is represented by shares of stock. A joint enterprise of this sort can accomplish things no individual could, but only if others can deal with it as a single entity instead of having to deal with the individual owners, of whom there may be millions. For many purposes, therefore, the law treats the corporation as if it were a person itself, independent of its owner-shareholders. This legal fiction makes it possible for corporations to own property, enter into contracts, sue and be sued, and be taxed, all in their own name.

In most business situations this is a convenience for all concerned. In one situation, it is not: if the business gets into a position where it doesn't have enough money or assets to cover its debts, then the creditors would like to be able to collect directly from the owners. After all, the corporation is just a stand-in for the owners; everything it does is on their behalf. They share in the corporation's profits; they should share in its debts. But the possibility of becoming liable for all the debts of a large company—or even for just a proportionate share of them—might discourage investment. Therefore, along with artificial personhood for corporations, legislatures have granted limited liability to corporations and their shareholders. This normally limits the corporation's liability for its obligations to the value of its assets, leaving the owners free of any responsibility for the debts or wrongdoings of their enterprise. At worst, if the company goes bankrupt, the value of the shareholders' stock might drop to zero; but even then, they get to keep all the profits they have received over the years, while the losses from unpaid obligations of the company are borne by those who did business with the company or were injured by it or—in the case of environmental disasters—by the public at large.

This legal barrier preventing creditors or injured parties from seeking compensation from the corporation's owners—even when there is only one owner, and that owner is a large, rich corporation itself and could easily make good on the debt—is referred to as the *corporate veil*. Occasionally, however, for reasons of fairness, a person with a claim against a corporation will be allowed to reach beyond the company's own inadequate assets to the assets of the shareholders or of a related corporation. This might occur, for example, if the claimant was misled about whom he or she was dealing with, or the corporation was deliberately underfunded by the shareholders. There is no fixed rule for when this will be allowed; the courts approach the issue flexibly as a matter of equity (see CHANCELLOR'S FOOT). When it does happen, courts allow the claimant to *pierce the corporate veil*. (In England, lawyers often speak instead of *lifting the corporate veil*—a less violent way of reaching the otherwise unreachable.)

The vividly visual terms *pierce* and *veil* are both natural choices for metaphorical use, and were used together at least as long ago as 1589, when poet Thomas Lodge wrote of nightfall, when the moon "with radient light begins / To pierce the vaile of silence with her beames." And American lawyers have put *corporations* and *veils* together practically since the country began. In a U.S. Supreme Court argument back in 1809, a lawyer attempted to discredit his adversary's position, characterizing that argument as saying that "you may raise the veil which the corporate name interposes, and see who stands behind it." (Perhaps he should not have been so eloquent: the court ruled in favor of the adversary.) In 1840, the governor of Michigan urged the legislature to protect the public from banks that issued worthless paper money: "Take from them . . . the corporate veil, which now encourages, and at the same time, conceals and protects their frauds and villainies." An 1895 tax treatise spoke of circumstances where a court might "look through the corporate veil." In 1901 a law review writer warned that "sheltered from public scorn by a corporate veil, men not infrequently commit acts of unrighteousness which otherwise they would not dare commit."[1]

It is unclear who put *pierce, veils,* and *corporations* together for the first time. The combination is so natural it may have happened independently over and over. We do know that it was a man named I. Maurice Wormser, a law professor and corporate lawyer, who made *pierce the corporate veil* a popular phrase. His 1912 law review article, "Piercing the Veil of Corporate Entity," is jam-packed with metaphors, many based on the image of the corporation as a person and the corporate form as its clothing: garments of little Red Riding Hood's grandmother, cloaks, the veil of corporate existence, disguises, the corporate robe, and legal armor-plate. In addition to being pierced, Wormser's veil is drawn aside, torn aside, penetrated, shaken aside, brushed aside, stripped off, and lifted. But the most prominent image was the one in the title, and when Wormser republished his article in a book fifteen years later, courts began to talk with some regularity about piercing the corporate veil.[2]

Today lawyers, judges, and academics use the phrase routinely. A search of the LEXIS legal database of U.S. cases, just for the ten years from 2000 through 2009, reveals more than five thousand state and federal cases referring to piercing the corporate veil. Wormser would no doubt be pleased that his metaphor is still thriving after a century of use. As a vigorous advocate of limits on the concept of "corporate personality," however, he

Corporate Entity

In the 1920s, the young poet Archibald MacLeish, having been indoctrinated in the concept of the corporation as an independent legal being a few years earlier as a brilliant student at Harvard Law School, put pen to paper to ridicule the idea. Almost fifty years later, addressing an assemblage of powerful lawyers at the eighty-fifth anniversary banquet of the Harvard Law Review, the now celebrated poet was unrepentant. Considering the financial involvement of corporations in politics, he said, "I have begun to wonder whether I was not too timid" in mocking, all those years before, "the legal conception of the corporate entity—the enchanting fiction that a corporation has an existence of its own distinct from the existence of its employees, its officers, and even its owners." The poem in question, published in 1926, takes the form (up to the sarcastic concluding couplet) of articles of incorporation of a hypothetical art-reproduction company called the Oklahoma Ligno and Lithograph Co. (A lignograph is a wood engraving.)

CORPORATE ENTITY
The Oklahoma Ligno and Lithograph Co
Of Maine doing business in Delaware Tennessee
Missouri Montana Ohio and Idaho
With a corporate existence distinct from that of the
Secretary Treasurer President Directors or
Majority stockholder being empowered to acquire
As principal agent trustee licensee licensor
Any or all in part or in parts or entire

Etchings impressions engravings engravures prints
Paintings oil-paintings canvases portraits vignettes
Tableaux ceramics relievos insculptures tints
Art-treasures or masterpieces complete or in sets—

The Oklahoma Ligno and Lithograph Co
Weeps at a nude by Michael Angelo.

From *Streets in the Moon,* by Archibald MacLeish (New York: Houghton Mifflin Co., copyright © 1926), 94; reprinted (sans the dash) in *Collected Poems, 1917–1982,* by Archibald MacLeish, copyright © 1985 by The Estate of Archibald MacLeish, 88. Reprinted here by permission of Houghton Mifflin Harcourt Publishing Company. All rights reserved. The poet's remarks at the *Harvard Law Review* banquet on March 25, 1972, were published as Archibald MacLeish, "Apologia," 85 *Harvard Law Review* 1505, 1507 (1972).

would certainly be shocked at the extremes to which that concept has been taken in the twenty-first century, as in the controversial 5–4 Supreme Court decision in 2010 holding that the freedom of speech clause of the First Amendment gives even the largest profit-making corporation—with untold millions of dollars to spend—the same rights as ordinary "persons" to promote or oppose candidates for public office. Justice John Paul Stevens, writing for the dissenters in that case, pointed out that "corporations are different from human beings," and are given special legal benefits such as limited liability that make it possible for them to amass resources far beyond anything a real person could ever achieve. "Their 'personhood,'" Stevens said, "often serves as a useful legal fiction. But they are not themselves members of 'We the People' by whom and for whom our Constitution was established."[3] As Wormser put it in 1927, the legal concept of the corporate entity "as a personality, separate and distinct from its stockholders," is a fiction that "must be employed with common sense and applied so as to promote the ends of justice. It must not be converted into a fetish. . . . There is always danger, when a fiction (whether corporate or otherwise) becomes so deeply rooted in the case law, that judges no longer remember its object and purpose, and apply the fiction to an extent where they refuse to consider and to penetrate into the actual facts behind it."[4]

EGT

play the race card

The phrase *play the race card* swept through the media—and into the consciousness of millions of Americans—during the O. J. Simpson murder case of 1994–95. Simpson was a football legend, a movie star, and African American. He was charged in the bloody double murder of his glamorous ex-wife Nicole Brown Simpson and her friend Ronald L. Goldman, both white. The prosecution claimed that the murder was motivated by sexual jealousy. The defense claimed that the prosecution—or at least the conduct of the police officer who claimed to have found the most dramatic piece of evidence, a bloody glove near the Simpson mansion—was motivated by racial hatred.

The bodies—and the glove—were found on the night of June 12–13, 1994. Simpson hired Los Angeles attorney Robert L. Shapiro, whose roster of celebrity clients over the years had included professional athletes, rock stars, and even, in the case that first brought him to prominence, porn star Linda Lovelace. Shapiro assembled a team of high-powered lawyers including Alan Dershowitz and F. Lee Bailey, both of whom had been instrumental in gaining acquittals for famous clients accused of the murder or attempted murder of their wives. The media promptly christened it the Dream Team.

Within barely a month, the lawyers had unearthed negative information about the officer who came up with the glove, Mark Fuhrman, and despite some internal disagreement over how much to make of this, had begun leaking the information to the press and floating the idea that Fuhrman had framed Simpson. Jeffrey Toobin, in the first of what would turn out to be many articles chronicling the case for the *New Yorker,* reported that "the defense will assert that Mark Fuhrman's motivation for framing O. J. Simpson is racism. 'This is a bad cop,' one defense lawyer told me. 'This is a racist cop.'" Toobin concluded: "By one reckoning, the new strategy may simply be a sign of desperation; the race card may be the only one in Simpson's hand. But it appears that his defense team will be playing it."[1]

Toobin's article hit the newsstands on about July 18, 1994. By July 19 the *Daily Telegraph* of London was sporting the headline "Simpson's

Lawyers to Play Race Card."[2] Within days the phrase appeared, in one variation or another, in newspapers across the United States.

In the months of drama that followed, race did indeed come to play a major, some say decisive, role in the case—and a divisive role on the defense team. Shapiro, who favored a less racially oriented approach to the case, was displaced as lead attorney by one of the lawyers he had recruited, Johnnie Cochran. Although Cochran had not yet joined the team when defense lawyers first planted the story of racial animus, once on board he seized upon the issue and made it a centerpiece of his strategy. After a nine-month televised trial that kept much of America glued to the screen, Simpson was acquitted on October 3, 1995. In a television interview that night, Shapiro, who had remained on the team in a subordinate position and had dutifully kept his silence, finally vented the disgust he had been harboring over the racial strategy, capping more than a year of public discussion about the "race card" with this escalation of the metaphor: "Not only did we play the race card, we dealt it from the bottom of the deck."[3]

But while the Simpson trial popularized this phrase in America, for the origins of the metaphor we must look much further back.

Card playing—with its mixture of chance and skill, bluffing and forthrightness, strategy and blunder, winning and losing—imitates life. This may account for its lasting appeal. Card games are believed to have existed for well over a millennium; they have been played in Europe since at least the fourteenth century. Card-playing metaphors have probably been in use since the day the first card game was played. We can play our cards close to the vest, tip our hand, lay our cards on the table. We can keep a poker face, have an ace up our sleeve, stack the deck. When someone leads, we follow suit. Just when the other side thinks we're done for, we play our trump card.

And this last example brings us close to the phrase at hand. The analogy between playing a card and making a particular strategic move in life—or in law—has proved particularly powerful. You can play your cards right, play your best card, play your last card. Of course, your best is sometimes not good enough; as one court sadly remarked in terminating a mother's parental rights, "In a metaphor, Emily was not dealt a good hand in life and has played her few cards very poorly."[4]

The metaphor is particularly well suited to the structured, rule-based, adversarial setting of the courtroom, where, as noted in a nineteenth-century

decision, once a jury is empaneled both sides must "play out their cards."[5]
It is therefore common in judicial contexts to encounter remarks like "In
short, the defendant's trial counsel played every card available to the defendant."[6]

Indeed, it was in the context of a legal matter that this card-playing
metaphor may first have been expanded to include a non-card-playing
term. In the first decade of the nineteenth century, a British trader named
John Bellingham encountered legal problems that landed him in a Russian
prison. When he finally made it back to England he petitioned the prime
minister, Spencer Perceval—among many others in the government—for
compensation on the ground that Britain's ambassador to Russia at the
time, Lord Granville Leveson-Gower, had improperly failed to intervene
on his behalf. Bellingham's petitions were politely but invariably denied,
and on Monday, May 11, 1812, he wrote to a friend, "Every thing, in point
of law, is in my favour; but Mr. Perceval and the Ministry have shewn
themselves more inclined to favour Lord Gower, than to do justice to me:
however, as I am resolved on having justice in case of need, I will very
shortly play a court card to compel them to finish the game." That afternoon Bellingham took in an exhibition of watercolors at the European
Museum, then strolled over to the House of Commons, waited a short
while for Mr. Perceval to arrive, and shot him dead. Two days later Bellingham had his DAY IN COURT—literally—at the Old Bailey, where, speaking in his own defense, he finally had the opportunity he apparently craved
to lay out his grievance in full for all the world to hear. The other players
then played out the game exactly as Bellingham had cryptically predicted:
the jury found him guilty, the chief justice sentenced him to death, and on
May 18, a week to the day after the assassination, he was hanged, "the exe-
cutioner being below pulling his legs, that he might die quickly."[7]

Linguistically, Bellingham was ahead of his time: it was at least another
three-quarters of a century before non-card-playing terms began appearing with any frequency in such an expression. Since then, the field has
been open to the substitution of virtually any word suggesting the subject
or nature of a strategic ploy—though as Bellingham's example illustrates
only too well, the meaning always depends on the context. A random
sampling from legal contexts in the years before the Simpson trial includes playing the "constitutional card," the "obscenity card," the "court

card," and even, in a discussion of pre–Civil War racial politics, the "mulatto card."[8]

The particular phrase "play the race card" apparently arose first in England, where at least one isolated occurrence can be found as early as 1974.[9] It became a staple of British political discourse in the late 1980s, but remained virtually unknown in the United States until the 1990s, when it finally began to appear with some frequency in contexts ranging from racially charged school financing issues in Boston ("Flynn also rapped the committee for 'playing the race card,' by confronting about 250 teachers with the possibility of layoffs") to debates over AFFIRMATIVE ACTION (" 'It's in the best interests of the Democrats to have Bush sign this bill' to prevent the GOP from 'playing the race card,' he said") to the hotly disputed nomination of Clarence Thomas to the Supreme Court of the United States ("Mr. Danforth [Republican Senator John C. Danforth], who has acted as Judge Thomas's sponsor on Capitol Hill this week, accused the black lawmakers of 'playing the race card' in much the same way Republicans have exploited the quota issue in the civil rights debate").[10] So when the Simpson case came along, the phrase had recently gained a foothold in American usage. It was just waiting to be picked up and popularized.

JEC

politically correct

In the twentieth century the phrase *politically correct* evolved from a term of approbation into one of opprobrium, and from an ad hoc juxtaposition of words into a vogue phrase complete with its own abbreviation: *PC*.

The first person known to have put these words together was the first Justice of the Supreme Court of the United States, James Wilson—a signer of the Declaration of Independence, a principal drafter of the Constitution, and probably the only sitting Supreme Court Justice ever to be put in jail. (In his last two years of life, while still a member of the Court, he was hounded by creditors and twice imprisoned for debt: first in New Jersey and then in North Carolina.) In 1793, in a seminal case on the relation between the states and the new federal government, Wilson argued that the national government derives its power not from the separate states but rather from the people of all the states together, as expressed in the opening words of the Constitution: "We the People of the United States . . ." Wilson bemoaned the imprecision of conventional language that made it sound as if the fundamental political unit in the country were the state rather than the individual: "Sentiments and expressions of this inaccurate kind prevail in our common, even in our convivial, language," he wrote. "Is a toast asked? 'The United States,' instead of the 'People of the United States,' is the toast given. This is not *politically* correct"—in other words, not an accurate characterization of the political structure established by the Constitution.[1]

Although Justice Wilson happened to hit upon a wording that two centuries later would become a popular and controversial expression, in his day there was nothing particularly noteworthy about the phrase. It was routine in eighteenth- and nineteenth-century discourse to characterize favored political ideas and actions as *correct* or, more often, *right*, in all the connotations of those words—"accurate," "just," "appropriate," "expedient," "desirable," "in conformity with accepted norms." One reads, for example, of "a correct political creed" (1785), "the first correct and rational idea of a political constitution . . . recorded in history" (1790), or, conversely, "very incorrect ideas of the political compact" (1799).[2] The most influential use of such language occurred in 1786, when Benjamin Rush, an eminent Philadelphia physician and another signer of the Declaration of Independence, delivered an oration dedicated to Benjamin Franklin: "Nothing," he declared, "can be *politically right*, that is morally wrong; and no necessity can ever sanctify a law, that is contrary to equity."[3] The words were tailor-made for the antislavery movement in the next century, which had to contend with the prevailing view in nonslave states that the evil of slavery had to be accommodated as a matter of political expediency in order to maintain national unity and political tranquility. Dr. Rush's words were incorporated into Quaker antislavery resolutions and repeated in tract after tract.

In a young nation built upon revolutionary new political ideas, it was seen as essential to inculcate these ideas in the young. Thomas Jefferson had this in mind when, after his service as president, he founded the University of Virginia. In 1825, the year the university opened, he wrote, "I fear not to say that within twelve or fifteen years from this time, a majority of the rulers of our State will have been educated here. They shall carry hence the correct principles of our day." This concern for correct political thinking and indoctrination even found voice in fiction; in an 1847 tale by the Vermont lawyer, politician, educator, abolitionist, and part-time novelist Daniel P. Thompson, a candidate for a teaching position is asked, "What are your views of the propriety of instilling correct political principles into the minds of your pupils, who are the rising generation, and soon to wield the destinies of our glorious republic?"[4] Even though this was fiction, it shows that the issue of "political correctness" in education was by no means a new one when it became the source of controversy in the United States a century and a half later.

Well into the twentieth century, *politically right* and *politically correct* remained unambiguously positive terms. But the rise of totalitarianism, with its enforced adherence to rigid political dogma, cast them in a new light. One read that journalists in Hitler's Germany "must have a permit . . . granted only to pure 'Aryans' whose opinions are politically correct," and that the Soviet army was hampered because "Stalin has killed off or exiled hundreds or thousands of the older officers who, though they might not follow the Stalinist party line, knew far more about battle lines than some of the politically correct young zealots who have replaced them."[5]

In the 1970s the term *politically correct* reappeared in the United States among campaigners for a new political order that would, among other things, recognize the rights and contributions of blacks and women. A few on the extreme left probably used the phrase seriously, but among the majority of social activists during that period it had a distinctly wry quality. It was a convenient shorthand for "consistent with our political and social ideals" and thus useful in internal debates, but it was uttered with implicit quotation marks around it—and often with deliberate humor or even as an explicit criticism of rigidity or dogmatism.[6] In the 1980s, the phrase was picked up by conservatives as a shorthand for the liberal positions that they opposed and as a device for characterizing those positions as rigid, dogmatic, and intolerant.[7] In the 1990s, the conservative sense of "political correctness" was popularized by the public media and became the rallying cry for a widespread attack on efforts to root out offensive language and practices and to expand educational curricula to include cultures and perspectives that had traditionally been disregarded.

In the courts, "political correctness"—at least in speech—is still generally regarded as a good thing. The courts were unsympathetic to a doctor who, while performing surgery in the presence of an African American nursing instructor whose duties required her to be there, allegedly kept up a running commentary on race that included such remarks as "You don't see 'no colored allowed' signs posted on doors anymore. I hate all this politically correct crap. . . . A pure white race, that's how it should be. Not zebras!" (The hospital, on the other hand, responded to the instructor's complaints by terminating the program of which she was a part.) And a much-cited federal appellate decision noted that racial discrimination has become harder to prove because, though no one would claim that discrimination no longer exists, at least the kind of overt racism exhibited by that doctor is largely a thing of the past: "In today's politically correct workplace environment such admissions are rarely, if ever, made or encountered."[8]

In most contexts, however, *political correctness* now carries a negative connotation. An education professor, searching for the words to criticize history textbooks that fail to deal in an honest and forthright way with racial issues, describes them as "politically correct multicultural mush."[9] Perhaps the ultimate example of this reversal of meaning was provided by Lynne V. Cheney, the chairman (her word) of the National Endowment for the Humanities in the administration of President George H. W. Bush when the Endowment commissioned a body of educators to devise national standards for the teaching of history in primary and secondary schools. When the draft standards were finally released, she hated them. In a statement that would have confounded both Thomas Jefferson (for whom *correct* meant "ideologically desirable") and James Wilson (for whom it meant "accurate"), Cheney said, "I've received dozens of phone calls from people . . . worried that the standards represent not only a politically correct version of history, but a version of history that's not true."[10]

JEC

posse

What is more American than the posse? A fixture of movie westerns since Thomas Edison founded the genre in 1903 with *The Great Train Robbery*, the posse—part upstanding citizenry, part lynch mob—symbolizes the struggle for law and order in the Wild West.

Yet neither the word nor the concept is an American creation. In Anglo-Saxon times, the able-bodied men of each shire in England were obliged, at the king's summons, to rally to the defense of the land under the leadership of the sheriff or another local official. After the Norman Conquest in 1066, shires came to be referred to by the French word *counte* or *countee* (literally, "the domain of a count"), which became the English *county*. The sheriff, as the king's representative, was expected to call upon the men of the county as needed to keep the peace. Statutes to this effect, written in French, referred to the manpower available for this purpose by such phrases as "la force du Countee" (the strength of the county) or "le poair de Counte" (the power of the county).[1] In Latin this was rendered as *posse comitatus*— *posse* (power), a noun use of the classical Latin verb that meant "to be able," plus *comitātūs* (of the county).

By the end of the seventeenth century the phrase *posse comitatus*—or *posse* for short—was established in the English language, and the duty of the sheriff to summon a posse when needed (and of the populace to respond when summoned) was established in English law.

The Anglo-Saxon *sheriff,* the French *county,* and the Latin *posse* were all incorporated into American law and public administration as part of the country's English heritage. And just as each county sheriff has the power to raise a posse to enforce state law within the county, under federal law the United States marshal for each federal judicial district is authorized to raise a posse to enforce federal law within the district. Posses have been an essential resource for law enforcement in times and places where there was no organized police force; but they have also been a lightning rod for controversy.

The most infamous use of a federal posse occurred on June 2, 1854, when the U.S. marshal for the District of Massachusetts employed federal military troops in the state as a posse to enforce the Fugitive Slave Act of

1850. A formidable body of men and arms was arrayed to hold the enraged citizenry of Boston at bay while the escaped slave Anthony Burns, whose case had galvanized the city, was paraded to the ship that would carry him back to Old Virginia—and to certain cruelty.[2]

After the Civil War, the tables were turned. In the period of Reconstruction, federal troops stationed in southern states were called upon to help enforce the rights of former slaves. But the Reconstruction ideal of ensuring full citizenship rights for blacks was doomed. The army was spread too thin, southern resistance was too pervasive, and northern support for the rights of blacks was too evanescent. The death knell was struck in the presidential election of 1876. A bitter dispute over the counting of votes from three southern states was finally resolved just a week before Inauguration Day by means of a compromise between northern Republicans (the party of Lincoln) and southern Democrats, which gave the presidency to Republican Rutherford B. Hayes in return for assurances that all remaining federal troops would be removed from the South. Hayes was inaugurated in March 1877, and in April he withdrew the troops—bringing Reconstruction to an end and abandoning southern blacks to generations of oppression, discrimination, and disfranchisement.

The next year, still bitter about Reconstruction, the Democrats who controlled the House of Representatives refused to agree to any further appropriation for maintenance of the army except with a rider making it unlawful, with limited exceptions, "to employ any part of the Army of the United States, as a posse comitatus, or otherwise, for the purpose of executing the laws." In effect, this meant that any federal or state law enforcement official in need of military assistance would have to rely upon the state militia (in 1903 confusingly renamed the National Guard)—which in the South in those days could be counted on to remain loyal to the white power structure. This rider, slightly reworded, is still in force, and is known as the Posse Comitatus Act.[3] Despite its origin as a device to ensure that the federal government would be impotent to deal with state suppression of black rights, it is now almost universally viewed as a valuable bulwark against military involvement in domestic matters—protecting civilians from military control and the military from diversion of resources into matters unrelated to defense.

The unspoken assumption in 1878 that local southern posses and troops would invariably support whites against blacks proved not always to be true. Even in one of the most infamous cases of racial injustice in American history—the 1931 case of the Scottsboro Boys, nine black youths falsely accused and wrongly convicted of raping two white women—an Alabama posse barricaded itself in the jail where the prisoners were held and, together with the sheriff and his deputies, held off a lynch mob until troops from the Alabama National Guard arrived to disperse what remained of the crowd.[4]

The classic American posse, however, remains the western posse—the kind we see in the movies, the kind associated with legendary lawmen like Bat Masterson and his friend Wyatt Earp. But while the posses were real, the movie images are not. Wyatt Earp was not always the ideal lawman portrayed by Burt Lancaster in John Sturges's 1957 movie *Gunfight at the O.K. Corral*. His celebrated shootout—which, to be historically accurate, should be called "The Gunfight in the Vacant Lot Beside Fly's Boardinghouse a Few Doors Down from the Driveway Leading to the Back of the O.K. Corral" —was in reality an ambiguous event, which pro- and anti-Earp partisans have been arguing about since the moment the smoke cleared.

Five of the six Earp brothers—James, Virgil, Wyatt, Morgan, and Warren—along with Wyatt's best friend, Doc Holliday, found their way to the mining town of Tombstone in the extreme southeast corner of the Arizona Territory in 1879 and 1880, and quickly became major figures in the small town. Virgil soon was serving as both the Tombstone town marshal (essentially chief of police) and the deputy U.S. marshal for southeastern Arizona, and all of his brothers except James had roles in law enforcement. In ranches out in the countryside was a group known as the Cowboys, who made their living mainly by rustling cattle. Within two years it was clear to everyone that the two groups were headed for a showdown.

It happened on October 26, 1881. The town, in an effort to instill a degree of public safety and civil peace, had banned the carrying of firearms. On this day, a group of Cowboys—some of whom had been openly making threats against the Earps and Holliday—refused to park their weapons. Virgil Earp formed a posse consisting of himself, brothers Wyatt and Morgan, and Holliday to disarm the Cowboys or, failing that, to have it out with them. As soon as the two groups faced each other, gunfire rang out. In thirty seconds it was over: three of the four members of the posse were

VIRGIL EARP, 1885

WYATT EARP, ABOUT 1885

JAMES EARP, 1881

MORGAN EARP, 1881

The four Earp brothers who were present in Tombstone, Arizona, on the day of the shootout. James, a businessman, was not directly involved in the hostilities between his brothers and the Cowboys; Doc Holliday, who was, made a fourth for Virgil's posse. This gallery of family photos is from the 1931 biography of Wyatt Earp written with the subject's cooperation: *Wyatt Earp: Frontier* wounded (only Wyatt was unscathed), and three of the four Cowboys were dead.[5]

The surviving Cowboy pressed murder charges against the Earps and Holliday, but after a month-long hearing a judge gave the lawmen the benefit of the doubt, holding that while Virgil had been "injudicious" in choosing for his posse men who had a personal feud with the Cowboys, it was understandable that he chose "staunch and true friends, upon whose courage, coolness and fidelity he could depend" in carrying out what was, after all, his duty to enforce the law. In any event, the judge decided that the Cowboys had reached for their guns first, and ordered the four defendants released.[6]

Far from settling the matter, this outcome inflamed the Cowboy faction to exact their own form of justice. They shot Virgil Earp, crippling him for life; they killed Morgan Earp. Wyatt responded by having himself appointed to replace Virgil as deputy U.S. marshal and, backed up by a posse consisting of his brother Warren, Holliday, and other supporters, shooting Morgan's alleged killer to death at point-blank range, then tracking down and killing at least two other Cowboys. In December 1881—even before all these shootings—the acting governor of the Arizona Territory had asked President Chester A. Arthur to seek repeal of the Posse Comitatus Act so that the military posted nearby could be called in to impose peace. The president did so, but Congress ignored his request.

The violence finally wound down in 1882 when Wyatt Earp, who had joined the first posse in this story and led the second, found himself being chased by a third posse—this one armed with a warrant to arrest him for murder—and had the wisdom to call it quits and leave the territory. He ultimately found his way to Los Angeles, cultivated his image as a straight-shooting lawman who never killed a man who didn't deserve it, and died in 1929, at the age of eighty, with nary a blemish on his body or his legal record for all his gun battles.

JEC

Marshal (Boston: Houghton Mifflin) by Stuart N. Lake. (Courtesy of Carolyn Lake. Photograph by Enrique Ortiz, courtesy of Butler Library, Columbia University.)

pound of flesh

The metaphor *pound of flesh* refers to a technically legal but unreasonable demand for payment. The phrase comes from Shakespeare's *Merchant of Venice*. In the play, Antonio (the Venetian merchant of the title) agrees to guarantee a loan so that his friend Bassanio can court Portia, a rich heiress. They seek the loan from Shylock, a wealthy Jewish moneylender, although there is no love lost between him and Antonio. Indeed, Shylock notes that Antonio has kicked and spit on him for being Jewish: "You call me misbeliever, cut-throat dog, and spet upon my Jewish gaberdine . . . . You . . . did void your rheum upon my beard, and foot me as you spurn a stranger cur over your threshold." Antonio, despite asking a favor, is unapologetic about his behavior: "I am as like to call thee so again, to spet on thee again, to spurn thee too."[1]

Shylock does make the loan, but only on condition that if he is not repaid on time, Antonio will forfeit "an equal pound of your fair flesh, to be cut off and taken in what part of your body pleaseth me." When Antonio fails to make timely payment, Shylock takes him to court to demand enforcement of the penalty under the terms of their contract, insisting, "The pound of flesh which I demand of him is dearly bought; 'tis mine, and I will have it." The Duke of Venice, presiding over the trial, calls in a young lawyer (Portia in disguise) to help rule on the issue. Portia finds the contract to be enforceable but interprets it strictly: the agreement was only for flesh, not blood. Shylock can have his pound of flesh only if he can cut it off without shedding Antonio's blood. Because this is not possible, Shylock must forfeit what he is due under the contract. Worse, he loses half his property and is forced to convert to Christianity.[2]

To a modern reader, this is a disturbing tale. The play's treatment of Jews and its stereotyping of Shylock as a greedy moneylender were shaped by the social and religious beliefs of England in the 1590s, when Shakespeare was writing *Merchant of Venice*. Stereotypes at that time painted the Jewish people as obsessed with money and vengeful against Christians; the more extreme (but not uncommon) prejudices blamed Jews for the plague and accused them of using the blood of Christian children for their rituals.

Acting on such religious hatred, King Edward I had expelled all Jews from England in 1290 (and seized their property); they were not allowed to return until well after Shakespeare's death. Thus neither Shakespeare nor his audience would have had openly Jewish acquaintances to temper the prevailing prejudices. Further, anti-Semitism was rampant throughout Europe. Venice, the setting for Shakespeare's play, was one of the few places where Jews were allowed to live openly, and even there they were confined to a ghetto. Lending money (and charging interest) was often one of the few occupations open to Jews—who were then despised for being moneylenders. Nor did Shakespeare invent the idea of a pound of flesh as payment; the motif portraying Jewish lenders as heartless users of that form of guaranty appears in tales that predate *The Merchant of Venice*.[3]

A heated dispute continues to rage as to whether Shakespeare's art ameliorates the play's anti-Semitism. Elements of the characterization clearly reinforce odious stereotypes, and Shylock is given virtually all the qualities that Elizabethan playgoers associated with Jews. Yet the Christian characters in the play also behave abominably, and Shakespeare gives Shylock an eloquent speech emphasizing his humanity:

Hath not a Jew eyes? hath not a Jew hands, organs, dimensions, senses, affections, passions? fed with the same food, hurt with the same weapons, subject to the same diseases, healed by the same means, warmed and cooled by the same winter and summer, as a Christian is?—if you prick us, do we not bleed? if you tickle us, do we not laugh? if you poison us, do we not die? and if you wrong us, shall we not revenge?[4]

Nevertheless, it is hard to escape an overall impression that Shylock is a personification of the anti-Semitic stereotype of Shakespeare's age, albeit a more fully human character than those created by Shakespeare's contemporaries.

The phrase *pound of flesh* is no longer confined to fictional trials, however, and in its modern usages is not meant to be taken literally. It appears frequently in reported legal decisions, originally in cases involving the lending of money. It was only 1807 when a U.S. case first used the metaphor. In resolving a breach of contract dispute regarding a land sale, the court considered the remedy sought by the plaintiff: that the defendant must forfeit both his interest in the land and all the money he had already paid. The court found this to be inequitable and likened it to "the exaction of the pound of flesh by a Shylock, and the enforcing of a hard and unconscientious bargain, at which the feelings of every honest mind would revolt."[5]

In more recent times, however, use of *pound of flesh* is more problematic, as courts may infer an anti-Semitic meaning when borrowers' lawyers fling the accusation at lenders. In a 2009 case challenging the enforcement of a judgment, the debtor's brief quoted extensively from the trial scene in *Merchant of Venice.* The judge advised counsel to remove such rhetoric from future briefs: "Counsel . . . may not be aware that *The Merchant of Venice* is a play known for its anti-Semitic tone. . . . The Court takes this opportunity to advise the [debtors] that such an introduction, complete with references to 'Jew,' 'Christian blood,' and 'pound[s] of flesh,' may well distract from the substance of their argument, and suggests that they would be better served by exclusion of such inflammatory references in their briefing."[6]

But *pound of flesh* is so versatile that it is used to describe everything from hamburgers to the death penalty. In a case involving McDonald's, for instance, the court worried that the winning party might get not full recovery but only "a quarter pound of flesh." And in one of the many capital punishment cases in which the phrase has appeared, the U.S. Supreme Court ruled in 1947 that Louisiana could try a second time to electrocute a prisoner (after the electric chair failed to kill him on the first try) without imposing "cruel and unusual punishment." Concurring in this 5–4 decision, Justice Felix Frankfurter stated that "this Court must abstain from interference with State action no matter how strong one's personal feeling of revulsion against a State's insistence on its pound of flesh."[7]

Beyond case law, contemporary writers use *pound of flesh* to characterize anything taken from the unwilling, especially if they regard it as excessive. Hence they say that the government, in collecting taxes, is exacting its pound of flesh, that credit card companies demanding inflated interest rates and fees seek a pound of flesh, that payday lenders whose impoverished customers never escape from the endless cycle of renewals and fees also demand their pound of flesh. Nor is the phrase confined to monetary payments.

Critics wanting to embarrass politicians are said to seek a pound of flesh, as are prosecutors who charge political or business leaders with corruption. In short, the phrase thrives today as a rhetorical device to taint an action that is legally proper as unsavory, cruel, or disproportionate. A popular authority or claimant may collect what is owed, but the unpopular are just after that pound of flesh.

EGT

rainmaker

In 1775 two gentlemen—a trader and a surveyor—who had lived and traveled among the Choctaw, Chickasaw, and other indigenous peoples of southeastern North America, independently published books describing the cultures they had observed. These books introduced the English-speaking world to the personages revered in those cultures for their apparent power to bring about rainfall. The authors referred to them as *rain-makers* or *rainmakers*—a literal translation (or "loan translation"; see GREEN CARD) of their native titles, as in the Choctaw *umba* (rain) *ikbi* (maker).[1] In the nineteenth century the term was applied to tribal practitioners of the art of producing rain in Africa—the focus of a great deal of attention from missionaries—and also to individuals who claimed to have scientific methods or theories for causing rainfall. By the end of the century there were so many charlatans roaming the country claiming to be scientific "rainmakers" that in 1897 one paper actually used the term to *mean* "charlatan," "huckster," or "con man": referring to a presidential appointee who insisted on promoting a proposed international currency agreement that the paper regarded as a political sham and manifestly impossible to achieve, the paper derided him as a "financial rain maker." The latter part of the twentieth century brought new uses for the term. By 1960 it was being applied to pilots who attempted to induce rain by seeding clouds. Soon thereafter the "rain" to be induced was stretched from literal to metaphorical—from the water essential to agrarian culture to the money and contacts craved by modern business. In 1970 the *Wall Street Journal* referred to "lobbyists and other influence peddlers—'rainmakers,' in the

Washington jargon—[who] may brag of having Senator X or Official Y in their pocket."[2]

By 1978, this new sense of the term had entered the realm of law. Reporting on the business and culture of the nation's top law firms, *Fortune* magazine noted that for a partner to reach the highest stratum within the firm, "it helps to be a 'rainmaker,' who brings in a lot of business." But the concept of a partner who specializes in obtaining clients—as distinguished from actually doing their legal work—long antedates the arrival of this colorful label. The earlier term was the prosaic *business getter*. As early as 1908, a practitioner observed that "in nearly every large firm in our great cities the indispensable partner is 'the business getter.'" An extended 1925 satirical sketch describes the business-getter as a type that "has waxed and swelled, until his work constitutes a profession in itself, and he bestrides the legal world like a colossus"; technically a lawyer, "actually, he is a peripatetic electric signboard, a prospectus that walks like a man, a barker with a modulated voice, a glorified sandwich-man, a solicitor in more senses than one, broadcasting the virtues of his law firm in waves more subtle than those of Marconi." Describing senior corporate lawyers in 1933, the legal realist scholar Karl Llewellyn observed: "Above all, he is, and he is valued as, a business-*getter*. The measure of him is the business he can summon from the vasty corporation deep. He is to attract more orders for services than he or twenty like him can supply. . . . He cashes in, then, as an enterpriser, putting his own label on the work of others."[3]

Researching large Chicago firms in about 1980, sociologist Robert Nelson encountered a humorous folk categorization of big-firm lawyers into "the finders, the minders, and the grinders"—those who acquire new clients, those who attend to existing ones, and those who grind out the work product. By 1986, this is described as an "old saw."[4] A few years later some accounts add to this triad a fourth rhyming term, *binders,* that is less steady in meaning: sometimes it refers to those who promote cohesion within the firm; sometimes it is a synonym for *minders*.[5] And occasionally, and less aptly, it replaces *finders*: the legal ethicist and law professor Geoffrey Hazard refers to "a trilogy familiar in professional jargon. The 'binders' attract the clients, the 'minders' supply the professional skills and a corps of 'grinders' does the supportive scut work."[6]

Both *rainmaker* and the *finders* trilogy appeared in the late 1970s just when the law firms were growing rapidly and entering an era of increased lateral mobility, more differentiation of partner rewards, and more visibility to the wider public and to each other. In this new, more competitive legal environment, in which law firms no longer could rely on enduring retainer relationships with large clients, business-getters were more valued than ever. A 1979 article on law-firm salaries quoted "a Chicago-based legal executive search consultant—also known as a headhunter" as stating that "the real push these days is for the 'rainmakers,' . . . who bring in the clients." The rise of the legal *headhunter*—another modern adaptation of an anthropological term—facilitated movement by lawyers from firm to firm. A Washington lawyer discerned "an era where talented lawyers with large books of business will be 'at play' . . . with firms bidding for their services. . . . Star lawyers are the new 'free agents' in our society, just like professional sports."[7] The term *book of business,* current in the insurance field since at least the 1960s, had entered law-firm jargon by the mid-1980s to describe client relationships and legal matters "controlled" by a particular partner, reflecting growing acceptance of the view that the legal profession is a business like any other.[8]

Twenty-first-century rainmakers enjoy continued ascendancy over their colleagues, but they may have to work harder and display greater talent than the business-getters of old. Professor Hazard detects a shift in the identity of rainmakers (the "binders" in his terminology): "In the old days, the binders were lawyers who had long-established relationships with long-term clients of the firm—the senior lawyers who took senior management of important clients down to the club and out to the golf course." But in the intensely competitive modern legal environment, the lawyers who attract and keep the biggest clients are stars distinguished by visibility, technical legal skills, and reputation for results rather than affability, seniority, or social eminence.[9]

Native American rainmakers may not have possessed supernatural powers, but the word *rainmaker* itself has a bewitching appeal. It has featured in the titles of innumerable books, plays, TV movies, animated shorts, and silent movies, and no less than five feature-length Hollywood films since the advent of the talkie, most notably the 1956 film *The Rainmaker,* starring

Burt Lancaster as an itinerant con man who almost magically changes the life of a lonely ranch girl played by Katharine Hepburn.[10] It was not until 1997, however, that such a movie came close to being about a rainmaker in the law-firm sense—and even then the title was ironic. The movie, based on John Grisham's 1995 novel *The Rainmaker,* revolved around an impecunious new law school graduate whose appeal as a character derives from the fact that he is the very antithesis of a celebrated or well-connected lawyer capable of attracting large amounts of business. However significant well-heeled business-getters are in the modern legal world, moviemakers know that they are not remotely as interesting as the Native American notables and charismatic con men of old, who promised real, honest-to-goodness, down-to-earth rain.

MG

rap

Rap is a very old and very versatile word. One of its uses comes from the world of slang about crime. You can take the rap (accept the blame), beat the rap (avoid conviction), or get stuck with a bum rap (be blamed even though innocent). A person who has a history with law enforcement will have a RAP SHEET (police record). These uses of *rap*, in the sense of a criminal charge or punishment, evolved gradually but naturally through the centuries and are now broadly used even outside the context of the criminal justice system.

In the beginning, *rap* was probably a word of echoic origin (it imitated the sound of the thing it represented). It referred to a blow to a person or sharp tap on an object. By the late sixteenth century, both senses were so well known that Shakespeare could use the confusion as a joke. In *The Taming of the Shrew*, Petruchio asks his servant Grumio to rap on a door for him, and in response Grumio pretends that Petruchio has asked to be hit:

PETRUCHIO: Here, sirrah Grumio, knock, I say.
GRUMIO: Knock, sir? Whom should I knock? Is there any man has rebused your worship?

PETRUCHIO: Villain, I say, knock me here soundly.

GRUMIO: Knock you here, sir? Why, sir, what am I, sir, that I should knock you here, sir?

PETRUCHIO: Villain, I say, knock me at this gate,
And rap me well, or I'll knock your knave's pate.

GRUMIO: My master is grown quarrelsome. I should knock you first,
And then I know after who comes by the worst.[1]

The effectiveness of a painful knock on the knuckles as a corrective for a minor misdeed—for example, when a child tries to grab a forbidden object—surely has been known from time immemorial. In the seventeenth century the phrase "rap on the knuckles" began to appear in print—first in the sense of an actual physical blow, but later as a common figurative expression for a rebuke or mild punishment. By the end of the eighteenth century the word *rap* alone was becoming sufficient in American usage to convey the idea of criticism or punishment or blame—"on the knuckles" being either too well understood to require saying or simply unnecessary to convey the sense of a rebuke. By the end of the nineteenth century, to *get the rap* for something was an American slang expression meaning "get the blame"—and the rebuke or reprimand that goes with it.

As the twentieth century began, *rap* in this relatively innocuous sense was absorbed into criminal slang and extended to the distinctly more serious misdeeds that are the subject of criminal law. In the underworld culture, *rap* meant not just blame for some minor matter but accusation of a crime; when used in the sense of "punishment," it meant not just a rebuke but a stretch in prison.

Once established in the fertile soil of underworld slang, *rap* was easily combined with other terms to generate new slang expressions, to the endless fascination of the popular press. A 1911 article about a prominent pickpocket noted that he was known for "never deserting a member of his 'mob' when such member would fall into the grip of the police. He has always sent for a lawyer to look after the defense, and has supplied his unfortunate associates with every possible help in an endeavor to beat the 'rap,' which is a crook's term for an official complaint." In 1913, another serial pickpocket, known as "Eddie the Immune," tried to convince Chicago reporters that he was going straight—and that if he should happen to be rearrested after leaving "the 'stir,' " it could only be because the "mugs" (police) were corrupt: "They will nail me the first time I make a show on the street. They'll frame a 'bum rap' on me before I've been out of stir a week." The *Chicago Daily Tribune,* in 1920, reported the story of a generous thief, who was trying to take sole blame for a robbery: "Here I am trying to shield this sucker because he's got a wife and she is going to be a mother soon. I'm willing to take all the blame. And he takes the rap with me. Plumb useless."[2]

With the help of such newspaper stories, underworld slang uses of *rap* quickly spread to the public at large. In 1926, for example, the *New York Times* provided this translation for yet another twist on the word: "In order to understand the news of the day the innocent must continually familiarize themselves with new words from the bright lexicon of crime. The newest is 'rap,' meaning identification. When one is singled out from a line of suspects as the dip who slid with the ticktick, one is the victim of a 'rap.' " Hard-boiled detective fiction such as Dashiell Hammett's stories, also popular at the time, helped familiarize the public with criminal slang. It wasn't long before *rap* needed no explanation, so that by 1929 Hammett could write in his first novel, *Red Harvest,* "I wondered if the little gambler had done it, or if this was another of the wrong raps that Poisonville police chiefs liked to hang on him."[3]

By the middle of the twentieth century and later, *rap* was such a familiar term that no one would have associated it particularly with underworld slang. The plot of Lisa Scottoline's thriller *Moment of Truth* (2000) revolves around a man who frames himself for murder. As the book jacket tantalizingly tells the potential reader, "When attorney Jack Newlin discovers his wife dead in their elegant home, he's convinced he knows who killed her—and is equally determined to hide the truth. He decides to take the rap, and to seal his fate he hires the most inexperienced lawyer he can find." *Rap* also continued to be understood to mean blame more generally, allowing former United Nations Ambassador Jeane Kirkpatrick to describe her attitude thus: "We entered with the absolute conviction that it was not America's God-given role in the world to take the rap. America was not, in fact, responsible for all the ills of the world. . . . We took off the 'kick me' sign."[4]

Rap, of course, has many nonlegal meanings. By the 1800s rap had become a term for talk, and in the latter half of the twentieth century that use became particularly linked to African American culture and a specific stylized repartee. This in turn evolved into rap music and associated hip-hop culture. The two *raps* came together beautifully in 2007. Responding to criticisms that rap music is a source of racist speech, one newspaper headline asked this question: "Is hip-hop getting a bum rap?"[5]

EGT

rap sheet

Rap sheet is a convenient name for a list of an individual's arrests and convictions. The term belongs to the same family tree as criminal slang phrases like "beat the rap" and "bum rap" (see RAP), but it emerged somewhat later and was coined by the law enforcers rather than the lawbreakers. This happened easily because by the time *rap sheet* came along, the word *rap*—in the sense of a criminal charge—had already been absorbed into mainstream speech, albeit with a slightly edgy, slightly jocular feel. As we shall see, however, familiarity with *rap* has not prevented the recent emergence and widespread acceptance of an entirely false etymology for *rap sheet*.

The earliest reference to "rap sheet" we have found is in the oral history of a California shipyard during World War II, published in 1947. When discussing hiring practices, the Employment Manager noted that "from the F.B.I. offices in Washington, D.C. we used to secure a 'rap sheet'—that is, an individual's criminal record. . . . One exciting experience was when we checked our files against the criminal reports sent out by the state and discovered that one of the men in the yard was wanted for theft. We notified the Sausalito Police Department and they took over from there."[1]

The first published judicial opinion to use "rap sheet" was a 1949 appellate decision in Oklahoma—still a "dry" state at the time—in the case of a man whose car had been found to contain twenty-four cases of whisky and who was thereupon convicted of unlawfully transporting liquor. The defendant complained that his trial was unfair, because the prosecutor had improperly signaled to the jurors that he had a history of liquor-law violations by saying in their presence, "Where is that 'rap sheet', I thought I had it right here." (The court agreed that the prosecutor's comment was improper but concluded that it didn't matter, considering that when the defendant's own lawyer called the defendant's wife to the stand and asked what her husband's occupation was she answered, "Whisky business.")[2]

Rap sheet got a boost in popular awareness in 1954. That was the year that a career criminal named James Henry "Blackie" Audett, who purported to be a compatriot of the likes of John Dillinger and Pretty Boy Floyd, wrote a highly exaggerated but colorful autobiography titled *Rap Sheet*. Blackie's own rap sheet was a long one, including multiple convictions for bank robbery, auto theft, and prison escapes. According to one crime historian, however, because of all the book's lies, "Blackie Audett's greatest crime was writing *Rap Sheet*."[3]

Today a rap sheet is more likely to be digital data than a piece of paper, as law enforcement agencies computerize their records to make criminal history information more easily searchable. Each state has its own method of collecting information about arrests and prosecutions and its own official name for the resulting records—usually not "rap sheet." The FBI collects the information in a central location to enable national searches for names and fingerprints. When television crime investigators say they're checking "NCIC" (National Crime Information Center) or "IAFIS" (Integrated Automated Fingerprint Identification System), they're referring to those centralized FBI records, which include things with names like "Electronic Rap Sheet" (ERS) and "Ten-Print Rap Sheet" (TPRS, which is keyed to a full set of fingerprints). The FBI's more formal name for the records, though, is "Criminal History Record" (CHR), and it is stored in the "Interstate Identification Index" (III).

In a law enforcement world awash with such initialisms ("FBI" itself is an initialism for "Federal Bureau of Investigation"), perhaps it was inevitable that someone would think that the *rap* in "rap sheet" was an acronym—a pronounceable word created from the initials of some phrase. In recent years many unofficial and even official sources have claimed that it stands for "Record of Arrest and Prosecution" or "Record of Arrests and Prosecutions." The fact that no such phrase was associated with rap sheets until decades after the term had become established shows that it is not a genuine acronym. This particular kind of etymological myth—the after-the-fact association of a word with a phrase—has become so common that it has acquired a whimsical name: *backronym*. The difference is timing: which came first, the phrase or the word? *Scuba,* for example, is a true acronym, evolved from "self-contained underwater breathing apparatus." *Golf,* on the other hand—contrary to widely circulated myth—does not stand for "Gentlemen Only, Ladies Forbidden." That's a backronym. Other backronyms wrongly believed to be actual etymologies include "Constable On Patrol" and "For Unlawful Carnal Knowledge." One enterprising computer programmer has even created a backronym generator, for those who would like to create their own amusing but fake derivations.

In the case of *rap sheet,* the earliest association with "record of arrest and prosecution" seems to be a 1980 case in which the Louisiana Supreme Court made the connection in a footnote.[4] (It is, in fact, the only reported case to have connected "rap sheet" to this fictional history.) The false etymology now appears—represented as actual etymology—in sources as diverse as blogs, advice columns, and law review articles. Recently, several states—including Maryland, Missouri, Nebraska, New York, Oklahoma, and Washington—have formally adopted the phrase "Record of Arrest and Prosecution" or the like for their rap sheets, thus converting linguistic myth into quasi-reality and slang into the official title for criminal history records. These states then refer to the record as a RAP Sheet or R.A.P. Sheet, turning the simple, earthy *rap* into an unwieldy, pretentious series of initials.

EGT

read the riot act

To *read the riot act* to someone is to issue a stern warning that continued misconduct or poor performance will not be tolerated. A parent whose child has been misbehaving at school might warn of severely reduced privileges, or a board of directors might give a manager six months to remedy certain problems in an organization or face firing.

The threat in the real Riot Act, which gave rise to this expression, was death. In August 1714, Queen Anne, the last member of the Stuart dynasty, which had ruled England for most of the preceding century (and Scotland since 1371), was succeeded by King George I, the first of the Hanoverian line. But there were still many in Great Britain who hoped to see the Stuarts restored to the throne in the person of Anne's half brother James Francis Edward Stuart, who was then in exile in France. As governments are wont to do when they feel insecure, George's government attempted to protect itself with stricter laws.

In particular, as one of its first acts in the reign of George I, Parliament in 1715 adopted "An Act for preventing Tumults and riotous Assemblies, and for the more speedy and effectual punishing the Rioters"—popularly known as the Riot Act. Enacted in response to what Parliament claimed were "many rebellious Riots and Tumults" fomented "with an Intent to raise Divisions, and to alienate the Affections of the People from his Majesty," the statute authorized justices of the peace and various other officials to order any group of twelve or more persons, "being unlawfully, riotously, and tumultuously assembled together, to the Disturbance of the Publick Peace," to disband. The act provided that those who failed to obey the command "shall suffer Death as in Case of Felony."[1]

Although the penalty was extreme, the Riot Act was notable for its attention to due process. To ensure that people throughout the kingdom had ample warning of it, Parliament specified "That this Act shall be openly read at every Quarter-Sessions, and at every Leet or Law-Day"—in other words, at regular sessions of courts, which in those days were public events of considerable note in the countryside, typically held on market days, when most of the populace would be in town. In addition, the act included a one-year statute of limitations, so that participation in a riot could not be dredged up as a pretext for trying someone more than a year later.

But most significantly, the act provided that no rioter could be prosecuted under it unless he or she remained on the scene for more than an hour after the crowd had been warned by an appropriate authority to disperse. And that warning was to consist of a reading, or at least a close paraphrase, of language specified in the act itself. In the words of the statute:

> The Justice of the Peace, or other Person authorized by this Act to make the said Proclamation, shall, among the said Rioters, or as near to them as he can safely come, with a loud Voice command, or cause to be commanded Silence to be while Proclamation is making, and after that, shall openly and with loud Voice make or cause to be made Proclamation in these Words, or like in Effect:
>
> > Our Sovereign Lord the King chargeth and commandeth all Persons, being assembled, immediately to disperse themselves, and peaceably to depart to their Habitations, or to their lawful Business, upon the Pains contained in the Act made in the first Year of King *George,* for preventing Tumults and riotous Assemblies.
>
> > *God save the King.*

The act did not prove especially effective in preventing riots, though some people were indeed hanged pursuant to it, often despite their understandable objection that they never heard the warning over the noise of the mob. After years of disuse the act was repealed in 1973, but its formula of fair but stern warning followed by serious consequences if the warning is not heeded lives on in the idiom.

And occasionally the idiom is applied—wittingly or unwittingly—to a situation surprisingly close to the original. Referring to coach Jan Gruden of the Oakland Raiders football team, a sports writer reported: "Gruden . . . was unhappy with his team during the morning workout. After a second

Reading the Riot Act to a Rainmaker

This joke is of a type that has been told of important people in various business environments—from sports stars to movie directors—since the 1920s. For a while in the 1980s and 1990s it was being told about lawyers, as in this version. Unlike most lawyer jokes, this did not become widely popular, perhaps because it is something of an inside joke—more likely to be told by lawyers to each other than by nonlawyers about lawyers.

The law firm's managing partner summoned the firm's highest-billing attorney to his office. "I realize you brought in five million dollars of new business last year, but you've been rude to the other partners and abusive to your assistants. You've bribed judges, had rival attorneys beaten up, and I know about the affair you've been having with my daughter."

"I'm sorry to say this," continued the managing partner, "but one more lapse and we'll have to think about the future of our relationship."

fight broke out, Gruden called an early halt to the session, gathered the team together and read them the riot act. The action took place on the far field, and the battle was quickly joined by dozens of players, so it was hard to distinguish the initial combatants. 'I'd seen enough,' Gruden said . . . . 'If drastic measures have to be taken, drastic measures will be taken . . . and I let them know.' "[2]

JEC

RICO

In 1950–51 America was mesmerized by the televised hearings of a congressional committee headed by Senator Estes Kefauver of Tennessee, which was investigating organized crime. When the committee issued its report, it noted, "One of the most perplexing problems in the field of organized crime is presented by the fact that criminals and racketeers are using the profits of organized crime to buy up and operate legitimate business enterprises."[1] When racketeers elbow their way into a business, it is bad for the business and bad for consumers. Two decades later, Congress, still grappling with this intractable problem, passed the Organized Crime Control Act of 1970. One part of that act, Title IX, was captioned "Racketeer Influenced and Corrupt Organizations." But everybody just calls it *RICO*.

RICO made it illegal to buy into, take over, or run any enterprise through a pattern of repeated criminal conduct. The statute was deliberately written in broad terms so as to cover any manner of criminal infiltration or manipulation of business, governmental, or other organizations. Violations are punishable by fines, imprisonment, and forfeiture of one's interest in the enterprise, and anyone harmed by such conduct can sue the wrongdoer for treble damages. It took a few years for prosecutors to get comfortable with the technicalities of the new law, but once they did they began to realize that nothing in the law limited it to the Mafia or other gangsters. Its comprehensive terms applied equally to "legitimate" business people—and even government officials—who had succumbed to corruption.

When prosecutors began using the statute against "respectable" people who just happened to have engaged in a pattern of criminal conduct, there were howls of outrage. Executives, no matter how many millions of dollars they might have stolen through their financial manipulations, did not feel that they should be tarred as racketeers. A prominent defense attorney groused, "You know as well as I do that Congress never would have passed it if it ever thought they were going to use it against governors and people like that."[2]

It was in the context of these arguments over the proper scope of the RICO statute that a pair of reporters, one from *Newsday* and one from *Newsweek,* first noted the interesting similarity between the name of the statute and the name of the gangster played by Edward G. Robinson in the 1931 Warner Brothers–First National Pictures film *Little Caesar.* The character is named Cesare Enrico Bandello. But in the film everybody just calls him Rico.

Little Caesar chronicles Rico's rapid rise and sudden fall as a ruthless mobster, ending with his incredulous dying words: "Mother of Mercy— Is this the end of Rico?" The reporters suggested that perhaps the drafters were thinking of this movie when they chose the somewhat convoluted name of the statute. They noted that, in any event, "there is no question that many members of Congress had people like Rico in mind" when they voted for the law.[3] The Supreme Court ultimately ruled in favor of a broader interpretation, however. The statute covers all modern-day Al Capones, whether they are mobsters or moguls.

But the Supreme Court could not resolve the more interesting question about the statute: Was it or was it not named after Rico Bandello? The person who knows is Notre Dame law professor G. Robert Blakey. He was chief counsel of the Senate subcommittee responsible for the Organized Crime Control Act of 1970 and is generally understood to be its principal drafter. And he's not telling. Professor Blakey has published a detailed explanation of the legislative development and legal significance of the name with no mention of the movie;[4] but he himself notes that his explanation is "not necessarily inconsistent" with the theory that the specific wording was chosen with *Little Caesar* in mind.[5] And he does admit to being a movie buff.

If it were ever established that the similarity in names is merely a coincidence, it would be a big disappointment to the legal community, which has had great fun with the presumed connection. When many states enacted their own laws modeled on RICO, those were promptly dubbed "Little RICO" statutes in emulation of "Little Caesar." At least two different articles about threats to the RICO statute, including one by Professor Blakey himself, have used the line "Is This the End of RICO?" in their titles, and Blakey's article works what amounts to an entire essay on movies into its footnotes. Another writer, discussing the point at which a civil claim under RICO comes into being, titled his article in part "Is This the Beginning of RICO?" And in a gem of legal satire, a law professor seized upon the name of another classic gangster movie (released by a competing studio the year after *Little Caesar*) as the name for a hypothetical statute, which she then used as the basis for a serious legal exploration of some troubling double-jeopardy issues raised by RICO. The name of the make-believe statute is the "Syndical Crime and Racketeering Forces Act—Compound Enforcement." But you can just call it SCARFACE.[6]

JEC

rule of thumb

A *rule of thumb* is a rough but practical principle or guideline based on experience, as distinguished from an inflexible rule or a precise measure. The expression was already a familiar one in the seventeenth century, when a popular Scottish preacher observed that "many profest Christians are like to foolish builders, who build by guess, and by rule of thumb, (as we use to speak [that is, as we customarily say]) and not by Square and Rule."[1] The phrase undoubtedly derives from the use of the thumb as a measuring tool; *thumb* and *thumb's breadth* were early synonyms for *inch*. Similar use of the body for measurement is reflected in words like *foot* and *mile* (from Latin *mille passuum*, "a thousand [double] paces"), and the French *pouce*, meaning both "thumb" and "inch." (And see CHANCELLOR'S FOOT.)

Few idioms have proved more versatile and durable than the homely *rule of thumb*. It has been applied in every conceivable context over the centuries. In the latter part of the twentieth century, however, this everyday expression became taboo in many circles as word spread that, for all its seeming innocence, it had a sinister significance: the phrase, it was said, actually originated in a common-law rule specifying the thickness of a thumb as the size of a stick with which a man was permitted to beat his wife. The spreading of this myth is an object lesson in bad legal scholarship, sloppy journalism, and irresponsible rumormongering. To put it into context, we must step a considerable distance back in time.

Writing in the 1760s, William Blackstone, that great expositor of the English common law, noted that under "the old law" a husband "might give his wife moderate correction," though he was prohibited from using unreasonable violence. But Blackstone went on, "In the politer reign of Charles the second [the years 1660–85], this power of correction began to be doubted: and a wife may now have security of the peace against her husband," citing a 1674 ruling by the great jurist Sir Matthew Hale, chief justice of the King's Bench, holding that a husband may only admonish an extravagant wife and confine her to the house, not beat her.[2] Thus by the time America achieved independence, any purported authority for wife beating under English law was ancient history.

Of course, theory and practice are two different things. Wife beating did go on. Only the most highborn women could realistically hope for legal protection, and not all judges could be relied upon to be sympathetic. In 1782, one judge in particular—Francis Buller of the King's Bench—was rumored to have made a remark from the bench condoning a husband's beating of his wife with a stick no bigger than his (perhaps the judge's, perhaps the husband's) thumb. The remark was never recorded, and ninety years later a historian noted that "after a searching investigation by the most able critics and antiquaries, no substantial evidence has been found that he ever expressed so ungallant an opinion."[3]

But misunderstood or not, Buller's purported statement was so absurd, and so far from any reasonable understanding of the law, that word of it spread like wildfire. Buller was dubbed "Judge Thumb" by satirists, and was lampooned in jokes and cartoons. According to one story, "A witty countess is said to have sent the next day to require the measurement of the [judge's] thumb, that she might know the extent of her husband's right."[4]

Although Judge Buller's alleged remark served mainly to provide a few months' entertainment at his expense in the popular press and had no effect on the law of England (let alone of America, which by then was independent), a vague memory of it lingered in the collective legal unconscious and cropped up in a confused way in three isolated American cases over the next century. In each case there was a passing reference to what the court evidently believed to have been an old rule or guideline about thumbs and sticks—though none of the opinions referred to it as a "rule of thumb" or anything of the sort. And while each of these courts expressed a willingness to turn a blind eye to wife beating so long as it did not result in serious injury, none of them espoused any rule or principle relating to stick size. To the contrary, in the one case of these three in which the husband

(opposite) Cartoon published November 21, 1782, lampooning Judge Francis Buller as "Judge Thumb." Buller, in his judicial wig and robe, is portrayed as a street hawker carrying a sheaf of sticks—each with a thumb on the end—and saying, "Here's amusement for married Gentlemen or, a Specific for a Scolding Wife; Who buys of me." In the background a husband has raised a stick to beat his wife, who cries, "Oh Murder! Murder! Oh Cruel Barbarian." The husband

answers, "Cruel ha, 'tis according to Law, you Jazabel." The caption states that the cartoon was published by I. Cooke; a British Museum catalogue speculates that it might have been drawn by a cartoonist named Hixon. (Courtesy of the British Museum)

was actually allowed to go unpunished, even as the court explained that "we will not interfere with family government in trifling cases" it took pains to state: "It is not true that . . . a husband has a right to whip his wife. And if he had, it is not easily seen how *the thumb* is the standard of size for the instrument which he may use . . . . The standard [for judicial intervention] is the *effect produced,* and not the manner of producing it, or the instrument used." Moreover, as the court noted in this 1868 decision, the "old law of moderate correction" referred to by Blackstone "has met with but little favor . . . in the United States."[5]

Not long after that decision was rendered, powerful forces for social change in both England and America focused attention on the status of women and the problem of wife beating; among other efforts to stem the problem, many states seriously considered, and three states actually enacted, statutes providing for convicted wife beaters to be whipped.[6]

Social movements and concerns ebb and flow, and early in the twentieth century concern with wife beating ebbed. But a new tide of activism on the old problem of family violence rose up with the resurgence of feminism in the 1970s. It was then—some three centuries after the phrase came into use—that *rule of thumb* made its first appearance in connection with wife beating.

At first the phrase was used in jest—bitter jest, to be sure, but jest. In 1976, Del Martin, co-coordinator of the National Organization for Women's newly formed National Task Force on Battered Women/Household Violence, wrote: "Our law, based upon the old English common-law doctrines, explicitly permitted wife-beating for correctional purposes. However, certain restrictions did exist . . . . For instance, the common-law doctrine had been modified to allow the husband 'the right to whip his wife, provided that he used a switch no bigger than his thumb'—a rule of thumb, so to speak."[7]

This was before the history behind the "thumb" references in American cases had been studied, and Martin was extrapolating from a very sketchy secondary source, which she properly disclosed. Although her statement reflected serious misunderstandings about the law, no one could reasonably read her as saying that the purported doctrine about switch size was called "the rule of thumb." But it is likely that Martin's book, or some encounter with Martin or her ideas, was in journalist Terry

Too Serious for God

The hardened social and legal attitude toward wife beating in the latter part of the nineteenth century was reflected even in the humor of the period. A story first recorded in 1892, while poking fun at judges' self-importance, treats wife beating as a serious matter:

In a case of an assault by a husband on his wife, the injured woman was reluctant to prosecute and give her evidence.

"I'll lave him to God, me lord," she cried.

"Oh, dear, no," said the judge; "it's far too serious a matter for that."

12 *The Green Bag: An Entertaining Magazine for Lawyers* 53 (1900); similarly, 4 *Green Bag* 42 (1892).

Davidson's mind when Davidson penned the lead article for a book on battered women published the following year. Davidson wrote:

One of the reasons nineteenth century British wives were dealt with so harshly . . . was the "rule of thumb." Included in the British Common Law was a section regulating wifebeating. . . . The old law had authorized a husband to "chastise his wife with any reasonable instrument." The new law stipulated that the reasonable instrument be only "a rod not thicker than his thumb."[8]

Despite the fifty footnotes in Davidson's article, there was nothing to indicate where she got these particular ideas—even the ones she put in quotation marks. With respect to the phrase *rule of thumb* itself, it is unclear whether she thought that was an established name or whether she was deliberately giving a new name to this purported "rule." In any event, she wrote with confidence, and it is understandable that ordinary readers would take her at her word. It is less understandable that readers with a professional or scholarly interest in the topic should have done so. That lawyers would do so is unfathomable. Even apart from the conspicuous absence of citations to cases, statutes, or other legal authorities, the reference to "a section" of the "British Common Law"—as if the common law were a statute rather than a set of principles derived from centuries of judicial opinions—was sufficient to tip off any reader with three weeks of law school training that the writer had no idea what she was talking about.

Nevertheless, the idea that the thumb-stick rule was an actual rule of law, and that it was known as the "rule of thumb," caught on—even among legal writers, who often cited Davidson as their authority. In addition to countless repetitions and elaborations in newspapers, magazines, books, and ultimately even textbooks, the tale was perpetuated in scores upon scores of law review articles. It even found its way into a Senate Judiciary Committee report on the Violence Against Women Act, and into the very title of a report of the United States Commission on Civil Rights: *Under the Rule of Thumb: Battered Women and the Administration of Justice* (a 1982 report citing Davidson as its authority on the "rule of thumb").[9]

The unreality of all this did not escape notice everywhere. In the mid-1990s, at least three writers with different perspectives independently took on the mythology of the "rule of thumb": conservative social critic Christina Hoff Sommers in the course of a book-length broadside against contemporary feminism, English professor Henry Ansgar Kelly in a scholarly article, and law student Sharon Fenick in a long and witty posting to the alt.folklore.urban newsgroup.[10]

The point of most such efforts is not to minimize the persistent problem of spouse abuse and domestic violence but precisely the opposite: to arm activists and scholars with reliable information that can be used in making sound, defensible, intellectually honest arguments and analyses. Continued reliance on a palpably false legend to argue a cause—no matter how good the story—does the cause a disservice: at best it shows the proponent to be ill-informed; at worst it makes him or her out to be unconcerned with truth and accuracy. Either way it discredits the cause. And reliance on a misunderstanding of legal history merely clouds analysis of current legal options and issues. It is much more enlightening—and sobering—to realize that wife beating has persisted for centuries despite legal disapproval that has ranged from tepid to draconian than to dismiss past violence as the product of a legal "rule" approving it.

But a good urban legend is impossible to root out, and this "rule of thumb" story apparently is a great one. Our own survey of U.S. law review articles published during the decade 2000–2009 found that fifty-four of the sixty-two articles mentioning this supposed "rule of thumb" repeated the myth as gospel, and four of the remaining eight allowed that it might be true. In perhaps the ultimate irony, in January 2000 it was reported that British police trainees were being taught to avoid the "offensive" phrase *rule of thumb* because it "originally referred to the width of a stick with which a man was allowed to beat his wife."[11] In less than a quarter century, the American folk tale about the origin of *rule of thumb* had spread its tendrils all the way back to England and taken root in the place where, more than two centuries earlier, the very notion of such a rule was so roundly ridiculed.

JEC

scofflaw

Despite its Shakespearean ring, the word *scofflaw* is a modern creation. Almost uniquely among words in general use, it came into being as the winning entry in a contest.

It all started with Prohibition. The Eighteenth Amendment to the Constitution, prohibiting "the manufacture, sale, or transportation of intoxicating liquors . . . for beverage purposes," was adopted on December 18, 1917. Its ratification a little over thirteen months later ushered in an era of disregard for law that was at once the most joyful and the most violent in United States history. When the solicitor general of the United States was tapped to give the presidential address at the 1921 annual meeting of the American Bar Association in place of its recently deceased leader, he chose as his topic "The Spirit of Lawlessness." Nothing in his sober oration betrayed any awareness that his title might be taken as a pun on *spirit* in the sense of alcoholic drink. At the same meeting, the association's Judicial Section (made up entirely of judges) presented a report decrying the flouting of Prohibition even at the highest levels of society: "When, for the gratification of their appetites, or the promotion of their interests, lawyers, bankers, great merchants and manufacturers, and social leaders both men and women disobey and scoff at this law, or any other law," wrote the judges, "they are aiding the cause of anarchy and promoting mob violence, robbery and homicide."[1]

In Quincy, Massachusetts, Delcevare King, scion of an old, wealthy, and socially prominent Boston-area family, was not content only to bemoan the lawlessness. King's job as executive vice president in his father's bank left him plenty of time to pursue his interests in social reform. He had been an active supporter of the cause of woman suffrage, a founder of the American Federation for Sex Hygiene (aimed at controlling venereal disease), treasurer of the New England Watch and Ward Society (aimed at controlling moral corruption), chairman of the Massachusetts Anti-Cigarette League, and treasurer of the Massachusetts No-License League (an anti-liquor organization), and by 1922 he was vice president of the Massachusetts branch of the Anti-Saloon League, the nation's leading advocacy group for Prohibition. In late 1923, Delcevare King had an inspiration. As he explained to a local student newspaper,

> I believe the whole atmosphere about prohibition can be changed—that lawless drinking can be made "bad form"—just by getting into general use a word describing the present day drinker that will bite as does the word "scab." In a strike men are held in line by fear of that word and during the war, men were driven to doing things by fear of being called "slacker."
>
> What then is that word or coined word which expresses the idea of "lawless drinker," or "menace," or "scoffer," or "bad citizen," or whatnot, with the biting power of "scab" or "slacker"? I offer one hundred dollars in gold for the best word.[2]

By January 2, 1924, the prize had been raised to two hundred dollars, and the *New York Times* reported that King had received five thousand letters containing twenty thousand suggestions "from every State in the Union and many provinces of Canada" for the single word that would, as King put it, "stab awake the conscience of the lawless, scoffing drinker."[3]

In retrospect, King's choice of the words *lawless* and *scoffing* foretold the outcome of the contest. Among the words already received were such colorful, punchy terms as *boozshevik, lawjacker,* and *patrinot.*[4] But on January 15, 1924—in a move clearly coordinated with the fifth anniversary of ratification of the Prohibition Amendment the next day—the publicity-savvy King announced that he and the two other judges had selected the word *scofflaw,* splitting the prize between two local individuals who had submitted it: Kate L. Butler of Dorchester (between Quincy and Boston) and Henry Irving Dale of Shawsheen Village (on the other side of Boston).[5] Miss Butler was a significant figure in local social work, and Mr. Dale had appeared as an actor in Boston society fund-raising events. It has never been suggested that the contest was fixed, but the coincidence that the two winning submissions were from virtual neighbors of King whose professional and social worlds intersected with his, and that they consisted of the very words he had been toying with, makes it easy to believe that King himself coined the term and contrived to have it submitted.[6]

The result of the contest was published far and wide, and the term met with immediate derision, not only among "wets" (opponents of Prohibition) but undoubtedly also among some "drys" (supporters of Prohibition). United Press sports reporter Westbrook Pegler (later to gain fame as a syndicated columnist) wrote from New York, " 'Scofflaw!' The terrible epithet crackled above the clank of bottles, decanters and glasses in all well-ordered speakeasies like the awesome thunder of rose-petals in a June breeze."[7] Newspaper columnists and letter writers suggested their own new words ("GINGRATE—One who scoffs at your synthetic gin when it is not contained in original Gordon Gin bottles"); cartoonists had a field day ("SCOFF-LAW!" a dry accuses a wet, who, on his knees, pleads, "NO, NO, ANYTHING BUT THAT"); writers of doggerel likewise ("I want to be a scofflaw / And with the scofflaws stand . . .").[8]

In King's own backyard, students at Harvard seized the opportunity for a bit of fun. Delcevare King, class of 1895, was a loyal but not uncritical son of his alma mater. In 1920 he had written letters to the *Harvard Crimson* suggesting that extra officials be posted in the stands at football games so that infractions visible to the crowd but missed on the field could be properly penalized and urging that the football players wear numbers, no doubt the better to identify the offenders. In October 1923 King wrote to the college Glee Club to protest the singing of "Johnny Harvard" ("Drink, drink, drink, drink, and pass the wine cup free . . .") by the University Double Quartet at the Harvard-Oxford debate. When he announced his new epithet for non-law-abiding wets three months later, the university's

Comic strip by Clare Briggs, published about two weeks after the word *scofflaw* was unleashed upon the public. Briggs was an extremely popular cartoonist in the 1920s, working for the *New York Tribune,* which syndicated his cartoons and comic strips in hundreds of papers. (This copy of his strip is from the *Atlanta Constitution* of February 1, 1924.) Briggs's cartoons fell into many different categories, one of which was "Wonder What _____ Thinks About"—a Bass Drummer, the Wife of a Movie Hero, a Bird on Seeing an Aeroplane, and so on. In this contribution to that series, Briggs simultaneously poked fun at the new word and, through syndication, helped spread it throughout the land.

literary magazine, *The Harvard Advocate,* retaliated by announcing that it would pay ten dollars "to the man contributing the best word of like nature stigmatizing Drys."[9]

The *Advocate* was not the first to make such an offer. Three days after King's announcement, Mrs. Rose R. Scott of Saugatuck, Connecticut, had offered one hundred dollars for "the best coined word that will in effect mean one who scoffs at the God-given privileges of liberty and the pursuit of happiness." The *Advocate* raised its offer to twenty-five dollars, but Mrs. Scott attracted the most attention, ultimately drawing over thirty thousand entries, including *killright, meddlebug, pokenose,* and *dictamaniac.* In the end, the *Advocate* awarded its prize to the sixty-seven-year-old woman who submitted *spigot-bigot,* and a team of judges assembled by Mrs. Scott settled on *banbug.*[10]

By then, however, for all the scoffing, *scofflaw* was already becoming entrenched. In an age when every day brought another story of Prohibition violators arrested or sentenced, it filled a need. It was short, and all the publicity assured that it would be understood. Just three days after it hit the newspapers, it was in use: a two-sentence arrest notice in the *Hartford Courant* was captioned matter-of-factly, "Another Scofflaw." (The arrest report stated, "A small amount of alleged wet goods was seized as evidence.") Contrary to predictions that the word would never last, within three and a half years a new dictionary was being promoted as the first to include "such common words" as *rayon, halitosis, loud-speaker, bus boy,* and *scofflaw.*[11]

But while the drys won the war of words, the wets won the war. The word did not deter drinking. On the very day of King's proclamation of *scofflaw,* the American Bar Association itself, despite great expressions of outrage in the United States Senate, stood by its choice of a British ocean liner instead of an American one for a planned trip by some thousand American lawyers to meet with their British counterparts. The association's announcement "denied that the question of liquor aboard ship had influenced the decision," but a newspaper columnist said what many felt: "The American Bar Association . . . won't even inquire whether there's a bar on board until after the 3-mile limit has been passed, but if there shouldn't be it is surmised that the chairman of the entertainment committee will need a whale for a ferry boat."[12] In 1932 the Democratic Party swept into power on a platform of repealing Prohibition. On February 20, 1933, Congress adopted the Twenty-first Amendment doing just that, and a scant nine and a half months later—much faster than in the case of Prohibition itself—the amendment was ratified by the states and the Noble Experiment was over.

Nothing in the word *scofflaw* inherently limited it to those who disregarded Prohibition. Barely a year after the word had been introduced it could already be found in other contexts, as when an Illinois legislator called colleagues who had voted against a long-overdue reapportionment bill "scofflaws" because "they have violated their oaths of office to support the constitution."[13] But the term was overwhelmingly used in its original sense, and when that became obsolete and World War II put memories of the Prohibition era far behind, it all but dropped out of the language. In 1952, however, the word gained a new lease on life when a *New York Times* editorial applied it to persistent traffic and parking violators.[14] The term became popular all over again, and for several decades was thought of primarily as an epithet for motor vehicle offenders who ignored their tickets.

By the year 2000, that use of the term, too, was on the wane, as computer technology finally provided a way for authorities to keep track of tickets and track down offenders. But computer technology itself provided new pastures for the word. By 2003, the *Harvard Crimson* could be found referring to "student scofflaws who illegally download music and movies," while a court on the West Coast referred to an elusive Internet gambling operation as "an international e-business scofflaw, playing hide-and-seek with the federal court."[15] Every generation will have its persistent lawbreakers, and *scofflaw* is flexible enough to cover all of them. It appears that Mr. King's word is here to stay.

JEC

separate but equal

There is no more reviled phrase in American law than *separate but equal*. It manages to represent simultaneously both an odious system of racial segregation and the hypocritical characterization of that system as a form of equality.

Yet the words themselves are not inherently offensive. The opening paragraph of the Declaration of Independence proudly proclaims the intent of the American people to assume "the separate and equal station to which the Laws of Nature and of Nature's God entitle them." And given the legal and social status of women in the nineteenth century, it was actually a sign of progress that the University of Michigan Medical Department, instead of limiting enrollment to men, advertised in 1873 that it offered "A Course separate, but equal, for women."[1] In the context of race, however, the Thirteenth and Fourteenth Amendments, adopted after the Civil War for the specific purpose of abolishing relics of slavery and guaranteeing people of color full and equal participation in American life, should have prevented both the phrase and the concept of *separate but equal* from gaining a foothold. Instead, for many decades the Supreme Court systematically thwarted every effort to integrate the former slave class into the culture at large and to establish genuine equality of rights and opportunities.

The nation's first court challenge to segregation of African American children into separate but purportedly equal schools took place long before the phrase *separate but equal* came into use. In 1848, Robert Morris, who just the previous year had become the second African American ever admitted to the bar, sued the city of Boston on behalf of a five-year-old black child whose father wished to send her to a nearby white school instead of farther away to one of the city's two schools for students of her race. When the court ruled against the girl, the abolitionist lawyer, orator, and lifelong civil rights advocate Charles Sumner joined Morris in appealing to the Supreme Judicial Court of Massachusetts. The city argued that the separate school was just as good as the white school; but Sumner, arguing for the plaintiffs, declared:

> It is not in fact an equivalent. It . . . inflicts upon [the pupils] the stigma of caste; and although the matters taught in the two schools may be precisely the same, a school exclusively devoted to one class must differ essentially, in its spirit and character, from that public school known to the law, where all classes meet together in equality.[2]

The case was lost, but Sumner's argument was published and helped to mobilize sentiment that led the Massachusetts legislature to outlaw segregated public schools in 1855. Two decades later, as a senator from Massachusetts in the post–Civil War era, Sumner persuaded the Senate to pass a civil rights bill prohibiting segregation in public accommodations and publicly supported schools and cemeteries. But the national outcry against "mixed schools" and integrated cemeteries was so great that the House of Representatives stripped those provisions out of the final bill—the doomed Civil Rights Act of 1875 (see BADGE OF SLAVERY)—effectively ending any governmental effort at the national level to integrate the nation's woefully unequal segregated schools for the next seventy-five years.

In the meantime, in the late nineteenth century a wave of laws swept the South requiring (in a phrasing that had long been used in the context of education) "equal, but separate" accommodations for blacks and whites on trains passing through those states. It was in this new context that the phrase *separate but equal* caught on—and more than that, secured the imprimatur of the U.S. Supreme Court. The first such law was enacted in Mississippi in 1888, and it was the attorney general of that state who turned the expression around and provided the first known instance of the phrase in a racial context. Defending the law against a claim that it interfered with interstate commerce, he argued disingenuously (but nonetheless successfully) that the law had no effect on interstate commerce because it required only that the railroads "provide separate but equal accommodations *in the state for passengers within the state.*"[3] The fact that this required the railroads to segregate their passengers throughout their routes in order to avoid reshuffling them at the Mississippi state line did not trouble the courts. But it was a case from Louisiana a few years later that squarely presented the question of whether legally enforced segregation of railway accommodations (which, like the schools, were grossly *un*equal in quality) violated the Thirteenth and Fourteenth Amendments. And it was in that infamous case, *Plessy v. Ferguson,* that the Supreme Court bestowed its official blessing on state-mandated racial discrimination.[4] Although the precise phrase *separate but equal* never appeared in the Court's opinion (though it occurred once in the dissent), *Plessy* stood for almost sixty years for the proposition that just about any form of state-sponsored racial inequality was permissible so long as it was cloaked in that deliberately deceitful phrase.

In 1954 the Supreme Court finally did the right thing. In *Brown v. Board of Education,* the Court considered a raft of modern studies showing the detrimental psychological effects of segregation, and unanimously concluded: "In the field of public education the doctrine of 'separate but equal' has no place. Separate educational facilities are inherently unequal."[5] The Court need hardly have gone to all that trouble; this is exactly what Charles Sumner said in that first school desegregation case more than a hundred years earlier. All the modern academic studies in the world could add nothing to what anyone with a willingness to look past glib bromides like *separate but equal* could see from the start.

But the story does not end here—nor even with the ultimate acceptance of the *Brown* decision by the nation as a whole after a long period of bitter resistance. (See DELIBERATE SPEED.) For after half a century of more or less consistent support for the ideal of desegregated public schools, the Supreme Court took another turn. In 2007, a reconstituted Court with two new Justices ruled by a vote of five to four that school districts in Kentucky and Washington State that had done a good job of establishing integrated school systems could not take race into account in placing students so as to maintain the rough racial balance that had been achieved. During oral argument, the new Chief Justice, John Roberts, asked the attorney for the Seattle School District, "How is that [Seattle's use of race as a "tie-breaker" in assigning students among equally desirable schools] different from the separate but equal argument?" The attorney must have been stunned. "Well," he answered, "because the schools are not racially separate. The goal is to maintain the diversity that existed within a broad range in order to try to obtain the benefits that the educational research show flow from an integrated education." But in the most extreme portion of his opinion in the case, the Chief Justice, joined by three of the four Justices who voted with him on the outcome, flatly rejected racial integration as a justification for race consciousness in allocating students to schools. Notwithstanding the purposes for which the Fourteenth Amendment was enacted, he was unable to perceive any difference, from a constitutional standpoint, between racial awareness for the purpose of maintaining integration and equality and racial awareness for the purpose of maintaining segregation and inequality.[6] (For how the dean of Chief Justice Roberts's alma mater, Harvard Law School, regarded this kind of thinking a century ago, see the remarks of James Barr Ames quoted in THINKING LIKE A LAWYER.) If the view now held by four members of the Supreme Court prevails, it will be extremely difficult for many school districts, having come to understand that integrated education is the best education, to avoid slipping back into a system of schools that are substantially separate and inherently unequal.

JEC

shadow of the law

The *shadow of the law* has been a popular image with writers for centuries. But as befits something as murky as a shadow, you sometimes have to look closely to see what the phrase actually signifies.

From at least the sixteenth century on, one meaning of *shadow* has been "hint," "trace," "merest bit," as in the familiar phrase "without a shadow of a doubt." This sense comes through in the description by Harriet Jacobs, an escaped slave writing in the 1850s under an assumed name, of the harrowing life of a girl in slavery, for whom "there is no shadow of law to protect her from insult, from violence, or even from death; all these are inflicted by fiends who bear the shape of men."[1] In the same vein, actions that were claimed to be entirely without legal justification were once routinely described in legal pleadings by such phrases as "without any shadow of law or justice" or "without shadow of law or authority."[2] But *shadow* could also mean "pretense," as in the description of the execution of a sheriff of London in 1685 on a trumped-up charge of treason as a "barbarous murder, under shadow of law."[3] (Today we would say, "under color of law.") Thus the same wrongful legal action could be described as simultaneously "under shadow of law" (that is, purportedly based upon legal authority) and "without shadow of law" (that is, lacking even a glimmer of actual legal authority).

Both of those legal phrases have long since fallen out of use. For the past two centuries, the *shadow of the law* has been used principally as a literary figure of speech depicting the law as a looming, lowering presence in the lives of those who run afoul of it or become entangled in it. In the 1930 Paramount film *Shadow of the Law,* for example, William Powell plays a man who, having innocently come to the assistance of an attractive young woman only to find himself convicted of murdering her husband, escapes from prison and lives on the lam while trying to clear his name. Newspaper and magazine stories refer to illegal activities such as the narcotics business as operating "in the shadow of the law."[4] The phrase appears in article after article about the lives of undocumented aliens in the United States, in such statements as "While Aguilar is now a legal resident, his family is living, like thousands of other illegal immigrants, in the shadow of the law."[5] But it was Charles Dickens who penned the darkest literary depiction of this shadow. In *Bleak House*, his fiercest novelistic attack on nineteenth-century English law, Dickens referred to the legal district of London as the "perplexed and troublous valley of the shadow of the law, where suitors generally find but little day"—ominously echoing the biblical "valley of the shadow of death."[6]

But a shadow can be protective as well as sinister; so alongside this thread is a parallel but less common usage in which the shadow of the law is not troubling but comforting. Not surprisingly, judges have tended to favor this benevolent view of the law's influence, saying things like "The party before a court of equity . . . should have his decree if he clearly stands within the shadow of the law" and "The government which fails to protect character from unjust and unprovoked aspersion, is as imperfect as one that fails to protect life. The one is as dear as the other, and ought as much to be placed under the protecting shadow of the law."[7] In this usage, *shadow* means "scope," "ambit," "protective cover." (For a special term for this sense of *shadow,* see PENUMBRA.)

Sometimes the law's shadow can be simultaneously beneficent *and* menacing: salutary for the person protected by it, but threatening to the person who would violate it. Nowhere is this better illustrated than in Harriet Jacobs's artful description of her vulnerability as a fifteen-year-old slave in the home of a lustful master: there was "no shadow of law" to protect her and deter her master.

In recent decades a new shade of meaning for "shadow of the law" has taken hold in academia. In this usage, the shadow is neither negative nor positive; it is simply a fact of life. As one court put it in 1930, "Law is a rule of civil conduct and in our every activity of life we are constantly coming into the shadow of some law that limits the freedom of our movements."[8] In this regard the laws of society affect us in much the same way as the laws of nature: consciously or unconsciously, our conduct is shaped by our legal environment. This environment includes not only the laws them-selves but the entire legal system—the likelihood that a law will be enforced, the possible outcomes if a case goes to court, and so on. In 1979 a law review article about the ways in which legal rules affect settlement negotiations in divorce cases was published under the title "Bargaining in the Shadow of the Law."[9] The article attracted a good deal of attention among legal schol-ars, and soon "the shadow of the law" was popping up in article after article as a catchphrase for the influence of the legal system on private negotiations, relationships, and behavior.

The result of all this is that in legal writing *shadow of the law* can refer to any aspect of the law or legal system and can connote something good, bad, or indifferent. In the popular media, the phrase is much simpler: it almost always refers to the law as a threatening presence.

JEC

shyster

Shyster is about the worst name you can call a lawyer. It labels him (the term is applied mostly to males) as unscrupulous, untrustworthy, under-handed, dishonest, dishonorable, and a host of other *un*'s and *dis*'s. This does not necessarily mean that he is ineffective; he may actually be a shrewd manipulator of the legal system. In fact, an American Bar Association study using focus groups found that however much the public disdains sharp practitioners, "when they do seek a lawyer, they may want one who most fits the shyster image."[1] Still, nobody wants to be called a shyster.

This epithet burst into the language in the mid-1800s and drove ety-mologists crazy for most of the next century and a half. The first theory about the term's origins to find its way into dictionaries was that it came from the German word *Scheiss* or *Scheisse* (which modern German-English dictionaries unabashedly translate into the English cognate "shit") or the related word *Scheisser* (defecator)—presumably altered under the influence of the English ending *-ster* as in *seamster, gangster,* or *punster*. As early as 1855 this unprintable etymology had been hinted at by what was then called the *New-York Daily Times*. With a wink and a nod to readers with a knowledge of German, the paper described the term as "completely untranslatable, but signifying to the Teutonic mind whatever is basest, meanest, vilest in humanity."[2]

A popular etymology that appeared in dictionaries somewhat later had it that *shyster* came from *Scheuster*, the name of an attorney often rebuked for his conduct. (It turns out that this Scheuster never existed.) Over the years, more than a dozen etymologies were advanced, including a derivation from the character of Shylock in *The Merchant of Venice* (see POUND OF FLESH) and derivations from four different senses of the word *shy*. The key to the mystery was finally found in the archives of the New-York Historical Society in the 1970s, and publicized in studies by etymologist Gerald Leonard Cohen in the 1980s.[3] The tale that emerged illustrates how the study of word origins is in reality the study of cultural history.

The story takes place in the 1840s—long before the practice of law was regulated or regularized in any meaningful way in the United States. The setting is the cells, corridors, courtrooms, and nearby taverns of New York City's new jail and court complex—officially named the "Halls of Justice" when it opened in 1838, but soon known to one and all as "that dread and famous place, the Tombs."[4] This dour popular name arose from the fact that the facade was in a style reminiscent of an Egyptian mausoleum; but the epithet so eloquently captured the atmosphere inside that it has endured to this day, though the building itself has been replaced several times.

The principal characters in the story are a scrappy reform-minded newspaperman named Mike Walsh and the de facto dean of the self-styled "lawyers" who hung out at the Tombs, one Cornelius W. Terhune. The criminal justice system to which petty thieves, drunks, vagrants, and innocent arrestees were subjected in the Tombs was criminal indeed—one of payoffs and corruption at every level. And the "Tombs lawyers," many of whom had qualified for admission to the bar by the simple expedient of paying off the judges, were the very heart of this system; it was they who extracted bribe money as "fees" from the detainees and distributed it to the jailers, police officers, clerks, and magistrates involved—always keeping, we may be sure, as much as they could for themselves.

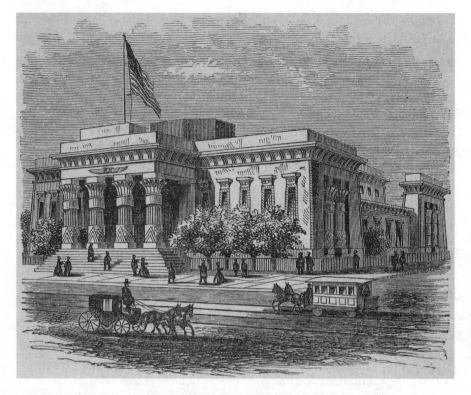

"The Tombs" (New York City's Halls of Justice) as it appeared in the 1860s. The Egyptian Revival architectural style of this court and jail complex, designed by the Philadelphia architect John Haviland, gave rise to the building's nickname: "the Egyptian Tombs," soon shortened to just "the Tombs." (*Manual of the Corporation of the City of New York* [1864], 83.) (Courtesy of Avery Classics Collection [Rare Books], Avery Architectural & Fine Arts Library, Columbia University. Photograph by Dwight Primiano.)

On July 22, 1843, Mike Walsh tore into this system—and especially the legal practitioners at its center—in his weekly newspaper *The Subterranean*. Walsh described the lawyers—that "disgraceful gang of pettifoggers who swarm about [the Tombs's] halls"—as "ignorant blackguards, illiterate blockheads, besotted drunkards, drivelling simpletons, *ci devant* mountebanks, vagabonds, swindlers and thieves," and detailed the process by which the guilty and the innocent alike were subjected to "the same extortion. In either case, if he be *flush*, he is free; if poor, in nine cases out of ten, condemned!"[5]

Cornelius Terhune—the most notorious manipulator of them all—took offense. When he ran into Walsh in a local tavern a few days later, he took the opportunity to state his case, which Walsh detailed in a witty follow-up article in the next issue of *The Subterranean*.[6] The heart of the matter was that Terhune did not appreciate being lumped with the other Tombs lawyers, whom he regarded as his inferiors by many degrees. He readily conceded that most of them deserved

> all you can give 'em, but ven you do it, just give the names, so I won't be confounded with sich *shyseters* as Magee, Peck, Camp and Stevenson, because I'm down on sich suckers as them—*I* am. If I wanted an innocent man, vat I was opposed to, you know, sent up—I'd just hire one of them *shiseters* to defend him, vich is just as sure as packing a jury against him.

The word that Walsh twice italicized was new to him—so new that he was still experimenting with different phonetic spellings for it. (He continued to vacillate in numerous articles over the next few months, finally settling for good on *shyster* in November 1843.)

Walsh was a great fan of slang and used it liberally in his newspaper. Others might simply have understood that Terhune was using some sort of derogatory term and let it go at that, but invective was Walsh's stock in trade. So he changed the subject from law to philology and asked Terhune to explain the term. Continuing his account of the conversation, he reported to his readers: "The Counsellor expressed the utmost surprise at our ignorance of the true meaning of that expressive appellation, 'shiseter', after which, by special request, he gave us the definition, which we would now give our readers, were it not that it would certainly subject us to a prosecution for libel and obscenity."

This means that after all the etymologies suggested over the years, it turns out that the first one—the "Teutonic" etymology alluded to by the *Times* in 1855—was right all along. Whatever Terhune's exact words were, what they clearly amounted to was: "It means 'shitter.' "

It has been proposed that the term most likely came from German by way of the British slang term *shiser* or *shicer* (worthless fellow), which was first recorded in England three years later (so far as is currently known) but could theoretically already have been brought to New York by criminals from England.[7] There is no need to construct such a round-about theory, however. New York's large German population was well represented in the Tombs;[8] the odds are that the term came straight from them.

The final piece of the *shyster* puzzle is the *t:* How did *Scheisser* acquire that *-ster* ending? Here it has been suggested that Walsh probably just didn't hear Terhune correctly.[9] But Walsh's fascination with Terhune's re-peated use of the term, his specific conversation about it with Terhune, and his meticulous rendering of Terhune's speech in all other respects—"give 'em," "ven," "sich," and so on—rule that explanation out. As between Walsh and Terhune, it is more likely that Terhune, a young man whose English was still heavily influenced by the language he had grown up with in a rural Dutch community in New Jersey, would unconsciously add a *t* to make the word sound more like its Dutch equivalent, *schijter*.[10] But there is no reason to assume that either of our leading characters was the source. Most likely it was someone less attuned to foreign languages than Terhune and less attuned to pronunciation than Walsh who unthinkingly conformed the ending of *Scheisser* to English words ending in *-ster.*

Most slang terms enjoy a brief vogue and then drop out of use. Walsh, however, picked up *shyster* and ran with it, and through circulation of his newspaper and personal influence turned it into an enduring part of the language. When the legal system struck back at Walsh a few weeks after his exposé by charging him with criminal libel, he made liberal use of the term to describe the district attorney and his other adversaries. When an obviously corrupt jury found him guilty and he was imprisoned—in the Tombs, no less—he relished the opportunity to report from the inside on what came to be known as the "shyster system."

Most uses of *shyster* today have nothing to do with law; the term can be applied to people in any business or field, and in fact to just about anyone you wouldn't want to buy a used car from. But because of its history, it has a singularly nasty ring when applied to a lawyer—so much so that under the law today, to write that a lawyer is a shyster is libelous per se.[11]

We have therefore changed course exactly 180 degrees since 1843. In that year, Mike Walsh popularized a brand-new word by using it as an epithet to lash back at the lawyer who was prosecuting him for libel. To-

Standard Operating Procedure

The modus operandi of the Tombs lawyers—and of some of the judges in that system—was not too different from the legal stereotype represented by this joke from 1915, similar examples of which have been repeated ever since:

"Why do you want a new trial?"
"On the grounds of newly discovered evidence, your Honor."
"What's the nature of it?"
"My client dug up $400 that I didn't know he had."

The truth about the system, however, was no laughing matter. This heart-rending editorial from the New-York Daily Times *in 1855 shows that a dozen years after Mike Walsh's muckraking articles, nothing had changed:*

A SAD SPECIMEN OF A LAWYER.
Perhaps the worst class of harpies in the community are those who prey upon the sins and sorrows of the wretched individuals whom indigence and hunger have driven to the commission of crime—not that indigence and hunger can excuse, though they may somewhat palliate offences. There is a class of attorneys in this City, whom popular contempt denominates "Tombs lawyers" and "shysters." These fellows get admission to the cells of newly committed prisoners and persuade the unfortunates, that unless their services are retained, there is no possible shield from the condign terrors of the law. If the prisoners or their friends have money, these "shysters" squeeze them as a strong man might squeeze a wet sponge. All that can be got out of them is obtained—money, if they have it—if not, furniture, jewelery, wearing apparel, anything that is convertible into money at the second-hand stores, pawnbrokers' shops, or junk shops. On Friday, at the Court of Special Sessions, one of these harpies was exposed in his dirty practice. We do not publish his name on this occasion. A wretched woman was tried for stealing four dollars and a half. She had four children, who were as miserable as such children could be—very hungry, in fact, starving. The sole earthly possession of this woman was a blanket, which the "shyster" caused her to get

> pawned for *two dollars,* that he might pocket the paltry sum for her defence.
> The Recorder suspended judgment in her case, and she left the Court to see
> after her children. When the lawyer left the Court, he had the woman's blan-
> ket—no, the two dollars it produced—in his pocket. The respectable mem-
> bers of the legal profession are outraged by such conduct. Cannot the Mayor,
> Recorder or City Judge move in the matter?
>
> Gus C. Edwards, *Legal Laughs: A Joke for Every Jury,* 2nd ed. (1915; Buffalo:
> Hein, 1993), 299, item 804; *New-York Daily Times,* May 14, 1855, 4. (The *Times*'s
> spelling *jewelery*—a hybrid of American *jewelry* and British *jewellery*—was
> occasionally used in the nineteenth century.)

day, if you use this old familiar word as an epithet against a lawyer, she
just might lash back by suing *you* for libel.

JEC

Star Chamber

In England in the fourteenth century, citizens sometimes petitioned the
king for help that they could not get from the court system, either because
the law was inadequate or because it could not be enforced against powerful individuals. The King's Council resolved these disputes and, as time
went by, its judicial function gradually evolved into more formal courts.
Two of those courts were the Court of Chancery (see CHANCELLOR'S FOOT)
and the Court of Star Chamber. For a long time these courts retained the
discretionary powers of the monarch, and the resulting decisions might
either right wrongs or perpetrate injustice. To label a case a "Star Chamber proceeding" today is a terrible insult—an accusation of gross procedural unfairness and abuse of power. But the story of the real Court of
Star Chamber is considerably more complicated.

The cloud of misunderstanding surrounding the court begins with the
name itself—why *Star Chamber?* The name refers both to a specific room

and to the building containing it, built on the grounds of Westminster Palace during the reign of Edward III in the mid-fourteenth century and used for meetings of the king and his council. As the court evolved out of the council, it continued to meet in that same room. Records in those days were kept almost entirely in Latin or French; the name of this room is found in Latin as *Camera Stellata* (the starred chamber) in 1355, and in French as *la Chaumbre du conseil esteillee* (the starred council chamber) in 1366 and, with varying spellings, as *la Chaumbre des esteilles* (the chamber of the stars) from 1367. In English there have been two basic forms, also with varying spellings—"star chamber" and "starred chamber." Although the *star* form appears to have occurred as early as 1378 or 1379, the *starred* form predominated well into the sixteenth century. The palace complex included other rooms with names like "the Painted Chamber" and "the White Chamber," and the natural assumption is that the Starred Chamber likewise was named for its decor. What's more, a set of illuminated manuscripts from 1504—INDENTURES between Henry VII and various officials embodying their promises with respect to a new chapel founded by the king—supports that interpretation. The manuscripts include exquisite miniature paintings depicting a ceremonial exchange of the indentures in the Star Chamber, which is represented as having ornate wall patterns, multiple windows divided into many small panes, and a lovely blue ceiling with bright gold stars. The fourteenth-century ceiling could not have stayed that bright for a century and a half; but it might have been repainted, or the manuscripts' illuminator might have brightened it up.[1]

But there is a mystery about those depictions. Just a little over forty years later, when Thomas Smith became clerk of the Privy Council in 1547 and then secretary of state in 1548, he undoubtedly attended many a meeting in the Star Chamber, and evidently saw no sign of stars on the ceiling. Writing about the Court of Star Chamber in the 1560s, he treated the name as a matter for speculation, saying that the room was "called the starre chamber, either because it is full of windowes, or because at the first all the roofe thereof was decked with images of starres gilted."[2] This opens up the possibility that while the windows depicted in the 1504 illuminations were certainly real enough, the starry sky painted on the ceiling might have been merely symbolic, for it is hard to imagine that Smith would have suggested that the room might have been named for the

Þis indenture
made betwene the
moost cristen and moste
excellent Prince kyng
henry the seuenth by
the grace of god kyng of
Englande and of ffrance
and lord of Irlande the
xvj · daye of July ·
the nynetene · yere of
his moost noble reigne

and John Islipp Abbot of the monastery of Saynt Petre of Westm͂ ·
and the Priour and Conuent of the same monastery Witnesseth
that the said Abbot Prior and Conuent by thaire all entier and comen
assent and consent conuenuten and graunten for theym and their ·
successours · and theym and thair Successours bynden to oure saide
soueraityn lord the king his heires and successours by these p͂sentes that
the same Abbot Prior and Conuent and thair successours shall from

windows if he had seen stars—or even the remnants of stars—right there in the room.

Other writers seized upon the uncertainty over the name and suggested other possible explanations, proving that etymological speculation is not just a modern pastime. By the 1590s, at least two different theories had been floated involving words that could be confused with *star* or its Latin equivalent. King James I (the "James" of the King James Bible) pronounced himself an agnostic on the question; in a speech in the Star Chamber in 1616 he said, "I will not play the Criticke to descant on the name," and contented himself with noting that it is "a name from heaven." In 1621, William Hudson, the preeminent legal practitioner in the Court of Star Chamber and clearly more interested in flattering the court than in etymological plausibility, suggested that the chamber's "stars" were the judges, shining in the reflected light of the king as the "sun."[3]

The great eighteenth-century legal scholar William Blackstone could not resist offering, as he put it, his own "conjectural etymology, as plausible perhaps as any of them." His theory, set out at some length in 1769, was that the room got its name from its proximity to a storage area for "Jewish contracts" (contracts made with Jews, especially contracts releasing debts) referred to in English as *starrs*.[4] Blackstone was tremendously influential, and almost two and a half centuries later his theory lives on in

(opposite) Indenture dated July 16, 1504, between King Henry VII and church officials regarding the founding of a chapel at Westminster. (Note the characteristic scallops across the top. See INDENTURE.) Inside the initial *T* is an image of the king in a red cloak giving the indenture to the church officials and monks in the Star Chamber, depicted as having gold stars on a bright blue ceiling. The text begins, "This indenture made betwene the moost cristen and moste excellent Prince kyng Henry the seventh by the grace of god kyng of Englande and of France and lord of Irelande the xvi daye of July the nynetene yere of his moost noble reigne and John Islipp Abbot of the monastery of Saynt Petre of Westm. [Westminster] and the Priour and Convent of the same monastery . . ." The occurrence of "moost" and "moste" (for *most*) three words apart highlights the variability of spelling in times past. (British Library, Harley MS 1498, folio 1.) (Courtesy of the British Library)

cyberspace (though usually as only one of several possible explanations for the name), despite having been convincingly refuted a few years later by a historian named John Caley. Caley's conclusion was that "though no actual proof can be at this time produced," taking all the evidence into account "there appears . . . no reason to depart from the usual derivation; which is, that the roof of the star chamber was anciently ornamented with gilded stars."[5]

There is still no direct proof, but a gem of new linguistic evidence was unearthed a century later by an assiduous researcher named William Paley Baildon, who was trying to discover when the building housing the Star Chamber was constructed (the answer: 1347–48). In poring over ancient records of expenditures for Edward III's construction projects, Baildon came upon a record from 1348 (or January 1349 at the latest) showing payments to tilers for repair of the roof after a windstorm, and that record referred to the building as the house called "Sterred Chambre." Baildon's discovery, first published in 1894, shows that people used the English *starred* form of the name, at the latest, within a few months of when the building was complete—and at least three decades before the first known instance of the *star* form. If this is true, then the name could not have arisen from a word that sounds like *star* (as distinguished from *starred*) in any language. This effectively rules out all serious theories about the name except the original two concerning the windows and the decor. Few have ever taken the windows theory seriously; after all, having windows through which one could see the stars was scarcely a distinguishing feature of a room in the days before gaslight or electricity. Often the simplest explanation for a word or phrase is the correct one, and here the evidence supports the simple explanation. Writers about the Star Chamber still often go beyond the evidence, assuming, for example, that the stars were gilded. But Baildon's simply stated conclusion is virtually irrefutable: "The Star Chamber was so called because it was decorated with stars."[6]

The more important mystery surrounding the Court of Star Chamber is whether it deserves its wretched reputation. The court evolved over hundreds of years and eventually became a focal point in the seventeenth-century political battles between king and Parliament. The final clash came during the reign of Charles I, who employed Star Chamber proceedings in his eleven-year effort (beginning in 1629) to reign without

Parliament. The court convicted and punished people who criticized Charles's policies, refused to collect his taxes, or resisted religious conformity. Charles lost his battle with Parliament (and ultimately his head), and Parliament abolished the Court of Star Chamber in 1641. The first generation of politicians, judges, and historians to comment on the court thereafter were on Parliament's side—and so tended to emphasize the abuses that had occurred under Charles I. Because actual records of Star Chamber proceedings were limited, later historians relied on the biased secondhand accounts, and so we inherited a picture of Star Chamber that was very negative indeed. More recent scholars have examined available records in detail and provide much more balanced accounts of the court's work during its multi-century existence.

For many years, the Court of Star Chamber handled both civil and criminal matters. Most cases of either kind were brought by private parties against private parties. Some writers suggest that the court made it possible for ordinary citizens to bring claims against the rich and powerful. And the court's civil jurisdiction, most of which involved disputes about trade and property, was generally unproblematic and had largely disappeared by the late sixteenth century.

It was the court's criminal jurisdiction that became controversial. Because of its ties to the king, the court was able to create new law: as time went on, Star Chamber criminalized conduct such as libel, perjury, conspiracy, and unsuccessful attempts to commit crimes. Some of these new laws were necessary to rein in commercial dishonesty, protect the integrity of the court system, and provide security against those whose disrespect for the country's legitimate rulers would lead to dangerous unrest. On the other hand, those same laws squelched political dissent and turned the expression of unwelcome opinion into a crime.

Jurors from common-law courts, whose verdicts had absolved a defendant, many times found themselves the defendants in Star Chamber proceedings; they were accused of perjury and if convicted were imprisoned, fined, or pilloried for their verdicts. Because these were trials about trials, without better records and fuller context it is hard to tell whether the prosecutions of jurors encouraged local juries to resist pressures to acquit the powerful or subverted justice by attacking legitimate judgments. Probably both were true.

The Court of Star Chamber used procedures that were both innovative and problematic but certainly not as draconian as its present-day reputation implies. The court's strength lay in its attempt to frame the issues and gather evidence, including sworn written testimony and relevant documents. Although its aim was admirable, its methods—one-sided examinations leading to written summaries used as evidence—could lead to error and unfairness. Star Chamber defendants possessed fewer rights than modern ones: the court did not allow defendants to refuse to talk to investigators, to produce documents, or to testify; and the loyalty of their lawyers was compromised by the fact that the lawyers themselves might be punished should the court be offended by the defendant's pleas. Judges, not juries, decided the cases, a procedure which some depict as a safeguard against jury corruption and others view as a deprivation of the protection of a jury trial. The most serious criticisms of Star Chamber procedure— that it regularly used torture to force confessions and gather information, and that it used in evidence the statements that other bodies acquired through torture—are rejected by modern historians as untrue. Finally, it is worth noting that the other courts of this period also fell far short of modern procedural ideals, and that unlike them the Court of Star Chamber could not impose the death penalty.[7]

During the reign of Charles I, the less savory aspects of the Court of Star Chamber surfaced in a dramatic way. Using charges like "seditious libel" and "dispersing false and dangerous rumors," the Star Chamber censored political and religious tracts and prosecuted gentlemen who criticized the government, the Anglican church, or the court itself. During this period the court also increased the penalties for convictions. In addition to ruinous fines and imprisonment for life (although these penalties were sometimes reduced), convicted defendants could be publicly humiliated, whipped, or pilloried, and have all or part of their ears cut off, face branded, or nose slit. These physical punishments may be one source of the belief that the court used torture, but they were penalties rather than investigative methods. Star Chamber process also became notorious for its use of the "ex officio oath," a religious oath imported from heresy trials in church courts allowing roving interrogation without a proper charge being filed, which had not previously been allowed in criminal cases against the laity. Because there was no right not to testify, the use of the oath created a lose-lose-lose proposition for religious and political dissidents: 1) they would be punished for contempt if they refused to swear to answer truthfully any question put to them; 2) they would be punished for their opinions and actions if they admitted them; and 3) they would be punished for perjury by the court and would endanger their immortal souls if they took a religious oath and then denied holding those opinions. (During this time period, defendants in criminal cases in the common-law courts were not examined under oath—in fact, they were forbidden to testify on oath even if they wanted to.)

So, did the Court of Star Chamber deserve its bad reputation? Yes and no. Much of its work, especially in the early days, was essentially benign, filling gaps in the developing common law and helping to keep order in a politically perilous and violent age. The court's effort to gather relevant evidence was laudable, though its secrecy and lack of protections for the defendant were not. Even Star Chamber's barbarous corporal punishments were not unusual for their time; the court's reputation for cruelty in its later years arose from the fact that these punishments were meted out not only to common criminals but also to gentlemen who were political or religious protestors. The Court of Star Chamber never escaped the political nature of its origins and so never developed the kind of judicial independence that a court needs. Increasingly over its history, rulers misused the court to suppress and punish political and religious dissent, and by the time of Charles I it was a ruthless tool through which the established church and the monarchy wielded power.

It is process rather than power that is the focus of today's rhetorical references to the Star Chamber. Modern American ideals of due process require advance notice of the charges against a defendant, the right to confront accusers, witnesses who are present to give oral testimony in open court, and an independent and unbiased decision maker. Courts are constitutionally required to provide these protections, but private groups are not—and when it is arguable that they have not, the resulting process is often compared to the Star Chamber, usually in comic exaggeration. For example, critics have attacked investigations by the National Collegiate Athletic Association, the deliberations of the national movie-ratings board, and even instant-replay reviews of umpires' calls in baseball by calling them Star Chamber proceedings.

When the epithet is applied to judicial proceedings, it is a far more serious accusation. In twenty-first century America, this charge has most often been leveled at proceedings targeting individuals suspected of involvement with terrorist organizations or plots. America's intensely secretive Foreign Intelligence Surveillance Court—which authorizes government spying on non-Americans in the United States and on Americans everywhere—is often likened to the Star Chamber, although the Surveillance Court's need for secrecy is generally acknowledged and the Star Chamber's deliberations were actually much more public. The treatment of terrorism suspects imprisoned without trial (see DAY IN COURT) also evokes comparisons with the Star Chamber at its worst.[8] And a terrorism-related departure from basic due process rights shares something else with the Star Chamber: its justification. As Justice John Paul Stevens stated in one such case involving a U.S. citizen, "At stake in this case is nothing less than the essence of a free society. . . . Unconstrained executive detention for the purpose of investigating and preventing subversive activity is the hallmark of the Star Chamber."[9]

EGT

testify

Legend has it that the word *testify* is derived from an ancient Roman custom that required a man to grasp his testicles with his right hand while reciting an oath—thus swearing by something that he quite literally held dear.

As etymological myths go, this one is especially easy to knock down, on both linguistic and historical principles. Linguistically, the English suffix *-fy* comes from the Latin combining form *-ficāre*, "to make," or *-ficārī*, "to be made," "to become." If the *test* in *testify* had anything to do with testicles, *testify* (from Latin *testificārī*) would mean something like "to become a testicle." Even if the Romans were in the habit of clutching their scrotums while swearing an oath, they would not have referred to it as becoming a testicle. In any event, the Romans were prolific writers whose culture is well known to us, and the simple historical fact is that they never had such a custom.

The real meaning of *testificārī* is "to be made a witness," "to give evidence" (from *testis,* "witness," "one who attests")—in a word, to testify. The Latin *testis* in this sense stems from the Indo-European roots *trei-,* "three," and *stā-,* "to stand": a witness is a third party standing by.

It is true, however, that *testis*—almost always in the plural, *testēs*—was also a Latin word for "testicle"; in fact, our word *testicle* itself comes from Latin *testiculus,* a diminutive form meaning "little testis." An early theory to account for this use of the word was that the testicles must have been regarded as "witnesses of virility," mutely testifying to their owner's masculinity—an implausibly abstract metaphor for so concrete an object. A more recent and more plausible theory is that the word came from the Greek *parastatēs* (from roots for "stand alongside"), which meant "comrade" or "defender" but was used in the plural to refer to pairs of objects standing side by side, and in particular as a medical term for testicles. Much Roman technical and medical terminology was translated from Greek. And because the Latin *testis,* in the sense of a witness on one's behalf, was a reasonable translation for the Greek *parastatēs* in the sense of a legal defender, the Romans might well have used that same word to translate *parastatēs* in its specialized medical sense, even though the etymological connection that linked the different meanings in the Greek— the concept of two people or things standing side by side—did not exist in the Latin.[1]

Whatever the origins of the anatomical meaning of *testis,* there is no question which meaning of the word is involved in *testify.* But although the Romans most assuredly did not confuse being a witness with being a testicle, the opportunities for punning presented by this double meaning were not lost on them. The Latin poet Martial (Marcus Valerius Martialis), for example, wrote wickedly of a fellow named Postumus, who was rumored to have suffered the indignity of being soundly poked in the mouth by one Caecilius at a dinner party. (That itself was a pun: Martial strongly implied that the "poking" was not done in the usual way, but rather that Caecilius had used Postumus sexually.) Postumus denied the whole thing, to which the poet replied: "quid quod habet testes, Postume, Caecilius?" (What about the fact, Postumus, that Caecilius has *testes?*)—meaning both that

Caecilius had witnesses and that, figuratively speaking, in contrast to the unmanly Postumus, Caecilius had balls.[2]

People seeking to explain how the legend about Romans grasping their testicles got started often suggest that the originators or perpetuators had in mind evidence of a similar custom alluded to in the Old Testament, which refers in a couple of places to the gesture of a slave or a child making a solemn promise to his master or father in terms such as this: "And the servant put his hand under the thigh of Abraham his master, and sware to him concerning that matter" (Gen. 24:9). This of course was a far earlier time and a far distant place from classical Rome and has nothing to do with anybody grasping his own genitals.

But there are those who believe that it might at least have to do with *somebody's* genitals. The Hebrew word for *thigh* that is used in these passages is *yarek.* It can mean "thigh," but it can also be used euphemistically to refer to the genitals or pubic area as the seat of procreative power. Thus when we read in the Bible that "Ehud made him a dagger . . . and he did gird it under his raiment upon his right thigh" (Judg. 3:16), we know that he bound it to his upper leg. But when we read that a wife who has been unfaithful shall suffer "the Lord [to] make thy thigh to rot," whereas if she is innocent she "shall conceive seed" (Num. 5:5–31), we know that the focus is a little higher. This double function has a parallel in the English word *loins,* which in fact is sometimes used in the King James Bible to translate *yarek* in its procreative sense: "All the souls that came with Jacob into Egypt, which came out of his loins, . . . were threescore and six" (Gen. 46:26).

So the question is, where exactly did the Old Testament scribes visualize these oath takers putting their hands? No one knows for sure. But considering the oath takers' subordinate status, it is easy to imagine them kneeling before their parent or master in a posture of supplication, with one arm outstretched toward the general vicinity of the thigh. The notion that the superior in that situation would direct the underling to grasp his genitals—or, frankly, get anywhere near them—is not only hard to believe but unsupported by any textual evidence. As with the legend of the Roman oath takers, the likely truth is less colorful than the fanciful story. But that's life. Sometimes a thigh is just a thigh.

JEC

thin blue line

We noted in BLUE WALL OF SILENCE the historical distinction between the red uniforms of the British army and the blue of British and American police. A striking example of the iconic significance of police blue is the image of the *thin blue line,* in which police, clad in blue, form a shield between the law-abiding populace and the criminal elements and forces of evil.

Yet it is to the red-coated British army that we ultimately owe the expression *thin blue line*—and specifically to the valor of the 93rd Highlanders, a Scottish infantry regiment in the Crimean War. On October 25, 1854, as the Russian cavalry prepared to make a run at the British-controlled port of Balaklava, the Highlanders—a few hundred Scotsmen arrayed in black kilts and red jackets with bayoneted rifles—were formed into a line of defense just two deep. In a report published twenty days later in *The Times* of London and then in many other newspapers, William Howard Russell, the paper's correspondent, painted a vivid tableau of the Russians' first probing assault as viewed from the heights above: "The ground flies beneath their horses' feet; gathering speed at every stride, they dash on towards that thin red streak topped with a line of steel." The soldiers stood their ground, and to everyone's surprise, after a couple of pro forma rifle volleys from the Scots, the Russians turned around without ever having come within 150 yards of the line. In the end it was a gratifyingly uneventful incident in a morning that was to end with the disastrous and horribly bungled charge of the Light Brigade, for which the Battle of Balaklava would become famous. But like that pointlessly suicidal charge, the Highlanders' stand evinced the bravery of the troops; and on January 23, 1855, when the House of Lords was debating who should receive medals for their parts in the Crimean War, the earl of Ellenborough, as reported in newspapers throughout Britain in the ensuing days, argued for medals not only for those in "the glorious charge" but also for "the services of that 'thin red line' which had met and routed the Russian cavalry."[1]

Ellenborough was probably quoting Russell's description as he remembered it but instinctively condensed it into a more pithy expression. His phrase caught on with a public always receptive to romantic images of war, and *thin red line*—sometimes with "of heroes" added for good measure— became a rhetorical appellation for the British army and British military might and grit generally. This was captured most famously in "Tommy," Rudyard Kipling's 1890 ode to the low-level British soldier, so scorned during peacetime yet so celebrated when sent off to war:

> Then it's Tommy this, an' Tommy that, an' "Tommy, 'ow's yer soul?"
> But it's "Thin red line of 'eroes" when the drums begin to roll.[2]

And the popular phrase proved to be an inexhaustible resource for writers on other, often more lighthearted, topics. Before the century was out one could see references to a thin red line of freemasons in crimson collars, a thin white line of bishops, a thin blue line of public schoolboys in blazers and straw hats, a thin brown line of Egyptian soldiers (a reference to skin color), and so on.

The first such extension of the phrase, less than seven months after Ellenborough's speech, was to policemen. In this context the heroic tones were missing, as a writer describing Queen Victoria's welcome in Paris noted that similar English festivities paled in comparison. "We can scarcely hang out a flag gracefully, and the thin blue line of policemen which usually guards our streets on such occasions . . . is not very captivating to the eye." An 1862 society column discussing horse races similarly describes police, who "walk in a 'thin blue line,' as best they can, and cry, 'Clear the course.'" Yet in 1900 we find *thin blue line* extended to the police as protectors of the people generally, just as *thin red line* had been extended to the army generally. In a speech to the annual meeting of supporters of the Birmingham Police Institute, as reported by the *Birmingham Daily Post,* the bishop of Coventry stated that he had "often felt that the police force wanted its Rudyard Kipling, who would . . . make the force occupy that place in the public esteem which it deserved as fully as the army. Perhaps, when the war was over [Britain's war du jour was the Second Boer War, in South Africa], Mr. Rudyard Kipling would make the public realise the debt it owed to the thin blue line. (Applause)."[3]

The bishop could not have imagined that his Kipling would arrive two decades later in the form of a businessman in New York City. In the United

States, although the phrase "thin red line" was not unknown, it understandably lacked the resonance it had in Britain. The spinoff "thin blue line," on the other hand, found occasional use in references to blue-clad military troops in various situations, including Union troops at the Battle of Gettysburg, the Prussians in the Franco-Prussian War, and American soldiers in the Spanish-American War. The most dramatic example described the Rough Riders' charge up San Juan Hill. "They walked to greet death at every step, many of them, as they advanced, sinking suddenly or pitching forward and disappearing in the high grass, but the others waded on, stubbornly, forming a thin blue line that kept creeping higher and higher up the hill."[4] Thus heroism came to the blue line.

Other uses of the phrase occurred occasionally, as in 1917 when the president of the National Baseball League (and former governor of Pennsylvania), John K. Tener, lavished praise on the sport's umpires, who he said "form the thin blue line between honesty and corruption in the game." The watershed date for our story, however, is January 11, 1921. On that day the Merchant Truckmen's Bureau of New York, a newly formed association of trucking executives who had banded together in part to form a united front in dealings with their drivers, evidently feeling that good relations with the police would be in their interest, adopted a resolution expressing "unqualified appreciation . . . of the efficient manner of the administration of our police under Commissioner Enright" (New York City police commissioner Richard E. Enright). The resolution declared that "it shall be a moral obligation of every man here present to refute slanderous attacks and unfair criticism of that—thin blue line—which has served us so faithfully and so well." The bureau's president, James J. Riordan, communicated this resolution forthwith in a letter to Enright, who filed it away with other letters of a similar nature to await a time when they would be useful to him.[5]

Enright judged that time to have arrived fifteen months later, in April 1922, when he was under fire from various quarters because of a crime wave and for allegedly "feathering his own nest" to the detriment of the police department. Enright responded with a public-relations blitz that included releasing his surprisingly large collection of almost suspiciously adulatory correspondence, prompting a page 1 article in the *New York Times* headlined "Enright, in Defense, Quotes Letters of Praise, Mostly Old."

The phrase from Riordan's letter, as a metaphor for the police generally, apparently caught the fancy of police officials, politicians, newspapers, and Enright himself, and it began to pop up with some regularity. In October of that year, for example, the mayor of Chicago lauded the city's police as "a thin blue line between crime and our three millions of population" in his address to the banquet of the National Poultry, Butter and Egg Association at the Hotel Sherman; in January 1924, Enright, not to be outdone, spoke of the "thin blue line of 1,700 patrolmen [who] stand on the battle line of law and order" to a meeting at the Biltmore Hotel of the Seaside Home for Crippled Children Association. And in case any police department had not yet picked up on the expression, it is a sure bet that Enright used it at the international conference of police chiefs that he hosted in New York City in May 1925, just as he did in an article about the conference published immediately before it opened, making extensive comparisons between police work and war and prompting the headline writer to characterize the conference as one about "Establishing a Blue Line of Defense Against the Common Enemy, Crime."[6]

The Los Angeles media were equally entranced with the image of the thin blue line. Thus when Chicago's chief of police persuaded the city council to fund the hiring of more officers in 1922, the *Los Angeles Times* reported, "The 'thin blue line' between life and property in Chicago and the crime band was almost doubled today." A few years later, that same newspaper praised the accomplishments of the Los Angeles police: "Over the largest city front in the world, 441 square miles, a thin blue line of police officers is fighting, and according to statistical data, winning its never-ending battle with crime although woefully weak in numbers, equipment, money and sometimes unsupported by the very people the officers are attempting to protect."[7]

William H. Parker, who joined the Los Angeles Police Department in 1927 and became its chief in 1950, saw the potential uses of this metaphor, and he exploited them so brilliantly that he is often erroneously credited with coining the phrase. The heroic identity implicit in *thin blue line* was just what Parker was after. Inheriting a department known to be a corrupt, patronage-ridden force, Parker wanted to transform the police into a professional organization, independent of politicians, and composed of committed, honest, disciplined officers. Parker was a master of public relations; he worked with Jack Webb to shape the television cop show *Dragnet* into a public-relations bonanza for the LAPD, and he made frequent use of the speechwriting talents of a young police officer named Gene Roddenberry, who many years later went on to create the television series *Star Trek*, in which, according to Roddenberry's authorized biographer, the character of Mr. Spock was based on Chief Parker. Parker's many speeches, reports, and other media events helped popularize the concept of the thin blue line. Most notably, when the LAPD faced criticism for police brutality, Parker produced (with the local NBC affiliate) a weekly television show to bolster public confidence in the department, and he named it *The Thin Blue Line*.[8]

In 1988, however, the image suffered a setback with the release of Errol Morris's movie *The Thin Blue Line*, a devastating documentary showing how an innocent man had been arrested, convicted of murdering a police officer, and sentenced to the electric chair with the help of suppressed evidence, perjured testimony, and an emotional closing argument for the prosecution. As the trial judge recounted it in the film, the "final argument was one I had never heard before about the thin blue line of police that separated the public from anarchy. And I have to concede that there my eyes kind of welled up when I heard that." Because of facts revealed by the film, the defendant, Randall Dale Adams, was released after more than twelve years in prison.[9] In the meantime, the real killer, left free because of the prosecutor's obsession with convicting and executing the wrong man, had killed again—a crime for which he was executed in 2004.

But the phrase proved too good to give up; within a year, New York City mayor Edward I. Koch was thanking the police union for endorsing him for reelection by saying, "You stand between us and the murderers and the rapists and the assaulters. You are that thin blue line." By 1993, an attorney for one of the white Los Angeles police officers charged with civil rights violations in the incendiary case in which they were videotaped brutally beating an African American, Rodney King, invoked the phrase in his own summation, describing the defendants, according to the *Washington Post*, as "embodiments of the 'thin blue line' that protects civilized society from 'the criminal element.'"[10]

The phrase never entirely recovered from the effects of Morris's documentary, and in the twenty-first century it sometimes has negative connotations; one can read in a newspaper of "the 'Thin Blue Line'—the brotherhood . . . that protects its own, right or wrong," or in a judicial opinion of evidence of police department retaliation against "officers who cross 'the thin blue line'" by disclosing improper police behavior. But the metaphor is overwhelmingly used in a positive way, and the late bishop of Coventry would be pleased to know that, well over a century after he suggested the idea in Birmingham, the phrase is so well established in England that it needed no explanation when, in 2009, the chairman of the English police union's West Midlands branch—headquartered on Coventry Road in Birmingham—spoke of the importance of the criminal justice system standing behind "that Thin Blue Line that helps keep society stable."[11]

EGT

thinking like a lawyer

The phrase *thinking like a lawyer* refers to a set of qualities of mind prized by lawyers. These include precision, caution, relevance, focus, resourcefulness, practicality, ability to make pertinent and sometimes startling distinctions, clearheaded detachment, lack of sentimentality, and prudent judgment. Because of the variety of ingredients, the expression can be served up in various flavors, both approving and critical.

Admirers of lawyerly thinking often emphasize its roots in practical experience. Thus in an academic debate about legal ethics, one law professor chides another for claiming to be "'thinking like a lawyer' about these ethical questions" when "most of his examples reflect abstract, academic thinking, more than lawyerly analysis based on experience and common sense."[1]

Although the phrase may be taken to extol the nonacademic origins and practical orientation of distinctively lawyerlike thinking, its emergence is intimately connected with the development of the modern law school at the end of the nineteenth century. As the university-affiliated law school displaced the earlier system of law office apprenticeship as preparation for the profession, particularly for its higher echelons, the case method of instruction invented by Christopher Columbus Langdell at Harvard in 1870 became the dominant mode of instruction. In 1894, James Keener, a Columbia professor, told the Section on Legal Education of the recently founded

American Bar Association that the study of cases ensured "a complete check upon any tendency to become speculative and visionary, or academically learned, as distinguished from a scientific lawyer capable of applying the principles of law as they exist."[2]

This modern view that legal education should stress legal analysis rather than mere legal rules was highlighted, fittingly, in connection with the dedication of a new law school building at the dawn of the new century. Addressing a dinner commemorating the new law building at the University of Pennsylvania in 1900, law professor (and later U.S. senator) George Wharton Pepper stated, "The Law School aims to train a man to think like a lawyer, to catch the spirit of the law's development, to analyze an authority and to determine its significance, to grasp the relation of our law to our political and economic development." And in a speech at the dedication ceremony the previous day, James Barr Ames, dean of the Harvard Law School, keenly described as the law professor's goal that "his students shall be able to discriminate between the relevant and the irrelevant facts of a case, to draw just distinctions between things apparently similar, and to discover true analogies between things apparently dissimilar, in a word, that they shall be sound legal thinkers."[3]

In his famous 1930 lectures to first-year law students, Columbia professor Karl Llewellyn used deliberately provocative language to emphasize the importance of rigorous thinking in law:

> The first year . . . aims, in the old phrase, to get you to "thinking like a lawyer." The hardest job of the first year is to lop off your common sense, to knock your ethics into temporary anesthesia. Your view of social policy, your sense of justice—to knock these out of you along with woozy thinking, along with ideas all fuzzed along their edges. You are to acquire ability to think precisely, to analyze coldly, to work within a body of materials that is given, to see, and see only, and manipulate, the machinery of the law.

The fictional Professor Kingsfield, who terrorized first-year Harvard law students in the 1973 film *The Paper Chase,* summed it up in a single blunt pronouncement: "You come in here with a skull full of mush and you leave thinking like a lawyer."[4]

Life, or at least law school, concurs with art: on their Web sites, law schools boast of "thinking like a lawyer" as the signature accomplishment of their curricula. Thus the University of Chicago Law School has said that it strives "to teach our students to 'think like lawyers.' This rather mysterious notion consists of a complex mix of rigorous objectivity, precise articulation, sound judgment, sensitivity to precedent, insight, intuition, imagination, and a host of other subtle and not so subtle attributes. However hard it may be to define 'thinking like a lawyer,' you know it when you see it and, perhaps even more important, you know it when you don't." More earthily, an online guide for students reduces the concept to "Four Strategies to Think like a Lawyer":

1. Accept ambiguity
2. Don't be emotionally tied to a position
3. Argue both sides
4. Question everything[5]

A more expansive and flattering sense of thinking like a lawyer is implied by the notion that lawyers do or should possess a distinctive faculty of complex, nuanced judgment, delicately articulated to context— something akin to the practical wisdom celebrated by a long succession of thinkers beginning with Aristotle. Contemporary observers who mourn the passing of the "lawyer-statesman," a paragon of professional virtue and prudential wisdom who supposedly flourished in the recent past, call for renewed cultivation of these lawyerly qualities.[6]

Critics both within and outside the profession, however, find much to dislike about thinking like a lawyer. Some see lawyers' most central and distinctive trait as their tunnel vision and insensitivity to context, codified in a witticism by Harvard professor Thomas Reed Powell, who reportedly observed, "If you think you can think about a thing that is inextricably attached to something else without thinking of the thing which it is attached to, then you have a legal mind."[7] Some view lawyers as "argumentative nitpickers."[8] Others see conventional legal thinking as disabling lawyers from embracing new technologies and business arrangements.[9] Still others view *thinking like a lawyer* as denoting a compartmentalization

The Legal Mind

There is no aspect of "thinking like a lawyer" that has escaped becoming the subject of a lawyer joke. Consider, for example, arguing both sides: Good lawyers have not only the ability to argue either side of an issue but also a psychological tendency to convince themselves that the better argument lies on whichever side they happen to have been hired to represent. Both their willingness to argue any position and their confidence in their own arguments are mocked in this joke from the 1990s:

A lawyer dies and goes to heaven, where he is brought before God. "A lawyer, eh?" says God. "We've never had a lawyer in heaven before. Argue a point of law for my edification."

The lawyer goes into a panic and says, "Oh, God, I cannot think of an argument worthy of your notice. But I'll tell you what . . . you argue a point of law and I'll refute you."

Even the whimsical ability to "think about a thing that is inextricably attached to something else without thinking of the thing which it is attached to"—first mentioned in print in 1935—was anticipated by this joke at least twenty years earlier:

A lawyer was defending a man accused of housebreaking, and said to the court: "Your Honor, I submit that my client did not break into the house at all. He found the parlor window open and merely inserted his right arm and removed a few trifling articles. Now, my client's arm is not himself, and I fail to see how you can punish the whole individual for an offense committed by only one of his limbs."

"That argument," said the judge, "is very well put. Following it logically, I sentence the defendant's arm to one year's imprisonment. He can accompany it or not, as he chooses."

The defendant smiled, and with his lawyer's assistance unscrewed his cork arm, and, leaving it in the dock, walked out.

and fragmentation of experience that is morally incapacitating and personally destructive.[10]

In sum, a century of use has not brought clarity. The phrase *thinking like a lawyer* is invoked to suggest both affinity with common sense and separation from it. It is used to signify both prudential wisdom that can wrestle with complex and intractable moral problems and a blinkered and mechanical outlook that makes for a diminished capacity to solve them. The ambiguity of the phrase mirrors the timeless mixture of appreciation and disdain for lawyers, even among themselves.

MG

third degree

The term *third degree*—referring to harsh and often violent police interrogation methods—now serves mostly as a jocular or deliberately exaggerated characterization of persistent or unwelcome questioning about some aspect of one's personal life. For much of the twentieth century, however, it was a serious business indeed. And the diversity of stories in circulation regarding the origin and meaning of the term illustrates how tales about word origins can arise and spread—through speculation, self-serving invention, and everyone's love of a good yarn.

The term came into use in the 1880s in connection with the activities of New York police inspector Thomas F. Byrnes, who was famous for his talent at extracting confessions. Byrnes made his name in 1879 when, as a police captain, he cracked a major bank robbery case by inducing a gang member to confess. A few months later, in 1880, he was put in charge of New York City police detectives, and over time he acquired a national reputation as a sort of combination of Sherlock Holmes and Svengali—an image that he continued to cultivate long after he left the force, and one that the newspapers devoured. For example, in 1894—by which time Byrnes had been promoted to superintendent (chief) of police—a typically fawning article recounted, with considerable embellishment, the story of one of Byrnes's earliest successes as inspector: the conviction and hanging of a murderer named Michael McGloin. Under the headline "The Third Degree: How It Was

Worked on Suspects by Inspector Byrnes," the writer spun out an elaborate tale of the ingenious staging of an interrogation, from precise placement of the chairs to artful display of the murder weapon to a strategically timed parade of witnesses. This, together with a "searching glance" from Byrnes's "penetrating eyes," did the trick. The suspect "literally sprang from his chair, and falling to his knees clasped Byrnes about his legs, crying like a child, confessing and begging the inspector not to have him hanged."[1]

By the turn of the century, legendary tales of Byrnes's working of the third degree were augmented by legends about the origin of the term *third degree* itself. A purported explanation in the *New York Times* in 1901 held that the term had to do with the location of the examination, with progressive degrees signifying interrogations by higher-level officers at more central

Examining a "Crook."

Illustration from a history of the New York City Police Department published in 1885 for the benefit of the Police Pension Fund. This shows the examination of a suspect by Inspector Byrnes (seated) as Byrnes and the department wanted the public to envision it. The picture is signed "Karst" or "V. Karst." (Augustine E. Costello, *Our Police Protectors* [New York, 1885], 406.) (Courtesy of Lyle Pearsons. Photograph by Dwight Primiano.)

locations, culminating with the chief of detectives at police headquarters. According to that article, the term was coined by "a newspaper writer" in reporting on the case of a criminal named Brunt in the early 1860s. In 1932 the same newspaper featured an article again attributing the term to an unidentified reporter, but this time claiming that it was coined in the early 1880s in the case of a sailor named "Frenchy" whom Byrnes had put away—though that case in reality occurred in 1891.[2] Various theorists assert that the term is derived from degrees of torture in the Spanish Inquisition, that it is a pun on its leading practitioner's name (Byrnes/burns), that it was coined by Byrnes himself, that it was coined by the president of the International Association of Chiefs of Police in 1910 (the year of Byrnes's death), and so on. All the stories advanced over the years—though typically recited with great confidence—have been either pure speculation or deliberate fabrication, and they were stated with complete certainty.[3]

A common thread in many such accounts is that the term must be a reference to Freemasonry—a fraternal order much given to secret rites. Its members progress from lower to higher levels, called degrees, of which the third and highest is Master Mason. To be elevated to the third degree the candidate must go through an elaborate ceremony, including ritual questioning. It has long been suggested—though never with any supporting evidence—that the most intense police interrogation, or interrogation at the highest level, got its "third degree" label from this source. On its face this seems an unlikely theory. By the mid-1880s, the New York City police force was predominantly Irish Catholic, and Freemasonry had been denounced by one pope after another since 1738. It would seem ironic, to say the least, for the police technique modeled by Dublin-born Tom Byrnes to be named for a rite so thoroughly condemned by the church.

But the New York City police force in those days was virtually an arm of Tammany Hall—the city's Democratic political machine—and many a back-room deal was made in the secrecy of the Masonic lodge. An obscure article on the status of Freemasonry in New York in December 1896 (apparently almost unnoticed until now) lifted the lid of the lodge and allowed the readers to peer in: "When it comes to policemen it will be hard to find one of any reputation who does not belong to some Masonic body. . . . It used to be said that the police force through Masonry, especially through the Shrine [a society open only to Master Masons], ruled the city." As to

Byrnes himself, the article reported, "The attitude of [his] church is given as the explanation of ex-Superintendent Thomas Byrnes' standing toward Masonry. Ten years ago Byrnes was a Mason of high degree. . . . He was one of the best-known members of the Shrine. About six years ago [at the end of 1890] he cut loose from all Masonic bodies." Evidently the latest papal denunciation, an encyclical by Pope Leo XIII issued on October 15, 1890, declaring the Masonic fraternity to be "animated by the spirit of Satan, whose instruments they are" and "consumed, like their inspirer, with a mortal and implacable hatred against Jesus Christ and his work," had finally forced Byrnes to dissociate himself from the society. But by then the stamp of Freemasonry was irretrievably upon his work—and thanks to historical materials that became available in searchable electronic form only in 2008, we can now say why: as some have speculated but none before could prove, it was Byrnes himself who gave his method its name. On February 5, 1883, the *New-York Tribune* reported that Byrnes had broken another gang of criminals: "When taken to Police Headquarters and put through what Inspector Byrnes styled 'the third degree of initiation,' or 'pumping process,' they all confessed their guilt."[4]

The image of a Masonic induction ceremony neatly conveyed how Byrnes wanted people to think of his sessions with suspects: taking place behind closed doors, involving procedures that were mysterious and almost magical, posing questions and requiring answers, but without the slightest hint of physical abuse. In 1905, ten years after his departure from the force, Byrnes—aware of growing criticism of police methods and still honing his image—wrote a lengthy description of his method as purely a battle of wits, in which he first put suspects off guard with what "might be called 'The Sympathetic Talk'" and then patiently drew out information: "This," he said, "is the much discussed, much criticized 'Third Degree.' Never has it done injustice to the innocent." In 1910, the International Association of Chiefs of Police devoted a session of their annual meeting to discussion of the growing public distrust of the "third degree." The president of the association trotted out the claim that the "third degree" is merely a reference to the location of the questioning; another member declared that the process had a bad reputation only because of "shyster lawyers" who coached their clients to claim in court that they had been mistreated, when in truth they had confessed voluntarily out of a guilty conscience.[5]

But no one involved in the criminal justice system in those days—including those police chiefs—was under any illusion about what was going on. Byrnes's own chief until 1885, George Walling, in his memoirs published in 1887, intimated that Byrnes's methods were a good deal more efficient than the public was led to believe. Referring to an officer beckoning a suspect into Byrnes's office, Walling wrote: "This indicates that the prisoner is going to pass a bad quarter of an hour, or what is known in police slang as 'getting the third degree.'" The press was in on the game. Police reporter turned social reformer Jacob Riis, who had covered the department during Byrnes's entire tenure as chief of detectives, acknowledged in his autobiography that Byrnes had made clever use of psychological techniques, but said that "his famous 'third degree' was chiefly what he no doubt considered a little wholesome 'slugging.' He would beat a thief into telling him what he wanted to know." One reporter even took the rare step of reporting this while Byrnes was still in office, quoting a convicted thief who said—not without a touch of admiration—"I tried [to lie], and he smashed me across the teeth with a pair of handcuffs." Nor were the judges who relied on these confessions ignorant of the circumstances. Information collected years later revealed that "following their interrogation, Byrnes' suspects regularly appeared in Magistrate's courts badly injured, bruised and bandaged, some so weak they could hardly stand."[6]

In Byrnes's time, however, the third degree, in the sense of "a little wholesome 'slugging,'" was regarded by almost everyone as a normal and necessary element of effective policing. When a reform-minded Board of Police Commissioners headed by Theodore Roosevelt was appointed in 1895 to clean up the police department, it demanded Byrnes's resignation not because he tolerated violence but because he headed a thoroughly corrupt organization—although they never succeeded in proving that the stunning personal fortune Byrnes himself had amassed during his career was the direct result of corruption. Over the succeeding decades, public tolerance, or at least indifference, in regard to coerced confessions remained high even as the third degree methods used to extract them became worse and legal and journalistic opposition mounted. Then in 1931, a national commission appointed by President Herbert Hoover to consider ways to deal with increasing lawlessness in the Prohibition era (informally called the Wickersham Commission after the name of its chairman) stunned the law enforcement world by issuing the book-length *Report on Lawlessness in Law Enforcement*. The report revealed and condemned the fact that "the third degree—that is, the use of physical brutality, or other forms of cruelty, to obtain involuntary confessions or admissions—is widespread." The commission documented every manner of torture inflicted to extract confessions, from the ubiquitous rubber hose to the inconspicuous sleep-deprivation method to the fast-acting "water cure, a species of torture well known to the bench and bar of the country . . . which consisted of placing the victim on his back and slowly pouring water into his nostrils until he nearly strangled."[7]

The Wickersham report was greeted with howls of outrage, denial, and defensiveness from police officials nationwide, such as the director of public safety in Philadelphia, who complained that "the forces of the law wouldn't get to first base in combatting criminal elements if we adhered strictly to the letter of the law."[8] Nevertheless, this report was a turning point: over time, public opinion, Supreme Court decisions, and police procedures all turned away from torture as an information-gathering technique as other methods proved to be not only more humane and more consonant with the Constitution but also more reliable. But the turn of another century—and specifically the terrorist attacks of September 11, 2001—gave the concept new currency, both in the popular imagination and in actual practice. The vocabulary changed—the perennial war on crime became the permanent "war on terror," the water cure became "waterboarding," the third degree became "enhanced interrogation"—but the rationale was straight out of the 1880s. The popular Fox television series *24*, which by happenstance took to the airwaves eight weeks to the day after the September 11 attacks and ran through the decade, consistently showed fictional antiterror agent Jack Bauer torturing prisoners in order to gain information, depicting this as a patriotic activity and an infallible intelligence-gathering technique that, as Byrnes himself put it, "never has . . . done injustice to the innocent." Military officials condemn the tactics depicted in the show, but poll after poll showed that a great many Americans in the first decade of the twenty-first century believed, just as police in the nineteenth century did, that torture is sometimes called for—so long as they themselves are not the ones believed to be withholding information. Yet both the practical and the philosophical objections that brought the third degree substantially to an end in domestic policing apply as well to international security. As commentator Sarah Vowell put it, "Not only because we would hope our captive soldiers would be treated with reciprocal human decency, or because the information gleaned from torture usually turns out to be a . . . sham, but mostly, Americans reject torture because we are not satanic monster scum."[9]

EGT

three-fifths rule

The United States Constitution, at its birth and for some eighty years thereafter, to the eternal disgrace of the nation, counted slaves as three-fifths of a person. But the meaning of the Constitution's *three-fifths rule* is often misunderstood, and its impact has only recently been analyzed.[1]

The three-fifths fraction, often referred to while it was in effect as the "federal ratio," first reared its head in 1783, when the Congress of the recently formed confederation of thirteen former colonies was struggling to find a way to raise revenues from the member states in a way that all the states could agree was fair. Apportionment of taxes on the basis of land values had proved unworkable, but the southern states had objected to apportionment on the basis of population—at least if slaves were regarded as part of the population. Their slaves, they said, were property, and should no more be counted as persons for the purpose of assessing taxes on the basis of population than the northerners' sheep and horses. The northerners, however, thought the slaves more analogous to northern laborers and wanted them included in the population count. This was not a debate about the humanity of the slaves; it was a fight over money. Each side simply wanted to shift as much as possible of the confederation's tax burden onto the other. A compromise was reached in which the slaves would be counted for tax purposes as three-fifths of a person. In the end, the tax plan fell two states short of the unanimous approval required by the Articles of Confederation; but when issues of apportionment arose in the Constitutional Convention just four years later, this compromise ratio naturally came to mind.

In the Constitutional Convention, however, the issue arose in a very different way. There the question was whether slaves should be counted as part of the state's population for the purpose of allocating representation in Congress. The Articles of Confederation had given the states equal representation in Congress. In this new context, the southerners suddenly became very solicitous of their slaves. "Blacks ought to stand on an equality with whites," said Charles Pinckney of South Carolina—neglecting to mention that, since slaves could not vote, the extra representatives gained for the state by including them in the population count would represent only the interests of their white masters. Many northerners in the Constitutional Convention opposed slavery on principle—the institution had already been abolished in two northern states and was being phased out in three others—and almost to a man they were opposed to the South's gaining political advantage simply by accumulating slaves. Pennsylvania delegate Gouverneur Morris argued that counting slaves for the purpose of allocating congressional seats

> when fairly explained comes to this: that the inhabitant of Georgia and South Carolina who goes to the Coast of Africa, and in defiance of the most sacred laws of humanity tears away his fellow creatures from their dearest connections and damns them to the most cruel bondages, shall have more votes in a Government instituted for protection of the rights of mankind, than the Citizen of Pennsylvania or New Jersey who views with a laudable horror, so nefarious a practice.

And Elbridge Gerry of Massachusetts, not the strongest opponent of slavery on the northern side but always alert for possible political advantage, turned the southerners' former arguments against them: "Blacks are property," said Gerry, "and are used to the southward as horses and cattle are to the northward; and why should their representation be increased to the southward on account of the number of slaves, [more] than horses or oxen to the north?"[2]

It was like a football game in which the teams had switched ends at halftime and were both now trying to push the ball in the opposite direction from before. Now the South was pushing to count slaves in full, and the North to disregard them. But just as before, the humanity of the slaves was not the principal concern on either side. This was about political power. And in the end the South got the better of the contest. The compromise allowed southern states to count three of every five slaves as part of their population—a substantial boost for a region where slaves constituted one-third of the population. When the convention turned to the executive branch, the delegates settled upon a mechanism for presidential elections that incorporated the three-fifths rule (see ELECTORAL COLLEGE). And since the president would appoint the judges, that power carried over into the judiciary branch as well—a clean sweep of the three branches of government.

As if this were not enough, other proslavery clauses were added to the Constitution, including provisions guaranteeing that importation of slaves from Africa would be allowed to continue for at least twenty years (which would increase southern political power because of the three-fifths rule), requiring free states to return slaves seeking refuge from slave states, and requiring the national government, upon request, to protect the states against "domestic Violence" (such as a slave rebellion). And in a crowning act of hypocrisy, in order to make the resulting package more palatable to ratifying conventions in the northern states, the Constitution was carefully kept free of all explicit references to slaves and slavery. The three-fifths clause, for example, stated that "Representatives . . . shall be apportioned among the several States . . . according to their respective Numbers, which shall be determined by adding to the whole Number of free Persons . . . three fifths of all *other persons*."[3]

The great irony of the three-fifths rule is that rather than hurting the slaves' cause by failing to count them as full persons, it hurt them by counting them at all. For example, it was only by reason of the three-fifths rule that the Virginia slave owner Thomas Jefferson, a consistent supporter of slavery policies, defeated the non-slave-owning New Englander John Adams in the presidential election of 1800. When accusations surfaced shortly thereafter that Jefferson had fathered several children by his slave

Sally Hemings (a story bolstered but not definitively proved by DNA analysis in 1998), a satirist published a lengthy poem filled with wicked gibes such as these:

> A southern negro is, you see, man,
> Already three fifths of a freeman,
> And when Virginia gets the staff,
> He'll be a freeman and a half!

> Great men can never lack supporters,
> Who manufacture their own voters;
> Besides, 'tis plain as yonder steeple,
> They will be *fathers* to *the people*.[4]

The consequence of the three-fifths rule was that for seven decades—the formative years for the country under its new constitution—American government was dominated by slaveholder interests. Eleven of the fifteen presidents before Lincoln were present or former slave owners, including every pre–Civil War president elected to a second term. The highest positions in the House of Representatives were overwhelmingly filled by slaveholders. Nineteen of the thirty-four Supreme Court Justices appointed during this time were present or former slaveholders (including five of the seven Justices who ruled against the slave Dred Scott in the infamous 1857 case that bears his name), as were untold numbers of lower-court judges. The "slave power," as northerners called the extra power granted to the slave states by the three-fifths clause, was responsible for the extension of slavery into new states as they were added to the Union, the reinstitution of slavery in areas acquired from Mexico (which had abolished it), and—in myriad subtle ways—the entire tone and substance of national policy up to the Civil War.

It is sometimes said that while the Constitution was admittedly extremely tolerant of slavery, at least it included a mechanism—the amendment process—by which that peculiar institution could ultimately be abolished. But history proves that statement wrong. The U.S. Constitution is far more difficult to amend than those of other democratic nations, and in the end it required a civil war to purge this country of slavery—and of the three-fifths rule.

What followed from that was in some ways the bitterest irony of all: the Fourteenth Amendment, ratified in 1868, made the former slaves citizens and ensured that they would be counted as whole persons; but after only a few years of Reconstruction the South's intransigence and the North's indifference combined to deprive the former slaves and their descendants of the vote throughout the South for almost another full century (see ONE PERSON, ONE VOTE). By losing the Civil War, the South finally obtained in full measure what it had asked for in the Constitutional Convention eighty years before: representation in Congress and in presidential elections based upon a full count of the blacks in their midst, while still depriving those blacks of any say in who should represent them. Not until adoption of the Voting Rights Act of 1965—achieved only after another prolonged period of violent white resistance, during the civil rights campaign begun in the late 1950s—did most African Americans in the South finally obtain full political rights to go with their full personhood.

JEC

versus

The contemporary English word *versus* has two general senses: "against" (Ali versus Frazier, the Yankees versus the Red Sox) and "compared with," "in contrast to," "as an alternative to" (free will versus determinism, nature versus nurture). We use it all the time, with no realization that the English language took this word from the language of law.

In classical Latin the preposition *versus* simply meant "toward"; the related word for "against" or "compared with" was *adversus*. But in the form of Latin used for legal purposes in medieval England, the distinction between the two words was lost, and *versus* was regularly used to mean "against." The scholars responsible for one older law dictionary, mindful of the difference between the two words in classical Latin and perhaps eager to justify the use of the seemingly "wrong" word in law, posited that the *versus* of Law Latin was actually "an abbreviation of the Latin *adversus*."[1] Yet the very first comprehensive treatise on English law, written in Latin in the first half of the thirteenth century and credited to a judge and priest named Henry de Bracton (though it is now believed to have been the combined work of several writers), consistently used *versus* to mean "against," with *adversus* appearing only a handful of times in the entire work. It appears that this is a simple case of normal language change.

When pleadings were written in Latin, the name of the case would naturally be written in Latin as well. Thus a case brought by Mr. Smythe against Mr. Fitzwilliams would be captioned *Smythe versus Fitzwilliams*. And even when English became fully established as the language of law in England, this familiar formula—like many others such as *habeas corpus* (the writ for challenging the legality of a detention) and *nolle prosequi* (the formal abandonment of a criminal case by the prosecutor)—remained intact.

For a considerable time *versus* remained almost exclusively a legal term, used in ordinary writing only when referring to court cases by name. But lawsuits and criminal cases always make for interesting news and tasty gossip; therefore, unlike most legal jargon, *versus* in case names was seen with some regularity in the popular media. Moreover—also unlike most legal jargon—this word had a simple, clear meaning applicable in any number of everyday situations. So it was inevitable that over time the word would creep into use in nonlegal contexts. And since a word meaning "against" easily expands to include "as against," "as compared with," and the like, once the word came into general use that extension of the meaning followed.

The surprise is that this process took so long. *Versus* did not appear in Noah Webster's 1838 *American Dictionary of the English Language;* if he thought about the word at all, he probably viewed it as a Latin term. At least one editor had seized upon the term as early as the 1790s and used it in the captions for two stories (mimicking the captions in legal papers and reports): "Short Coats versus Long Coats" (1790), a whimsical piece about the amount of material wasted because of the fashion for wearing long jackets, and "Whisky versus Government" (1792), a satirical essay in the form of an antigovernment diatribe signed with the pen name "Whisky."[2] The first of these is the earliest instance we have found of the extended meaning of *versus* (short coats *as compared with* long coats); the second uses the original meaning (against), but in reference not to adversaries in a lawsuit but rather to an individual purporting to be in philosophical opposition to a political institution.

These linguistic leaps might not have been unique—one can never be sure—but if similar uses existed they were extremely rare. In 1852 a particularly zealous New Hampshire lawyer could still think that it was worth a shot to argue that a conventional form of pleading against his client should be thrown out because its caption violated the statutory requirement that pleadings be in English. The issue went to the state's highest court, which held:

> It is said in the argument that the plea is not wholly in the English language; that "*vs.*" stands for "*versus*," and that "*versus*" is not an English word; that the plea should have been entitled Smith *against* Butler. But "*vs.*" and "*versus*" have been too long used in legal practice, and their meaning is too well understood, to be open to the objection stated. They have, in fact, become engrafted upon the English language, at least so far as they are used in this country in legal proceedings. Their meaning is well understood, and their use quite as appropriate as the word "against" could be.[3]

Over the course of the nineteenth century, use of the word in nonlegal contexts and with extended meanings grew. Even so, awareness of the legal origin of the term was never far from the surface. One finds, for example, in 1845, "Fancy *versus* Fact. This is the suit. So far as this point is concerned, we beg leave to enter a '*nolle prosequi*'" (note the italics indicating which words were regarded as non-English), and in 1894, "The Rambler *vs.* the Lumberman; an indictment for the larceny of a path." By the end of the century, even a writer in the *Harvard Law Review* was not above having a little fun with the word; he titled his article comparing two Supreme Court decisions "Swift *v.* Tyson versus Gelpcke *v.* Dubuque."[4]

By the early twentieth century, just about the only place you could be sure *not* to find some use of *versus* in an expanded or nonlegal sense was in the courts. A federal circuit court broke the ice in 1914, referring to "the question of mechanical skill versus invention" in a patent case,[5] but expanded uses of the term did not become common in the courts until the 1930s. The judiciary's slowness in getting on the bandwagon illustrates the general linguistic conservatism of the law, and especially of judges; the new uses of the term probably struck many judges as slangy and inappropriate for formal writing. The U.S. Supreme Court did not use the term in any such sense (save when it had to quote others) until 1947, when Justice Hugo Black wrote an opinion referring to "the barge versus rail competitive situation." That broke the unconscious taboo, and from then on *versus* was used with increasing frequency in the Supreme Court in all the same ways that it is now used by everyone else. Some recent examples include "the independent-contractor-versus-employee issue," "individual versus systematic thrust," "branded versus nonbranded mushrooms," "electrocution versus other methods of execution," and "porch versus, e.g., front walk."[6] In fact, the one context in which the word *versus* is almost never seen in the Supreme Court these days is the one that started it all: *versus* in case names. The long-established convention is to reduce that to *v.* (in contrast to *vs.*, the customary abbreviation in other contexts).

Yet even though the Supreme Court has now joined the rest of the English-speaking world in its use of *versus,* it still clings to one archaic practice. A century or two back, *versus* was regarded as a non-English word and therefore—following a typographic convention still used for foreign words today—was usually italicized. Applying that same rule to an abbreviation, the name of a case brought by Roe against Wade would have been written "Roe *v. Wade.*" Now that *versus* is well established in English, it is no longer italicized in ordinary writing. In case names, however, the Supreme Court—virtually alone among legal institutions—still italicizes it. Or at least it *would* do so, were it not for two other typographic conventions. First, because prior judicial opinions are so central to legal argument, the modern practice is to italicize case names in legal text to make them easy for lawyers to pick out. Second, when italicizing a phrase (such as the title of a book) that contains a foreign word that is already italicized, it is customary to "reverse italicize" that word by changing it back to plain roman type. Applying these principles to case names, the Supreme Court writes them in italics but meticulously *un*italicizes each little *v.,* so that the names come out in the form "*Roe* v. *Wade.*"

Perhaps this is the century in which the highest court in the United States will finally come to realize, as the highest court in New Hampshire did in 1852, that the *versus* in case names—once just a Latin legalism—is now part of the English language.

JEC

wall of separation

Few phrases in the law stir so much passion, and so much controversy, as Thomas Jefferson's "wall of separation between church and state."

The history of this phrase is really the history of the United States. The American colonies were established by individuals and groups of varying religious persuasions—many of them religious dissidents—who with few exceptions promptly set out to enforce their own beliefs in the new land. But religious uniformity proved as difficult to maintain in the colonies as it had been in England, and by the time the Constitution was being drafted there were minority sects in every state, many of whose adherents chafed at paying taxes to support the schools and churches of the state-approved denominations and at being denied such civil rights as the right to hold public office. In addition, the Western world had undergone that revolution in thought known as the Enlightenment, whose ideas underlay the American Revolution and gave rise to deism, a religious philosophy that rejected most of the Christian theology—including most fundamentally the divinity of Jesus—that had been common to all the colonial establishments. Enlightenment philosophers tended to distrust not only state control of religion but also its inseparable converse, religious control of state functions. Several of America's leading political and intellectual figures in the years before and after the Revolution, including Benjamin Franklin, Thomas Paine, and the country's first four presidents—George Washington, John Adams, Thomas Jefferson, and James Madison—either were avowed deists or at least evidenced clear reservations about conventional Christianity.

It was obvious to most of those who were putting the Constitution together in 1787 that a group of states as religiously diverse as America's could never "form a more perfect Union" if the national government endorsed religious views or played favorites among religions. They conspicuously rejected the custom, embodied in all state constitutions then and now, of mentioning God in the Preamble; they included a clause prohibiting the imposition of any religious requirement for the holding of any office or employment in the national government; they even provided that officeholders need not swear an oath to support the Constitution, thus implicitly invoking God, but may (for what is traditionally referred to as the "oath of office") recite a simple affirmation instead.[1] (When the Confederate States seceded, they drafted their own constitution by editing the U.S. Constitution. They first remedied the original framers' omission in the Preamble by inserting the words, "invoking the favor and guidance of Almighty God." Thus reassured that God was guiding their hand, they proceeded to add several clauses guaranteeing the right to own slaves.)[2]

Despite all this, many states were still not satisfied that the framers had done enough to ensure that the federal government would stay out of religion. The first session of Congress therefore adopted what two years later became the First Amendment to the Constitution, opening with the words "Congress shall make no law respecting an establishment of religion, or prohibiting the free exercise thereof."

The new government's deliberate neutrality on religion soon stood it in good stead in a way that the framers could not have foreseen. In his second term as the first president, George Washington dispatched a representative to negotiate treaties with the Barbary States of North Africa, to protect American shipping from Barbary pirates. In negotiations with the bey (governor) of Tripoli, it proved helpful to be able to point out that the U.S. government had no quarrel with the Islamic religion. The English version of the resulting treaty, executed in the waning months of Washington's presidency, stated:

> As the government of the United States of America is not in any sense founded on the Christian religion—as it has in itself no character of enmity against the laws, religion or tranquillity of Musselmen [Muslims]— . . . it is declared by the parties, that no pretext arising from religious opinions shall ever produce an interruption of the harmony existing between the two countries.[3]

The treaty made its way back to the United States, where in 1797 it was submitted for the Senate's advice and consent by President John Adams, read aloud and printed for the senators, ratified a few days later by a unanimous vote, signed and proclaimed by the president, and published in newspapers.

This of course does not mean that the people of the United States were not overwhelmingly Christian. When Adams's vice president, Thomas Jefferson, sought to succeed him as president, considerable opposition was raised against him because of his personal, as well as political, religious neutrality. Jefferson was on record as having said, "It does me no injury for my neighbour to say there are twenty gods, or no god"—though he had not yet confided, as he did later on, that in his view the wisdom of Jesus's actual words was as separable from the supernatural claims made about Jesus by the Gospel writers "as the diamond from the dunghill."[4] A vigorous campaign was mounted to defeat Jefferson on account of his "disbelief of the Holy Scriptures," "rejection of the Christian Religion," and "Deistical principles," as a result of which his election would "destroy religion, introduce immorality, and loosen all the bonds of society."[5]

But many evangelicals, still disadvantaged by *state* establishments of religion even though the *federal* government was barred from discriminating against them, supported Jefferson for his strong stand against government involvement in religion. They knew that it was Jefferson who had drafted the stirring Virginia Statute for Religious Freedom, whose enactment in 1786 had served as an inspiration for the drafting of the First Amendment just three years later. When Jefferson won the election, one such group, the Danbury Baptist Association, representing twenty-six churches in Connecticut and New York, wrote him an elaborate letter hailing his election, praising his past services, bemoaning their "degrading" status as a religious minority in a state where Congregationalism was the official state religion, and expressing the hope "that the sentiments of our beloved President, which have had such genial Effect already, like the radiant beams of the Sun, will shine & prevail through all these States."[6]

Jefferson could have tossed off a formulaic response thanking the association for its sentiments, but he did not. This was an issue he cared deeply about, and he viewed the letter as an opportunity to advance his views (already adopted at the federal level) at the state level. He drafted a response and circulated it to two of his political advisers—the attorney general and the postmaster general—saying that he wished to use it as an occasion for "sowing useful truths & principles among the people." Upon receiving their comments, Jefferson revised the letter, and on January 1, 1802, he sent it out. In its final form, the letter assured the Danbury Baptists of Jefferson's "sovereign reverence" for the action of the American people as a whole in adopting the First Amendment, "thus building a wall of separation between Church & State." Almost three centuries later, Supreme Court Justice (later Chief Justice) William Rehnquist, an ardent foe of strict separation, dismissed Jefferson's letter as nothing more than "a short note of courtesy."[7] Nothing could be further from the truth.

Jefferson was not the first to come up with the metaphor of a *wall of separation*. More than a century and a half earlier, Roger Williams, the Baptist founder of the colony of Rhode Island, had written of the importance of a "hedge or wall of Separation between the Garden of the Church and the Wildernes of the world," and just ten years before the American Revolution the English reformer James Burgh, in an essay whimsically addressed to "the Good People of Britain of the Twentieth Century," had advised those far-distant people to "build an impenetrable wall of *separation* between things *sacred* and *civil*."[8] Burgh was known and admired by Jefferson and his fellows, and it is often speculated that Jefferson got the *wall of separation* metaphor from Burgh. But there is no reason to assume that. The phrase had long been used for both literal and metaphorical walls in every sort of context—as when King Charles I unwisely rejected an offer to meet with Parliament at the outset of the English Civil War in 1642, and instead denounced Parliament for creating "a Wall of Separation betwixt Us and Our People."[9] (On January 30, 1649, the parliamentarians created a separation between Charles's body and his head, making his royal "Us" singularly appropriate.) It was not necessary for Jefferson to have remembered the phrase from anywhere in particular, or even to have remembered it at all.

Jefferson could scarcely have imagined how successful his effort to sow the principle of separation of church and state would be. In 1879 the Supreme Court, in a unanimous opinion written by the Chief Justice, said of Jefferson's letter, "Coming as this does from an acknowledged leader of the advocates of the [First Amendment], it may be accepted almost as an authoritative declaration of the scope and effect of the amendment thus secured."[10] Ironically, the Court in that case ruled *against* the party complaining of interference with his religion, holding that Mormons had no right to practice polygamy. Evidently the Court did not believe, as a latter-day Jefferson might have put it, that "it does me no injury for my neighbour to have twenty wives, or no wife."

The Supreme Court returned to Jefferson's metaphor in 1947, strongly stating (again in language agreed to by all nine Justices) that the establishment clause of the First Amendment—extended to the states by virtue of the Fourteenth Amendment—is a complete barrier to public support for "any religious activities or institutions . . . whatever form they may adopt to teach or practice religion. . . . The First Amendment," the Court declared, "has erected a wall between church and state. That wall must be kept high and impregnable." Once again, the ironic result of the case was a ruling against the party claiming the benefit of the First Amendment: over passionate dissents from four of its members, the Court approved the use of tax dollars to reimburse parents for the cost of busing their children to school, even when it is a parochial school. Justice Robert Jackson, one of the dissenters, noting what he regarded as a conflict between the majority's rhetoric and its result, remarked that "the most fitting precedent" for the decision was the case of Julia in Lord Byron's *Don Juan*, who (wrote Byron) "whispering 'I will ne'er consent,'—consented."[11]

But from then on, the First Amendment and the *wall of separation* metaphor were inextricably bound together—to the dismay of antiseparationists like Justice Rehnquist but to the great benefit of legal scholars, who as a result have no end of opportunity for exploiting the metaphor in article titles. In view of the strong shift to the right in Supreme Court decisions in the latter part of the twentieth century and early part of the twenty-first, most of those titles now concern the weakening of Jefferson's wall: "The Wall of Separation Crumbles," "The Decline and Fall of the Wall of Separation," "The Writing Is on the Wall of Separation," and so on.[12]

But all the disputes over the wall of separation are as nothing compared with the conflicts that would embroil the nation if religious beliefs were subject to legislation. The historian Leonard W. Levy summed it up: "Despite its detractors and despite its leaks, cracks, and its archways, the wall ranks as one of the mightiest monuments of constitutional government in this nation."[13]

JEC

wet foot, dry foot

On June 29, 1999, the city of Miami, center of the largest concentration of Cubans outside Cuba, was in tumult. Six Cuban refugees in a fourteen-foot rowboat—evidently launched from a smuggler's vessel a mile or two offshore—were trying to make landfall just north of Miami Beach. The United States Coast Guard, with a fleet of four Coast Guard and police boats, was trying to repel the invasion. A television station broadcast the David and Goliath struggle live from a helicopter as crowds gathered on the beach to cheer the refugees on. The refugees swung their oars to fend off the Coast Guard; the Coast Guard fought back with a fire hose. The refugees finally jumped into the water and swam for it, zigzagging desperately in an effort to evade their pursuers. Miraculously, two of them made it to shore, where they were promptly taken into custody by the Border Patrol; the other four were captured in the water and detained on a Coast Guard vessel. Later in the day, hundreds of protesters from the Cuban community took to the streets, shutting down an expressway and a causeway for a considerable time during rush hour.

By then the *Miami Herald* had dispatched a slew of reporters to cover the event from every possible angle; it would publish seven stories and columns on the incident and its aftermath the next day and eleven the day after that, plus an editorial each day. The paper's reporter Yves Colon was interviewing Dan Geoghegan, assistant chief of Border Patrol in Miami. Though he probably did not put it this way, the obvious question was, "Why go to all that trouble? Why not just wait for the Cubans to land and pick them up?" The answer, as both the would-be migrants and their supporters on shore were keenly aware, is that different laws apply to Cubans who reach land and those stopped at sea—a distinction that Geoghegan set out to clarify.

Geoghegan had young children at the time, and some of their toys were in his office. His eyes fell on a set of Dr. Seuss flashcards designed to teach about opposites: *Wet Foot, Dry Foot, Low Foot, High Foot.* "It's sort of like Dr. Seuss," Geoghegan explained to Colon. Colon, struck by the clarity of the explanation, led with it in his article published the next morning: "Wet foot or dry foot. That's the short version of United States policy when it comes to Cuban refugees. If they're caught in the water, they're sent back to Cuba. If they touch ground, they get to stay." (The article went on to explain that there was actually a little more to the rule than that: those caught in the water would be given a chance to prove that they were entitled to political asylum, but grants of asylum in such cases were rare.)[1]

This simple characterization of a rather unintuitive policy was an instant hit. By the next day other Florida newspapers were referring to "the 'wet foot' policy," "a 'wet feet, dry feet' policy," and the like; one day later the *Miami Herald* itself reported that the ACLU and other groups would be working to overturn "the 'wet-foot, dry foot' rule." Three days after Colon's story first appeared, the motif hit the national media in a *Washington Post* article (a version of which was syndicated to other papers) referring to "the Clinton administration's policy, dubbed 'wet foot, dry foot.'" In that form (matching Dr. Seuss's wording and punctuation) the phrase remains the shorthand most often used to describe the current compromise in the long history of U.S.-Cuba immigration policy.[2]

The *wet foot, dry foot* dichotomy is more the result of history than of conscious policy decision. Beginning in 1959, after Fidel Castro's Communist revolution in Cuba, hundreds of thousands of Cuban nationals fled to the United States. These earliest immigrants were mostly educated people from the middle and upper classes. They may have expected that Castro's regime would fail quickly and they would be able to return. When that didn't happen, it gradually became clear that the Cuban immigrants needed some kind of formal status. Congress therefore passed the Cuban Adjustment Act (CAA) in 1966. The CAA created a unique deal for Cubans headed for the United States: instead of having to prove political persecution individually, they were assumed to be entitled to

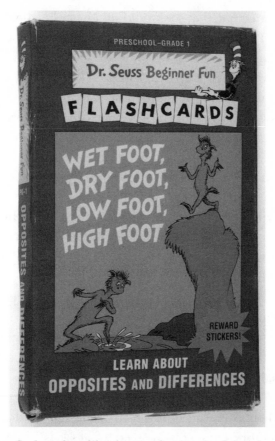

A 1998 Dr. Seuss flashcard set like the one that inspired the phrase *wet foot, dry foot* in 1999. (The original is vividly colored.) (*Dr. Seuss Beginner Fun Flashcards,* TM & © Dr. Seuss Enterprises, L.P. 1998. Used by permission. All rights reserved. Photograph by Dwight Primiano.)

asylum, and they could become permanent legal residents (receiving a GREEN CARD) after a short time in the United States. This rule applied whether the Cubans were rescued from boats or made it to shore.

The flow of Cuban immigrants continued, exacerbated at times by massive migrations such as the Mariel boatlift of 1980, in which 125,000 Cubans, many of them former prisoners, arrived in south Florida in a period of six months. Less prosperous Cubans arrived in large numbers, some after harrowing trips in small, overcrowded boats. In 1994 and 1995, negotiations between the United States and Cuba resulted in a new rule: Cubans intercepted at sea would no longer be allowed to enter the United States. This new agreement, however, did not repeal the CAA.

The functional result of these combined laws is the wet foot, dry foot rule. Cubans who make it to U.S. soil need not show persecution, only Cuban origin, in order to be on the fast track to legal residency. Those stopped at sea go back to Cuba unless they can show in an asylum interview that they have a well-founded fear of persecution (in which case they are resettled in countries other than the United States).

The wet foot, dry foot rule has some odd legal consequences. A boat carrying thirty-four Cubans got within a quarter mile of Grassy Key before hitting a sandbar. The fifteen who swam ashore (achieving dry feet) were allowed to stay. Those in the boat were returned to Cuba. In another incident, the Coast Guard found fifteen Cubans on a dilapidated bridge south of Marathon Key. This old bridge had collapsed in places and so was no longer connected to land on either end. Since the Cubans could not walk to land without returning to the water (wet foot), they were sent back to Cuba. After a federal judge disagreed with this application of the policy, the parties settled the case and the Cubans (except for one man with a criminal history) were given permission to return to the United States if Castro would allow them to leave Cuba.

The overwhelming need to reach dry land means that setting off in creaky vessels in the hope of being rescued at sea is no longer an option. Cubans desperate to achieve dry feet turn to well-paid professional smugglers with sleek "go-fast" boats instead of the old makeshift rafts. These trips can turn deadly. One Customs agent described the smugglers' disregard for their passengers' safety: "The passengers aren't human beings, they're contraband. That's how they are treated. It could be a bale of marijuana, a kilo of cocaine, or a human being." Deaths and injuries occur as the smugglers take extreme measures to elude the Coast Guard. And the smuggling business is extremely lucrative. In 2006 officials estimated the price for smuggling a Cuban to the United States at eight to ten thousand dollars; at those rates, if a smuggler squashed twenty-five immigrants into a speedboat, he could earn as much as a quarter million dollars in one trip.[3]

The wet foot, dry foot rule itself has controversial policy implications. Part of the criticism turns on its tendency to favor light-skinned immigrants; it excludes all other refugee groups, most notably those fleeing Haiti. *Miami Herald* columnist Carl Hiaasen has suggested that a different rhyme is involved: "'white foot, black foot' . . . if your foot is black, you're going back." White immigrants are welcome; black ones are not: "Pack about two hundred Norwegians—the whitest and blondest you can find—on a boat headed for Miami. I bet nobody would interdict them on the water, except perhaps to loan them some sunblock. I bet no army of police would be deployed to round them up once they came ashore."[4]

The operation of wet foot, dry foot seems at times more like Lewis Carroll than Dr. Seuss. While there is no Queen of Hearts to scream, "Off with their heads," there are plenty of rules that could come from an *Alice in Wonderland* world lacking common sense and coherent policy. It may take a person who can believe six impossible things before breakfast to decipher the finer points of the rules that govern this area. The importance of reaching dry land, though, is clear: if Cuban refugees are caught with their feet in the water, away they go.

EGT

white shoe

A *white-shoe* law firm is an old-line upper-crust firm—the kind that in bygone days selected its members using much the same criteria as an exclusive gentlemen's club. Imagine well-heeled men in navy blazers and white buck shoes relaxing over cocktails on the veranda of a restricted Long Island golf club in the 1950s, and you have a picture of the people and atmosphere evoked by this phrase.

White buckskin shoes have been associated with gentlemanly pursuits at least since the 1880s, when they became part of the all-white uniform worn by cricketers. In the 1950s they were so much a part of Ivy League student attire—particularly among those for whom college was more a social pursuit than an academic one—that in at least one university they gave rise to an entire sociolinguistic system. As described in a 1953 article in *Esquire*:

At Yale there is a system for pigeonholing the members of the college community which is based on the word "shoe." Shoe bears some relation to the word chic, and when you say that a fellow is "terribly shoe" you mean that he is a crumb in the upper social crust of the college . . . . You talk of a "shoe" fraternity or a "shoe" crowd, for example, but you can also describe a man's manner of dress as "shoe." The term derives, as you probably know, from the dirty white bucks which are the standard collegiate footwear . . . , but the system of pigeonholing by footwear does not stop there. It encompasses the entire community under the terms White Shoe, Brown Shoe, and Black Shoe.

White Shoe applies primarily to the socially ambitious and socially smug types.[1]

Socially well-connected Ivy Leaguers were exactly the kind of candidate sought by some of the most powerful and prestigious legal and financial firms on Wall Street—like Davis Polk & Wardwell, a law firm that in 1961 had thirty-eight partners, of whom twenty-six were listed in the *Social Register.* At most major New York law firms in those days it went without saying that only white male Protestants need apply; as an associate at one such firm put it, "They . . . want lawyers who are Nordic, have pleasing personalities and 'clean-cut' appearances, are graduates of the 'right' schools, have the 'right' social background and experience in the affairs of the world."[2]

An observer of the Wall Street legal scene in the early 1960s reported that "those offices where many of the associates and partners are listed in the *Social Register* or are 'social register types' (upper-class), are called social firms."[3] The rise of *white-shoe firm* as a common term for such firms shows the spread of college-boy slang into mainstream usage as the college boys themselves rose in the professions. This was no doubt abetted by the fact that the fashion of white shoes for casual wear in the summer—at the golf club, the sailing party, the weekend do at the summer house—continued to be a familiar feature of upper-class life.

But for some time this remained largely in-group jargon among lawyers and Wall Street types, and more a matter of oral tradition than of writing. The phrase showed up in a 1967 law review article and a 1973 book about

Wall Street law firms,[4] but such appearances were rare. General media coverage of law firms was relatively sparse until a 1977 Supreme Court opinion declared that lawyers have a First Amendment right to advertise, freeing them to discuss their business with the press. It was not until the 1980s that the phrase *white-shoe firm* began to appear regularly in print. The earliest instance we have found in a general-circulation organ occurred, fittingly enough, in a *Fortune* magazine article about the horsey set, in which the owner of the winning horse in a particularly rich race was described as "a litigator with the white-shoe law firm of Breed Abbott & Morgan in Manhattan."[5]

Ironically, by the time the "white-shoe" characterization finally entered general usage, it no longer really fit the firms to which it was applied. Society, business, and law had all undergone a revolution since the 1950s. It was no longer either legal or fashionable for firms to exclude candidates on the basis of race, sex, religion, or ethnicity. On a practical level—in part because of that 1977 decision on lawyer advertising—the business of law was becoming far more competitive; firms could no longer count on keeping or getting clients on the basis of school, social, and historical ties. Most significantly, brilliant lawyers who for a century or more had been foreclosed from establishment firms because they "wouldn't fit in"—often meaning that they were Jewish—had formed their own firms and developed them into formidable legal powerhouses, in many cases larger and richer and more sought after for corporate advice and representation than most of their purportedly more "upper-crust" competitors. No firm hoping to survive in the new business environment could afford to reject bright candidates simply because they did not fit the old white-shoe mold.

The historical roots of a firm could nevertheless affect its tone in almost subliminal ways; in 1982 it could still be said of the elite investment-banking firm of Morgan Stanley & Company, "They like to hire WASP types even if they are black or Jewish."[6] But as the ethnic and social makeup of legal and financial firms became more mixed over the years, *white shoe* became less a description of the social makeup of a firm and more an indication of its historical origins or its current status as powerful, well established, and well connected. In light of this more general meaning, the term has also expanded beyond the New York–centered region to which it was originally confined; one can now read, for example, of "one of the upper South's lead-ing white-shoe firms, Hunton & Williams," based in Richmond, Virginia.[7] And in what can only be described as poetic justice, the phrase is now frequently used in reference to firms that grew powerful by accepting those very lawyers who in bygone days were not regarded as "shoe" enough for admission to the traditional white-shoe firms.

JEC

the whole truth

By long custom throughout the English-speaking world—enforced by stat-ute in many states of the United States—every witness (except in unusual situations) must pledge to tell "the truth, the whole truth, and nothing but the truth." The formula is so familiar, and seems so clear, that we seldom pause to ask where it comes from or what it really means.

The phrase is certainly very ancient. Perhaps alone among verbal for-mulas of such length in the law, "Do you swear to tell the truth, the whole truth, and nothing but the truth, so help you God?" is entirely devoid of Latin or French influence: every word is of Anglo-Saxon origin. Like reli-gion, the law has been characterized from earliest times by rhythmic, repetitious language that lends itself to memorization and ritual use. "The truth, the whole truth, and nothing but the truth" emerged from that tra-dition.

It appeared in writing at least as early as 1593, in a book on procedure in manorial courts, and was brought to America as a part of English legal tradition and independently adopted in various colonies.[1] For example, the laws that William Penn drew up in England in 1682 for the colony that he had just been granted in America—named Pennsylvania in honor of his late father, Admiral Sir William Penn—provided that witnesses would give evidence "by solemnly promising to speak the truth, the whole truth, and nothing but the truth, to the matter, or thing in question."[2]

The words "solemnly promising" are significant. The traditional oath required a witness not merely to promise the court but to swear to God, and thereby put his immortal soul in jeopardy if the oath was violated (though penalties for perjury, in the form of fines or imprisonment, were provided in case the prospect of eternal damnation proved an insufficient deterrent). But Penn, a Quaker, founded his colony as a haven for Quakers and a place where people of all religions would be welcome; and one of the characteristics that made Quakers the subject of distrust and persecution in England was their refusal, on religious grounds, to swear oaths—even oaths of loyalty to the king. To the consternation of legal authorities, Quakers insisted that they were bound by the higher authority of Jesus Christ who, according to the new translation of the Bible authorized by King James earlier in that century, had preached in the Sermon on the Mount: "Ye have heard that it hath been said by them of old time, Thou shalt not forswear thyself [swear falsely], but shalt perform unto the Lord thine oaths: But I say unto you, Swear not at all" (Matt. 5:33–34; see also Jas. 5:12).

In deference to such scruples, the framers of the United States Constitution more than a century later were careful not to require any oath; instead, they provided that high government officers "shall be bound by Oath *or Affirmation,* to support this Constitution."[3]

But most colonies had not been so tolerant and had required that evidence be given on oath. This posed a problem in the colony of Virginia, where the requirement of sworn testimony stood in the way of receiving necessary evidence from non-Christianized slaves in cases against other slaves, particularly capital cases involving alleged conspiracies against slave masters. If the recently imported slaves did not worship (and fear) the Christian God, how could they swear an oath, and how could the usual criminal penalties for perjury—deemed a sufficient deterrent to perjury for white Christians—provide sufficient assurance of honesty?

The problem was resolved in 1723 by a Virginia statute permitting judges to receive testimony from "Negroes, Mulattos, or Indians, bond or free," but only after providing the following helpful explanation of their obligations as a witness:

> You are brought hither as a witness; and, by the direction of the law,
> I am to tell you, before you give your evidence, that you must tell the
> truth, the whole truth, and nothing but the truth; and that if it be

found hereafter, that you tell a lie, and give false testimony in this matter, you must, for so doing, have both your ears nailed to the pillory, and cut off, and receive thirty-nine lashes on your bare back, well laid on, at the common whipping-post.

There are records of the penalty being applied, and this law "remained the basis for the admission of evidence in capital trials of slaves in Virginia to the end of slavery in 1865."[4]

Of course, in a broad philosophical sense no one can testify to the "whole truth" of a matter, since everything is interconnected and so much is unknowable. As Carl Sandburg put it in his epic poem *The People, Yes:*

> "Do you solemnly swear before the everliving God that the testimony you are about to give in this cause shall be the truth, the whole truth, and nothing but the truth?"
>
> "No, I don't. I can tell you what I saw and what I heard and I'll swear to that by the everliving God but the more I study about it the more sure I am that nobody but the everliving God knows the whole truth and if you summoned Christ as a witness in this case what He would tell you would burn your insides with the pity and the mystery of it."[5]

But even in the more limited and practical sense of "all material facts" or "all facts directly relevant to the case," the whole truth is really not welcome in American courtrooms, and witnesses who attempt to flesh out their testimony in accordance with their oath are routinely instructed: "Just answer the question." Relevant information withheld from juries falls into two general categories: evidence the lawyers would like to introduce that is excluded by law, and evidence the law would allow that the lawyers choose not to introduce.

In the first category is evidence that might be helpful or even essential in a specific case but that is excluded for larger reasons of public policy. To preserve the sanctity of the confessional, for example, a priest cannot be asked to disclose what was said in confession; so as not to give the police free license to conduct unlawful searches, the prosecution usually is barred from using illegally obtained evidence; to ensure all litigants an adequate opportunity to cross-examine their accusers, there is a general rule against hearsay testimony. This category stems from America's emphasis on individual rights and due process.

The second category stems from the American tradition of lawyer-controlled litigation. In contrast to the continental European system (discussed at HEARSAY), judges in America are not expected to bring to light the relevant facts; if the lawyers choose not to pursue certain evidentiary threads, the evidence generally does not get in. Since there are always some facts that a lawyer would prefer that the jury not hear, the standard advice to clients who will be called as a witness is, "Don't volunteer information. Say only what is necessary to answer the question, then stop." If the jury is left with an incomplete or distorted picture because the opposing lawyer fails to follow up, that's just the way the game is played.

This system has its critics. A federal judge who has been described as "a leader in the movement to give truth a greater value in trials"[6] wrote, "Decisions of the Supreme Court give repeated voice to this concept . . . that 'partisan advocacy on both sides,' according to rules often countenancing partial truths and concealment, will best assure the discovery of truth in the end. . . . We . . . would fear for our lives if physicians, disagreeing about the cause of our chest pains, sought to resolve the issue by our forms of interrogation, badgering, and other forensics. But for the defendant whose life is at stake—and for the public concerned whether the defendant is a homicidal menace—this is thought to be the most perfect form of inquiry."[7] But whatever else one might say of this approach to the presentation of evidence in court, one cannot call it perjury. Despite the witness's oath to tell the whole truth, the general rule is that so long as the words spoken are true *as far as they go,* the mere fact that they may be a misleading half-truth is not a violation of the oath.

The Supreme Court made this clear in a case in which the owner of a company in bankruptcy, at a hearing held to determine what assets might be available to pay the company's debts, was asked whether he had ever had a Swiss bank account and answered, "The company had an account there for about six months, in Zurich." The only tiny detail that he left out was that he had also maintained a *personal* bank account in Switzerland for *five years*—which is precisely what he was asked about. It was a deliberate deception and a clear violation of the oath, and when the full story came out he was duly convicted of perjury. The Supreme Court reversed the

Not a Scholar

If this widely circulated "actual trial transcript" from England is to be believed, there is at least one individual in the English-speaking world who does not just blindly recite the words of the oath without thinking about what they mean:

CLERK: **Please repeat after me, "I swear by Almighty God . . . "**
WITNESS: **"I swear by Almighty God."**
C: **"That the evidence that I give . . ."**
W: **That's right.**
C: **Repeat it.**
W: **"Repeat it."**
C: **No! Repeat what I said.**
W: **What you said when?**
C: **"That the evidence that I give . . ."**
W: **"That the evidence that I give."**
C: **"Shall be the truth and . . ."**
W: **It will, and nothing but the truth!**
C: **Please, just repeat after me, "Shall be the truth and . . ."**
W: **I'm not a scholar, you know.**
C: **We can appreciate that. Just repeat after me: "Shall be the truth and . . ."**
W: **"Shall be the truth and."**
C: **Say, "Nothing . . ."**
W: **Okay. (*Witness remains silent.*)**
C: **No! Don't say nothing. Say, "Nothing but the truth."**
W: **Yes.**
C: **Can't you say, "Nothing but the truth"?**
W: **Yes.**
C: **Well? Do so.**
W: **You're confusing me.**
C: **Just say: "Nothing but the truth."**
W: **Okay, I understand.**
C: **Then say it.**

w: What?

c: "Nothing but the truth."

w: But I do! That's just it.

c: You must say: "Nothing but the truth"!

w: I WILL say nothing but the truth!

c: Please, just repeat these four words: "Nothing," "But," "The," "Truth."

w: What? You mean, like, now?

c: Yes! Now. Please. Just say those four words.

w: Nothing. But. The. Truth.

c: Thank you.

w: I'm just not a scholar.

conviction and put the blame entirely on the duped questioner. It said, "If a witness evades, it is the lawyer's responsibility to recognize the evasion and to bring the witness back to the mark, to flush out the whole truth with the tools of adversary examination."[8]

In sum, the phrase "the truth, the whole truth, and nothing but the truth," repeated with such ceremony, is in some respects just ceremony. Ceremonies are important in law; they emphasize the gravity of the proceedings. But this may be the only legal ritual in America whose very words are explicitly misleading. It puts witnesses and parties who have not been coached by a lawyer at a disadvantage because they may take the oath literally (one might even say seriously): a litigant who "believes the oath and volunteers information . . . will often be victimized by an opponent who understands and acts upon the real rules."[9]

JEC

Notes

abuse excuse

1. William Blackstone, *Commentaries on the Laws of England,* vol. 4 (Oxford, 1769), 75.
2. "Battle of Sexes Joined in Case of a Mutilation," *New York Times,* Nov. 8, 1993, A16; "Husband Tells of Mutilation as Wife's Trial Starts," *New York Times,* Jan. 11, 1994, A12.
3. Danny R. Tipton, letter to the editor, *Dayton Daily News,* Dec. 4, 1993, 12A ("Don't be so quick to believe every woman with an abuse excuse"); Ann Landers column, *Chicago Tribune,* Nov. 18, 1993, Tempo section, 3.
4. Alan M. Dershowitz, interview by Paula Zahn, *CBS This Morning,* Jan. 14, 1994; Alan M. Dershowitz, "The Abuse Excuse," *Albany Times Union,* Jan. 17, 1994, A6. The essay is reproduced with minor changes as the first chapter of a book published later that year: Alan M. Dershowitz, *The Abuse Excuse and Other Cop-Outs, Sob Stories, and Evasions of Responsibility* (Boston: Little, Brown, 1994).
5. *Geraldo,* syndicated television show, Jan. 26, 1994; *Nightline,* ABC television, Feb. 4, 1994.
6. Hank Grezlak, "Bobbitt Attorney Discusses Defense; Strategy Meshed Insanity and Self-Defense," *Legal Intelligencer,* Feb. 8, 1994, 1; Stephanie B. Goldberg, "Fault Lines," *ABA Journal,* June 1994, 40.
7. *Lyle v. Warner Brothers Television Productions,* 117 Cal. App. 4th 1164, 1178 & n.74 (2004) (bracketed change by the court), *rev'd,* 38 Cal. 4th 264 (2006).

affirmative action

1. "A Copy of a Letter Wrote by the Prophet Lodowicke Muggleton, to Mrs. Elizabeth Flaggetter, of Cork in Ireland, Bearing Date from London, June 25, 1683," in John Reeve, *Sacred Remains; or, A Divine Appendix* ([London?], ca. 1751), 394 (characterizing obedience to a negative commandment as "an affirmative Action"); *Mason & Hale v. Denison & Denison,* 15 Wend. 64, 72 (N.Y. 1835) (holding that certain contracts by minors are unenforceable even if the minor has not taken "affirmative action" to annul them).
2. Executive Order No. 10925, § 301, 26 *Federal Register* 1977 (March 8, 1961).
3. Nicholas Lemann, "Taking Affirmative Action Apart," *New York Times Magazine,* June 11, 1995, 36, 40 (ellipsis in original).

4. *Washington Post, Times Herald* [the combined newspaper now known as *The Washington Post*], Apr. 5, 1964, A8, and May 24, 1964, F6.

5. Lyndon B. Johnson, commencement address at Howard University: "To Fulfill These Rights," June 4, 1965, in *Public Papers of the Presidents of the United States: Lyndon B. Johnson* (Washington, D.C.: United States Government Printing Office, 1965), 2:636.

6. Martin Luther King Jr., "Remaining Awake Through a Great Revolution," sermon given at National Cathedral, Washington, D.C., Mar. 31, 1968, as reprinted in *A Testament of Hope: The Essential Writings and Speeches of Martin Luther King Jr.*, ed. James M. Washington (1986; San Francisco: HarperCollins, 1991), 271; also reprinted in *Congressional Record*, Apr. 9, 1968, 9395–97.

7. Martha S. West, "The Historical Roots of Affirmative Action," 10 *La Raza Law Journal* 607, 620 (1998).

age of consent

1. Edward Coke, *The First Part of the Institutes of the Lawes of England; or, A Commentarie upon Littleton* (London, 1628), 79b; [Thomas Edgar?], *The Lawes Resolutions of Womens Rights* (London, 1632), 223. The phrase occurs in French (*age de consent*) in the report of *Kenne's Case* (1606) in *La Sept Part des Reports Sr. Edw. Coke Chivaler, Chiefe Justice del Common Banke* [The Seventh Part of the Reports of Sir Edward Coke, Knight, Chief Justice of the Common Bench] (London, 1608), 42b, 43a–43b, in a context suggesting that the phrase was well established in the law.

2. *Humphrey v. Wilson,* 282 Ga. 520 (2007); Jeremy Redmon and Tammy Joyner, "Wilson Rejoices: 4–3 Decision Frees Genarlow," *Atlanta Journal-Constitution,* Oct. 27, 2007, 1A.

3. R. H. Helmholz, *Marriage Litigation in Medieval England* (London: Cambridge University Press, 1974), 98–99.

4. 3 Edw. I, ch. 13 (1275), 1 Statutes of the Realm 29.

5. 18 Eliz. I, ch. 7 (1575–76), 4 Statutes of the Realm 617–18; 9 Geo. IV, ch. 31, §§ 16, 17 (1828).

6. 24 & 25 Vict., ch. 100, §§ 48, 50, 51 (1861).

7. "We Bid You Be of Hope," *Pall Mall Gazette,* July 6, 1885. The title of the series, which began in that day's paper, was "The Maiden Tribute of Modern Babylon." The story of Stead's activities, and of the varied cast of social, religious, political, and criminal characters involved, is told by Ann Stafford in *The Age of Consent* (London: Hodder and Stoughton, 1964).

8. For statistics in this paragraph see Mary E. Odem, *Delinquent Daughters: Protecting and Policing Adolescent Female Sexuality in the United States, 1885–1920* (Chapel Hill: University of North Carolina Press, 1995), ch. 1 and n. 59; the Arkansas decision was *State v. Pierson,* 44 Ark. 265, 265–67 (1884).

aid and abet (and the like)

1. Letter to Joseph C. Cabell, Sept. 9, 1817, in *The Writings of Thomas Jefferson,* ed. Andrew A. Lipscomb, vol. 17 (Washington, D.C.: Thomas Jefferson Memorial Association, 1904), 418. For more of Jefferson's remarks on the subject, see David Mellinkoff, *The Language of the Law* (Boston: Little, Brown, 1963), 252–53.
2. *Wiegand v. Perper,* No. G031175, 2004 Cal. App. Unpub. LEXIS 4689, at *10 (Cal. Ct. App. May 13, 2004) (emphasis, brackets, and final ellipsis added).
3. Mellinkoff, *Language of the Law,* 186–92.
4. John Adams, letter to William Tudor, Sept. 10, 1818, in *Novanglus, and Massachusettensis* (Boston, 1819), 304.
5. Copy, in Jefferson's own hand, of the final draft of the Declaration of Independence as submitted to the full congress for action (emphasis added). This copy, one of a handful that Jefferson wrote out for friends, is in the collection of the New York Public Library. For a reproduction, see Julian P. Boyd, *The Declaration of Independence: The Evolution of the Text,* rev. ed. (Washington, D.C.: Library of Congress, 1999), document 7. Spelling and capitalization were changed in the final version of the Declaration.

attorney general

1. Francis Morgan Nichols, *Britton: The French Text Carefully Revised with an English Translation, Introduction and Notes* (Oxford, 1865), 2:356.
2. Court reporter's transcript of oral argument, *Davenport v. Washington Education Association,* No. 05-1589 (argued Jan. 10, 2007), 14; Web site of Office of the Attorney General, State of Mississippi, http://www.ago.state.ms.us/index.php/ sections/divisions (2011).
3. Michael Herz, "Washington, Patton, Schwarzkopf and . . . Ashcroft?" 19 *Constitutional Commentary* 663, 673 (2002); George W. Bush, remarks Remarks to the United States Attorneys Conference, Nov. 29, 2001, 37 *Weekly Compilation of Presidential Documents* 1726, 1726 (Dec. 3, 2001).
4. United States Department of Justice, *An Investigation into the Removal of Nine U.S. Attorneys in 2006* (September 2008), 325–26 (posted on the Department of Justice Web site at http://www.usdoj.gov/oig/special/s0809a/final.pdf).
5. See Mary Jane McCaffree, Pauline Innis, and Richard M. Sand, *Protocol: The Complete Handbook of Diplomatic, Official and Social Usage,* 25th anniversary edition (Dallas: Durban House, 2002), 20–22.

attorney vs. lawyer

1. J. H. Baker, "The Three Languages of the Common Law," 43 *McGill Law Journal* 5, 18 (1998).

badge of slavery

1. William Shakespeare, *Henry IV, Part 2* (ca. 1598), act 4, scene 3; Stephen Crane, *The Red Badge of Courage: An Episode of the American Civil War* (New York, 1895), ch. 9, p. 91.
2. "Junius," letter of May 28, 1770, in *A Complete Collection of Junius's Letters* (London, 1770), 166, 173.
3. *Congressional Globe,* 39th Cong., 1st Sess. 474 & 322 (1866).
4. *Blyew v. United States,* 80 U.S. 581, 585, 599 (1871) (Bradley, J., dissenting).
5. *Civil Rights Cases,* 109 U.S. 3, 21, 24–25 (1882); Malvina Shanklin Harlan, *Some Memories of a Long Life, 1854–1911* (New York: Modern Library, 2002), 108–14 (written in 1915; originally published in the *Journal of Supreme Court History,* 2001).
6. *Plessy v. Ferguson,* 163 U.S. 537, 562 (1896) (Harlan, J., dissenting); *Hodges v. United States,* 203 U.S. 1, 35 (1906) (Harlan, J., dissenting).
7. *Jones v. Alfred H. Mayer Co.,* 392 U.S. 409, 440 (1968).

billable hour

1. *Copeland v. Marshall,* 641 F.2d 880, 929 n.53 (D.C. Cir. 1980) (Wilkey, J., dissenting). Judge Wilkey, no doubt fearing that his opinion might inadvertently impugn some actual recently deceased lawyer, left the lawyer's name blank; we have supplied a fictitious name.
2. *O'Connor v. Richmond Savings & Loan Association,* 262 Cal. App. 2d 523, 527 (1968); ABA Special Commission on Legal Assistants, *Liberating the Lawyer* (1971), 47; Bob Kane, letter to the editor, *Student Lawyer,* Nov. 1972, 2–3. But see Joel A. Rose, "Simplified Timekeeping and Billing Management," *Legal Economics,* Spring 1975, 23 (still explaining concept of "billable hour" in 1975).
3. Deborah Rhode, quoted in Adam Liptak, "Stop the Clock? Critics Call the Billable Hour a Legal Fiction," *New York Times,* Oct. 29, 2002, G7.
4. Geoffrey Hazard, quoted in Niki Kuckes, "The Hours: The Short, Unhappy History of How Lawyers Bill Their Clients," *Legal Affairs,* Sept.–Oct. 2002.
5. Amy Miller, "Survey Shows the Bell Is Tolling for the Billable Hour," *Corporate Counsel Online,* Dec. 1, 2009, http://www.law.com/jsp/article.jsp?id=120243 5924167&slreturn=1&hbxlogin=1; Tamara Loomis, "Talkin' Revolution," *Corporate Counsel Online,* Aug. 20, 2009, http://www.law.com/jsp/cc/PubArticleCC .jsp?id=1202433183136.
6. Rhode, quoted in Liptak, "Stop the Clock?"

black letter law

1. Gerald Newton, *"Deutsche Schrift:* The Demise and Rise of German Black Letter," 56 *German Life and Letters* 183, 196–97 and plate 2 (photo of Bormann's memo) (2003).
2. William Blackstone, *Commentaries on the Laws of England,* vol. 3 (Oxford, 1768), 318.
3. John Holliday, *The Life of William Late Earl of Mansfield* (London, 1797), 127.
4. *Shorner's Case,* 22 F. Cas. 8, 9 (District of Pennsylvania 1812); *Mallery v. Dudley,* 4 Ga. 52, 60 & 57 (1848), quoting (without citing) James Kent, *Commentaries on American Law,* vol. 4 (New York, 1830), Lecture 53(4), 14, and Lecture 58(3), 206 note b.
5. *Rybolt v. Jarrett,* 112 F.2d 642, 644 (4th Cir. 1940); *Chestnut v. Ford Motor Co.,* 445 F.2d 967, 971 (4th Cir. 1971); *City of Indianapolis v. Edmond,* 531 U.S. 32, 49 (2000) (Rehnquist, J., dissenting).

blackmail

1. Scot. Act., Jam. 6, ch. 27 (1567) (Scot.); Scot. Act., Jam. 6, ch. 59, § 13 (1587) (Scot.); 43 Eliz., ch. 13, § 1 (1601) (Eng.).
2. Walter Scott, *Rob Roy,* ed. Ian Duncan (Oxford: Oxford University Press, 1998), ch. 26, p. 303. For a nonfiction account of Rob Roy's life, see David Stevenson, *The Hunt for Rob Roy: The Man and the Myths* (Edinburgh: John Donald, 2004).
3. Susan Forward, *Emotional Blackmail* (New York: HarperCollins, 1997).
4. Richard A. Posner, "Blackmail, Privacy, and Freedom of Contract," 141 *University of Pennsylvania Law Review* 1817, 1817 n.1 (1993); *Vegelahn v. Guntner,* 167 Mass. 92, 107 (1896) (Holmes, J., dissenting).
5. James Lindgren, "Unraveling the Paradox of Blackmail," 84 *Columbia Law Review* 670 (1984).

blood money

1. T. Christian Miller, "Everyone Wants a Piece of the $18-Billion Man in Iraq," *Los Angeles Times,* Aug. 23, 2004, A1.
2. David Wood, "Civilian Deaths Costly for U.S.; Iraqis' Claims Usually Rejected, Fueling Hostility," *Baltimore Sun,* Oct. 11, 2007, 1A.
3. *Rufo v. Simpson,* 86 Cal. App. 4th 573, 614, 616, 623–25 (2001); "Simpson Civil Case: Determining Damages," *Los Angeles Times,* Feb. 5, 1997, A17.
4. [Francis Grose], *A Classical Dictionary of the Vulgar Tongue* (London, 1785).
5. Charles Dickens, *Our Mutual Friend* (London, 1865), bk. 2, ch. 12, pp. 275 and 276–77.
6. David Paul Brown, *The Forum; or, Forty Years Full Practice at the Philadelphia Bar* (Philadelphia, 1856), 2:40.

7. Michael T. McCormack, "The Need for Private Prosecutors: An Analysis of Massachusetts and New Hampshire Law," 37 *Suffolk University Law Review* 497, 497 & n.5 (2004) ("Though common in England, only a few American states allow private prosecutions today.").

8. Jim Dwyer, Peter Neufeld, and Barry Scheck, *Actual Innocence: When Justice Goes Wrong and How to Make It Right,* updated with new material (New York: New American Library, 2003), 318.

9. For details, see Alexandra Natapoff, *Snitching: Criminal Informants and the Erosion of American Justice* (New York: New York University Press, 2009), 50–54.

10. Use by Ashcroft: John Mintz, "Muslim Charity Leader Indicted," *Washington Post,* Oct. 10, 2002, A14; Leonard Greene and Andy Soltis, " 'Terror' Charity— Feds Nab 5 over 'Blood Money' for Hamas," *New York Post,* July 28, 2004, 20. But see Greg Krikorian, "Weak Case Seen in Failed Trial of Charity," *Los Angeles Times,* Nov. 4, 2007, 22. Use by personal injury lawyers: Tom Baker, "Blood Money, New Money, and the Moral Economy of Tort Law in Action," 35 *Law & Society Review* 275, 276 (2001).

11. Joseph D. Diaz, "Blood Money: Life, Death, and Plasma on the Las Vegas Strip," *Electronic Journal of Sociology,* vol. 4, no. 2 (April 1999), available at http://www .sociology.org/archive.html (paid blood donors); Jeyling Chou, "Needling's Invited in This Business; In Summer Especially, Local Blood Bank Has a Shortage of Donors," *San Antonio Express-News,* Aug. 10, 2004, 1B (cost of blood).

blue laws

1. *New-York Mercury,* Mar. 3, 1755, 1. Thanks to Joel S. Berson for identifying this as the earliest known instance of "blue laws."

2. [Noah Welles], *The Real Advantages Which Ministers and People May Enjoy, Especially in the Colonies, by Conforming to the Church of England* (1762), 28–29.

3. George Otto Trevelyan, *The American Revolution,* Part 1 (London, 1899), 396–97 (appearance of Peters and other loyalists). For a thorough study of the life and writings of Samuel Peters, see Wayne Normile Metz, "The Reverend Samuel Peters (1735–1826): Connecticut Anglican, Loyalist, Priest" (Ph.D. diss., Oklahoma State University, 1974).

4. [Samuel Peters], *A General History of Connecticut, from Its First Settlement Under George Fenwick, Esq. to Its Latest Period of Amity with Great Britain; Including a Description of the Country, and Many Curious and Interesting Anecdotes . . . By a Gentleman of the Province* (London, 1781), 152, 325–35, iv–v, 43, 63–69. Later, slightly different, editions were printed in the United States in 1829 and 1877. See also J. Hammond Trumbull, ed., *The True-Blue Laws of Connecticut and New Haven and the False Blue-Laws Invented by the Rev. Samuel Peters* (Hartford, 1876), 30–31.

5. *Debates and Other Proceedings of the Convention of Virginia, Convened at Richmond, on Monday the 2d Day of June, 1788, for the Purpose of Deliberating on the Constitution Recommended by the Grand Federal Convention,* vol. 3 (1789), 152–53; Peters, *General History,* 63, 69–70.

6. *McGowan v. Maryland,* 366 U.S. 420 (1961).

blue wall of silence

1. News reports from Middleton and Colne, *Northern Star* (Leeds, England), May 2, 1840.

2. Augustine E. Costello, *Our Police Protectors: History of the New York Police* (New York, 1885), 127–29 (quoting police inspector Thomas W. Thorne and discussing uniforms generally).

3. Remarks of Congressman Nix in the House of Representatives on Apr. 8, 1965, 111 *Congressional Record* 7478; Arthur Niederhoffer, *Behind the Shield: The Police in Urban Society* (New York: Doubleday, 1967), 4; Jerry M. Flint, "Negroes Accuse Police in Detroit," *New York Times,* Nov. 10, 1968, 66.

4. David Burnham, "Graft Paid to Police Here Said to Run into Millions," *New York Times,* Apr. 25, 1970, 1, 18; testimony of police captain Daniel McGowan on October 29, 1971, as quoted in Barbara Davidson, "The Knapp Commission Didn't Know It Couldn't Be Done," *New York Times Magazine,* Jan. 9, 1972, 16.

5. Joseph B. Treaster, "A Station House Divided: Police Debate Officers' Indictments," *New York Times,* Oct. 31, 1975, 35, 66.

6. Sam Roberts, "Hit-and-Run Death Revives Debate over Police Officers' 'Code of Silence,'" Mar. 29, 1985, B1; Marcia Chambers, "3 City Officers Are Indicted in Park Ave. Hit and Run," *New York Times,* May 24, 1985, B3 (continuing cover-up by superior officers and others); David Burnham, "Violence and the Police," *New York Times Book Review,* Jan. 31, 1971, 4, 5 (reviewing William A. Westley, *Violence and the Police: A Sociological Study of Law, Custom, and Morality* [Cambridge: MIT Press, 1970]). See also Gabriel J. Chin & Scott C. Wells, "The 'Blue Wall of Silence' as Evidence of Bias and Motive to Lie: A New Approach to Police Perjury," 59 *University of Pittsburgh Law Review* 233, 237 (1998) (loyalty obligation underlies code of silence).

7. Selwyn Raab, "2 More Officers Charged in Inquiry into Torture at a Queens Precinct," *New York Times,* Apr. 25, 1985, A1; Selwyn Raab, "5 Police Officers Indicted by Jury in Torture Case," *New York Times,* May 3, 1985, A1; John M. Doyle, untitled Associated Press news story, May 15, 1985.

8. For a detailed account of facts surrounding the Louima assault, see *U.S. v. Bruder,* 103 F. Supp. 2d 155 (E.D.N.Y. 2000). The quotations in the final two paragraphs of this entry are from Michele McPhee, "Nurse Sought for Hosp Stories," *New York Daily News,* Aug. 20, 1997, 4 ("abnormal homosexual activities"); Dan Barry, "Officers' Silence Still Thwarting Torture Inquiry," *New York*

Times, Sept. 5, 1997, A1 ("learned virtually nothing"); William Glaberson, "News Analysis: Case Closed, Not Resolved," *New York Times,* Sept. 23, 2002, A1 ("without resolving"); Editorial, "An End to the Louima Case," *New York Times,* Sept. 24, 2002, A26 ("the longstanding tradition").

boilerplate

1. As early as 1778, the pioneering British engineer John Smeaton specified that certain parts of a diving bell designed for bridge building were "to be made of boiler plate." See letter to Jonathan Pickernell, Sept. 16, 1778, in *Reports of the Late John Smeaton, F.R.S.,* vol. 3 (London, 1812), 282.
2. See Carol Bast, "A Short History of Boilerplate," 5 *Scribes Journal of Legal Writing* 155, 156 n.4 (1994–1995), citing Albert A. Sutton, *Design and Makeup of the Newspaper* (New York: Prentice-Hall, 1948), 246–47. Early references to journalistic boiler plate include William B. Chisholm, "That Note in Bank," *The Century,* Sept. 1891, 800 (a poem mentioning popular nineteenth-century poets whose works have "adorned the boiler-plate"); *Congressional Record,* Aug. 18, 1893, 53rd Cong., 1st sess., 465 (remarks of Congressman Sibley, complaining that New York bankers were manipulating public opinion by distributing "tons of 'boiler plates'" containing editorials disguised as news).
3. *Dolph v. Lennon's, Inc.,* 109 Or. 336, 341 (1923); Ed McBain, *Doll* (New York: Delacorte, 1965), 113.
4. *National Equipment Rental, Ltd. v. Szukhent.* 375 U.S. 311, 330, 328 (1964) (Black, J., dissenting).

Chancellor's foot

1. John Selden, *Table Talk* (London, 1689), 18 (punctuation modernized). Selden died in 1654; this book of his sayings was published posthumously by his amanuensis Richard Milward.
2. *Gee v. Pritchard,* 36 Eng. Rep. 670, 674 (1818).
3. Charles Dickens, *Bleak House,* ch. 1, serialized in *Harper's New Monthly Magazine,* Apr. 1852, 650.
4. *Grupo Mexicano de Desarrollo S.A. v. Alliance Bond Fund,* 527 U.S. 308, 332 (1999) (misspelling of "Selden" in original. Justice Scalia was quoting the nineteenth-century legal scholar Joseph Story, although Story spelled "Selden" correctly).
5. Ibid. at 342 (Ginsburg, J., dissenting).

charter party

1. James E. Clapp, *Random House Webster's Dictionary of the Law* (New York: Random House, 2000), 79.

Chinese Wall

1. *NCK Organization, Ltd. v. Bregman,* 542 F.2d 128, 135 (2d Cir. 1976).
2. *Kesselhaut v. United States,* 214 Ct. Cl. 124, 555 F.2d 791 (U.S. Ct. of Claims 1977).
3. *Fund of Funds, Ltd. v. Arthur Andersen & Co.,* 435 F. Supp. 84, 96 (S.D.N.Y. 1977).
4. See, for example, Martin Lipton and Robert B. Mazur, "The Chinese Wall Solution to the Conflict Problems of Securities Firms," 50 *New York University Law Review* 459 (1975); Ralph F. Huck, "The Fatal Lure of the 'Impermeable Chinese Wall,'" 94 *Banking Law Journal* 100 (1977).
5. *Peat, Marwick, Mitchell & Co. v. Superior Court of Contra Costa County,* 200 Cal. App. 3d 272, 293 (1988) (concurring opinion).
6. *Portland General Electric Co. v. Duncan, Weinberg, Miller & Pembroke, P.C.,* 162 Or. App. 265, 267 n.2 (1999); Christopher J. Dunnigan, "The Art Formerly Known as the Chinese Wall: Screening in Law Firms: Why, When, Where, and How," 11 *Georgetown Journal of Legal Ethics* 291, 291 n.1 (1998).
7. A Minister of the Gospel, in Massachusetts [Horace Thomas Love], *Slavery in its Relation to God: A Review of Rev. Dr. Lord's Thanksgiving Sermon* (Buffalo, N.Y., 1851), 8; [Frederick Douglass], "Reconstruction," *Atlantic Monthly,* Dec. 1866, 761, 764.

color-blind

1. This famous statement was published by Du Bois in *The Souls of Black Folk: Essays and Sketches* (Chicago: A. C. McClurg, 1903), vii, but was "first made by Du Bois in his address, 'To the nations of the World,' in London at the first Pan-African conference, July 1900": W. E. B. Du Bois, *The Souls of Black Folk: Authoritative Text, Contexts, Criticism,* ed. Henry Louis Gates Jr. and Terri Hume Oliver (New York: Norton, 1999), 5 n. 1.
2. "Reconstruction: Wendell Phillip's [*sic*] Views on the Question," *New-York Times,* Dec. 28, 1864, 8; "Reviving Race Issues: The Supreme Court Denounced for Its Civil Rights Decision," *Washington Post,* Oct. 23, 1883, 1.
3. *Plessy v. Ferguson,* 163 U.S. 537, 559 (1896) (Harlan, J., dissenting); Martin Luther King Jr., "I Have a Dream" speech, delivered at the March on Washington for Jobs and Freedom, Washington, D.C., Aug. 28, 1963.
4. Paul Finkelman, "The Color of Law," 87 *Northwestern University Law Review* 937, 945 (1992).
5. Ibid., 980–81.
6. See *Parents Involved in Community Schools v. Seattle School District No. 1,* 551 U.S. 701 (2007), at 772–82 (concurring opinion of Justice Thomas), 730–31 & n.14 (plurality opinion), and 788 (separate opinion of Justice Kennedy, concurring in the judgment).

Comstockery

1. Special Cable to the New York Times, "Bernard Shaw Resents Action of Librarian," *New York Times,* Sept. 26, 1905; Editorial, "Comstockery," *New-York Times,* Dec. 12, 1895 (first published use of *Comstockery*).
2. "Who's Bernard Shaw? Asks Mr. Comstock," *New York Times,* Sept. 28, 1905.
3. Heywood Broun and Margaret Leech, *Anthony Comstock: Roundsman of the Lord* (New York: Albert and Charles Boni, 1927) (providing overall biographical information about Comstock, and quoting this excerpt from Comstock's diaries at 55–56); Margaret A. Blanchard and John E. Semonche, "Anthony Comstock and His Adversaries: The Mixed Legacy of This Battle for Free Speech," 11 *Communication Law & Policy* 317–65 (2006) (summary of Comstock's career); H. I. Brock, "Anthony Comstock Was Militant Puritanism Incarnate," *New York Times Book Review,* Mar. 6, 1927, 3 (review of Broun and Leech).
4. Broun and Leech, *Anthony Comstock,* 16. See generally Donna I. Dennis, "Obscenity Law and Its Consequences in Mid-Nineteenth-Century America," 16 *Columbia Journal of Gender & Law* 43, 60 (2007) (thorough discussion of nineteenth-century pornography prosecutions); Donna I. Dennis, "Obscenity Law and the Conditions of Freedom in the Nineteenth-Century United States," 27 *Law & Social Inquiry* 369 (2000) (Comstock and Comstock scholarship in historical context).
5. "Anthony Comstock—An Heroic Suppressor or an Unconscious Protector of Vice?" *Current Opinion,* Apr. 1914, 288, 289 (quoting the *Rochester Post-Express*).
6. *Regina v. Hicklin,* [1868] L. R. 3 Q. B. 360; *Miller v. California,* 413 U.S. 15, 24 (1973).
7. Glen O. Robinson, "Federal 'Comstockery' Commission," *Broadcasting & Cable,* Aug. 25, 2008, 30; *FCC v. Fox Television Stations, Inc.,* 129 S. Ct. 1800, 1818 (2009).

corpus delicti

1. *The Tryal of Captain Thomas Green and His Crew, Pursued Before the Judge of the High Court of Admiralty of Scotland* (Edinburgh, 1705), 17.
2. John Burnett, *A Treatise on Various Branches of the Criminal Law of Scotland* (Edinburgh, 1811), 529.
3. Matthew Hale, *Historia Placitorum Coronae: The History of the Pleas of the Crown* (London, 1736), 2:290 & note g. Usually this passage is erroneously cited to Hale's *Pleas of the Crown* (London, 1678), which is a different work.
4. The history, importance, and current status of the rule are given in David A. Moran, "In Defense of the Corpus Delicti Rule," 64 *Ohio State Law Journal* 817 (2003).

5. Agatha Christie, *And Then There Were None* (Cutchogue, N.Y.: Buccaneer, 2000), vi (originally published as *Ten Little Niggers* in 1939; title has varied over the years).
6. Lord Dunboyne, ed., *The Trial of John George Haigh (The Acid Bath Murder)* (London: William Hodge and Company, 1953), 17, 125–32.

CSI effect

1. Sharon Begley, "But It Works on TV! Forensic Science Often Isn't," *Newsweek*, Apr. 12, 2010, 26 (quoting the Innocence Project); Tom R. Tyler, "Viewing *CSI* and the Threshold of Guilt: Managing Truth and Justice in Reality and Fiction," 115 *Yale Law Journal* 1050–85 (2006); Richard Catalani, "A CSI Writer Defends His Show," *Yale Law Journal (The Pocket Part)*, Jan. 31, 2006, http://www.thepocket part.org/ylj-online/criminal-law-and-sentencing/34-a-csi-writer-defends-his-show.
2. *State v. Cooke*, 914 A.2d 1078, 1095 (Del. Super. Ct. 2007).
3. Joe Milicia, "TV Crime Dramas Aiding Real Life Killers," Associated Press, Jan. 29, 2006.

cut the baby in half

1. Jennifer 8. Lee, "Many Bidders May Pursue New Method to Carry TV," *New York Times*, April 30, 2002, C8; Thomas L. Fowler, "Of Moons, Thongs, Holdings and Dicta: *State v. Fly* and the Rule of Law," 22 *Campbell Law Review* 253, 254 (2000).
2. The full story is at 1 Kings 3:16–28.
3. *Gilmore v. Devlin*, 11 D.C. (MacArth. & M.) 306, 317 (1880).
4. *Schaffer v. Commissioner of Internal Revenue*, 779 F.2d 849, 852 n.2 (2d Cir. 1985), discussing *Cannon v. Commissioner of Internal Revenue*, 533 F.2d 959, 960 (5th Cir. 1976).
5. 1 Kings 2:24–46.
6. *Stewart v. Schwartz Brothers-Jeffer Memorial Chapel*, 159 Misc. 2d 884, 889, 606 N.Y.S.2d 965, 969 (N.Y. Sup. Ct., Queens County 1993).
7. Paul Gewirtz, "On 'I Know It When I See It,'" 105 *Yale Law Journal* 1023, 1033 (1996). For discussion of the first three interpretations of the story see Barbara Bennett Woodhouse, "Afterword: Deconstructing Solomon's Dilemma" in "Symposium: Solomon's Dilemma: Exploring Parental Rights," 26 *Connecticut Law Review* 1525, 1525–27 (1994); for an example of the last see Ann Althouse, "Beyond King Solomon's Harlots: Women in Evidence," 65 *Southern California Law Review* 1265 (1992).
8. Mark Twain, *Adventures of Huckleberry Finn (Tom Sawyer's Comrade)* (New York, 1885), ch. 14, p. 111. (First American edition. The first edition [London, 1884] had "neighbours.")

9. Story of Rahab: Joshua 2, 6:16–17, 6:21–25; Matthew 1:5. Solomon's wives and concubines: 1 Kings 11:3. Legal status of prostitutes today: *People v. Link,* 107 Misc. 2d 973, 976, 436 N.Y.S.2d 581, 584 (N.Y.C. Crim. Ct. 1981).

day in court

1. Magna Carta (1215), § 39 (translated from Latin).
2. William Blackstone, *Commentaries on the Common Law,* vol. 1 (Oxford, 1765), 131–32; *In re Oliver,* 333 U.S. 257, 273 (1948).
3. William Watson, *The Clergy-Man's Law* (London, 1701), 217 & 225. Similarly, see *The Law of Corporations* (London, 1702), 243 & 330; *The Law of Executors and Administrators* (London, 1702), 172, 185, & 454.
4. Marc Galanter, "The Vanishing Trial: An Examination of Trials and Related Matters in Federal and State Courts," 1 *Journal of Empirical Legal Studies* 459, 478 fig. 11 & 497 fig. 26 (2004) (2002 data).
5. William Shakespeare, *Hamlet* (ca. 1601), act 5, scene 1.
6. *Louisville & Nashville Railroad Co. v. Schmidt,* 177 U.S. 230, 239 (1900).
7. Marc Galanter, "A World Without Trials?" 2006 *Journal of Dispute Resolution* 7, 7–11 & figs. 1–4 (2006).
8. *Bordenkircher v. Hayes,* 434 U.S. 357 (1978).
9. *Boumediene v. Bush,* 553 U.S. 723, 787 (2008).
10. Barack H. Obama, remarks at the National Archives and Records Administration, May 21, 2009, in *Daily Compilation of Presidential Documents,* 2009 DCPD No. 388, 6, available at http://www.gpoaccess.gov/presdocs/2009/DCPD -200900388.pdf; Guantanamo Review Task Force, *Final Report,* Jan. 22, 2010 (released May 28, 2010), 24, available at http://www.justice.gov/ag/guantanamo -review-final-report.pdf.

death and taxes

1. Franklin, letter to Jean-Baptiste Le Roy, Nov. 18, 1789, in *The Writings of Benjamin Franklin,* ed. Albert Henry Smyth, vol. 10 (New York: Macmillan, 1907), 68, 69.
2. Sydney Smith, "Speech at Taunton in 1831 on the Reform Bill Not Being Passed," reprinted from the *Taunton Courier* of Oct. 12, 1831, in *The Works of the Rev. Sydney Smith,* 2nd ed. (London, 1840), 3:123.
3. *Select Tales and Fables, with Prudential Maxims* (Dublin, 1756), 2:160. (The date of 1746 on the cover of the second volume, which contains the quoted entry, is evidently incorrect.) Christopher Bullock, *The Cobler of Preston* (London, 1716), 14–15.
4. Allan Sloan, "Why Your Tax Cut Doesn't Add Up," *Newsweek,* Apr. 12, 2004, 41, 42.

death tax

1. Ed Gillespie and Bob Schellhas, eds., *Contract with America: The Bold Plan by Rep. Newt Gingrich, Rep. Dick Armey and the House Republicans to Change the Nation* (New York: Times Books, 1994), 130; Republican Party Platform adopted August 12, 1996, http://www.historycentral.com/elections/Conventions/RepPlat1996.html.

2. The history of the campaign is recounted in several places, including Bob Thompson, "Sharing the Wealth?" *Washington Post Magazine,* Apr. 13, 2003, W8 (which includes the Norquist quote); William H. Gates Sr. and Chuck Collins, *Wealth and Our Commonwealth* (Boston: Beacon, 2002); and David Cay Johnston, *Perfectly Legal* (New York: Portfolio, 2003), ch. 6.

3. Andrew Carnegie, "The Presidential Election—Our Duty," *North American Review,* Oct. 1900, 495, 504.

4. Richard S. Dunham, "When Is a Tax Cut Not a Tax Cut?" *Business Week,* Mar. 19, 2001, 38 (Spaeth quote); Nicholas Lemann, "The Word Lab," *New Yorker,* Oct. 16 and 23, 2000, 100, 108–09 (Luntz's work and findings on terminology).

5. Lizette Alvarez, "In 2 Parties' War of Words, Shibboleths Emerge as Clear Winner," *New York Times,* Apr. 27, 2001, A20.

6. John McCaslin, "Death Wish," *Washington Times,* Aug. 11, 1999, A7.

7. Photo accompanying Jonathan Weisman, "Linking Tax to Death May Have Brought Its Doom: Senate Passage Likely for Repeal of Inheritance Levy," *USA Today,* May 21, 2001, 4A.

8. Weisman, "Linking Tax to Death," (2001 figures); Paul Krugman, "The Tax-Cut Con," *New York Times Magazine,* Sept. 14, 2003, 54 (2003 figure).

9. Interview with Frank Luntz, Dec. 15, 2003, in "The Persuaders," episode of PBS documentary series *Frontline,* broadcast Nov. 9, 2004. Transcript of the show available at http://www.pbs.org/wgbh/pages/frontline/shows/persuaders/etc/script.html; full text of interview (quoted here) available at http://www.pbs.org/wgbh/pages/frontline/shows/persuaders/interviews/luntz.html.

10. Joshua Green, "Meet Mr. Death," *American Prospect,* May 21, 2001, 12.

deep pocket

1. Percy Fitzgerald, *Chronicles of Bow Street Police-Office* (London, 1888), 2:130.

2. [Henry Fielding], *Rape upon Rape; or, The Justice Caught in His Own Trap* (1730), act 2, scene 2; Grace Glueck, "Aspen Debates Its Image: Devotees of 'Deep Pocket' Tourists Fear Creation of a 'Hot Dog' Circuit," *New York Times,* Sept. 1, 1965, 31; Glen Justice, "For Deep-Pocket Givers, Crystal and Candlelight," *New York Times,* Jan. 21, 2005; Mitch Lawrence, "Russian billionaire Mikhail Prokorov has deep pockets to offer Nets," *New York Daily News,* Sep. 24, 2009.

3. *Short v. Stoy* (1836), an unreported case summarized in Henry Roscoe, *A Digest of the Law of Evidence on the Trial of Actions at Nisi Prius,* 5th ed., with additions by C. Crompton and E. Smirke (London, 1839), 54; *Hodsoll v. Taylor,* 9 Q.B. 79 (1873).

4. See *The Whole Proceedings at Large in a Cause on an Action Brought by the Rt. Hon. Richard Lord Grosvenor Against His Royal Highness Henry Frederick, Duke of Cumberland; for Criminal Conversation with Lady Grosvenor, Tried Before the Rt. Hon. William Lord Mansfield, . . . Faithfully Taken in Shorthand by a Barrister* (London, 1770), 77. Accounts such as these were the tabloids of their day, and this case generated an enormous amount of publicity. See Abby L. Sayers, "Publicizing Private Life: Criminal Conversation Trials in Eighteenth-Century Britain" (M.A. diss., Auburn University, 2010), 19 and n. 55.

5. *Clem v. Holmes,* 74 Va. 722, 726 (1880).

6. John A. Jenkins, "Betting on the Verdict," *New York Times Magazine,* Nov. 25, 1984.

7. Irvin Molotsky, "Drive to Limit Product Liability Awards Grows as Consumer Groups Object," *New York Times,* March 2, 1986.

8. Valerie P. Hans, "The Contested Role of the Civil Jury in Business Litigation," 79 *Judicature* 242 (1996); Robert J. MacCoun, "Differential Treatment of Corporate Defendants by Juries: An Examination of the 'Deep Pockets' Hypothesis," 30 *Law & Society Review* 121 (1996); Audrey Chin and Mark A. Peterson, *Deep Pockets, Empty Pockets: Who Wins in Cook County Jury Trials?* (Santa Monica: Rand, 1985), 25.

9. California Voters' Handbook, Proposition 51, quoted in Richard Alexander, "Limiting the Application of Proposition 51 in Cases Involving Public Policy and Employer's Negligence," http://library.findlaw.com/1999/Sep/15/126755.html; Walter Probert, "The Politics of Torts Casebooks: Jurisprudence Reductus," 69 *Texas Law Review* 1233, 1239 (1991).

deliberate speed

1. *Brown v. Board of Education of Topeka* (*Brown I*), 347 U.S. 483 (1954); *Brown v. Board of Education of Topeka* (*Brown II*), 349 U.S. 294, 300–01 (1955).

2. Holmes's use of the phrase: *Virginia v. West Virginia,* 222 U.S. 17, 19–20 (1911); letter from Oliver Wendell Holmes Jr. to Frederick Pollock, Mar. 7, 1909, in *Holmes–Pollock Letters,* 2nd ed., ed. Mark DeWolfe Howe (Cambridge, Mass.: Belknap, 1961), 1:152.

3. The Definitive Treaty of Peace 1783 [Treaty of Paris], Art. 7, available at http://avalon.law.yale.edu/18th_century/paris.asp.

4. Walter Scott, *Rob Roy,* edited with an introduction and notes by Ian Duncan (Oxford: Oxford University Press, 1998), ch. 36, p. 420.

5. See Byron's letters and diary entries for the years 1818–21 reproduced in Thomas Moore, *Life of Lord Byron, with his Letters and Journals,* new ed. (London,

1854), 4:128, 4:151, and 5:65 (referring to *Rob Roy*), and 4:143, 4:300, and 5:77 (using the phrase "with all deliberate speed," usually in quotation marks); see also 6:117 ("with all convenient speed"). All volumes are available at http://www .gutenberg.org (2011).

6. 1802 essay: Thomas Beddoes, M.D., "Essay on Personal Imprudence, Active and Passive . . . ," 94, which is the second essay (separately paginated) in the author's *Hygeia; or, Essays Moral and Medical, on the Causes Affecting the Personal State of Our Middling and Affluent Classes,* vol. 1 (Bristol, Eng., 1802). Thanks to Stephen Goranson of the Duke University Libraries for finding this early cite and bringing it to the attention of the American Dialect Society. 1844 case: *Murdock v. Washburn,* 9 Miss. 546, 558 (1844).

7. Frankfurter's markup of the draft decree is shown in the accompanying illustration; the rest of this chronology is detailed and documented in John Q. Barrett's introduction to "Supreme Court Law Clerks' Recollections of *Brown v. Board of Education II,*" 79 *St. John's Law Review* 823, 834–37 (2005).

8. Cass R. Sunstein, "Did Brown Matter?" *New Yorker,* May 3, 2004, 102, 103 (Marshall quote); *Griffin v. County School Board of Prince Edward County,* 377 U.S. 218, 234 (1964) (time has run out); Bernard Schwartz, *The Unpublished Opinions of the Warren Court* (New York: Oxford University Press, 1985), 469 (Warren's reflection).

9. *Secretary of State for the Environment v. Euston Centre Investments Ltd.,* [1995] ch. 200, 208 (1994).

electoral college

1. *U.S. Constitution,* Preamble.

2. Notes of James Madison in Max Farrand, ed., *The Records of the Federal Convention of 1787* (New Haven: Yale University Press, 1911), 2:56–57 (proceedings of July 19, 1787) and 2:32 (proceedings of July 17, 1787) (abbreviated state name spelled out).

3. *Bush v. Gore,* 531 U.S. 98, 104 (2000).

4. Remarks of Senator Abraham Baldwin of Georgia, 6 *Annals of Congress* 31 (debate in the U.S. Senate, Jan. 23, 1800); 3 United States Code §§ 4, 15 (the first derived from 5 Statutes at Large 721 [1845]).

5. "Electioneering," *The Constitutional Telegraphe* (Boston), Oct. 22, 1800, 3; 13 Statutes at Large 567, 568 (1865).

6. Letter from Thomas Jefferson to James Monroe (1800), quoted in American Bar Association, *Electing the President,* rev. ed. (Chicago: American Bar Association, 1977), 23.

7. Quoted in *McPherson v. Blacker,* 146 U.S. 1, 31–32 (1892).

8. Wyoming had 3 electoral votes for a population of 495,304. California had only 18.3 times as many electoral votes for 68.5 times as many people (55 electoral votes for a population of 33,930,798).

eye for an eye

1. All translations of the code in this entry are from Chilperic Edwards, *The Hammurabi Code and the Sinaitic Legislation* (London: Watts, 1904).
2. Leviticus 24:19–20. All Bible quotations in this entry are from the New Revised Standard Version. See also Exodus 21:22–25; Deuteronomy 19:19, 21. Regarding lex talionis as a limit on private vengeance, see Adele Berlin and Marc Zvi Brettler, eds., *The Jewish Study Bible* (New York: Oxford University Press, 2004), 154; Mary Douglas, *Leviticus as Literature* (Oxford: Oxford University Press, 1999), 212–13.
3. Matthew 5:38–39.
4. *In re Summers,* 325 U.S. 561, 576 (1945) (Black, J., dissenting).
5. *Furman v. Georgia,* 408 U.S. 238, 332 n.41 (1972) (Marshall, J., concurring); *People v. Harlan,* 109 P.3d 616, 622 (Colo. 2005); *Robinson v. Polk,* 438 F.3d 350, 358 (4th Cir. 2006) (North Carolina case); *Thornburg v. Mullin,* 422 F.3d 1113, 1140, 1142 (10th Cir. 2005) (Oklahoma case).
6. Phil Hirschkorn, "Jury spares 9/11 plotter Moussaoui," May 4, 2006, http://edition.cnn.com/2006/LAW/05/03/moussaoui.verdict; comment posted by kbiel on Wizbang.com, June 8, 2006, http://wizbangblog.com/content/2006/06/08/abu-musab-alzarqawi-reportedly.php ("rusty knife").
7. Associated Press, "Recruitment Killing Suspect Doesn't Think Killing Was Murder," June 9, 2009, available at http://www.foxnews.com/story/0,2933,525584,00.html. Although the "whole world blind" quotation is widely credited to Gandhi, it is not clear that he said it. The Gandhi Institute for Nonviolence states that the Gandhi family believes it is an authentic Gandhi quotation, but no one has discovered an example of Gandhi's actual use of the phrase. See Fred R. Shapiro, ed., *The Yale Book of Quotations* (New Haven: Yale University Press, 2006), 269–70 (also quoting Louis Fischer: "An-eye-for-an-eye-for-an-eye-for-an-eye . . . ends in making everybody blind").

fishing expedition

1. *Buden v. Dore,* 28 Eng. Rep. 284 (1752); *Renison v. Ashley,* 30 Eng. Rep. 724, 725 (1794).
2. *Newkirk v. Willett,* 2 Johns. Cas. 413, 413 (N.Y. 1800).
3. *George v. Solomon,* 14 So. 531, 533 (Miss. 1893).
4. *In re Abeles,* 12 Kan. 451, 453 (1874).
5. *Hickman v. Taylor,* 329 U.S. 495, 507 (1947); Alexander Holtzoff, "Instruments of Discovery Under Federal Rules of Civil Procedure," 41 *Michigan Law Review* 205, 215 (1942).
6. William H. Erickson, "The Pound Conference Recommendations: A Blueprint for the Justice System in the Twenty-First Century," 76 F.R.D. 277, 288 (1978). For a more complete discussion of the history and uses of "fishing expedition,"

see Elizabeth G. Thornburg, "Just Say No Fishing: The Lure of Metaphor," 40 *University of Michigan Journal of Law Reform* 1 (2006).

7. *In re IBM Peripheral EDP Devices Antitrust Litigation,* 77 F.R.D. 39, 42 (N.D. Cal. 1977).

8. The epigram appears to have been first attributed to Lord Mansfield seventy-nine years after his death, by Lord Westbury in *Knox v. Gye,* L.R. 5 H.L. 656, 675 (1872).

grand jury

1. See Andrew D. Leipold, "Why Grand Juries Do Not (and Cannot) Protect the Accused," 80 *Cornell Law Review* 260, 281–83 (1995).

2. Peter D. G. Thomas, *Tea Party to Independence: The Third Phase of the American Revolution, 1773–1776* (Oxford: Clarendon, 1991), 24.

3. *United States v. Dionisio,* 410 U.S. 1, 17 (1973).

4. See Niki Kuckes, "The Useful, Dangerous Fiction of Grand Jury Independence," 41 *American Criminal Law Review* 1, 8 (2004), and Roger Roots, "If It's Not a Runaway, It's Not a Real Grand Jury," 33 *Creighton Law Review* 821, 827 (2000).

green card

1. Alien Friends Act, ch. 58, § 1, 1 Stat. 570–71 (1798).

2. [Douglas] Larsen, "Nation's Capital News," *Altoona Mirror,* Dec. 3, 1956, 10. See also "Aliens Visiting Canada Need Registration Card," *Youngstown Vindicator,* June 28, 1955, 17 ("This is a green card . . . . The former card is white").

3. Article published as "Deberes del extranjero en Estados Unidos," *La Prensa* (San Antonio, Tex.), Feb. 4, 1953, 3, and as "La nueva ley de inmigración y nacionalidad," *Notas de Kingsville* (Kingsville, Tex.), Mar. 5, 1953, 7.

4. Ruben Salazar, " 'Commuting' Mexican Farm Workers Stir U.S. Dispute," *Los Angeles Times,* Nov. 25, 1962, H1–2. The remainder of the series was published over the succeeding three days.

5. Allan Wernick, "Columna de inmigración," *Al Día* (Dallas), Feb. 21, 2009; Matthew Waller, "Fe y albergue," *Al Día* (Dallas), Sept. 8, 2009; E-mail from Jorge Chávez to Elizabeth Thornburg (Feb. 25, 2009).

6. Silvia Garduño, "Repunta la legalización de paisanos," *Mural* (Guadalajara, Mexico), Mar. 28, 2009.

7. Special Agent Martin D. Ficke, quoted in Anthony Ramirez, "Immigration Net Snags 64 Sex Crimes Convicts," *New York Times,* Aug. 19, 2004, B3.

hanged for a sheep

1. John Ray, *A Collection of English Proverbs,* 2nd ed. (Cambridge, 1678), 350.

2. Everett Lloyd, "Law West of the Pecos . . . The Story of Judge Roy Bean,"

Dallas Morning News, Dec. 15, 1935, A2, quoted in Shawn E. Tuma, "Law in Texas Literature: Texas Justice—Judge Roy Bean Style," 21 *Review of Litigation* 551, 563 (2002). The "son-of-a-gun" in this account is a concession to the sensibilities of newspaper readers in 1935. Judge Roy Bean was not known for such delicacy of expression, and other versions of this widely varying story reflect that. See, e.g., ibid., 563–64 n.68.

3. Roberta M. Harding, "Capital Punishment as Human Sacrifice: A Societal Ritual as Depicted in George Eliot's *Adam Bede,*" 48 *Buffalo Law Review* 175, 257 (2000).

4. *Regina v. Spicer,* 169 Eng. Rep. 160 (1845).

5. *United States v. Anderson,* 59 F.3d 1323, 1339 (D.C. Cir. 1995) (Ginsburg, J., dissenting).

hearsay

1. Giles Du Wes, *An Introductorie for to Lerne to Rede to Pronounce and to Speke Frenche Trewly, Compyled for the Right High Exellent and Most Vertuous Lady the Lady Mary of Englande, Doughter to Our Most Gracious Soverayn Lorde Kyng Henry the Eight* (London, ca. 1533; facsimile reprint, Menston, Eng.: Scolar, 1972). The book is unpaginated; this passage occurs five pages from the end.

2. John M. Maguire and Edmund M. Morgan, "Looking Forward and Backward at Evidence," 50 *Harvard Law Review* 909, 921 (1937).

3. Eleanor Swift, "The Hearsay Rule at Work: Has It Been Abolished De Facto by Judicial Decision?" 76 *Minnesota Law Review* 473, 501 & n.98 (1992).

4. Karleen F. Murphy, Note, "A Hearsay Exception for Physical Abuse," 27 *Golden Gate University Law Review* 497, 522 n.175 (1997).

5. Ruling of Judge Lance Ito, quoted in Gordon Van Kessel, "Hearsay Hazards in the American Criminal Trial: An Adversary-Oriented Approach," 49 *Hastings Law Journal* 477, 538 (1998).

6. Jeremy A. Blumenthal, "Shedding Some Light on Calls for Hearsay Reform: Civil Law Hearsay Rules in Historical and Modern Perspective," 13 *Pace International Law Review* 93, 112 (2001).

7. John H. Langbein, "Historical Foundations of the Law of Evidence: A View from the Ryder Sources," 96 *Columbia Law Review* 1168, 1195 n.131 (1996).

8. General discussions of European procedure as it relates to hearsay evidence include Langbein, note 7 above, 1168–69; Blumenthal, note 6 above; and Mirjan Damaška, "Of Hearsay and Its Analogues," 76 *Minnesota Law Review* 425, 444–49 (1992).

9. Derek O'Brien, "The Rule Against Hearsay RIP," 146 *New Law Journal* 153 (Feb. 2, 1996).

hornbook law

1. William Shakespeare, *Love's Labour's Lost* (ca. 1594), ed. Wilbur L. Cross and Tucker Brooke, The Yale Shakespeare (New Haven: Yale University Press; London: Oxford University Press, 1925), act 5, scene 1. This version of the text incorporates a correction or revision of the earliest printed versions of the play introduced by Lewis Theobald in his scholarly edition of the complete plays of Shakespeare published in 1733. Theobald changed "the last of the five vowels" to "the third of the five vowels" on the ground that Shakespeare obviously did not intend Moth to refer to the same vowel (*U*) twice. Most modern scholarly editions of the play revert to the earlier text, and include convoluted notes attempting to explain how that could have been what Shakespeare actually meant to say.
2. T. Deckar [Thomas Dekker], *The Guls Horne-Booke* (London, 1609).
3. *Jim (a Slave) v. The State*, 3 Mo. 147, 173–74 (1832) (argument of counsel).
4. *Day v. Graham*, 6 Ill. 435 (1844), at 451 (argument of counsel) & 452 (opinion of court).
5. *Davis v. Zimmerman*, 67 Pa. 70, 74 (1871).
6. *Ex parte Virginia*, 100 U.S. 339, 352 (1880) (Field, J., dissenting).
7. *Grupo Dataflux v. Atlas Global Group, L.P.*, 541 U.S. 567, 570–71 & n.2 (2004) (citing the books).

hue and cry

1. The Statute of Winchester, 1285, 13 Edw. (Eng.).
2. *An Abridgement of the Laws In Force and Use in Her Majesty's Plantations; (Viz.) Of Virginia, Jamaica, Barbadoes, Maryland, New-England, New-York, Carolina, &c.* (London, 1704), 57.
3. William Blackstone, *Commentaries on the Laws of England*, vol. 4 (Oxford, 1769), 290.
4. Walter Dew, *I Caught Crippen* (London: Blackie and Son, 1938), 33; Philip Johnston, "We Pay to Deport Those Who'd Go Anyway," *Daily Telegraph* (London), Nov. 20, 2006, 22.

indict a ham sandwich

1. "Poison," episode 7 in season 1 of *Law & Order: Criminal Intent* (NBC, first broadcast Nov. 11, 2001). Fan sites on the Internet have identified at least three episodes of *Law & Order* (the series of which *Law & Order: Criminal Intent* was a spinoff) that also contain lines about indicting a ham sandwich.
2. Jan Hoffman, "No Longer Judicially Sacred, Grand Jury Is Under Review," *New York Times*, Mar. 30, 1996, 1 (estimated cost at that time: $47 million per year); David Rohde, "Saying System Is Unsound, Grand Jurors Urge Changes," *New York Times*, Oct. 9, 1998, B5.

3. William J. Campbell, "Delays in Criminal Cases" (address before the Conference of Metropolitan Chief District Judges of the Federal Judicial Center), 55 *Federal Rules Decisions* 229, 253 (1972); Marcia Kramer and Frank Lombardi, "New Top State Judge: Abolish Grand Juries & Let Us Decide," *Daily News,* Jan. 31, 1985, 3.

4. David Margolick, "Law Professor to Administer Courts in State," *New York Times,* Feb. 1, 1985, B2.

5. Tom Wolfe, *The Bonfire of the Vanities* (New York: Farrar Straus Giroux, 1987), ch. 30, p. 603.

6. See letters of July 8 and 9, 2002, from Barry Popik to American Dialect Society e-mail discussion list at http://listserv.linguistlist.org/cgi-bin/wa?A2=ind0207 B&L=ADS-L&P=R666 and http://listserv.linguistlist.org/cgi-bin/wa?A2=ind0207 B&L=ADS-L&P=R1606.

7. For extended accounts, see Linda Wolfe, *Double Life: The Shattering Affair Between Chief Judge Sol Wachtler and Socialite Joy Silverman* (New York: Pocket, 1994), and John M. Caher, *King of the Mountain: The Rise, Fall, and Redemption of Chief Judge Sol Wachtler* (Amherst, N.Y.: Prometheus, 1998).

8. See Bernard E. Harcourt, *The Illusion of Free Markets: Punishment and the Myth of Natural Order* (Cambridge: Harvard University Press, 2011), 222–25; see also U.S. Department of Justice, "Study Finds More Than Half of All Prison and Jail Inmates Have Mental Health Problems," news release, Sept. 6, 2006, available at http://www.ojp.usdoj.gov/newsroom/pressreleases/2006/BJS06064.htm.

9. For Wachtler's own reflections on the experience, see Sol Wachtler, *After the Madness: A Judge's Own Prison Memoir* (New York: Random House, 1997). On the "ham sandwich" quote and grand juries in general, see pages 292–95. The TV episode generally assumed to have been partially based on his case is "Censure," episode 80 (season 4, episode 14) of *Law & Order* (NBC, first broadcast Feb. 2, 1994). Chief Judge Kaye was quoted in Richard Pérez-Peña, "State's Top Court Orders a Portrait of Wachtler," *New York Times,* June 5, 2001, B4.

jailbait

1. Examples of this and other meanings are given in J. E. Lighter, *Random House Historical Dictionary of American Slang,* vol. 2 (New York: Random House, 1997), 243–44.

2. Warren Eyster, *Far from the Customary Skies* (New York: Farrar, Straus and Giroux, 1953), 336; George Mandel, *Flee the Angry Strangers* (Indianapolis: Bobbs-Merrill, 1952), 9.

3. *Horace Mann Insurance Co. v. Barbara B.,* 4 Cal. 4th 1076, 1079 n.2 (1993).

Jim Crow

1. "Kirby turned fiercely to the black, and said— 'Shut your oven [mouth], you crow.'" James Fenimore Cooper, *The Pioneers* (New-York, 1823), vol. 1, ch. 17, p. 249.

kangaroo court

1. Reported in a letter to the Random House *Maven's Word of the Day* Internet site, as quoted in a column on *kangaroo*, June 14, 2001, http://www.randomhouse .com/wotd/index.pperl?date=20010614.
2. See John B. Haviland, "A Last Look at Cook's Guugu Yimidhirr Word List," 44 *Oceania* 216, 216 & n.1, 229 (1974); Markman Ellis, "Tails of Wonder: Constructions of the Kangaroo in Late Eighteenth-Century Scientific Discourse," in Margarette Lincoln, ed., *Science and Exploration in the Pacific: European Voyages to the Southern Oceans in the Eighteenth Century* (Woodbridge, Suffolk, Eng.: Boydell, 1998), 163–82; Douglas Gray, "Captain Cook and the English Vocabulary," in E. G. Stanley and Douglas Gray, eds., *Five Hundred Years of Words and Sounds: A Festschrift for Eric Dobson* (Cambridge: Brewer, 1983), 49–62.
3. W. P. Andrews, letter to the editor dated Dec. 1, 1848, in *The Mississippian* (Jackson, Mississippi), Jan. 12, 1849, 3; "Drafts at Sight on the Southwest, VIII: Term-Time in the Backwoods, and a Mestang Court," *Literary World,* July 20, 1850, 46 (thanks to Stephen Goranson for finding this and calling it to the attention of the American Dialect Society discussion list); Sylvester Silversight, "Backwoods Scenes; or, Reminiscences of Early Times in Texas: No. 1, A 'New Comer' in a Tight Place," *Galveston Weekly News,* Apr. 1, 1851, 1 (thanks to Barry Popik for finding this and calling it to the attention of the American Dialect Society discussion list).
4. See generally *American Life Histories: Manuscripts from the Federal Writers' Project, 1936–1940,* http://memory.loc.gov/ammem/wpaintro/wpahome.html. The particular interviews referred to here are those of Tom Mills (by Florence Angermiller), R. A. Perry (by Annie McAulay), William Riley Angermiller (by Florence Angermiller), and Mollie Webb Privett, widow of Samuel Thomas Privett, a rodeo star known as Booger Red (by Elizabeth Doyle).
5. Josiah Flynt, "Club Life Among Outcasts," *Harper's New Monthly Magazine,* Apr. 1895, 712, 718–20.
6. See California Penal Code § 4019.5 (originally enacted in 1947), and *Bryant v. County of Monterey,* 125 Cal. App. 2d 470 (1954) (dismissing suit by prisoner blinded in one eye in beating by kangaroo court despite that statute).
7. *State of Nebraska ex rel. Nebraska State Bar Association v. Rhodes,* 177 Neb. 650 (1964); *In re Paulsrude,* 311 Minn. 303 (1976) (attorney disbarred).

kill all the lawyers

1. William Shakespeare, *Henry VI, Part 2* (ca. 1590–91) (except as otherwise noted, all quotations are from act 4, scene 2); Trish Foxwell, "Area Attractions Sell Trinkets, Treasures," *Washington Times,* June 1, 2000, M4; Ralph Blumenthal, "Wired: Forget Power, Fame and $3,000 Suits. Give That Man a Sandwich." *New York Times,* June 16, 2002, § 4, 5, excerpted from *The Gotti Tapes* (New York: Times Books, 1992) (tape of Jan. 4, 1990).
2. David Reinhard, "Yum: Turkey and Mashed Florida!" *The Oregonian,* Nov. 23, 2000, B9.
3. Stephen Kelson, "Violence Against Lawyers: The Increasingly Attacked Profession," 10 *Boston University Public Interest Law Journal* 260, 262–63 (2001).
4. Wesley Pruden, "Pruden on Politics: Deadly Soccer Moms Amok Among Us," *Washington Times,* Apr. 27, 2001, A4; *Walters v. National Association of Radiation Survivors,* 473 U.S. 305, 371 n.24 (1985) (Stevens, J., dissenting).
5. From full text as quoted in I. M. W. Harvey, *Jack Cade's Rebellion of 1450* (Oxford: Clarendon, 1991), 190.

the law is a ass

1. Henry Glapthorne, *Revenge for Honour,* act 3, scene 2. First performed in the 1630s or 1640s; first published in 1654 (after Glapthorne's death) as *"Revenge For Honour. A Tragedie,* by George Chapman"—the name of the more celebrated Chapman (author of the first translations of Homer into English, who died 1634) having been attached by the publisher in an apparent ploy to boost sales.
2. Charles Dickens, *Oliver Twist,* bk. 3, ch. 13, as originally published in *Bentley's Miscellany,* Mar. 1839, 285. Dickens revised this passage slightly in later editions, but not for the better. See, for example, the version in the authoritative Clarendon Press edition edited by Kathleen Tillotson (Oxford, 1966), ch. 51, p. 354.
3. William Blackstone, *Commentaries on the Laws of England,* vol. 1 (Oxford, 1765), 430, and vol. 4 (Oxford, 1769), 28, 29.
4. Jeremy Bentham, *The Elements of the Art of Packing as Applied to Special Juries, Particularly in Cases of Libel Law* (1821), reprinted in *The Works of Jeremy Bentham,* ed. John Bowring, vol. 5 (New York: Russell and Russell, 1962; reproduced from the Bowring edition of 1838–43), 92; Marjorie Stone, "Dickens, Bentham, and the Fictions of the Law: A Victorian Controversy and Its Consequences," 29 *Victorian Studies* 125, 136–37 (1985).
5. *Debra P. v. Turlington,* 654 F.2d 1079, 1088 (5th Cir. 1981) (Hill, J., dissenting).
6. *Estate of Wilson v. Aiken Industries, Inc.,* 439 U.S. 877, 879–80 (1978) (Blackmun, J., concurring in denial of certiorari).

lawyers, guns, and money

1. Kathy B. Weinman, "President's Page: Send Lawyers, ~~Guns~~, and Money," *Boston Bar Journal,* Jan./Feb. 2009, 2; Bryan G. Garth, "Two Worlds of Civil Discovery," 39 *Boston College Law Review* 597, 608–09 (1998); Francis J. Mootz III, "After the Battle of the Forms: Commercial Contracting in the Electronic Age," 4 *I/S: A Journal of Law and Policy for the Information Society* 271, 301 & n.40 (2008).

2. Editorial, "Lawyers' Feeding Frenzy Is Repulsive," *The Advocate* (Baton Rouge), Oct. 29, 1995; Comment to "Five Signs That the Apocalypse Is Upon Us," Sept. 2, 2009, http://open.salon.com/blog/capn_parrotdead/2009/09/02/five_signs_ that_the_apocalypse_is_upon_us. See also KILL ALL THE LAWYERS.

3. *In the matter of the Estate of Cornelia C. Sage,* 412 N.Y.S.2d 764, 795 (Surrogate's Court 1979).

make a federal case out of it

1. Judith Resnik, "Trial as Error, Jurisdiction as Injury: Transforming the Meaning of Article III," 113 *Harvard Law Review* 924, 968–75 (2000).

2. "Police Break In on Romance of the Range," *Chicago Daily Tribune,* May 22, 1936, 1.

3. Typed script of *The Camel Program,* Jan. 21, 1944, 9–10, available at http://www .otrr.org/FILES/Scripts_pdf/Jimmy%20Durante%20-%20Camel%20Caravan (ellipses in original, though in most cases typed with only two dots. The typed script was also all uppercase. "Shoo Shoo Baby" was a popular song of the day). The similar skits were aired on August 18, 1944, and May 6, 1949 (scripts available on the same Web site), and quoted in Jack Gaver, *There's Laughter in the Air! Radio's Top Comedians and Their Best Shows* (New York: Greenberg, 1945), 263. Joey Adams, *The Curtain Never Falls* (New York: Frederick Fell, 1949), 260.

4. Walter Winchell, "In New York," *New York Daily Mirror,* May 14, 1948, 10 (ellipsis in original). "Colyumist" is a humorous misspelling/mispronunciation of *columnist* that was popular for a while in the first half of the twentieth century.

5. See *Chicago Daily Tribune,* June 16, 1951, C2 (photo of Marcello with phrase as cut line in TV listings); C. E. Butterfield, "Video Introduced Marcello to Public," *Washington Post,* July 17, 1952, 31. See also "Berle's Man Marco," *Newsweek,* Mar. 5, 1951, 54.

6. Walter Haight, "They Pay Off $58, $11.80 in Features," *Washington Post,* Dec. 30, 1950, 11; Bill Bennings column, *Washington Post,* July 23, 1952, 19; Allen Drury, *Advise and Consent* (New York: Doubleday, 1959), 37; James A. Michener, *Hawaii* (New York: Random House, 1959), 880.

7. *Vermont Low Income Advocacy Council v. Usery,* 546 F.2d 509, 514 (2d Cir. 1976).

8. *Stapleton v. Mitchell,* 60 F. Supp. 51, 55 (D. Kan. 1945). The author of the opinion is the same Alfred P. Murrah after whom the federal courthouse in Oklahoma City—bombed in 1995 by Timothy McVeigh—was named.

one-bite rule

1. Bryan A. Garner, *A Dictionary of Modern Legal Usage,* 2nd ed. (New York: Oxford University Press, 1995), 619.
2. *People v. Navarro,* 204 Ill. App. 3d 1097, 1100 (1990); *Felix v. Commissioner of Internal Revenue,* T.C. Memo. 1981-99 (U.S. Tax Court Mar. 2, 1981).
3. William L. Reynolds, "The Iron Law of Full Faith and Credit," 53 *Maryland Law Review* 412, 415 (1994).
4. *In re Becker,* 20 P.3d 409, 414 (Wash. 2001) ("not a feast"); *Stephens v. State,* 806 S.W.2d 812, 819 (Tex. Crim. App. 1990) (rape case).
5. *Basu v. Leal,* 2002 Cal. App. Unpub. LEXIS 10752 (2002).

one person, one vote

1. Abigail Adams to John Adams, Mar. 31, 1776; John Adams to Abigail Adams, Apr. 14, 1776. Images of the actual letters together with complete transcripts are available at http://www.masshist.org/digitaladams/aea/letter/.
2. Florida politician speaking in 1872, quoted in *Johnson v. Bush,* 353 F.3d 1287, 1296 (11th Cir. 2003).
3. John Cartwright, *The People's Barrier Against Undue Influence and Corruption* (London, 1780), 5; "Reform Demonstration at Manchester," *Liverpool Mercury,* June 3, 1867, 6.
4. *Colegrove v. Green,* 328 U.S. 549, 556 (1946).
5. *Buckley v. Hoff,* 234 F. Supp. 191, 197 (D. Vt. 1964).
6. *Gray v. Sanders,* 372 U.S. 368, 381 (1963).
7. These and other measures aimed at overturning the one person, one vote principle are detailed in C. Herman Pritchett, "Representation and the Rule of Equality," and Jerry B. Waters, "Reapportionment: The Legislative Struggle," both in Robert A. Goldwin, ed., *Representation and Misrepresentation: Legislative Reapportionment in Theory and Practice* (Chicago: Rand McNally, 1968).
8. John Lewis with Michael D'Orso, *Walking with the Wind: A Memoir of the Movement* (San Diego: Harvest, 1998), 238–39.
9. *Long v. State,* 42 Ala. App. 476, 476 (1964); Lewis, *Walking with the Wind,* 218.
10. Gerhard Casper, "Apportionment and the Right to Vote: Standards of Judicial Scrutiny," 1973 *Supreme Court Review* 1, 7 (1973). For more such comments, see the citations collected by Jerry R. Parkinson in Note, "Reapportionment: A Call for a Consistent Quantitative Standard," 70 *Iowa Law Review* 663, 663 n.3 (1985).

oyez

1. Rule V(B) of the Rules of the Seventeenth Judicial District Court, Parish of Lafourche (in effect 2001; superseded by uniform statewide rules in 2002).

2. *State v. Taylor,* 311 N.C. 266, 267 (1984); *Lombardo v. United States,* 29 F.2d 445, 447 (District of Columbia Court of Appeals 1928).

3. The same proclamation is set out in the entry for *crier* in William C. Anderson, *A Dictionary of Law* (Chicago, 1889), 293.

4. William Blackstone, *Commentaries on the Laws of England,* vol. 4 (Oxford, 1769), 334 note s.

5. James A. Ballentine, *The College Law Dictionary, Second Students Edition, Self-Pronouncing* (Rochester, N.Y.: Lawyers Co-operative, 1948), 601.

6. "For the Record: News & Views from the Hallways of Government," *Hartford Courant,* Apr. 28, 2000, A6.

7. "Election 2000; The Presidency; The Day in Court," *Newsday,* Nov. 20, 2000, A19.

paper chase

1. "Hare and Hounds in Westchester," *New-York Times,* Nov. 28, 1883, 2; "Mrs. Astor in Paper Chase," *New York Times,* Feb. 26, 1916, 9.

2. Lewis Funke, "Will the 'Bus Stop' Here?" *New York Times,* Dec. 17, 1972, D3.

3. *Bowen v. Sentry Insurance Co.,* 134 Ga. App. 88, 91 (1975).

4. *Charbonnier v. Amico,* 367 Mass. 146, 153 (1975).

penumbra

1. *Textile Workers Union v. Lincoln Mills of Alabama,* 353 U.S. 448, 457 (1957).

2. *Springer v. Government of Philippine Islands,* 277 U.S. 189, 209 (1928) (Holmes, J., dissenting).

3. *Griswold v. Connecticut,* 381 U.S. 479, 484, 485–86 (1965).

4. *Whalen v. Roe,* 429 U.S. 589, 598 n.23 (1977).

Philadelphia lawyer

1. Ray Hackett, "Seniors: New Medicare Bill Does Nothing for Middle Class," *Norwich* (Connecticut) *Bulletin,* Jan. 23, 2004, 1B; Forrest S. Clark, "FEMA Helped During Storms, but Many Did Not Get Much Assistance," *The Ledger* (Lakeland, Florida), Sept. 27, 2004, F3; Matthew Eisley, "Back from the Dead, Man's Struggles Continue," *The News & Observer* (Raleigh, North Carolina), Feb. 2, 2005, A1.

2. Becky Ehmann, "QA Folks Want Hard Line on Growth," *The Capital* (Annapolis, Maryland), Jan. 31, 2005, B2; Bill Herald, "Bowling's Rules Need New Set of Guidelines," *Sarasota* (Florida) *Herald-Tribune,* Oct. 14, 2004, C4.

3. "Humorous Description of the Manners and Fashions of London; in a letter from a Citizen of America to his Correspondent in Philadelphia," *Columbian*

Magazine, Apr. 1788, 181, 182; Editorial, *Charleston* (West Virginia) *Daily Mail,* Mar. 8, 2004, 4A.

pierce the corporate veil

1. Thomas Lodge, "The Discontented Satyre," in his collection *Scillaes Metamorphosis* (1589), D2; *Bank of the United States v. Deveaux,* 9 U.S. 61, 75 (1809) (argument of counsel); State of the State message of Governor Stevens T. Mason, Jan. 7, 1840, in George N. Fuller, ed., *Messages of the Governors of Michigan,* vol. 1 (Lansing: Michigan Historical Commission, 1925), 289, available at Making of America, http://quod.lib.umich.edu/m/moagrp; Roger Foster and Everett V. Abbot, *A Treatise on the Federal Income Tax Under the Act of 1894* (Boston, 1895), 55; B. J. Ramage, "The Growth and Moral Attitude of Corporations," 49 *American Law Register* 221, 226 (1901).
2. I. Maurice Wormser, "Piercing the Veil of Corporate Entity," 12 *Columbia Law Review* 496 (1912), reprinted as chapter 2 of Wormser, *Disregard of the Corporate Fiction and Allied Corporation Problems* (New York: Baker, Voorhis, 1927), 42–85.
3. *Citizens United v. Federal Election Commission,* 130 S. Ct. 876, 971, 972 (2010) (Stevens, J., dissenting).
4. Wormser, *Disregard of the Corporate Fiction,* 23–24.

play the race card

1. Jeffrey Toobin, "An Incendiary Defense," *New Yorker,* July 25, 1994, 56, 58, 59. See also Peggy Peterman, "Confronting the Issue of Race and O.J.," *St. Petersburg* (Florida) *Times,* July 17, 1994, 1F (discussing the growing divide between black and white opinion on the case: "The race card is at play here whether we want to acknowledge it or not").
2. *Daily Telegraph,* July 19, 1994, International Section, 10 (citing the *New Yorker* as a source).
3. Robert L. Shapiro, interview by Barbara Walters, ABC News special, Oct. 3, 1995, as quoted in David Margolick, "Not Guilty: The Overview," *New York Times,* Oct. 4, 1995, 1.
4. *In the Interest of Michael L.,* 1999 Conn. Super. LEXIS 263, at *4 (Feb. 2, 1999).
5. *Stith v. Lookabill,* 71 N.C. 25, 30 (1874) (attributing the quote to the great eighteenth-century chief justice of the King's Bench, Lord Mansfield).
6. *Commonwealth v. Bertrand,* 385 Mass. 356, 369 (1982). On metaphors in litigation generally, see Elizabeth G. Thornburg, "Metaphors Matter: How Images of Battle, Sports, and Sex Shape the Adversary System," 10 *Wisconsin Women's Law Journal* 225 (1995).

7. Bellingham letter quoted in *The Observer* (London), June 7, 1812, 4; "Behaviour and Execution of Bellingham," *The Observer,* May 24, 1812, 4. The transcript of the trial is in *Proceedings of the Old Bailey,* May 13, 1812, 5, available at http://www.oldbaileyonline.org/browse.jsp?div=t18120513-5.

8. John D. Ayer, "Rethinking Absolute Priority After *Ahlers,*" 87 *Michigan Law Review* 963, 997 (1989) (constitutional card); Joseph Nocera, "The Big Book-Banning Brawl," *New Republic,* Sept. 13, 1982, 24 (obscenity card); Marc Galanter, "Reading the Landscape of Disputes: What We Know and Don't Know (and Think We Know) About Our Allegedly Contentious and Litigious Society," 31 *UCLA Law Review* 4, 60 (1983) (court card); J. Morgan Kousser, "'The Supremacy of Equal Rights': The Struggle Against Racial Discrimination in Antebellum Massachusetts and the Foundations of the Fourteenth Amendment," 82 *Northwestern University Law Review* 941, 982 (1988) (mulatto card).

9. "Powell Lost Heath 6 Seats," *The Observer* (London), Mar. 3, 1974, 4: "But there is substantial evidence that . . . Mr Powell enabled many anti-coloured voters to identify with the Conservatives (although the Tory leadership declined to play the race card) and may even have tipped the scales to Mr Heath in 1970."

10. Michael Rezendes, "Threat of Shorter Class Year Angers Flynn and Iannella," *Boston Globe,* June 30, 1990, 24; Thomas B. Edsall, "Civil Rights Bill May Hold Pitfalls for Democrats; Strong Feelings about Affirmative Action Programs Divide Voters Along Racial Lines," *Washington Post,* July 23, 1990, A5 (quoting Democratic strategist Robert Beckel); Richard L. Berke, "Black Caucus Votes to Oppose Thomas for High Court Seat," *New York Times,* July 12, 1991, 1.

politically correct

1. *Chisholm v. Georgia,* 2 U.S. 419, 462 (1793) (Wilson, J., concurring; the Court reporter's italicization of "United States" for stylistic reasons throughout the report of the case has been removed to avoid unintended emphasis).

2. *A Key to the Parliamentary Debates: Being an Humble Attempt to Render Them Intelligible* (London, 1785), viii; [David Williams], *Lessons to a Young Prince , on the Present Disposition in Europe to a General Revolution* (London, 1790), 42; [William Griffith], *Eumenes: Being a Collection of Papers . . . Exhibiting Some of the More Prominent Errors and Omissions of the Constitution of New-Jersey* (Trenton, N.J., 1799), 24.

3. Benjamin Rush, *An Oration, Delivered before the American Philosophical Society* (Philadelphia, 1786), 40 (emphasis added).

4. Letter from Thomas Jefferson to William B. Giles, Dec. 26, 1825, in *The Writings of Thomas Jefferson,* vol. 16, ed. Andrew A. Lipscomb, Montecello Edition (Washington, D.C.: Thomas Jefferson Memorial Association, 1904), 151;

[Daniel P. Thompson], *Locke Amsden; or, The Schoolmaster: A Tale* (Boston, 1847), ch. 7, p. 136.

5. Frederick T. Birchall, "Personal Liberty Vanishes in Reich," *New York Times,* Dec. 31, 1934, 4; Joseph H. Baird, "The Red Fiasco: Why the Finnish Campaign Has Flopped," *Washington Post,* Jan. 21, 1940, B9.

6. See Ruth Perry, "A Short History of the Term *Politically Correct,*" in Patricia Aufderheide, ed., *Beyond PC: Toward a Politics of Understanding* (1992), 77.

7. John K. Wilson, *The Myth of Political Correctness: The Conservative Attack on Higher Education* (Durham, N.C.: Duke University Press, 1995), 4.

8. *Williams v. Vartivarian,* No. B155653 (Cal. Ct. App. Feb. 20, 2003) (unpublished; available through LEXIS) (internal quotation marks added); *Jordan v. City of Gary, Indiana,* 396 F.3d 825, 832 (7th Cir. 2005).

9. Diane Ravitch, *The Language Police: How Pressure Groups Restrict What Students Learn* (2003; New York: Vintage, 2004), 148.

10. Carol Innerst, "History Rewritten for the Classroom: Draft Guidelines Faulted as 'PC,'" *Washington Times,* Oct. 26, 1994, A1 (ellipsis in original).

posse

1. Statute of 17 Richard II, ch. 8 (1393–94), 2 Statutes of the Realm 89; Statute of 13 Henry IV, ch. 7 (1411), 2 Statutes of the Realm 169.

2. For a description of the procession of federal troops and guns, see *Ela v. Smith,* 71 Mass. 121 (1855). For the larger story, see Paul Finkelman, "Legal Ethics and Fugitive Slaves: The Anthony Burns Case, Judge Loring, and Abolitionist Attorneys," 17 *Cardozo Law Review* 1793 (1996).

3. Army Appropriations Act of June 18, 1878, ch. 263, § 15, 20 Statutes at Large 145, 152; Posse Comitatus Act, Title 18, United States Code, § 1385.

4. Dan T. Carter, *Scottsboro: A Tragedy of the American South,* rev. ed. (Baton Rouge: Louisiana State University Press, 1979), 7–10.

5. For books that undertake to sort out the complex series of events leading up to the gunfight and the details of the gunfight and its aftermath—all of which have been the subject of generations of conflicting accounts and some outright mythmaking—see Casey Tefertiller, *Wyatt Earp: The Life Behind the Legend* (New York: Wiley, 1997), and Allen Barra, *Inventing Wyatt Earp: His Life and Many Legends* (1998; reprinted with a new introduction, Lincoln: University of Nebraska Press, 2008).

6. Steven Lubet, "The Forgotten Trial of Wyatt Earp," 72 *University of Colorado Law Review* 1, 40–43 (2001), expanded as *Murder in Tombstone: The Forgotten Trial of Wyatt Earp* (New Haven: Yale University Press, 2004), 182–87.

pound of flesh

1. William Shakespeare, *The Merchant of Venice* (ca. 1596), act 1, scene 3.
2. Ibid., act 1, scene 3 ("equal pound of your fair flesh"); act 4, scene 3 ("I will have it").
3. For a thorough discussion of the mythology and fictional portraits of Jews that would have been available to Shakespeare, see Hermann Sinsheimer, *Shylock: The History of a Character* (New York: Benjamin Bloom, 1947). See also Amanda Mabillard, "Shakespeare's Sources for *The Merchant of Venice*," *Shakespeare Online* (2000), http://www.shakespeare-online.com/sources/merchantsources .html.
4. Shakespeare, *Merchant of Venice*, act 3, scene 1.
5. *Shortz v. Quigley*, 1807 Pa. LEXIS 54 (1807).
6. *Savig v. First Nat'l Bank of Omaha*, 2009 U.S. Dist. LEXIS 57593 (D. Minn. 2009) (bracketed change by the court). See also *Bloch v. Frischholz*, 533 F.3d 562, 568-69 (7th Cir. 2008) (Wood, J., dissenting) (describing as "shocking" the defendants' assertion that the plaintiffs sought their "pound of flesh" in suit alleging religious discrimination against Jews).
7. *Gillis v. McDonald's Corp.*, 1992 U.S. Dist. LEXIS 14239 (E.D. Pa. 1992); *Louisiana ex rel. Francis v. Resweber*, 329 U.S. 459, 471 (1947) (Frankfurter, J., dissenting).

rainmaker

1. James Adair, *The History of the American Indians* (London, 1775), 85 (a book primarily about the Chickasaws); Bernard Romans, *A Concise Natural History of East and West Florida* (New York, 1775), 85 (a passage specifically about the Choctaws). Regarding the original Choctaw name, see H. B. Cushman, *History of the Choctaw, Chickasaw, and Natchez Indians* (Greenville, Tex., 1899), 260. The Chickasaw and Choctaw languages are closely related.
2. *Milwaukee Journal*, Dec. 8, 1897, 4, quoting *La Crosse* (Wisconsin) *Chronicle* ("financial rain maker"); Alan L. Otten, "He Who Gets Bugged," Politics and People, *Wall Street Journal*, Jan. 14, 1970, 10.
3. Peter W. Bernstein, "The Wall Street Lawyers Are Thriving on Change," *Fortune*, Mar. 13, 1978, 104; Champ S. Andrews, "The Law—A Business or a Profession?" 17 *Yale Law Journal* 602, 608 (1908); Beverly Waugh Smith, "The Business-Getter," *American Mercury*, June 1925, 199, 199–200; Karl N. Llewellyn, "The Bar Specializes—With What Results?" 167 *Annals of the American Academy of Political and Social Science* 177, 178 (1933).
4. Robert L. Nelson, "Practice and Privilege: Social Change and the Structure of Large Law Firms," 1981 *American Bar Foundation Research Journal* 95, 119 (1981); Phyllis Weiss Haserot, "How to Get Associates into the Act: A Neglected Resource," *National Law Journal*, Aug. 26, 1986, Special Section, 15 ("old saw").

5. Chris Blackhurst, "The Lawyers Take Over; Corporate Takeover Boom," *The Sunday Times* (London), Aug. 20, 1989 (*binders* added); "Prerequisites for a Workable Partner Compensation Plan," *Law Office Management & Administration Report*, Oct. 1998, 5, 6 (binders as promoting cohesion); Phyllis Weiss Haserot, "Tapping a Valuable Resource: Involve Associates Early," *The Rainmaker's Review*, June 1986, 1 (*binders* as synonym for *minders*).

6. Geoffrey C. Hazard Jr., "Look at Lawyers, See Stars," *National Law Journal*, Apr. 23, 2001, A-17.

7. Laura A. Kiernan, "Battle for 'Brahmins' Requires Big Bucks," *Washington Post*, Nov. 19, 1979, B1, B3; Saundra Torry and B. H. Lawrence, "Star Lawyers Become Field's 'Free Agents'; Traditional Loyalty to Firms Gives Way to Bidding War Mentality," *Washington Post*, Feb. 27, 1989, A1 (first ellipsis in original).

8. *Heit v. Bixby*, 276 F. Supp. 217, 233 (E.D. Mo. 1967) ("book of business" in insurance); Mary Ann Galante, "Westward Expansion," *National Law Journal*, Aug. 25, 1986, 1 ("book of business" in law).

9. Hazard, "Look at Lawyers, See Stars."

10. The five are *The Rainmaker* (1926), *The Rainmakers* (1935), *Henry, the Rainmaker* (1949), *The Rainmaker* (1956), and *John Grisham's The Rainmaker* (1997).

rap

1. William Shakespeare, *The Taming of the Shrew* (ca. 1593), act 1, scene 2.

2. "Made $150,000 at One Touch: Black Prince, World's Greatest Negro Crook, Has Had Remarkable Career in Crime," *Washington Post*, Sept. 17, 1911, MS2; "Will Study Law in Prison," *Chicago Daily Tribune*, June 5, 1913, 5; "Honor Among Thieves? Well, Look This Over," *Chicago Daily Tribune*, Jan. 22, 1920, 15.

3. L.H.R., "Footnotes on Headlines: Concerning Dry Orders, Orgy Tubs and So Forth," *New York Times*, May 30, 1926, XX2; Dashiell Hammett, *Red Harvest* (New York: Knopf, 1929), 215.

4. Jeane J. Kirkpatrick, *Legitimacy and Force: Political and Moral Dimensions* (New Brunswick, N.J.: Transaction, 1988), 1:328.

5. George Varga, "Is Hip-Hop Getting a Bum Rap in the Wake of Imus Controversy?" *San Diego Union-Tribune*, Apr. 27, 2007, E-1.

rap sheet

1. George Keeney, "Hiring Hall," in Richard Finnie, ed., *Marinship: The History of a Wartime Shipyard, Told by Some of the People Who Helped Build the Ships* (San Francisco: Marinship, 1947), 51.

2. *Taylor v. State*, 208 P.2d 185, 189 (Okla. Crim. App. 1949).

3. Edward Butts, *Running with Dillinger* (Toronto: Dundurn, 2008), 80, attributing the opinion to Robert E. Bates, author of "The Truth About Blackie Audett," *On the Spot Journal,* winter 2006.
4. *State v. Douglas,* 389 So. 2d 1263, 1267 n.6 (La. 1980).

read the riot act

1. 1 Geo. I, Stat. 2, ch. 5 (Eng.). The name in the text is correct: there is no "of" before "the Rioters." The date of 1714 that is often associated with this act refers to the calendar used by Parliament at the time, under which the new parliamentary year did not begin until March 25, 1715. The statute actually became law when the king gave his "Royal Assent" to it on July 20, 1715 (see entry for that date in *London Gazette,* July 23, 1715, 1). Capitalization and punctuation of the act vary slightly among different sources. The source used in this entry is *The Statutes at Large, from Magna Charta to the Seventh Year of King George the Second, Inclusive,* ed. William Hawkins, vol. 4 (London, 1735), 600–02.
2. David Bush, "Gruden's Agent Says Coach's Deal Just Fine," *San Francisco Chronicle,* Aug. 1, 2001, B3.

RICO

1. Senate Report No. 141, 82d Cong., 1st Sess. 33 (1951), quoted in G. Robert Blakey and Brian Gettings, "Racketeer Influenced and Corrupt Organizations (RICO): Basic Concepts—Criminal and Civil Remedies," 53 *Temple Law Quarterly* 1009, 1014 n.21 (1980).
2. William G. Hundley, quoted in Tony Marro and Elaine Shannon, "Are Prosecutors Going Wild over RICO?" *Legal Times of Washington,* Oct. 8, 1979, 32.
3. Marro and Shannon, "Are Prosecutors Going Wild over RICO?"
4. Blakey and Gettings, "Racketeer Influenced and Corrupt Organizations," note 1 above, 1025–26 n.91.
5. G. Robert Blakey, "The RICO Civil Fraud Action in Context: Reflections on *Bennett v. Berg,*" 58 *Notre Dame Law Review* 237, 237 n.3 (1982).
6. Joseph E. Bauerschmidt, Note, "'*Mother of Mercy—Is This the End of Rico?*'—Justice Scalia Invites Constitutional Void-for-Vagueness Challenge to RICO 'Pattern,'" 65 *Notre Dame Law Review* 1106 (1990); G. Robert Blakey and Thomas A. Perry, "An Analysis of the Myths That Bolster Efforts to Rewrite RICO and the Various Proposals for Reform: 'Mother of God—Is This the End of RICO?'" 43 *Vanderbilt Law Review* 851, 982–87 & nn.435–43 (1990) (Blakey's title is based on the last line of the book on which the movie was based, which had "Mother of God" rather than the movie's toned-down "Mother of Mercy"); Paul B. O'Neill, Note, "'Mother of Mercy, Is This the Beginning of RICO?': The Proper Point of Accrual of a Private Civil RICO Action," 65 *New York University Law Review* 172

(1990); Susan W. Brenner, *"S.C.A.R.F.A.C.E.*: A Speculation on Double Jeopardy and Compound Criminal Liability," 27 *New England Law Review* 915 (1993).

rule of thumb

1. James Durham (1622–1658), *Heaven upon Earth* (sermons published posthumously, Edinburgh, 1685), 217.
2. William Blackstone, *Commentaries on the Laws of England,* vol. 1 (Oxford, 1765), 432–33, citing *Lord Leigh's Case,* 3 Keble 433, 84 Eng. Rep. 807 (1674).
3. Edward Foss, *Biographia Juridica: A Biographical Dictionary of the Judges of England from the Conquest to the Present Time, 1066–1870* (Boston, 1870), 137.
4. Thomas Wright and R. H. Evans, *Historical and Descriptive Account of the Caricatures of James Gillray, Comprising a Political and Humorous History of the Latter Part of the Reign of George the Third* (London, 1851), 14.
5. The three cases are *Bradley v. State,* 1 Miss. 156 (1824), *State v. Rhodes,* 61 N.C. 453 (1868), and *State v. Oliver,* 70 N.C. 60 (1874). The case quoted is *Rhodes,* 61 N.C. at 459 & 456.
6. Elizabeth Pleck, "Criminal Approaches to Family Violence, 1640–1980," 11 *Crime and Justice* 19, 40–41 (1989).
7. Del Martin, *Battered Wives* (San Francisco: Glide, 1976), 31, citing Robert Calvert, "Criminal and Civil Liability in Husband-Wife Assaults," in Suzanne K. Steinmetz and Murray A. Straus, eds., *Violence in the Family* (New York: Dodd, Mead, 1975), 89. The article attributed to Calvert is little more than a set of notes with partial quotations (containing many small inaccuracies) from cases. A note attached to the article (p. 88) says, "Edited for this volume by Murray A. Straus from draft papers prepared by Robert Calvert."
8. Terry Davidson, "Wifebeating: A Recurring Phenomenon Throughout History," in Maria Roy, ed., *Battered Women: A Psychosociological Study of Domestic Violence* (New York: Van Nostrand Reinhold, 1977), 18 (no citation given). The statement that "the old law had authorized a husband to 'chastise his wife with any reasonable instrument'" was evidently taken from an impassioned (but in this regard confused) article cited by Davidson for a different proposition, written by the nineteenth-century British women's-rights advocate Frances Power Cobbe: "Wife-Torture in England," *The Contemporary Review,* Apr. 1878, 55, 64. An entirely unacknowledged source of Davidson's, though not for the specific passage quoted here, was the article attributed to Robert Calvert ("Criminal and Civil Liability in Husband-Wife Assaults"). Davidson evidently used Calvert's transcriptions of several passages from cases (at p. 19 of her article), copying his errors and adding several of her own. The designation of the purported rule about sticks and thumbs as the "rule of thumb," however, appears to be Davidson's own.

9. Senate Report No. 138, 103d Cong., 1st Sess. 41 (1993), citing as its authority on the purported "rule of thumb" an article published earlier that year by Committee Chairman (later Vice President) Joseph R. Biden: "Domestic Violence: A Crime, Not a Quarrel," *Trial,* June 1993, 56. United States Commission on Civil Rights, *Under the Rule of Thumb: Battered Women and the Administration of Justice,* Jan. 1982, at 2 & nn.10–12.

10. Christina Hoff Sommers, *Who Stole Feminism? How Women Have Betrayed Women* (New York: Simon & Schuster, 1994), 203–07; Henry Ansgar Kelly, *"Rule of Thumb* and the Folklaw of the Husband's Stick," 44 *Journal of Legal Education* 341 (1994); Sharon Fenick, 1996 newsgroup posting—happily still available at this writing—at http://tafkac.org/language/etymology/rule_of_thumb.html.

11. Yvonne Ridley, "Why It's Strictly Non-PC for a PC to Get Down to the Nitty Gritty," *The Independent* (London), Jan. 9, 2000, 3.

scofflaw

1. James M. Beck, "The Spirit of Lawlessness," 7 *American Bar Association Journal* 441, and Judicial Section report, 484–85 (1921).

2. "Reward of $100 for Single Word," *The Tech* (Massachusetts Institute of Technology), Dec. 26, 1923, 4.

3. "Stinging Epithet Sought to Stigmatize Wets," *New York Times,* Jan. 3, 1924, 1.

4. Ibid.

5. "Are You a Scofflaw?" *Boston Evening Globe,* Jan. 16, 1924, 1. The name "Henry Irving Shaw," which appeared in the Associated Press account published the same day (usually without attribution) in newspapers throughout the country, was no doubt the result of momentary confusion with the name "Shawsheen Village."

6. When interviewed, however, Butler told a persuasive story of having received cards announcing the contest and coming up with this word—and a few others—at the last minute: "'Scofflaw' Wins Half of $200 Prize for Miss Kate Butler, Dorchester," *Boston Daily Globe,* Jan. 17, 1924, 3. For earlier publicity about Butler and Dale, see "Vacation School Will Close Term," *Christian Science Monitor,* Aug. 20, 1912, 10 (Butler in charge of summer activities for children); "Fiesta of San Giorgio: Annual Stunts Given by Copley Society," *Boston Daily Globe,* Apr. 27, 1911, 11 (Dale as performer); "Amateurs Aid Charity," *Boston Daily Globe,* Dec. 13, 1911, 11 (Dale as performer).

7. Westbrook Pegler, "Scofflaw Causes Wave of Giggles Among Scoffers," *Atlanta Constitution,* Jan. 27, 1924, 6C.

8. These three newspaper barbs, and a great many more, were found and transcribed (as quoted here) by word sleuth Barry Popik and posted on Dec. 7, 1997, on the American Dialect Society discussion list, http://www.americandialect .org/americandialectarchives/dec97190.html.

9. All facts and quotations in this paragraph are from *The Harvard Crimson,* letters and articles published Sept. 29 and Nov. 8, 1920, Oct. 11, 1923, Jan. 25, 1924, and Nov. 19, 1952. All information from the *Harvard Crimson* cited in this entry (and more advice to the school from Delcevare King) can be viewed by searching the newspaper's archive at http://www.thecrimson.com/search/.

10. "Now a $100 Price for Best Scoffer at 'Scofflaw,'" *Chicago Daily Tribune,* Jan. 19, 1924, 1 (prize offered by Mrs. Scott); "Harvard Proves Drier Than Delcevare King So Desperate Editors Raise the Ante," *Harvard Crimson,* Feb. 8, 1924 (*Advocate* increases its prize); "Dry Haters Coin Many Biting Words," *Hartford Courant,* Jan. 31, 1924, 2 (including long list of words received by Mrs. Scott; for still more, see Rodney F. Dutcher, "'Scofflaw' Sets Experts Hurling Epithetic Muss," *Atlanta Constitution,* Feb. 2, 1924, 4); "'Spigot-Bigots' Is Name to Toss at Dry Leaguers," *Atlanta Constitution,* Mar. 1, 1924, 1 (winner of *Harvard Advocate* contest); "'Banbug' Wins a Prize," *New York Times,* Mar. 17, 1924, 17 (winner of Mrs. Scott's contest, also listing the nine other words among the ten finalists).

11. The John C. Winston Company, advertisement for the *Winston Simplified Dictionary,* in *The Elementary School Journal,* vol. 27, no. 10, front matter (June 1927).

12. *Washington Post,* Jan. 16, 1924, 4 ("U.S. Bar Committee Approves Ship Choice") and 1 (George Rothwell Brown, "Post-Scripts").

13. Frank Butzow, "Fergus Whets Ax for Scofflaws of Constitution," *Chicago Daily Tribune,* Feb. 20, 1925, 13.

14. "The Ignored Summons," *New York Times,* May 30, 1952, 14.

15. Katharine A. Kaplan, "Lewis Warns Against Illegal Downloading," *Harvard Crimson,* Jan. 29, 2003; *Rio Properties, Inc. v. Rio International Interlink,* 284 F.3d 1007, 1018 (9th Cir. 2002).

separate but equal

1. Advertisement in *The American Journal of the Medical Sciences,* July 1873, 296.

2. *Roberts v. City of Boston,* 59 Mass. 198, 203 (argued 1849, decided 1850) (argument of counsel).

3. *Louisville, New Orleans & Texas Railway Co. v. State of Mississippi,* 66 Miss. 662, 668 (1889) (argument of counsel).

4. *Plessy v. Ferguson,* 163 U.S. 537 (1896). See also discussion of the case in BADGE OF SLAVERY.

5. *Brown v. Board of Education of Topeka,* 347 U.S. 483, 495 (1954).

6. *Parents Involved in Community Schools v. Seattle School District No. 1,* 551 U.S. 701 (2007). Transcript of oral argument, Dec. 4, 2006, at 44; plurality opinion by Chief Justice Roberts (joined by Justices Scalia, Thomas, and Alito), 551 U.S. at 730–31. Justice Kennedy, the fifth vote against the school districts, did not join in this part of the Chief Justice's opinion.

shadow of the law

1. Harriet Jacobs [Linda Brent, pseud.], *Incidents in the Life of a Slave Girl, Written by Herself* (Boston: published for the author, 1861), 45.

2. *Answers for Thomas Rannie, Tenant in Huntlaw, and James Pringle, Tenant in Limpuckwells, to the Petition of James Wight, Tenant in Duncrahill* (Edinburgh, 1768), 7; *Wilson v. State,* 80 Miss. 388, 391 (1902).

3. *Remarks on the Reprinted Tryal of Henry Cornish, Esq; for Conspiring the Death of King Charles the II . . .* (London, 1707?), 37.

4. Matthew Brzezinski, "Re-Engineering the Drug Business," *New York Times Magazine,* June 23, 2002, 24, at 26; Jörg Raab and H. Brinton Milward, "Dark Networks as Problems," 13 *Journal of Public Administration Research and Theory* 413, 420 (2003).

5. Susan Gilmore, "Immigrant 'Window' Closes in Four Days," *Seattle Times,* April 26, 2001, B1.

6. Charles Dickens, *Bleak House,* ch. 32, serialized in *Harper's New Monthly Magazine,* Jan. 1853, 235; Psalms 23:4.

7. *Stroff v. Swafford,* 79 Iowa 135, 138 (1890); remarks of Delegate Volney E. Howard, *Debates of the Texas Convention [of 1845]* (William F. Weeks, reporter) (Houston, 1846), 93, as quoted in *Ex parte Tucci,* 859 S.W.2d 1, 64 (Tex. 1993) (Phillips, Ch. J., concurring).

8. *Leymel v. Johnson,* 105 Cal. App. 694, 702 (1930).

9. Robert H. Mnookin and Lewis Kornhauser, "Bargaining in the Shadow of the Law: The Case of Divorce," 88 *Yale Law Journal* 950 (1979); see also Marc Galanter, "Justice in Many Rooms: Courts, Private Ordering and Indigenous Law," 19 *Journal of Legal Pluralism and Unofficial Law* 1 (1981) (noting that the shadow is cast not just by formal legal rules but also by other legal considerations such as the costs and risks of litigation).

shyster

1. James Podgers, "Public: 'Shyster' OK—If He's on Your Side," 67 *American Bar Association Journal* 695, 695 (1981).

2. "Shysters," *New-York Daily Times,* Oct 17, 1855, 4.

3. Gerald Leonard Cohen, *Origin of the Term "Shyster"* (Frankfurt am Main: Peter Lang, 1982). The crucial early uses of the term were found in a systematic search by the New-York Historical Society's newspaper librarian Roger Mohovich. Mohovich called them to the attention of Cohen, who compiled them and put them into historical and linguistic context in his 1982 monograph and subsequent writings. Among other things, Cohen analyzed twelve different etymologies that had previously been suggested (4–23). Yet another purported etymology was given in "Shyster: An Explanation of the Origin of the Word

Attributed to Hon. John Wentworth," *New-York Times,* Apr. 22, 1874, 5 (reprinted from the *Chicago Times*).

4. "Sketches from the Life School. Number Four: The Egyptian Tombs," *New-York Daily Times,* Oct. 4, 1852, 2.

5. Mike Walsh, "The Pettifogger," *The Subterranean,* July 22, 1843, 12, as quoted in Cohen, *Origin of the Term "Shyster,"* 47–48.

6. Mike Walsh, "The Pettifogger," *The Subterranean,* July 29, 1843, 22, as quoted in Cohen, *Origin of the Term "Shyster,"* 63–65.

7. This is Cohen's theory; see *Origin of the Term "Shyster,"* 14–15 & 100–01.

8. "Sketches from the Life School" ("Every nation, every color, is fairly represented [in the Tombs]—Irish, American, German, Negro . . ."). See also Stanley Nagel, *Little Germany: Ethnicity, Religion, and Class in New York City, 1845–80* (Urbana: University of Illinois Press, 1990), 42 (28 percent of New York City population in 1850 was German-born or German-American).

9. This is another part of Cohen's theory; see *Origin of the Term "Shyster,"* 100.

10. In previous accounts of this history by others, Terhune has been identified as a particular individual who was eighty-two years old at the time of these events; in addition, because of his accent, he was assumed to have been an immigrant from parts unknown. However, he was almost certainly Cornelius Wyckoff Terhune, who was baptized in the Dutch Reformed Church of Raritan, New Jersey, on February 28, 1808, and was thirty-five years old when these events occurred. Our thanks to genealogist Barbara Francis Terhune for intensive research making this identification possible.

11. W. Page Keeton et al., *Prosser and Keeton on the Law of Torts,* 5th ed. (St. Paul, Minn.: West, 1984), § 112, at 791.

Star Chamber

1. The Latin and French forms are documented in William Paley Baildon, ed., *Les Reportes del Cases in Camera Stellata, 1593 to 1609* (London, 1894), xlv and nn. 3–4, xlvi and n.1, available at http://openlibrary.org/books/OL24153202M/Les_reportes_del_cases_in_Camera_Stellata_1593_to_1609. The English form *Starre-Chamber* is cited in William Lambarde, *Archeion* (completed 1591, published 1635), 149 (attributing it to a document from the second year of the reign of King "Richard," without specifying which Richard); documentation cited by Cora L. Scofield, *A Study of the Court of Star Chamber* (Chicago: University of Chicago Press, 1900), 2 and n. 3, indicates that it was Richard II, whose second year on the throne ran from mid-1378 to mid-1379. The predominance of the *starred* form as late as the reign of Henry VIII (r. 1509–47) is attested to by A. F. Pollard in "Council, Star Chamber, and Privy Council under the Tudors: II. The Star Chamber," 37 *English Historical Review* 516, 523 (1922).

2. Sir Thomas Smith, *De Republica Anglorum* (London, 1583), 94 (completed in 1565).

3. Lambarde, *Archeion,* 154–55 (first report of two theories about terms confused with *star*); James I, "A Speach in the Starre-Chambre," June 20, 1616, in *The Workes of the Most High and Mightie Prince, James* (London, 1616), 549, 559; William Hudson, *A Treatise on the Court of Star Chamber* (1621), in [Francis Hargrave, ed.], *Collectanea Juridica,* vol. 2 (London, 1792), 1, 8–9.

4. William Blackstone, *Commentaries on the Laws of England,* vol. 4 (Oxford, 1769), 263 note a. *Starr* is derived from late Hebrew *sh'ṭār,* "a writing": *Oxford English Dictionary,* 2nd ed. (Oxford: Oxford University Press, 1989), at *starr.*

5. John Caley, "On the Origin of the Jews in England," 8 *Archaeologia* 389, 403–04 (1787).

6. Baildon, *Reportes del Cases in Camera Stellata,* xlv, xlvi, 462.

7. Regarding the history, jurisdiction, and practices of the Court of Star Chamber, see generally Thomas G. Barnes, "Star Chamber Mythology," 5 *American Journal of Legal History* 1 (1961), and John H. Langbein, Renée Lettow Lerner, and Bruce P. Smith, *The History of the Common Law* (New York: Aspen, 2009), 562–67. The U.S. Supreme Court discussed the forced-counsel rule in *Faretta v. California,* 422 U.S. 806, 821–23 (1975).

8. See James Bamford, "Washington Bends the Rules," *New York Times,* Aug. 22, 2002 (Foreign Intelligence Surveillance Court as "a modern Star Chamber"), and J. Wells Dixon, "Star Chamber at Guantanamo," Mar. 20, 2007, http:// jurist.law.pitt.edu/hotline/2007/03/star-chamber-at-guantanamo.php.

9. *Rumsfeld v. Padilla,* 542 U.S. 426, 465 (2004) (Stevens, J., dissenting, joined by Justices Souter, Ginsburg, and Breyer).

testify

1. This theory was advanced by philologist Carl Darling Buck in *A Dictionary of Selected Synonyms in the Principal Indo-European Languages: A Contribution to the History of Ideas* (Chicago: University of Chicago Press, 1949), § 4.49, at 257. The tendency of Latin writers to translate medical vocabulary from Greek is mentioned in J. N. Adams, *The Latin Sexual Vocabulary* (1982; Baltimore: Johns Hopkins Paperbacks, 1990), 227, though Adams himself (at 67) regards *testis*—and for that matter the Greek *parastatēs*—as a "personification" of the testicle.

2. Martial, Epigram 2.72. For the full epigram with a translation and analysis, see Craig A. Williams, *Martial: Epigrams, Book Two* (New York: Oxford University Press, 2004), 228–31. For additional discussion of the puns involved, see Adams, *Latin Sexual Vocabulary,* 212.

thin blue line

1. [William Howard Russell], "The War in the Crimea: The Operations of the Siege," *The Times* (London), Nov. 14, 1854; report of proceedings in House of Lords, *The Times* (London), Jan. 24, 1855.
2. Rudyard Kipling, "Tommy," *Scots Observer*, Mar. 1, 1890, 410.
3. "Her Majesty's Visit to France," *The Times* (London), Aug. 20, 1855; "Men, Women, and Horses: A Study at Ascot," *London Society*, Aug. 1862, 102; "Birmingham Police Institute," *Birmingham Daily Post*, May 4, 1900.
4. Richard Harding Davis, *The Cuban and Porto Rican Campaigns* (New York, 1898), 220.
5. "New Baseball Rules Mean Fun for Fans," *New York Times*, Feb. 4, 1917; "Enright, in Defense, Quotes Letters of Praise, Mostly Old," *New York Times*, Apr. 17, 1922, 1, 5. Commissioner Enright also denied the existence of THIRD DEGREE interrogation methods by the New York Police Department. See "No 3d Degree, Says Enright," *New York Times*, Jan. 21, 1922.
6. "Enright, in Defense, Quotes Letters of Praise," 5; "Mayor Thompson's Address," *National Poultry, Butter & Egg Bulletin*, Nov. 1922, 15; "Enright Praises His Force," *New York Times*, Jan. 19, 1924; Richard E. Enright, "Police of 40 Nations to Confer in New York: Even Fiji Sending Its Chief to Consult About Establishing a Blue Line of Defense Against the Common Enemy, Crime—Cooperation Becomes Imperative," *New York Times*, May 10, 1925.
7. "More Police for Chicago," *Los Angeles Times*, May 25, 1922, 1; "Major Crimes Decline Markedly Under Davis," *Los Angeles Times*, June 3, 1929, A2.
8. Alisa Sarah Kramer, "William H. Parker and the Thin Blue Line: Politics, Public Relations and Policing in Postwar Los Angeles" (Ph.D. diss., American University, 2007), 62–92, 114; John Buntin, *L.A. Noir* (New York: Random House, 2009), 190–91.
9. *Ex parte Adams*, 768 S.W.2d 281 (Tex. Crim. App. 1989).
10. Arnold H. Lubasch, "Koch Endorsed by Police Union for Re-Election," *New York Times*, Aug. 1, 1989; Lou Cannon, "Attorney Hails Beating Defendants as Embodiment of 'Thin Blue Line,'" *Washington Post*, Apr. 10, 1993.
11. "Two Views: DWB, TWB, BBWPASC and the LAPD," *Los Angeles Sentinel*, June 10, 1999; *Ventura v. Town of Manchester*, 2008 U.S. Dist. LEXIS 66957 (D. Conn. 2008); "Assaults Cost Police 1,166 Days," *Birmingham Evening Mail*, Apr. 18, 2009.

thinking like a lawyer

1. David N. Yellin, "'Thinking Like a Lawyer' or Acting Like a Judge? A Response to Professor Simon," 27 *Hofstra Law Review* 13, 18 (1998), replying to William H. Simon, "'Thinking Like a Lawyer' About Ethical Questions," 27 *Hofstra Law Review* 1 (1998).

2. William A. Keener, "The Inductive Method in Legal Education," 28 *American Law Review* 709, 718 (1894).

3. University of Pennsylvania, *The Proceedings at the Dedication of the New Building of the Department of Law, February 21st and 22nd, 1900,* compiled by George Erasmus Nitzsche (Philadelphia: University of Pennsylvania, 1901), 170 (remarks of George Wharton Pepper, Feb. 22, 1900) and 37 (address of James Barr Ames entitled "The Vocation of the Law Professor," Feb. 21, 1900). The latter address was reprinted in James Barr Ames, *Lectures on Legal History and Miscellaneous Legal Essays* (Cambridge: Harvard University Press, 1913), 354, 364.

4. Karl N. Llewellyn, *The Bramble Bush* (1930; New York: Oxford University Press, 2008), 107; *The Paper Chase* (Twentieth Century Fox, 1973). The film and a subsequent TV drama (broadcast on CBS in 1978–79, with a later version on Showtime from 1983 to 1986) were based on the 1971 novel of the same name by John Jay Osborn Jr. The quoted line of Professor Kingsfield does not appear in the novel.

5. University of Chicago Law School Web site (ca. 2000); Benjamin A. Templin at LawNerds.com, http://www.lawnerds.com/guide/mind.html (2011).

6. Anthony Kronman, *The Lost Lawyer: Failing Ideals of the Legal Profession* (Cambridge, Mass.: Belknap, 1993).

7. Thomas Reed Powell, as quoted in Thurman W. Arnold, *The Symbols of Government* (1935; New York: Harcourt, Brace and World, 1962), 101. In 1949, Powell confessed that he could not locate the place where he recalled having written something along this line, but credited Arnold's "paraphrase" as the source of later usage; see A. Simpleman, Jr. [Peter R. Teachout], "Sentimental Metaphors," 34 *UCLA Law Review* 537, 545 n.17 (1986).

8. Rosemary Harold, "Thinking Like a Lawyer Won't Warp You—But It Also Won't Give You All the Answers," *Student Lawyer,* Oct. 1990, 11.

9. Michael D. Freeborn, *"STOP Thinking Like a Lawyer:* Lessons from Law School to Un-Learn If We Are to Benefit from New Technologies," *The Docket* (American Corporate Counsel Association), Sept.–Oct., 1997.

10. James R. Elkins, "Thinking Like a Lawyer: Second Thoughts," 47 *Mercer Law Review* 511, 536–38 (1996).

third degree

1. "The Third Degree: How It Was Worked on Suspects by Inspector Byrnes," from the *New York Press,* as reprinted in *Idaho Avalanche* (Silver Spring, Idaho), May 19, 1894, *Woodland* (California) *Daily Democrat,* June 27, 1894, and no doubt other regional papers. For a contemporaneous account of the interrogation of McGloin—less creative but still dramatic—see "Traced by His Pistol: The Murderer of Hanier Caught; Patient and Skilful Work of Inspector Byrnes— The Prisoner's Confession," *New-York Tribune,* Feb. 2, 1882, 8.

2. T. O. McGill, "Third Degree in Police Parlance: What It Means, How It Is Operated and Some Famous Cases of Its Application," *New York Times Magazine Supplement,* Oct. 6, 1901, 12; Meyer Berger, "Third Degree Has Defenders as Well as Vigorous Critics," *New York Times,* July 24, 1932, XX3. As to Frenchy the sailor, see " 'Frenchy' Is Pardoned" and "What Ex-Supt. Byrnes Says," *New York Times,* Apr. 17, 1902, 2 (new evidence substantially exonerated convict long thought to have been "railroaded").

3. For various theories on the origins of *third degree,* see Jonathan Kirsch, "Vocabularies of Inquisition," http://www.wondersandmarvels.com/2009/02/vocabularies-of-inquisition.html ("five degrees of torture by which the Inquisition formally measured out the violence to its victims"); "Thomas F. Byrnes," *Wikipedia,* http://en.wikipedia.org/wiki/Thomas_F._Byrnes ("apparently coined by Byrnes"); "Third Degree (Interrogation)," Wikipedia, http://en.wikipedia.org/wiki/Third_degree_(interrogation) (pun on Byrnes or created by Chief Sylvester [see note 5 below]). The differing accounts even within Wikipedia are discussed (as of summer 2011) at "Talk: Thomas F. Byrnes," http://en.wikipedia.org/wiki/Talk:Thomas_F._Byrnes and "Talk: Third Degree (Interrogation)," http://en.wikipedia.org/wiki/Talk:Third_degree_(interrogation).

4. "Are Rarely Masons: Few Multi-Millionaires Take the Degrees," *Morning Oregonian* (Portland, Oregon), Dec. 29, 1896, 6; Pope Leo XIII, *Ab Apostolici* (translated from Latin); "Arrest of a Gang of Burglars: Their Capture by Inspector Byrnes," *New-York Tribune,* Feb. 5, 1883, 5.

5. Thomas Byrnes, "The 'Third Degree,' " *New-York Tribune Sunday Magazine,* Oct. 8, 1905, 3; remarks of Washington, D.C., police chief Richard H. Sylvester and Milwaukee police chief John T. Janssen in proceedings of the seventeenth annual convention of the International Association of Chiefs of Police (1910), quoted in John Henry Wigmore, *The Principles of Judicial Proof* (Boston: Little, Brown, 1913), 550–51, 552–53.

6. George W. Walling, *Recollections of a New York Chief of Police* (New York, 1887), 189; Jacob A. Riis, *The Making of an American* (New York: Macmillan, 1901), 341; Edward Marshall, "Greatest Detective: Superintendent of Police Thomas F. Byrnes of New York," *Galveston Daily News,* July 1, 1894, 12 (and in other newspapers under other headlines); Richard Angelo Leo, "Police Interrogation in America: A Study of Violence, Civility and Social Change" (Ph.D. diss., University of California, Berkeley, 1994), 20 (citing an interview with retired police inspector Daniel E. Costigan in the files of the Wickersham Commission, as to which see next paragraph).

7. National Commission on Law Observance and Enforcement ("Wickersham Commission"), *Report on Lawlessness and Law Enforcement* (Washington, D.C.: United States Government Printing Office, 1931), 4, 67.

8. Lemuel B. Schofield, quoted in "Philadelphia Defends Police," *New York Times,* Aug. 11, 1931, 12 (part of an extensive compilation of police reactions from around the country).

9. Sarah Vowell, "Down with Torture! Gimme Torture!" *New York Times,* Feb. 5, 2006, sect. 4, p. 13.

three-fifths rule

1. Modern scholarship on the origins and effects of the three-fifths rule includes Leonard L. Richards, *The Slave Power: The Free North and Southern Domination, 1780–1860* (Baton Rouge: Louisiana State University Press, 2000); Paul Finkelman, *Slavery and the Founders: Race and Liberty in the Age of Jefferson,* 2nd ed. (Armonk, N.Y.: Sharpe, 2001), and numerous law review articles by Finkelman; and Garry Wills, *"Negro President": Jefferson and the Slave Power* (Boston: Houghton Mifflin, 2003).

2. Max Farrand, ed., *The Records of the Federal Convention of 1787* (New Haven: Yale University Press, 1911), 1:542 (Pinckney's remarks on July 6 as recorded in notes of James Madison), 2:222 (Morris's speech on August 8 as recorded in notes of James Madison, with abbreviations and spelled out and including a spelling correction by Farrand), and 1:206 (Gerry's remarks on June 11 as recorded in notes of Robert Yates); see also 1:201 (James Madison's account of Gerry's remarks) and 1:208 (William Paterson's account, adding mules to the list).

3. *U.S. Constitution,* Art. 1, § 2, cl. 3 (three-fifths clause; emphasis added). See also Art. 1, § 9, cl. 1 (importation of slaves); Art. 4, § 2, cl. 3 (return of escaped slaves); Art. 4, § 4 (protection against slave uprisings).

4. Christopher Caustic [Thomas Green Fessenden], "The Jeffersoniad," in *Democracy Unveiled; or, Tyranny Stripped of the Garb of Patriotism* (Boston, 1805), 106–07.

versus

1. Walter A. Shumaker and George Foster Longsdorf, *The Cyclopedic Law Dictionary,* 2nd ed. (Chicago: Callaghan, 1922), at *versus.*

2. *The American Museum,* Apr. 1790, 203; Apr. 1792, 171.

3. *Smith v. Butler,* 25 N.H. 521, 523 (1852).

4. "Domestic Slavery, Considered as a Scriptural Institution," *Southern Literary Messenger,* Sept. 1845, 513, at 516; James Buckham, "The Path Through the Woods," *Outing,* Feb. 1894, 395, at 397; William H. Rand, Jr., "Swift *v.* Tyson versus Gelpcke *v.* Dubuque," 8 *Harvard Law Review* 328 (1895).

5. *Jones v. Evans,* 215 F. 586, 590 (7th Cir. 1914).

6. *Interstate Commerce Commission v. Mechling,* 330 U.S. 567, 571 (1947); *Clacka-mas Gastroenterology Associates, P. C. v. Wells,* 538 U.S. 440, 450 (2003); *Gonzaga University v. Doe,* 536 U.S. 273, 302 (2002) (Stevens, J., dissenting); *United States v. United Foods,* 533 U.S. 405, 428 (2001) (Breyer, J., dissenting); *Baze v. Rees,* 553 U.S. 35, 102 (2008) (Thomas, J., concurring in the judgment); *Illinois v. McArthur,* 531 U.S. 326, 335 (2001).

wall of separation

1. *U.S. Constitution,* Preamble; Art. VI, cl. 3; Art. I, § 3, cl. 6; Art. II, § 1, cl. 8. As to the oath of office, see also WHOLE TRUTH.

2. *Constitution of the Confederate States of America,* March 11, 1861, Preamble; Art. I, § 9, cl. 4; Art. IV, § 2, cl. 1 & cl. 3; Art. IV, § 3, cl. 3, available at http://avalon.law.yale.edu/19th_century/csa_csa.asp.

3. *Treaty of Peace and Friendship Between the United States of America, and the Bey and Subjects of Tripoli, of Barbary,* Art. XI, Nov. 4, 1796, ratified June 7, 1797, 8 United States Statutes at Large 154, 155. (The misspelling "emnity" in this official text has been corrected by us to conform to the spelling in other contemporaneous copies of the treaty.)

4. Thomas Jefferson, *Notes on the State of Virginia* (London, 1787), 265; Jefferson, letter to William Short, Oct. 31, 1819, in *Thomas Jefferson: Political Writings,* ed. Joyce Appleby and Terence Ball (Cambridge: Cambridge University Press, 1999), 313, 314.

5. [William Linn], *Serious Considerations on the Election of a President: Addressed to the Citizens of the United States* (New York, 1800), 4, 24.

6. All of the correspondence and drafting history relating to Jefferson's letter (as recited in this paragraph and the next) is reproduced in Daniel L. Dreisbach, "'Sowing Useful Truths and Principles': The Danbury Baptists, Thomas Jefferson, and the 'Wall of Separation,'" 38 *Journal of Church and State* 455, 457–69 (1997).

7. *Wallace v. Jaffree,* 472 U.S. 38, 92 (1985) (Rehnquist, J., dissenting).

8. Roger Williams, *Mr. Cottons Letter Lately Printed, Examined and Answered* (London, 1644), 45; [James Burgh], *Crito; or, Essays on Various Subjects,* vol. 2 (London, 1767), 119.

9. Letter from Charles I received by the House of Lords on Nov. 28, 1642, in *Journal of the House of Lords,* vol. 5: *1642–1643,* 463–64, available at http://www.british-history.ac.uk/report.aspx?compid=34964.

10. *Reynolds v. United States,* 98 U.S. 145, 164 (1879).

11. *Everson v. Board of Education of the Township of Ewing,* 330 U.S. 1, 16, 18 (1947) (majority opinion, by Justice Hugo Black); ibid., 330 U.S. at 19 (Jackson, J., dissenting). The quote from Byron is as rendered in Justice Jackson's opinion.

12. Missy McJunkins, Note, "Constitutional Law—First Amendment and Establishment Clause—The Wall of Separation Crumbles. *Agostini v. Felton,* 117 S. Ct. 1997 (1997)," 20 *University of Arkansas at Little Rock Law Journal* 813 (1998); F. King Alexander, "The Decline and Fall of the Wall of Separation Between Church and State and Its Consequences for the Funding of Public and Private Institutions of Higher Learning," 10 *University of Florida Journal of Law and Public Policy* 103 (1998); Catherine L. Crisham, "The Writing Is on the Wall of Separation: Why the Supreme Court Should and Will Uphold Full-Choice School Voucher Programs," 89 *Georgetown Law Journal* 225 (2000).

13. Leonard W. Levy, *The Establishment Clause: Religion and the First Amendment,* 2nd ed. (Chapel Hill: University of North Carolina Press, 1994), 250.

wet foot, dry foot

1. Yves Colon, "Touching Land Defines Who Stays, Goes," *Miami Herald,* June 30, 1999. Information about the origin of the phrase comes from e-mail exchanges between Elizabeth Thornburg and Yves Colon (July 2007), and Elizabeth Thornburg interview with Daniel Geoghegan (July 13, 2007).

2. Editorial, *Palm Beach Post,* July 1, 1999; "U.S.-Cuba Relations: Coast Guard Examines Actions," *St. Petersburg Times,* July 1, 1999; Frances Robles, "Incident May Be Spark Needed to Review Immigration Law," *Miami Herald,* July 2, 1999; Sue Anne Pressley, "Refugee Incident Spawns a Tempest; Miami in Uproar After Cubans' Arrest," *Washington Post,* July 3, 1999.

3. Mark Potter, "Profits Trump Safety in Cuban Smuggling," *MSNBC.com,* Sept. 15, 2006, http://www.msnbc.msn.com/id/14849572.

4. Carl Hiaasen, "Stance on Haitian Refugees Is Immoral," *Miami Herald,* Oct. 3, 2000, 5L; Carl Hiaasen, "What If Asylum Seekers Were Norwegian?" *Miami Herald,* Nov. 3, 2002, 7L. See generally Alberto J. Perez, Note, "Wet Foot, Dry Foot, No Foot: The Recurring Controversy Between Cubans, Haitians, and the United States Immigration Policy," 28 *Nova Law Review* 437 (2004).

white shoe

1. Russell Lynes, "How Shoe Can You Get? America's Premier Student of Snobs and Brows Peers Through the Ivied Windows at Hallowed Precincts and Their New Social Hierarchy of White Shoe, Brown Shoe, Black Shoe," *Esquire,* Sept. 1953, 59 and 128. Thanks to word sleuth Barry Popik for uncovering this article and bringing it to the attention of the American Dialect Society.

2. Erwin O. Smigel, *The Wall Street Lawyer: Professional Organization Man?* (New York: Free Press of Glencoe, 1964), 176 (Davis Polk statistics), 37 (quote).

3. Ibid., 176.

4. Abraham S. Blumberg, "Covert Contingencies in the Right to the Assistance of Counsel," 20 *Vanderbilt Law Review* 581, 591 (1967); Paul Hoffman, *Lions in the Street: The Inside Story of the Great Wall Street Law Firms* (New York: Saturday Review Press, 1973), 20.

5. Marilyn Wellemeyer, "The Richest Stakes in Horse Racing," *Fortune,* Oct. 6, 1980, 27.

6. Charles R. Wolf, professor of finance at the Columbia Graduate School of Business, quoted in Leslie Wayne, "The Heat's on Morgan Stanley," *New York Times,* Mar. 21, 1982, § 3, 1.

7. Nicholas Lemann, "The Newcomer," *New Yorker,* May 6, 2002, 62.

the whole truth

1. Jonas Adames, *The Order of Keeping a Court Leete, and Court Baron, with the Charges Appertayning to the Same: Truely and Playnly Delivered in the English Tongue* . . . (London, 1593), 4. An early appearance of the phrase in the colonies is found in an official compilation of Massachusetts statutes entitled *The Book of the General Lawes and Libertyes Concerning the Inhabitants of the Massachusets* (Cambridge, Mass., 1648), 58.

2. Charter of Liberties and Frame of Government of the Province of Pennsylvania in America, Article XXVI (1682), in *Colonial Origins of the American Constitution: A Documentary History* (Indianapolis: Liberty Fund, 1998).

3. *U.S. Constitution,* Art. VI, cl. 3 (emphasis added).

4. Thomas D. Morris, "Slaves and the Rules of Evidence in Criminal Trials," 68 *Chicago-Kent Law Review* 1209, 1216 (1993) (quoting and discussing the statute).

5. Carl Sandburg, *The People, Yes* (New York: Harcourt, Brace, 1936), ch. 73, p. 193.

6. Franklin Strier, "Making Jury Trials More Truthful," 30 *U.C. Davis Law Review* 95, 102 n.19 (1996).

7. Marvin E. Frankel, *Partisan Justice* (New York: Hill and Wang, 1980), 12.

8. *Bronston v. United States,* 409 U.S. 352, 358–59 (1973).

9. Stephen McG. Bundy and Einer Elhauge, "Knowledge About Legal Sanctions," 92 *Michigan Law Review* 261, 306–07 (1993).

Index

For additional words and phrases, see the table of contents.

ACLU (American Civil Liberties Union), 282
Adams, Abigail, 168
Adams, Joey, 162
Adams, John, 16, 100–01, 168, 270, 276, 278
adjectives, postpositive, 18–19, 58
affirmation, 277, 288–89
Afghanistan, 82
African Americans: in the 1960s, 6; legal treatment in century after Civil War, 24–26, 62–63, 142–43, 231–32; and rap, 211; and Reconstruction, 169, 198, 272; and segregation in schools, 93–94, 96–98, 231–34; and voting rights, 169, 171–74, 272. *See also* civil rights movement; slavery
Alabama, 172
Alderson, Edward Hall, 90, 120
Alien and Sedition Acts of 1798, 113
Alien Registration Act of 1940, 113
alliteration, 6, 16, 17, 147
Al-Qaeda in Iraq, 105
American Bar Association (ABA), 4, 28, 29, 31, 225, 229, 236, 259
Americans for Tax Reform, 86
American Tort Reform Association, 93
Ames, James Barr, 233, 259
Anglicanism, 16, 44, 248
Anglo-American legal tradition, 41, 80, 124
Anglo-French (a.k.a. Anglo-Norman) language, 10, 176, 177–78

Anglo-Saxon language. *See* Old English
anni nubiles, 8
Anthony, Susan B., 170
anti-Semitism, 32, 202–04, 286, 287
Arthur, Chester A., 201
Articles of Confederation, 185, 269
Ashcroft, John, 20, 43
Assize of Clarendon (1166), 109–10
Assize of Northampton (1176), 110
associates. *See under* law firms
attorney at law, 22, 23
attorney in fact, 23
Australia, 118, 143–44

backronyms, 213
Baildon, William Paley, 246
Bailey, F. Lee, 190
battered woman syndrome, 1–2
Bean, Roy, 118
Bellingham, John, 192
Bentham, Jeremy, 153, 156
Berle, Milton, 163
Berson, Joel S., 300n1
Bible: quotations and references, 41, 77–79, 104–05, 166, 235, 252, 289; use by jurors, 105; versions, xiii–xiv, 32, 41, 166, 252, 289, 310n2
Black, Hugo, 53, 104, 275
Blackmun, Harry, 157
Blackstone, William, 1, 34, 80, 131, 154–56, 177, 219, 245
Blakey, Robert, 218

Bleak House (Dickens), 56–57, 235
Bloody Code, 118
Bobbitt, John Wayne, 2–3, 4
Bobbitt, Lorena, 2–3
Bonfire of the Vanities, The (Wolfe), 138
book of business, 207
Book of Common Prayer, 16
Booth, Bramwell, 11
Bormann, Martin, 32
borrowing (in linguistics), 115
Boston, 111, 197–98, 226–27, 231
Boston Tea Party, 111
Bracton, Henry de, 273
Breyer, Stephen, 57
Brown v. Board of Education (1954, 1955), 64, 93–98, 171, 232–33
Buller, Francis, 220, 221
Burger, Warren, 108
Burns, Anthony, 198
Bush, George H. W., 196
Bush, George W., 20, 43, 82, 86, 90, 102
Bush v. Gore (2000), 99
business getters, 206–07
Butler, Josephine E., 11
Byrnes, Thomas F., 262–67
Byron, George Gordon, Baron, 95, 280

Cade, Jack: in history, 150–52; in Shakespeare, 150
California, 60, 92, 101, 114, 211
Campbell, William J., 137
Canadian law, 124
canon law, 8
capital punishment. *See* death penalty
Capone, Al, 161
Cardozo, Benjamin, 140
carnal knowledge, 10, 12
Carnegie, Andrew, 86
Cartwright, John, 170
Castro, Fidel, 282, 284
Catholicism, 264, 265
CBS Broadcasting, 3, 70
Chancery, 55–57, 94–95, 96–98, 242

Charles I, king of England, 55, 246–47, 248–49, 279
Charles II, king of England, 110, 219
charter, 58, 184
chattel real, 18
Chávez, Jorge, 115
Cheney, Lynne V., 196
Chertoff, Michael, 139
Chicago, 140
Chickasaw people and language, 205
Choctaw people and language, 205
Christie, Agatha, 72
Churchill, Winston, 162
Church of England, 16, 44, 248
civil law. *See* continental European law
Civil Rights Act: of 1866, 24–25, 26; of 1875, 25, 62, 128, 232; of 1964, 6
Civil Rights Cases (1882), 25
civil rights movement, 26, 63, 172–74, 272
Civil War, American, 24, 65, 272
Civil War, English, 55, 279
Clement, Paul, 19
Clinton, Bill, 86, 282
Cochran, Johnnie, 191
code switching, 115, 116
Cohen, Gerald Leonard, 237
Colledge, Stephen, 110
Colon, Yves, 281
colonial America: law and politics, 10, 24, 110–11, 118, 182–85; religion, 43–47, 188–89, 276; slavery and servitude, 130–31, 133–36, 289–90
common law: basic principle, 34, 118, 125, 224; particular examples, 12, 128, 131, 183. *See also* Blackstone, William; English law; joint and several liability
Comstock, Anthony, 65–68
Comstock Act (1873), 67, 68
condition precedent, 18
confession: false or forced, 50, 71–72, 82, 266–67; religious, 44, 290

Congregationalism, 44, 65, 278
Connecticut: colony, 44–46; state, 65, 278
Constantine I, emperor of Rome, 43
Constitution, Confederate, 277
Constitution, U.S.: amendment process, 101, 172, 271–72; Bill of Rights, 111, 181; and democracy, 99, 168–69, 174–75; and federal jurisdiction, 160, 165; Benjamin Franklin on, 83; need for interpretation, 180–81; Preamble, 189, 194, 277; and race or color, 63–64, 93; and religion, 276–77, 289; role of James Wilson, 193; and slavery, 268–72. *See also* constitutional amendments; Constitutional Convention of 1787
constitutional amendments: First (religion, speech, press), 47, 65, 184, 189, 277–81, 287; Fifth (federal grand jury, double jeopardy, federal due process), 80, 111, 112, 167; Sixth (defendants' rights), 80; Thirteenth (slavery abolished), 24–26, 62, 136, 231, 232; Fourteenth (equal protection, state due process), 63, 80, 169, 231, 232, 233, 272, 280; Fifteenth (black suffrage), 169, 171; Seventeenth (direct election of senators), 171; Eighteenth (Prohibition), 225; Nineteenth (woman suffrage), 170, 171; Twenty-first (repeal of Prohibition), 229; Twenty-third (District of Columbia suffrage), 99
Constitutional Convention of 1787, 98–99, 185, 269–70, 272
Continental Congress, 17, 168, 184
continental European law, 124, 291
"Contract with America," 85–86
Cook, James, Captain, 143–44
"Corporate Entity" (MacLeish), 188
corporations: bargaining power of, 53; as defendants, 92–93; limited liability

of, 186; as persons, 185–89; and taxes, 84
Cosby, William, 110, 182–83
court martial, 19
Coverdale, Miles, 41
cowboys, 144–45
Crimean War, 253
criminal conversation, 90–91
Cromwell, Oliver, 55
cruel and unusual punishment, 8, 204
Cuba, 82, 281–85
Cuban Adjustment Act of 1966 (CAA), 282, 284
Cuomo, Mario, 137

Danbury Baptist Association, 278–79
date certain, 19
Davidson, Terry, 222–24
Day, William Rufus, 26
death penalty: in America, 81, 118, 119; in England, 1, 10, 37, 41–42, 110, 118–19, 214–15, 248; specific instances of, 71, 105, 127, 192, 204, 257, 262–63
Declaration of Independence (1776), 12, 16–17, 168, 171, 184, 193, 194, 230
decree absolute, 18
deed poll/deed indented, 133
Delaware, 12
democracy, 20–21, 98–102, 168–75
Democratic Party, 198, 229, 264
Department of Justice, 19, 20
Dershowitz, Alan, 3, 4, 190
Dickens, Charles, 42, 43, 153–54, 156; *Bleak House*, 56–57, 235; *Oliver Twist*, 153–56; *Our Mutual Friend*, 42
diminished-capacity defense, 2
discovery (in litigation), 106–08, 167
District of Columbia, 94, 99
diya, 40
DNA evidence, 42, 75–76, 271
Don Juan (Byron), 280
Dorr, Thomas, 169
double jeopardy, 167, 218

Douglas, William O., 171, 181
Douglass, Frederick, 61
Dragnet (TV series), 75, 257
Dred Scott case (1857), 26, 271
Dr. Seuss, 282–83
Du Bois, W. E. B., 62
due process, 80, 124, 165, 214, 249, 250
Dunning, John, 35
Durante, Jimmy, 161–62
Durk, David, 49
Dutch language, 240

Earp, Wyatt, and brothers, 199–201
Edward I, king of England, 9, 203
Edward III, king of England, 243, 246
Eldon, John Scott, earl of, 56
electoral college, 98–102, 168, 175, 270
English language: characteristic features,
    17, 18, 21, 115; history, 21, 23, 37. *See
    also* Middle English, Old English
English law: age of consent, 8–11; Bloody
    Code, 118; collective responsibilities,
    130, 197; courts, 11, 54–57, 192, 242–50;
    crimes, 1, 9–10, 37, 68, 214–15; due
    process, 80; grand jury, 109–10, 112;
    languages used in, 16, 21, 22, 129;
    married women, status of, 90–91,
    154–56, 219–20, 221; procedure, 71,
    90–91, 106–07, 122, 124, 248–49;
    punishments, 1, 9–10, 110, 118–19,
    136, 192, 214–15, 247–48; seduction
    and criminal conversation, 90–91;
    wergild, 40
enhanced interrogation, 267. *See also*
    torture
Enright, Richard E., 255–56
equal protection, 63, 171
equity courts, 55–57, 106–07, 127–28,
    186
estate tax, 84, 85–89
ethical screen, 60
European Convention on Human
    Rights, 119

exemplary (punitive) damages, 41, 91
ex officio oath, 248

Farrell, James T., 140
FBI, 212
FCC, 69–70, 76
federal ratio, 268
Federal Rules of Civil Procedure, 108
Federal Rules of Evidence, 122
Federal Writers' Project, 144
fee simple absolute, 19
felon disenfranchisement, 169, 174
feminist movement, 10–11, 170, 174, 222
Fenick, Sharon, 224
Field, Stephen, 128
Fielding, Henry, 89
finders/minders/binders/grinders,
    206–07
Finkelman, Paul, 63
fleeting expletives, 69
Foreign Intelligence Surveillance
    Court, 250
forensic evidence, 74–76
Fraktur type, 32
France, 112
Frankfurter, Felix, 94, 96, 97, 171, 204
Franklin, Benjamin, 83, 133, 276
Freemasonry, 264–65
French language: evolution of, 176–77;
    influence of, 18, 21, 23, 176–77; as
    language of law, 18, 22, 34, 129; in
    legal vocabulary, 1, 13–15, 19, 21, 22,
    58, 121, 129–30. *See also* Anglo-
    French; Law French; Norman
    French; Old French
Friends (TV series), 4
Fugitive Slave Act of 1850, 197–98
Fuhrman, Mark, 190

Gandhi, Mahatma, 106
Garner, Bryan, 165
general counsel, 18
Geoghegan, Dan, 281–82

George I, king of England, 214
George III, king of England, 90, 99
Georgia, 8, 174
German, 236–37, 239
Germanic languages, 21, 36
Germany, 32, 195
Gerry, Elbridge, 269
Gettysburg Address, 17, 171
Gewirtz, Paul, 78
Gingrich, Newt, 87
Ginsburg, Ruth Bader, 57
Goldman, Ronald L., 40–41, 123, 190
Gonzales, Alberto, 20
Goranson, Stephen, 309n6, 315n3
Gothic type, 31, 32, 34
Goths, 32
Gotti, John, 148
Graham, Fred, 4
grand jury, 109–12, 136–38, 140
Great Awakening, Second, 65
Great Depression, 144
Great Train Robbery (film), 197
Greek, 41, 251
Grisham, John, 208
Griswold v. Connecticut (1965), 181
Gruden, Jan, 215–16
Guantánamo detainees, 82
Gunfight at the O.K. Corral (film), 199
Gutenberg, Johannes, 31–32
Guugu Yimithirr people and language, 144

habeas corpus, 273
Haigh, John George, 72–73
Hale, Sir Matthew, 71, 219
Hamilton, Andrew, 182–85
Hamlet (Shakespeare), 81
Hammett, Dashiell, 210
Hammurabi, Code of, 103, 104
Harcourt, Bernard E., 139
Harlan, John Marshall (1833–1911, the first Justice Harlan), 25–26, 63, 64

Harlan, John Marshall (1899–1971, the second Justice Harlan), 26
Harvard Advocate, 228–29
Harvard University, 227–28, 258
Hayes, Rutherford B., 198
Hazard, Geoffrey, 28–29, 206, 207
Hebrew, 252, 331n4
Hemings, Sally, 271
Henry II, king of England, 109
Henry IV, Part 2 (Shakespeare), 23
Henry VI, king of England, 150
Henry VI, Part 2 (Shakespeare), 148–52
Henry VII, king of England, 243
Henry VIII, king of England, 121
Hiaasen, Carl, 285
high treason. *See* treason
Hitler, Adolf, 32, 195
Holliday, John Henry ("Doc"), 199–201
Holmes, Oliver Wendell, Jr., 26, 39, 94–96, 181
Holtz, Lou, 162, 163
Hoover, Herbert, 266
Hoover, J. Edgar, 68
Hornbook Series, 129
"Hound of Heaven, The" (Thompson), 95
Howard University, 6
Huckleberry Finn (Twain), 78–79
Hutchinson, Thomas, 111

Illinois, 104, 171
Immigration and Nationality Act of 1952, 114
immigration policy, 112–17, 281–85
indecent exposure, 77
indentured servitude, 133–36
indictments, 111
Industrial Revolution, 170
infamous crime, 111
Ingersoll, Robert G., 62
Innocence Project, 75
Inns of Court, 149
Internal Revenue Code, 85

International Association of Chiefs of
Police, 264, 265
Iraq, 40, 105–06, 158
Islam, 277
Islamic law, 40
Italy, 32
Ito, Lance, 123

Jackson, Janet, 70
Jackson, Robert, 280
Jacobs, Harriet, 234, 235
jailhouse snitch, 42
James I, king of England, 55, 245
Jefferson, Thomas, 12, 16, 17, 100–01,
194, 270, 276–80
Jesus Christ, 41, 104, 105, 265, 276, 278,
289
John, king of England, 80
Johnson, Lyndon B., 5–6
joint and several liability, 92–93
Jump Jim Crow (song and dance),
141–42
jury: factors affecting decisions, 2, 74–76,
89–93, 105, 123–24, 290–91; grand
vs. petty, 109–10. *See also* grand
jury

Kaye, Judith, 140
Kelly, Henry Ansgar, 224
Kennedy, Anthony, 64
Kennedy, John F., 5, 6, 172
Kentucky, 25
Kerry, John, 102
King, Delcevare, 226–28
King, Martin Luther, Jr., 7, 63
King, Rodney, 257
King's Council, 242
Kipling, Rudyard, 254
Koch, Edward I., 257

Langdell, Christopher Columbus, 258
Latin: Antonin Scalia and, 70; in current
legal use, 71, 103, 166, 273; French

descended from, 176; as historical
language of law, ix, 8, 16, 18, 74, 131,
243, 273; influence in English, 18, 21,
23; legal terms derived from, 15, 22,
54, 78, 132, 197, 250–51, 272–73; in
post-Conquest England, 21, 23; puns,
251–52
law firms: associates in, 27, 29–30, 286;
billing, 27–31; business-getting,
205–08; structure, 285–88
Law French, 16, 34, 176
law merchant, 19
law vs. equity (systems of justice), 54–57,
127–28
lawyers: categorizations of, 206–07, 236,
285–88; duty of loyalty, 59; effect of
TV shows on, 74–76; hostility toward,
148–49, 159; modes of thought,
258–62; wordiness, 12–13. *See also*
law firms
legal education, 237, 258–59
legal fictions, 156, 185, 188, 189
Leo XIII, Pope, 265
letters testamentary, 19
Levy, Leonard W., 281
Lewis, John, 172–73, 174
lex talionis, 103
libel, 239, 240–42, 247. *See also* seditious
libel
Limbaugh, Rush, 106
limited liability, 186, 189
Lincoln, Abraham, 17, 171
"Lindbergh Law," 161
litigiousness, 159
Little Caesar (film), 217–18
Llewellyn, Karl N., 206, 259
loan translations, 115, 116, 121, 205
loanwords, 115, 116
Los Angeles Police Department, 256–57
Los Angeles Times, 114
Louima, Abner, 51–52
Love's Labour's Lost (Shakespeare),
125–27, 313n1

Low, Harry, 60
Luntz, Frank, 87–88

MacLeish, Archibald, 188
Madison, James, 98, 276
Mafia, 49, 217
Magna Carta, 80
Man and Superman (Shaw), 64
Mann Act (1910), 161
Mansfield, William Murray, earl of, 34, 35, 90–91, 109
Marcello, Marco ("Fatso Marco"), 163, 164
maritime law, 58
Marshall, Thurgood, 64, 96, 104
Martial (poet), 251–52
Martin, Del, 222
Martin, Jim, 87
Mary I, queen of England, 121
Massachusetts: colony, 111; state, 197–98, 231
Menendez, Erik and Lyle, 2, 3
mental illness, 139
Merchant of Venice (Shakespeare), 202–04, 237
Metropolitan Police Force (London), 48
Mexico, 114, 115–16, 271
Miami, 281
Middle English, 37
minstrel shows, 141–42
Miranda warning, 75
Mississippi, 232
Mohovich, Roger, 329n3
Mormons, 280
Morris, Errol, 257
Morris, Gouverneur, 269
Morris, Robert, 231
Moussaoui, Zacarias, 105
Mrs. Warren's Profession (Shaw), 65
murder: in American law, 1–2, 71–72, 123, 124; in English law, 1, 40, 71–73; murder cases, 2, 40–41, 72–73, 76, 123, 131, 190–91

Murrah, Alfred P., 165
mustang courts, 144

NAACP, 93–94, 96
National Guard, 198–99
National Organization for Women (NOW), 222
Nelson, Robert, 206
New Haven Colony, 45–46
New York: colony, 44, 110–11, 182–83; state, 136–37
New York City, 48–52, 237–40, 264–65
New-York Historical Society, 237
Nix, Robert N. C., 49
nolle prosequi, 273, 274
Norman Conquest, 21, 22, 23, 197
Norman French, 175–76
Norquist, Grover, 86

oath, 109–10, 122, 248–49, 277, 288–93
Obama, Barack, 82
obscenity, 64–70, 239
Old English, 13–15, 21, 23, 31, 37, 117, 288
Old English type, 31
Old French, 13, 15, 22, 36, 58, 109–10, 129, 132
Old Norse, 21, 36, 117
Old Testament law, 40, 104, 166
Oliver Twist (Dickens), 153–56
ordeal, trial by, 110, 112
Organized Crime Control Act of 1970, 217, 218
Osborn, John Jay, Jr., 179
Our Mutual Friend (Dickens), 42

Paine, Thomas, 276
Parker, William H., 256–57
Patrolmen's Benevolent Association (New York City), 51
Peasants' Revolt of 1381, 150
Pegler, Westbrook, 227
Penn, William, 288

Pennsylvania: colony, 183, 288; state, 46, 184
People, Yes, The (Sandburg), 290
Pepper, George Wharton, 259
Perceval, Spencer, 192
perjury, 51, 247, 249, 289–91
Perry Mason (TV series), 74–75
personification, 156
Peters, Samuel, 45–46
petit treason. *See* treason
Philadelphia, 182, 184–85, 267
Pinckney, Charles, 269
Plessy v. Ferguson (1896), 26, 63, 64, 232
police, 48–52, 253–58, 262–68
Pollock, Frederick, 95
Popik, Barry, 138, 314n6, 315n3, 327n8, 337n1
population shifts, 10, 170–71
posse comitatus, 197
Posse Comitatus Act (1878), 198, 201
Post Office Act of 1865, 66
postpositive adjectives, 18–19, 58
Powell, Thomas Reed, 260
presentments, 111
presidential elections, 85, 98–102, 168, 170, 175, 178, 198, 270–72
Prince Edward County, Va., 96
printing, 31–32
Prohibition, 225–30, 267
pronunciation, 22, 74, 176–78, 240, 317n4
prostitution, 11, 65, 79
punitive (exemplary) damages, 41, 91
Puritans, 44

Quakers, 194, 289
Quincy, M.E. (TV series), 75

rape, 2, 8, 9–10, 153, 160, 167
Rape upon Rape (Fielding), 89
Reagan, Ronald, 87
Reconstruction, 169, 198, 272
redundant language. *See* word pairs

Rehnquist, William, 36, 279, 280
religion. *See under* colonial America; Constitution, U.S.; constitutional amendments: First; slavery; Supreme Court, U.S. *See also* Bible; confession: religious; Virginia Statute for Religious Freedom (1786); *and individual religions*
republican form of government, 168
Republican Party, 85, 169, 198
res judicata, 166
Revenge for Honour (play), 153
reverse discrimination, 6
Revolutionary War, 45, 95, 184–85, 276, 279
Rhode, Deborah, 28, 30
Rhode Island: colony, 279; state, 169
Rice, Thomas Dartmouth ("Daddy"), 141–42
Riis, Jacob, 266
Riot Act (1715), 214
Rivera, Geraldo, 4
robbery, 36, 118, 160, 226
Roberts, John, 19, 233
Rob Roy, 37–38
Rob Roy (Scott), 38, 95
Rockefeller, Nelson, 137
Roddenberry, Gene, 257
Roosevelt, Theodore, 266
Rush, Benjamin, 194
Russell, William Howard, 253

Salazar, Ruben, 114
Salvation Army, 11
Sandburg, Carl, 290
Sanger, Margaret, 67–68
Scalia, Antonin, 57, 70, 129
Schwartz, Victor, 93
Scots language, 37
Scott, Dred, 26, 271
Scott, Rose R., 228–29
Scott, Walter, 38, 95
Scottish law, 37, 71, 124

Scottsboro Boys, 199
Scott v. Sandford (*Dred Scott* case, 1857), 26, 271
Securities and Exchange Commission (SEC), 106
seditious libel, 110, 183, 248
segregation. *See* African Americans
Selden, John, 56, 57
self-defense, 2
Selma, Ala., 172
Seneca Falls Convention (1848), 11, 170
September 11, 2001, attacks, 105, 267
Serpico, Frank, 49
Shaftesbury, Anthony Ashley Cooper, earl of, 110
Shakespeare, William, 149–50, 203; *Hamlet,* 81; *Henry IV, Part 2,* 23; *Henry VI, Part 2,* 148–52; *Love's Labour's Lost,* 125–27, 313n1; *Merchant of Venice,* 202–04, 237; *The Taming of the Shrew,* 208–09
Shapiro, Robert L., 190, 191
Shaw, George Bernard, 64–65, 66, 68
Shylock, 203–04
Silverman, Joy, 138–39
Simpson, Nicole Brown, 40, 123–24, 190
Simpson, O. J., 40, 123, 190–91
60 Plus Association, 87
slavery: and Confederate Constitution, 277; legal treatment of slaves, 127, 131, 197–98, 234–35, 289, 290; and religion, 61; slaves as property, 34–35, 268–69; and U.S. Constitution, 98–99, 168–69
Sloan, Allan, 84
Smith, Thomas (1513–77), 243–45
social purity movement, 11
Social Register, 286
Society for the Suppression of Vice, 66
solicitor general, 19, 20
Solomon, King, 77–79

Sommers, Christina Hoff, 224
"Sonnets upon the Punishment of Death" (Wordsworth), 119
Souter, David, 57
Southampton, Henry Wriothesley, earl of, 149
Spaeth, Merrie, 87
Spanglish, 115, 116
Spanish, 114–16
special/independent/outside counsel, 18
special prosecutor, 18
Statue of Liberty, 116–17
statutory rape, 8
Stead, William Thomas, 11
Stevens, John Paul, 57, 148, 189, 250
Stuart, James Francis Edward, 214
Student Nonviolent Coordinating Committee (SNCC), 172–73
suffrage: for African Americans, 98; equal, 168, 170; universal, 168, 170; for women, 11, 170, 226
Sumner, Charles, 231, 233
Sunday closing laws, 43, 44, 46–48
Supreme Court, U.S.: and capital punishment, 104, 204; and civil rights, 5–7, 24–26, 62–63, 93–96, 128, 142, 171, 174, 232–33; and corporate personhood, 187, 189; and elections, 99; as an institution, 161, 175, 271, 274–75; and obscenity, 68; and privacy, 181; and racketeering, 218; and religion, 47, 279–80; and right to a trial, 80–82; and slavery, 231, 271
syntax, 18–19, 121

Taming of the Shrew, The (Shakespeare), 208–09
Tammany Hall, 264
Taney, Roger, 26
taxes, 24, 83–84, 85–89, 169, 268, 276
Taylor, Hobart, Jr., 5–6
temperance movement, 11
temporary-insanity defense, 2, 3

Terhune, Cornelius W., 237–40
Texas, 114, 118, 144, 147
thief takers, 41–42
thin red line, 253–55
Thomas, Clarence, 64, 193
Thompson, Daniel P., 195
Thompson, Francis, 95
Tombstone, Ariz., 199
"Tommy" (Kipling), 254
Toobin, Jeffrey, 190
"tort reform" movement, 91
torture, 50, 51–52, 82, 159, 266–68
treason: high vs. petit, 1; particular
    cases, 17, 119, 169
Treaty of Paris (1783), 95
Treaty of Tripoli (1796), 277–78
trials, famous, 2–3, 77, 182–83, 190–91,
    202
Trumbull, Lyman, 24
Twain, Mark, 78
24 (TV series), 267
Tyler, Wat, 150

United States Commission on Civil
    Rights, 224
University of Chicago, 140, 260
University of Michigan, 231
University of Pennsylvania, 259
University of Virginia, 194
urbanization, 10, 170–71
U.S. Border Patrol, 281
U.S. Coast Guard, 281, 284

vaudeville comedians, 160, 161–63
Vermont, 171
Virginia: colony, 130, 198, 278, 289;
    state, 12, 96, 98, 101
Virginia Statute for Religious Freedom
    (1786), 278
voting rights. See under African
    Americans. See suffrage
Voting Rights Act of 1965, 272
Vowell, Sarah, 268

Wachtler, Sol, 136–40
Walsh, Mike, 237–42
Warren, Earl, 94, 96
Washington, George, 276, 277
waterboarding (a.k.a. water cure), 267.
    See also torture
Webb, Jack, 257
Webster, Noah, 273
wergild, 40
Westminster, First Statute of (1275), 9
Westminster Palace, 243
white letter (typestyle), 34
"white slavery," 11
White-Slave Traffic Act of 1910, 161
Wickersham Commission, 267
wife beating, 1, 219–24
William I, king of England (the
    Conqueror), 21, 175
Williams, Roger, 279
Wilson, Genarlow, 8
Wilson, James, 193–94
Winchell, Walter, 162
Wolfe, Tom, 138
woman suffrage movement, 11, 170
women: in the 1960s, 6; age of consent
    and, 9–10; battered, 1–2, 219–25; legal
    status when married, 90–91, 128,
    154–56, 219–22; segregation of, 230–31
Women's Christian Temperance Union
    (WCTU), 11, 12
women's rights movement. See feminist
    movement
word pairs, 13–17, 22, 129–30
Wordsworth, William, 38, 119
Wormser, I. Maurice, 187, 189
Wyoming: territory, 170; state, 101

Yale University, 286
Young Men's Christian Association
    (YMCA), 66

Zenger, John Peter, 110–11, 182–83
Zevon, Warren, 157–59